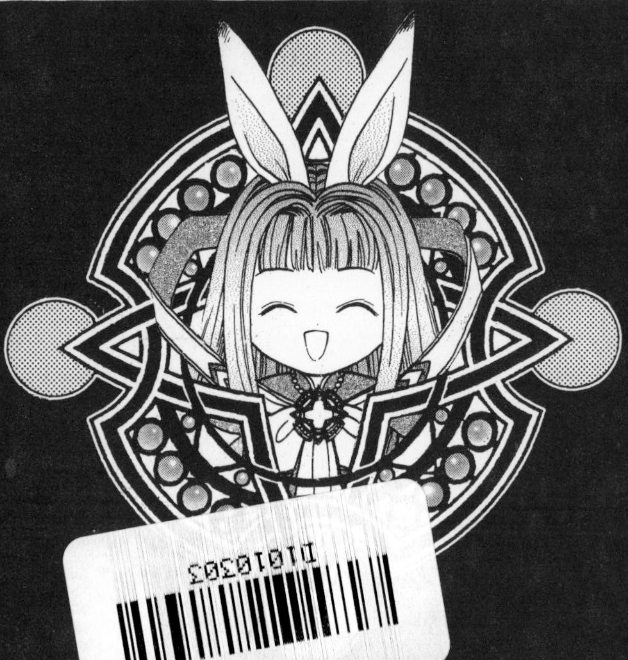

The Lost Word

Alice 19th™

story and art by **Yû Watase**

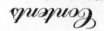

Alice 19th

TM

Story thus far

Having taken over the Metropolitan Building in Tokyo, Darva, the embodiment of evil, is slowly consuming Alice's sister Mayura. Strong in their resolve to find and rescue Mayura, Alice and the other young Lotis Masters enter the building, which has been transformed into an eerie otherworld. As they face fearsome Maram Masters and defeat them one by one, Alice and Kyô display exceptional strengths that arise from their compassion and purity of heart.

Frey and Chris are forced to face the demons of their pasts, and they confront and overcome their own inner darkness. The group of Lotis Masters is then suddenly transported to the Lotsuan Sanctuary in Frey's home country, Norway, where they find all the residents of the sanctuary, except for Frey's mentor Eric, slaughtered. Far from having a happy reunion with Eric, Frey discovers that his former teacher is responsible for the bloodshed, having turned to Darva and embraced Mara in a desperate hour of jealousy and fear. Alice, Kyô, Frey, Chris, Mei Lin, and Billy all try to use Lotis words to reach out to Eric and deliver him from the darkness, but their efforts are futile. As Darva taunts the Lotis Masters about their inability to save their comrade, Eric dies in Frey's arms. Darva also implies that Kyô may have already succumbed to the darkness in the past...

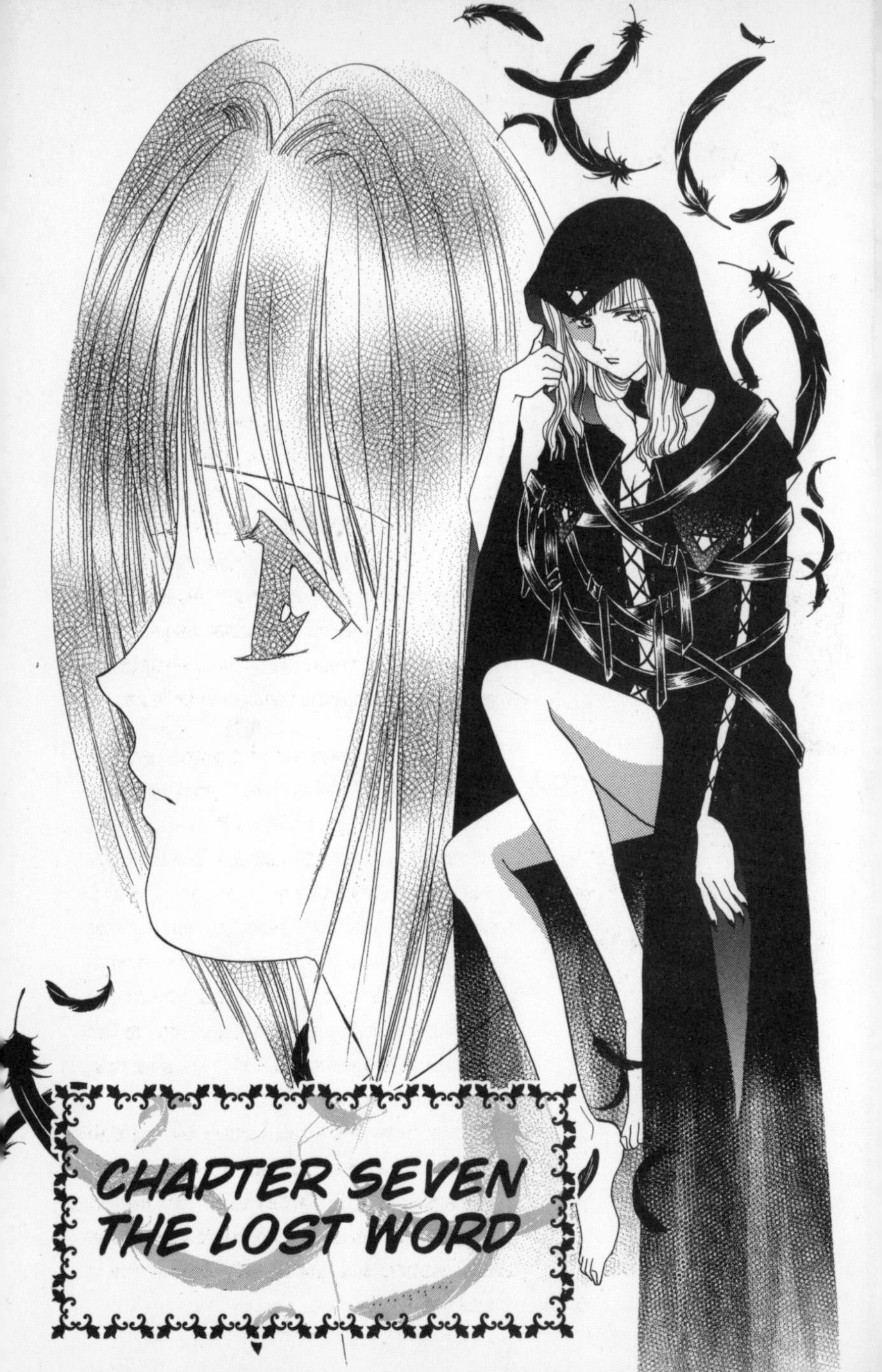
CHAPTER SEVEN
THE LOST WORD

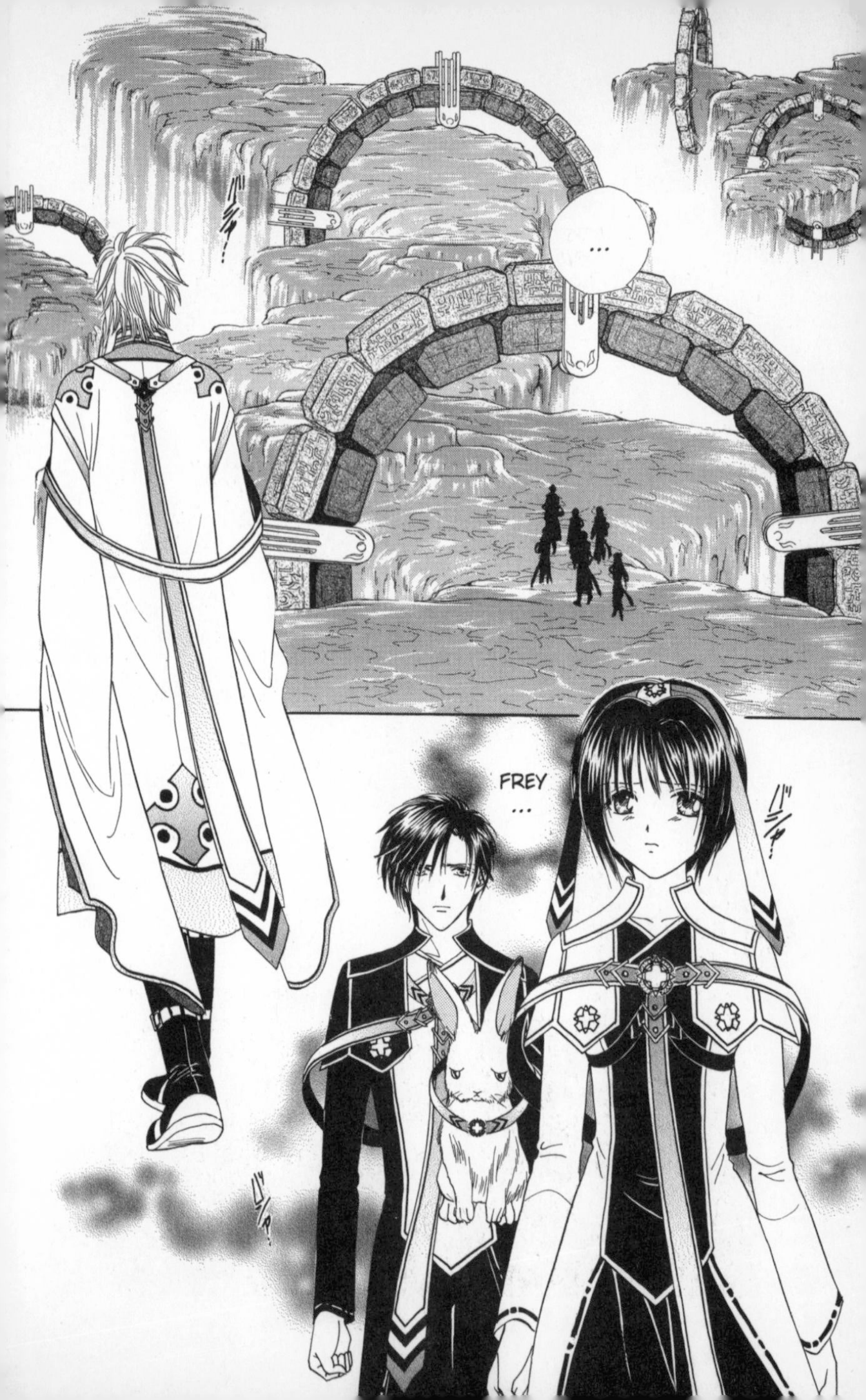
...
FREY ...

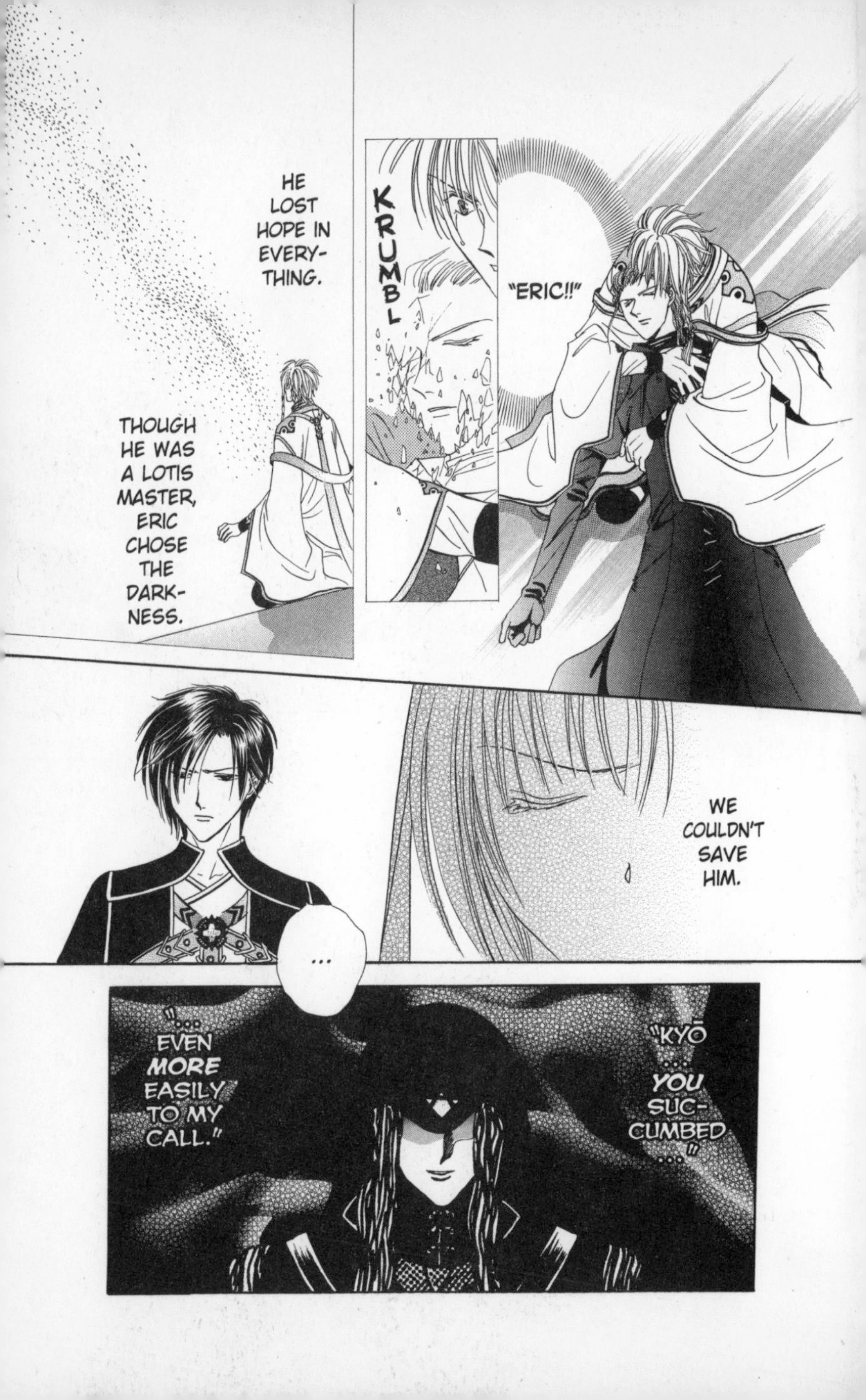
"ERIC!!"
KRUMBL
HE LOST HOPE IN EVERY-THING.
THOUGH HE WAS A LOTIS MASTER, ERIC CHOSE THE DARK-NESS.
WE COULDN'T SAVE HIM.
...
"KYŌ... *YOU* SUC-CUMBED..."
"...EVEN *MORE* EASILY TO MY CALL."

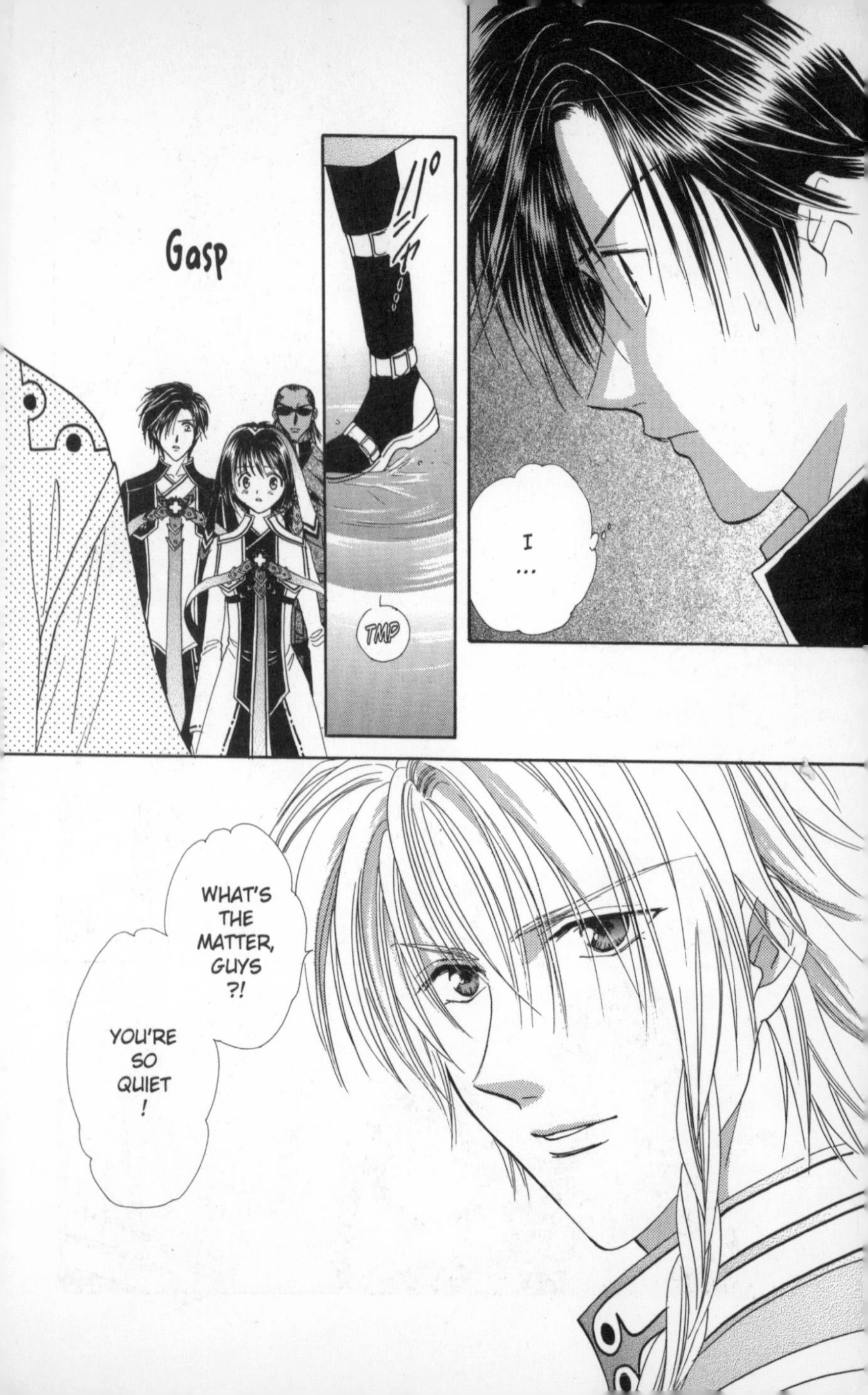
I ...
TMP
Gasp
WHAT'S THE MATTER, GUYS ?!
YOU'RE SO QUIET !

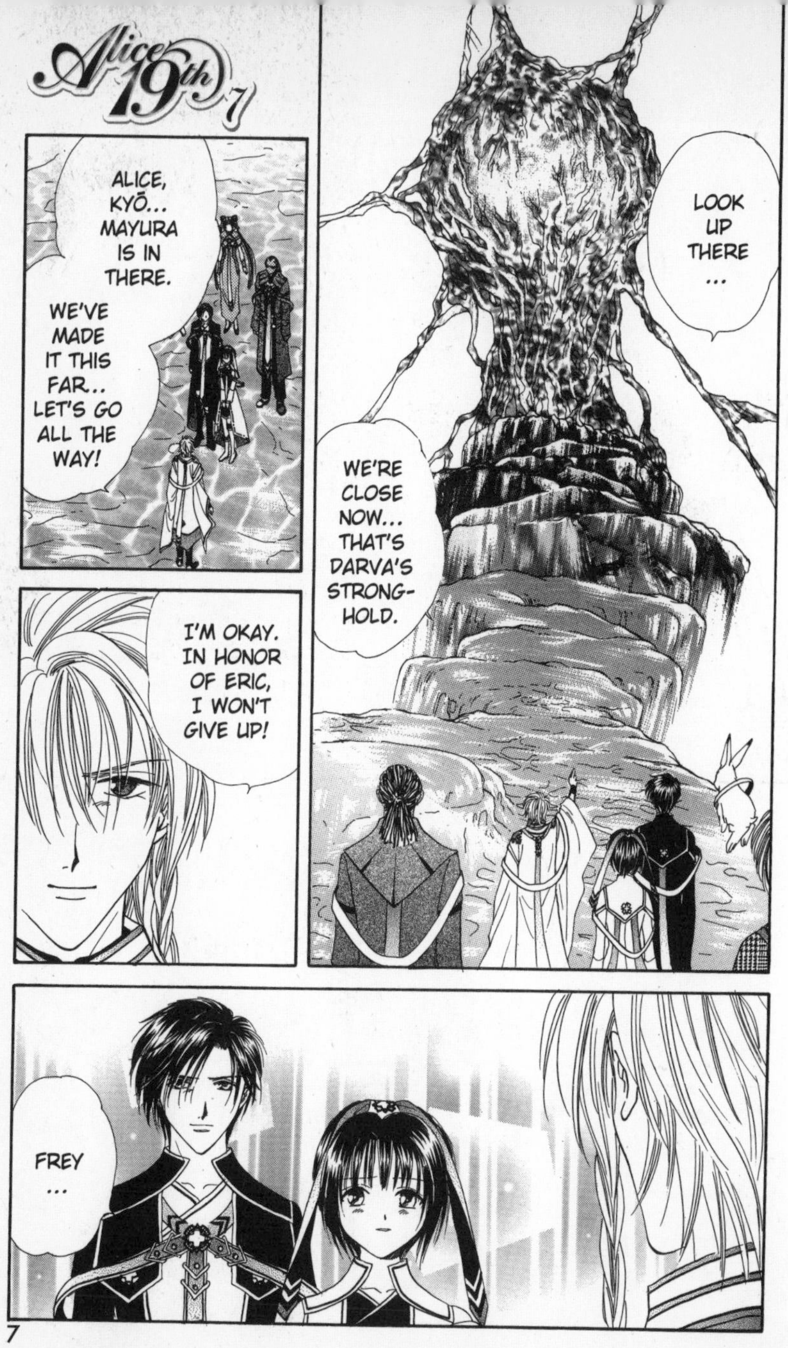
LOOK UP THERE ...
WE'RE CLOSE NOW... THAT'S DARVA'S STRONG-HOLD.
ALICE, KYŌ... MAYURA IS IN THERE.
WE'VE MADE IT THIS FAR.. LET'S GO ALL THE WAY!
I'M OKAY. IN HONOR OF ERIC, I WON'T GIVE UP!
FREY ...

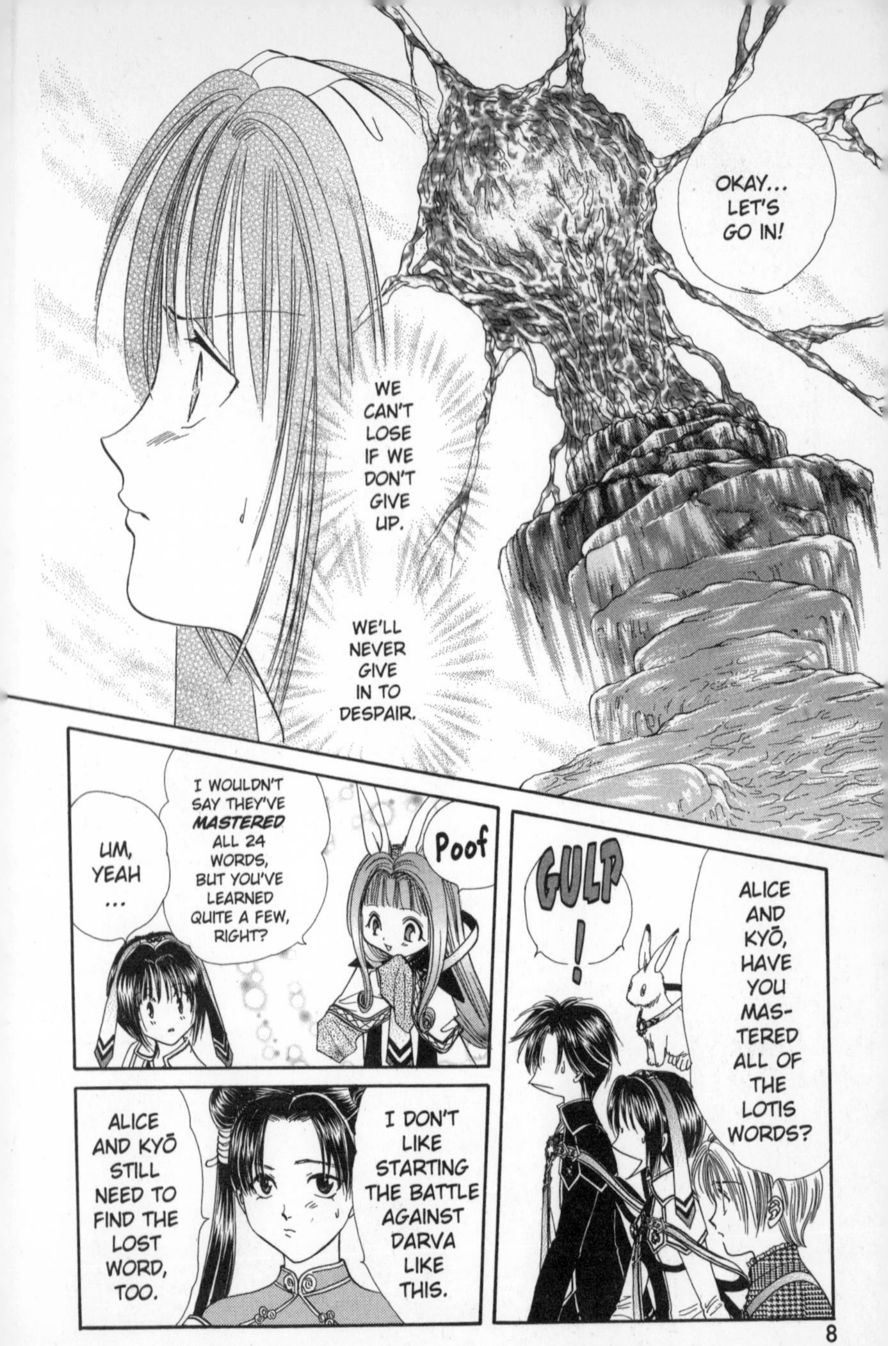
OKAY... LET'S GO IN!
WE CAN'T LOSE IF WE DON'T GIVE UP.
WE'LL NEVER GIVE IN TO DESPAIR.
ALICE AND KYŌ, HAVE YOU MASTERED ALL OF THE LOTIS WORDS?
GULP !
Poof
I WOULDN'T SAY THEY'VE MASTERED ALL 24 WORDS, BUT YOU'VE LEARNED QUITE A FEW, RIGHT?
UM, YEAH ...
I DON'T LIKE STARTING THE BATTLE AGAINST DARVA LIKE THIS.
ALICE AND KYŌ STILL NEED TO FIND THE LOST WORD, TOO.

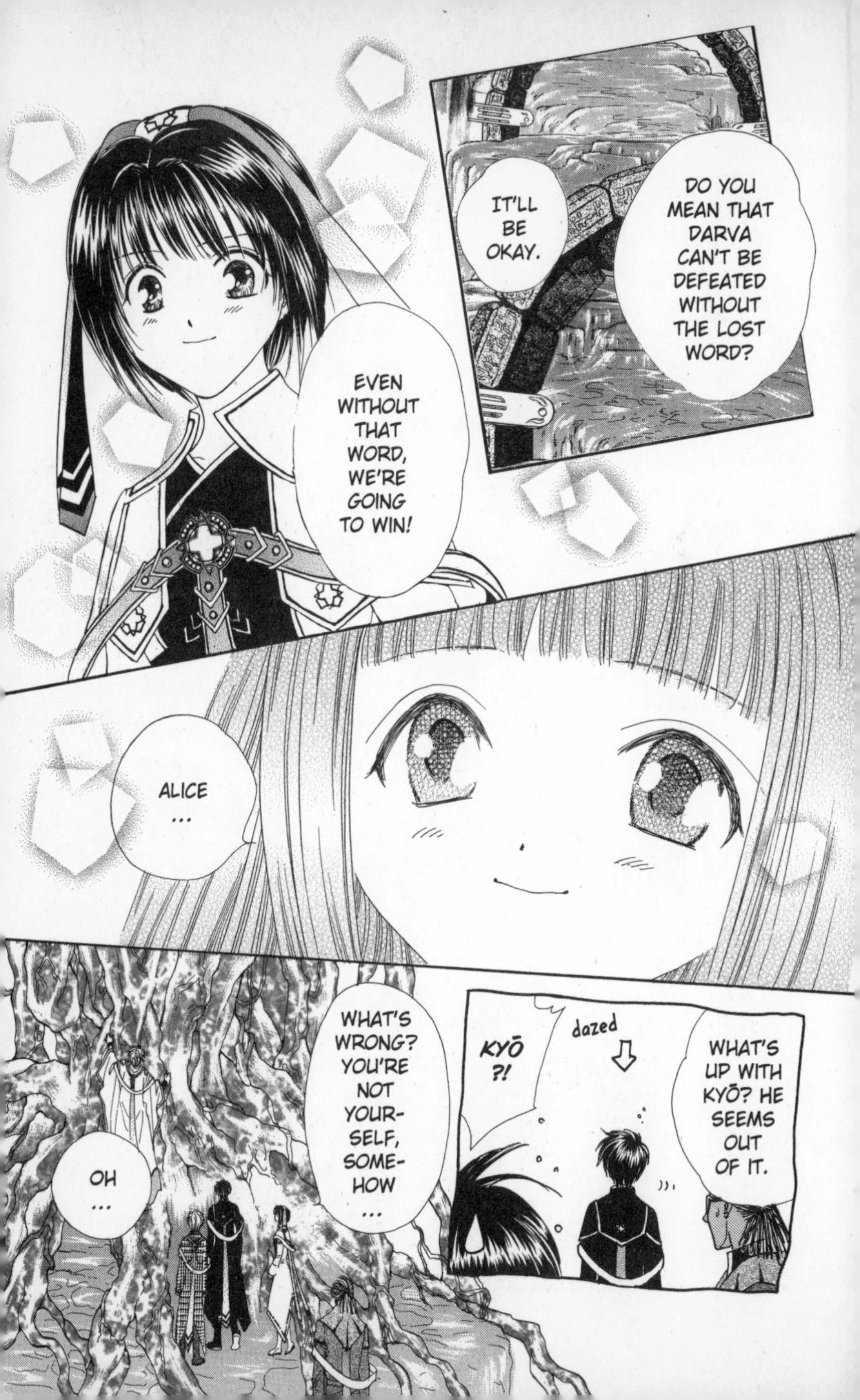
DO YOU MEAN THAT DARVA CAN'T BE DEFEATED WITHOUT THE LOST WORD?
IT'LL BE OKAY.
EVEN WITHOUT THAT WORD, WE'RE GOING TO WIN!
ALICE ...
WHAT'S UP WITH KYŌ? HE SEEMS OUT OF IT.
dazed
KYŌ ?!
WHAT'S WRONG? YOU'RE NOT YOURSELF, SOMEHOW ...
OH ...

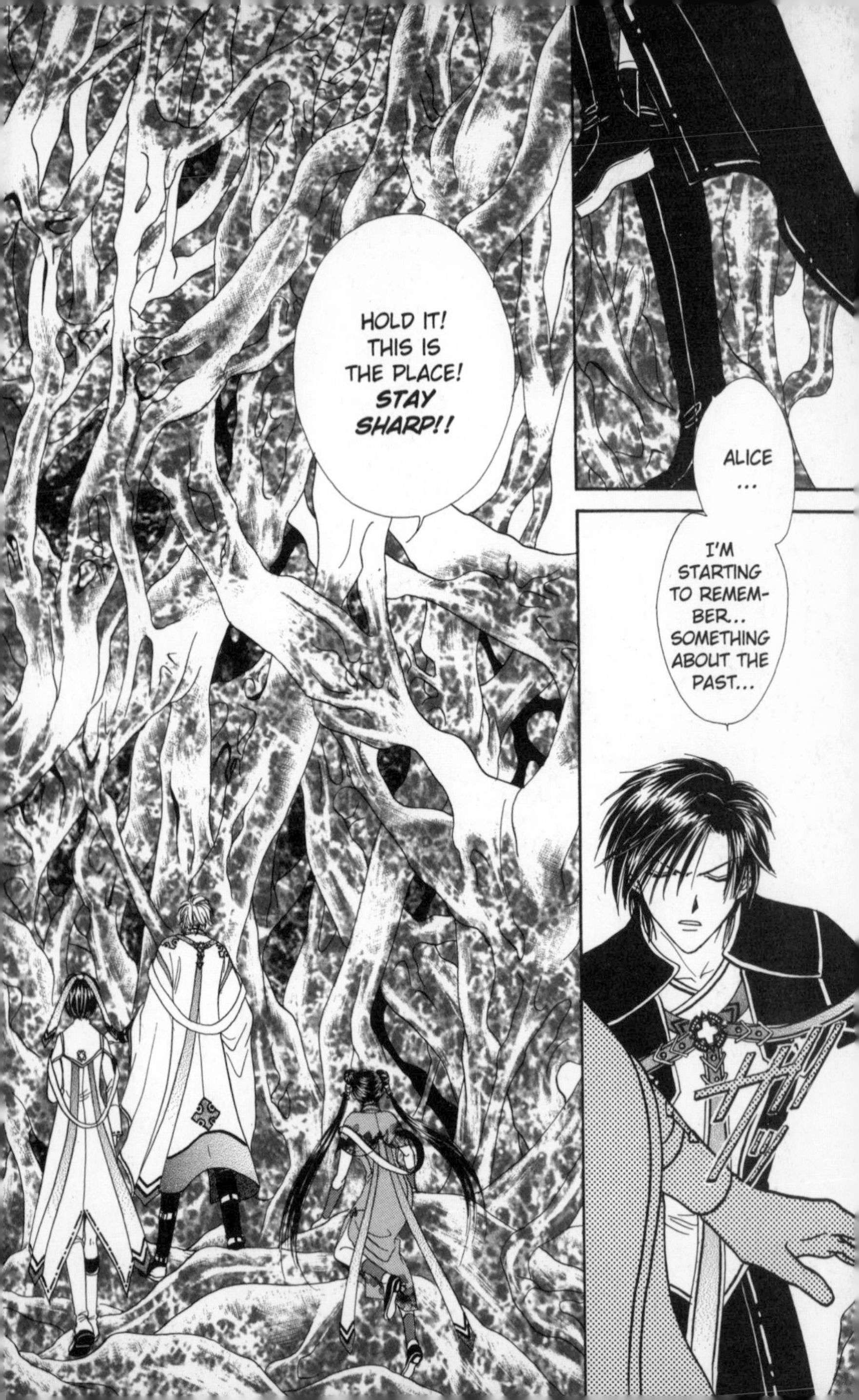
ALICE ...
I'M STARTING TO REMEM- BER... SOMETHING ABOUT THE PAST...
HOLD IT! THIS IS THE PLACE! **STAY SHARP!!**

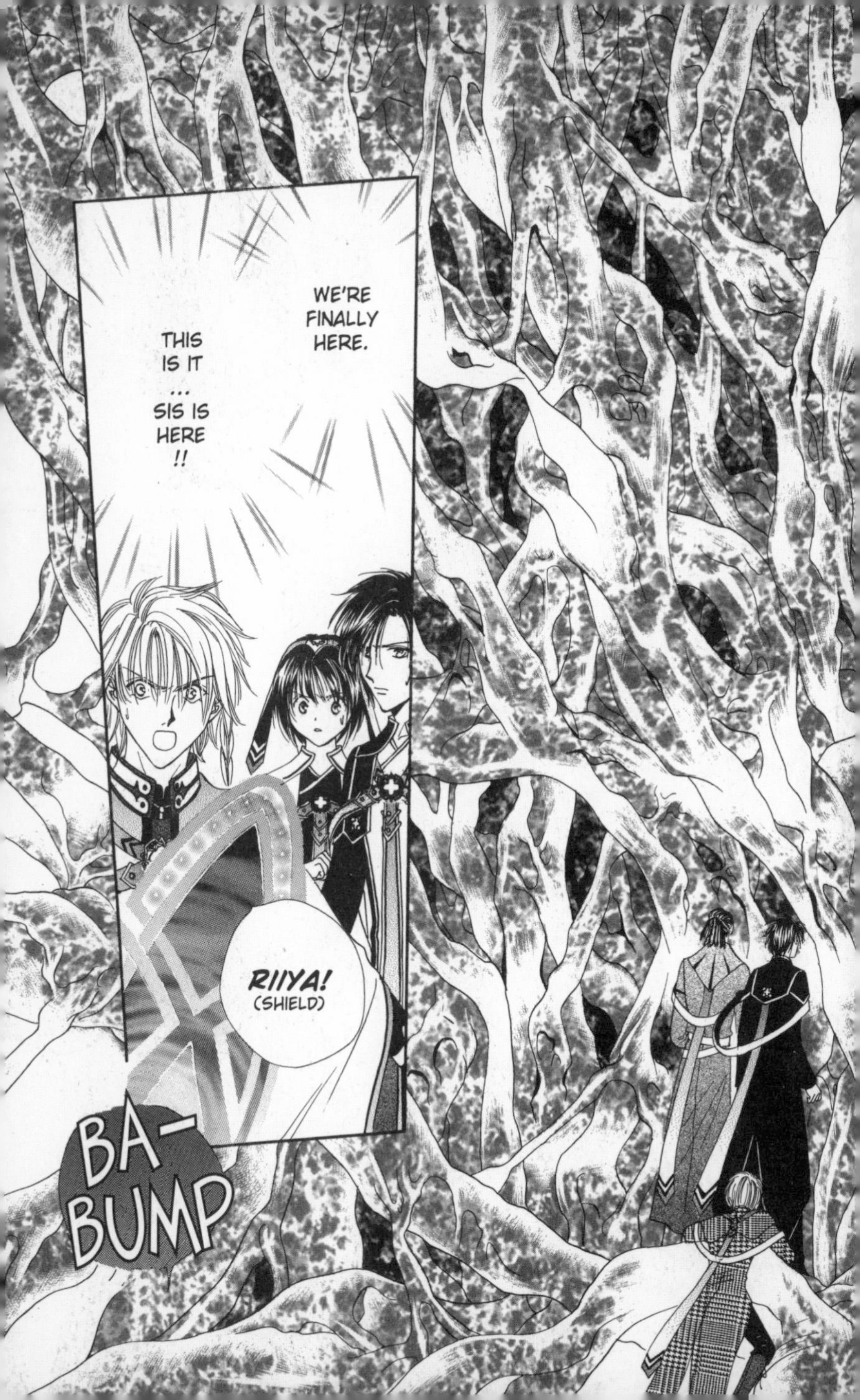
WE'RE FINALLY HERE.
THIS IS IT ... SIS IS HERE !!
RIIYA! (SHIELD)
BA-BUMP

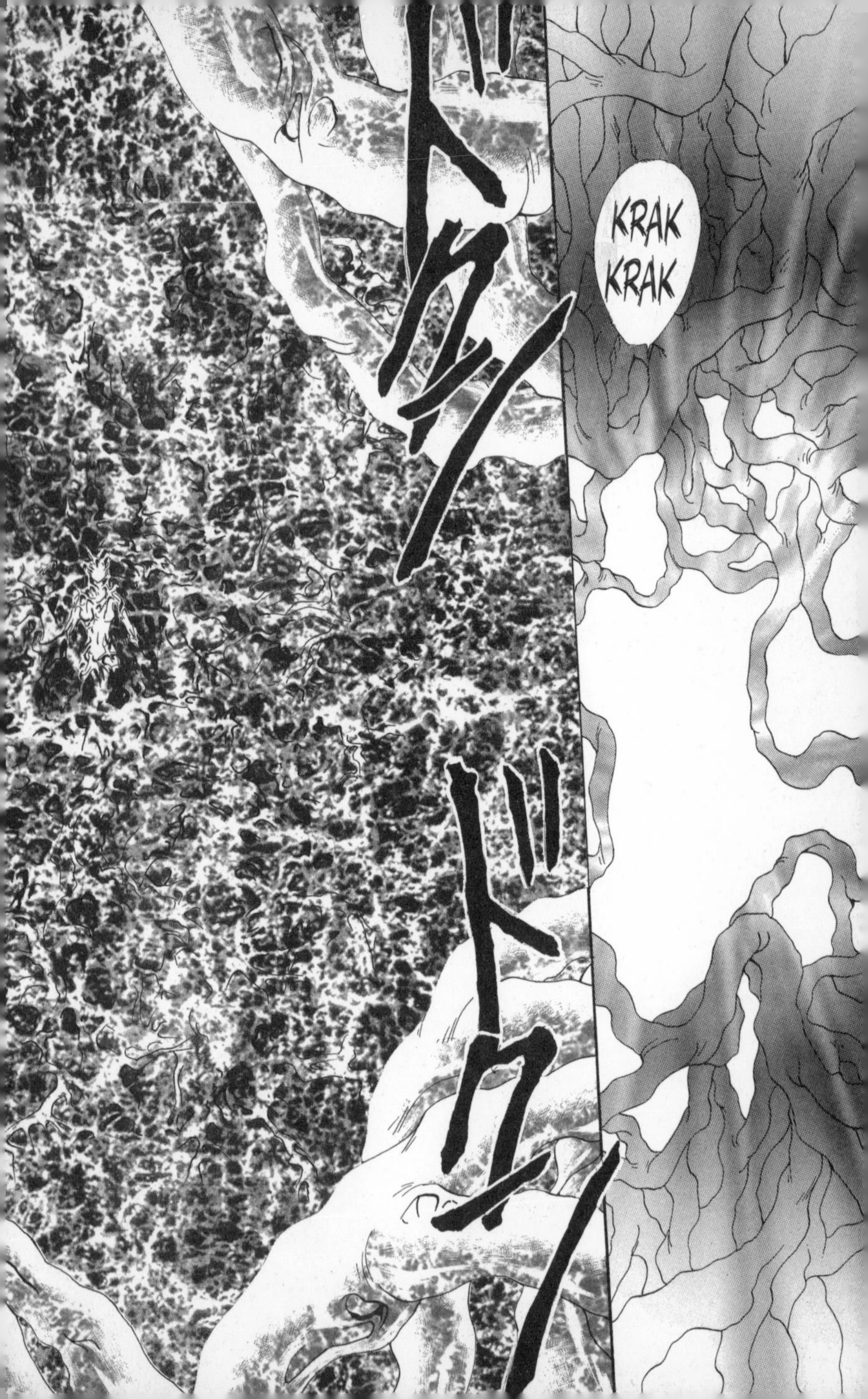
KRAK KRAK

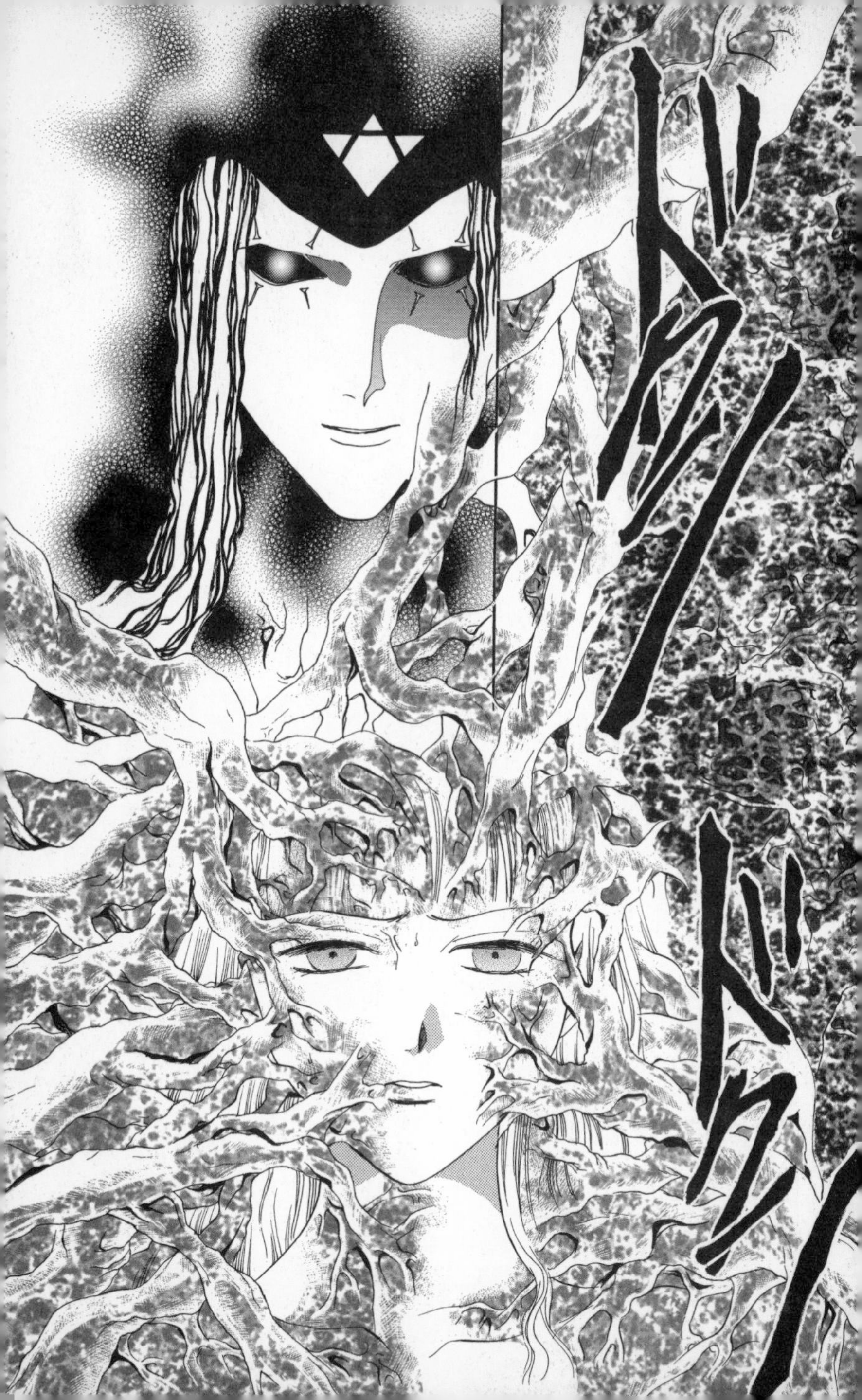
ドクン
ドクン

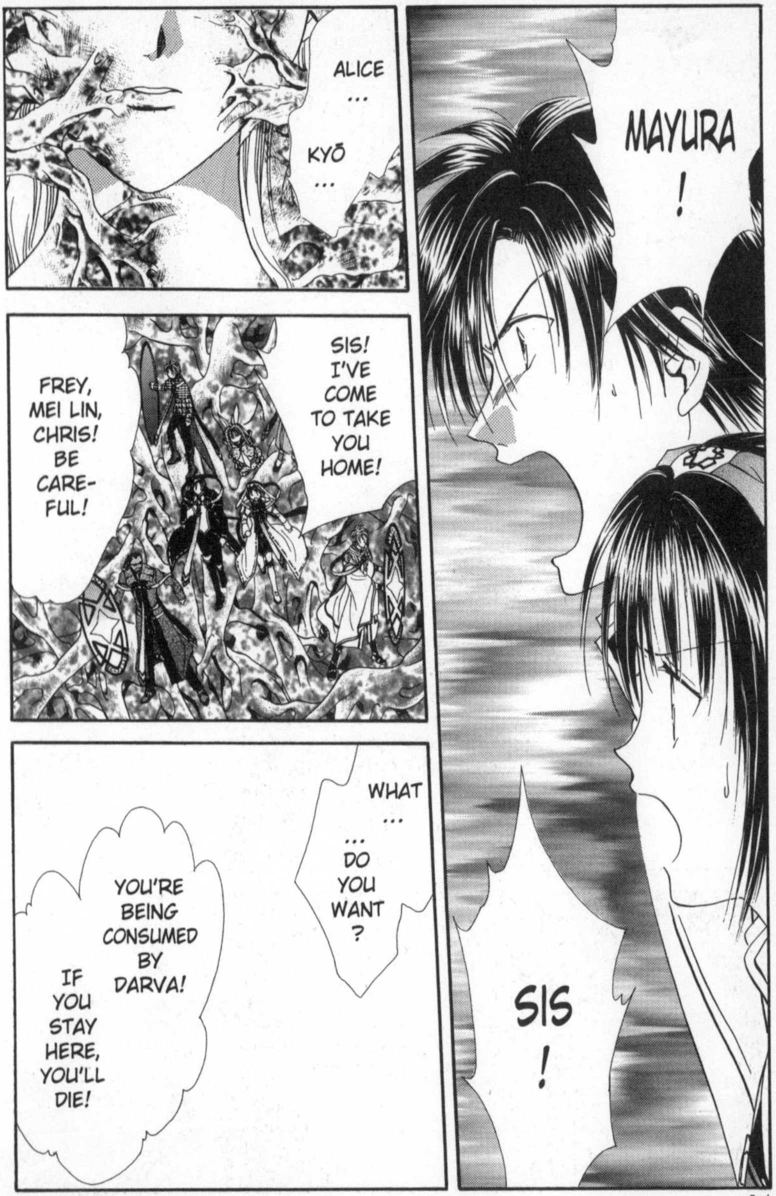

MAYURA!
SIS!
ALICE...
KYŌ...
SIS! I'VE COME TO TAKE YOU HOME!
FREY, MEI LIN, CHRIS! BE CARE-FUL!
WHAT... ...DO YOU WANT?
YOU'RE BEING CONSUMED BY DARVA!
IF YOU STAY HERE, YOU'LL DIE!

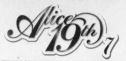

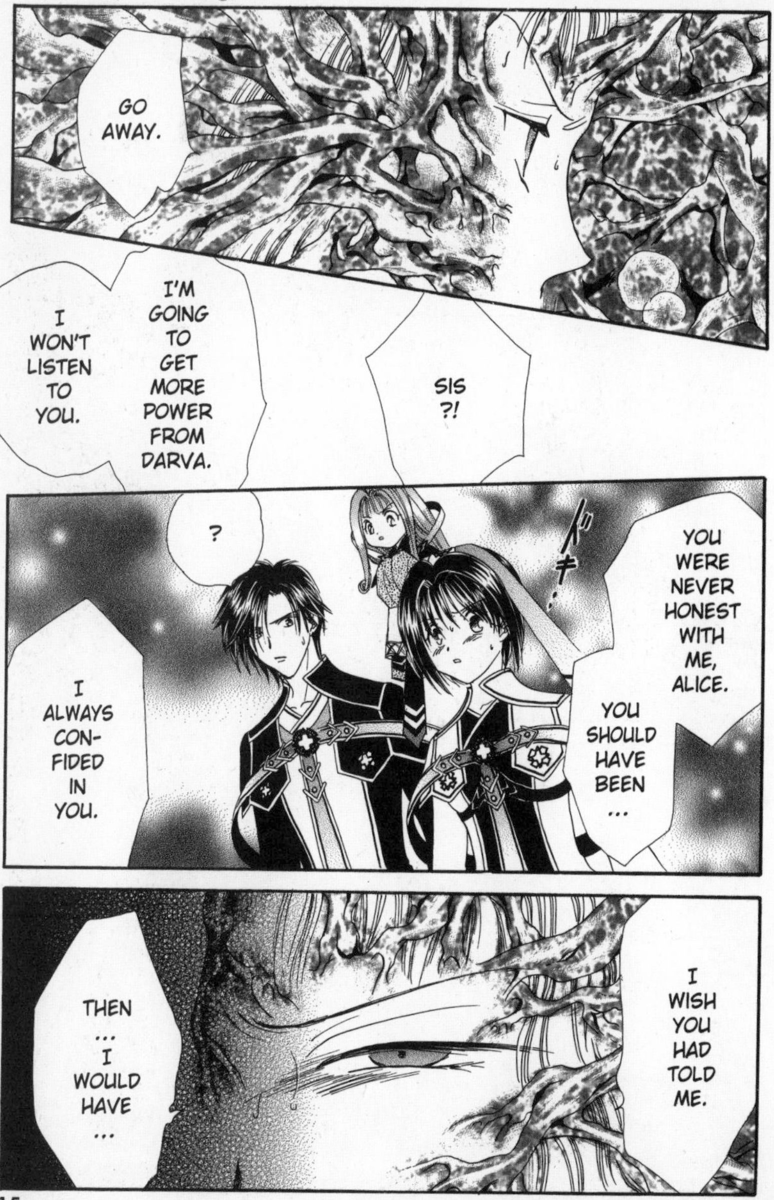
GO AWAY.
SIS ?!
I'M GOING TO GET MORE POWER FROM DARVA.
I WON'T LISTEN TO YOU.
ドキ…
YOU WERE NEVER HONEST WITH ME, ALICE.
?
YOU SHOULD HAVE BEEN ...
I ALWAYS CON-FIDED IN YOU.
I WISH YOU HAD TOLD ME.
THEN ... I WOULD HAVE ...

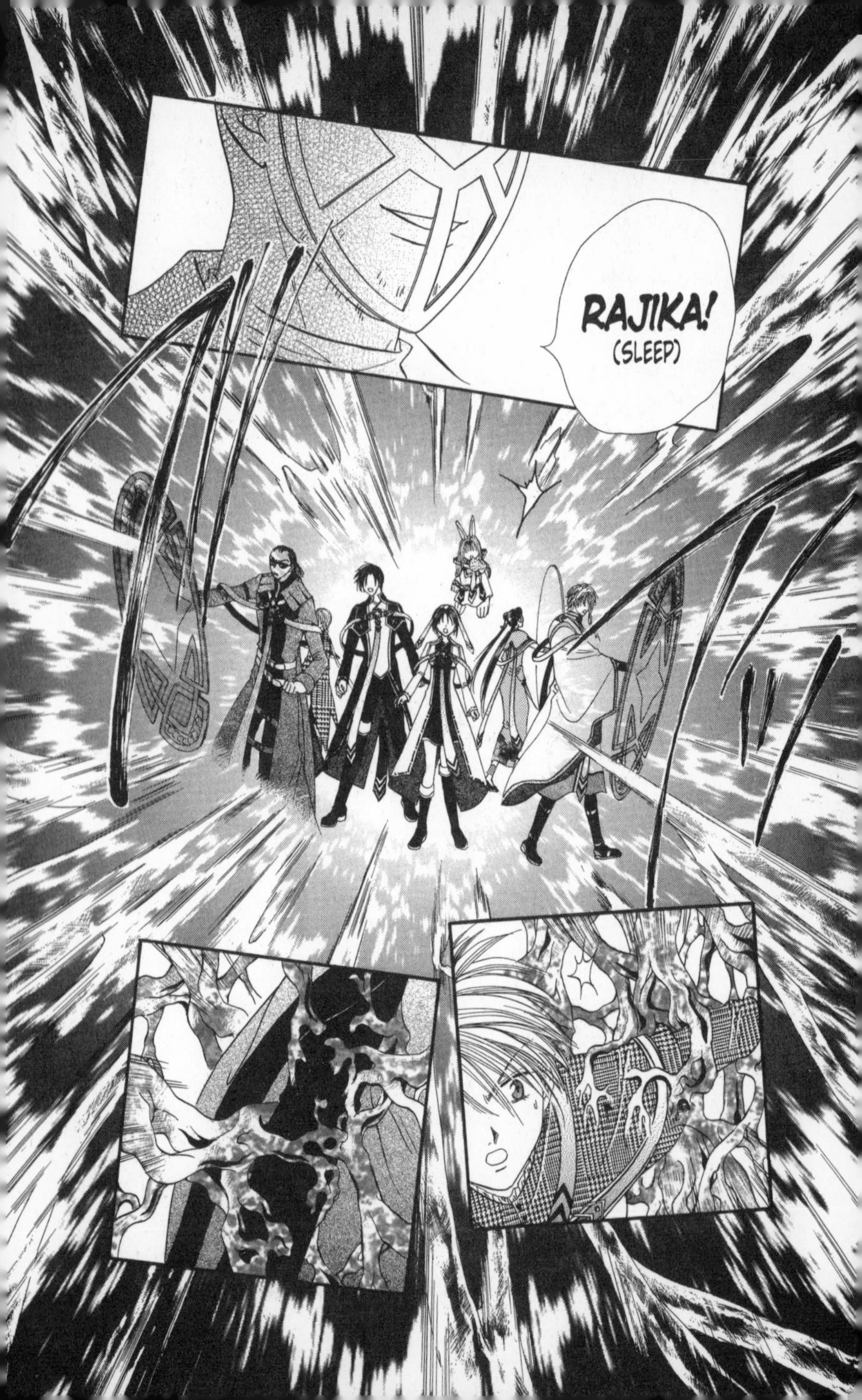
RAJIKA!
(SLEEP)

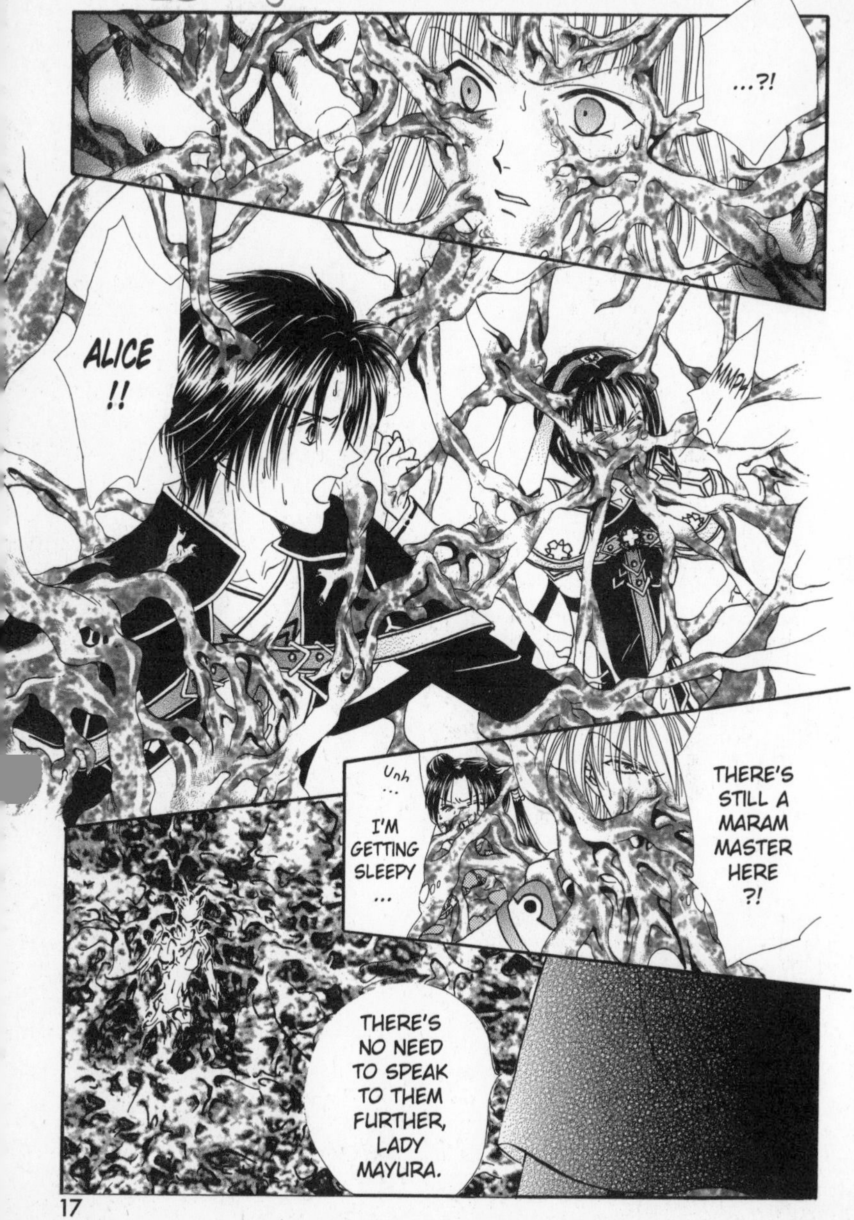
...?!
ALICE !!
MMPH !
THERE'S STILL A MARAM MASTER HERE ?!
Unh ...
I'M GETTING SLEEPY ...
THERE'S NO NEED TO SPEAK TO THEM FURTHER, LADY MAYURA.

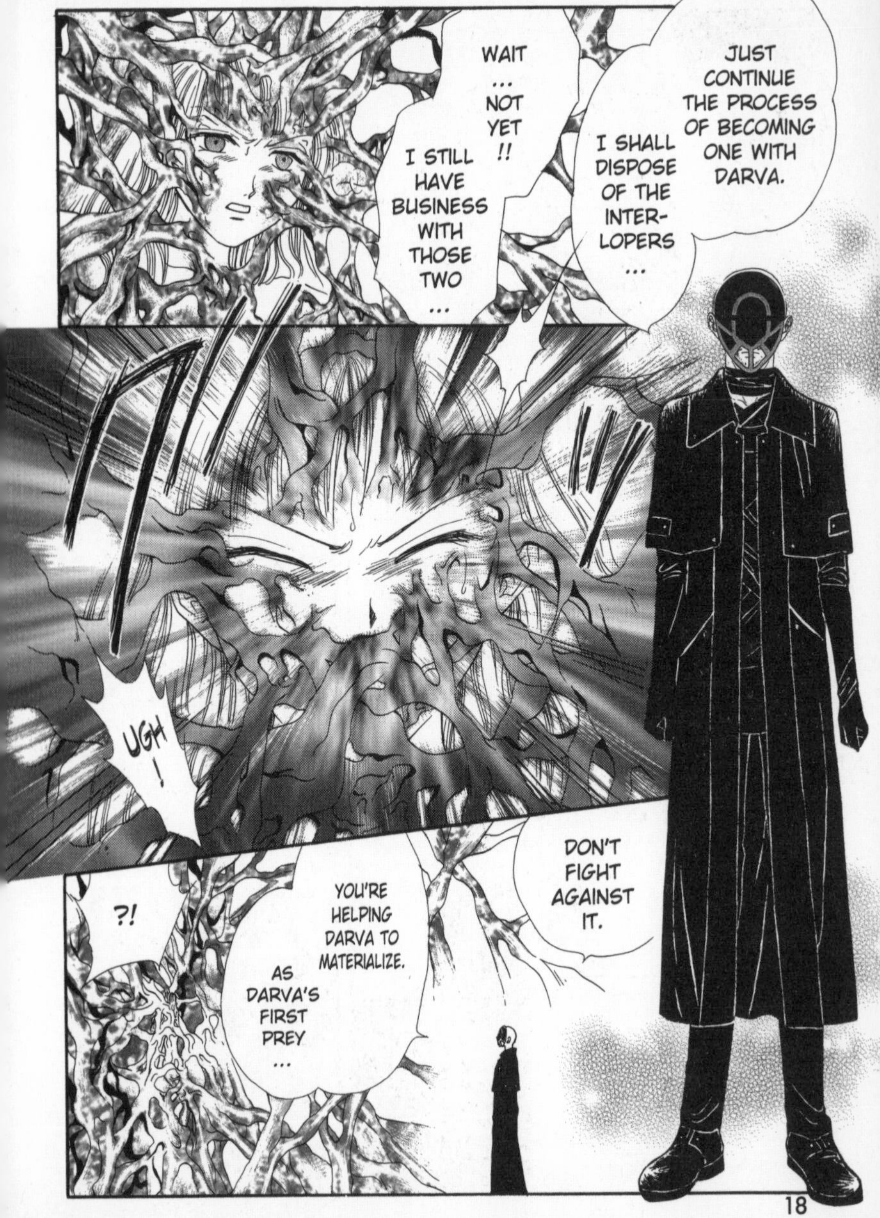
JUST CONTINUE THE PROCESS OF BECOMING ONE WITH DARVA.
I SHALL DISPOSE OF THE INTER-LOPERS ...
WAIT ... NOT YET !!
I STILL HAVE BUSINESS WITH THOSE TWO ...
UGH !
DON'T FIGHT AGAINST IT.
YOU'RE HELPING DARVA TO MATERIALIZE.
?!
AS DARVA'S FIRST PREY ...

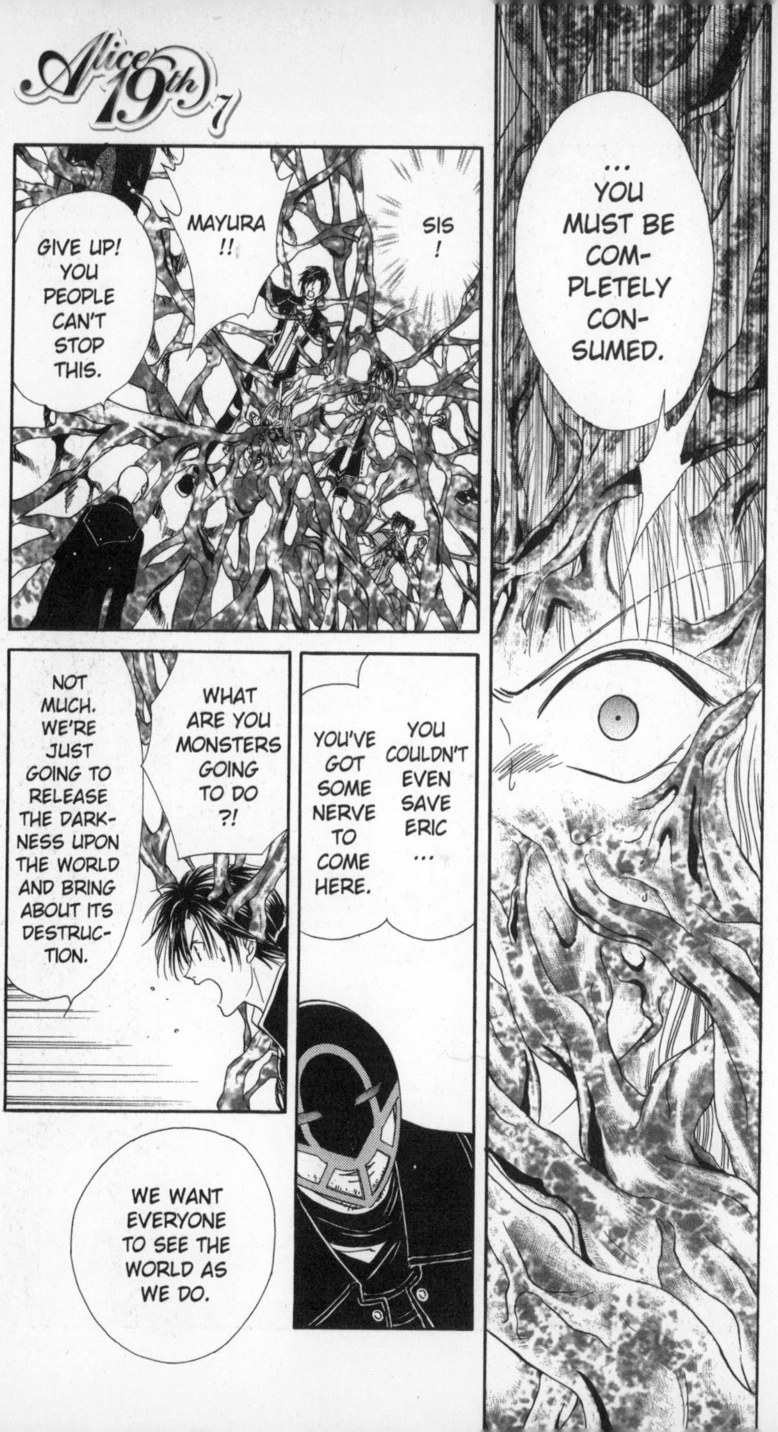

... YOU MUST BE COM-PLETELY CON-SUMED.
SIS !
MAYURA !!
GIVE UP! YOU PEOPLE CAN'T STOP THIS.
YOU COULDN'T EVEN SAVE ERIC ...
YOU'VE GOT SOME NERVE TO COME HERE.
WHAT ARE YOU MONSTERS GOING TO DO ?!
NOT MUCH. WE'RE JUST GOING TO RELEASE THE DARK-NESS UPON THE WORLD AND BRING ABOUT ITS DESTRUC-TION.
WE WANT EVERYONE TO SEE THE WORLD AS WE DO.

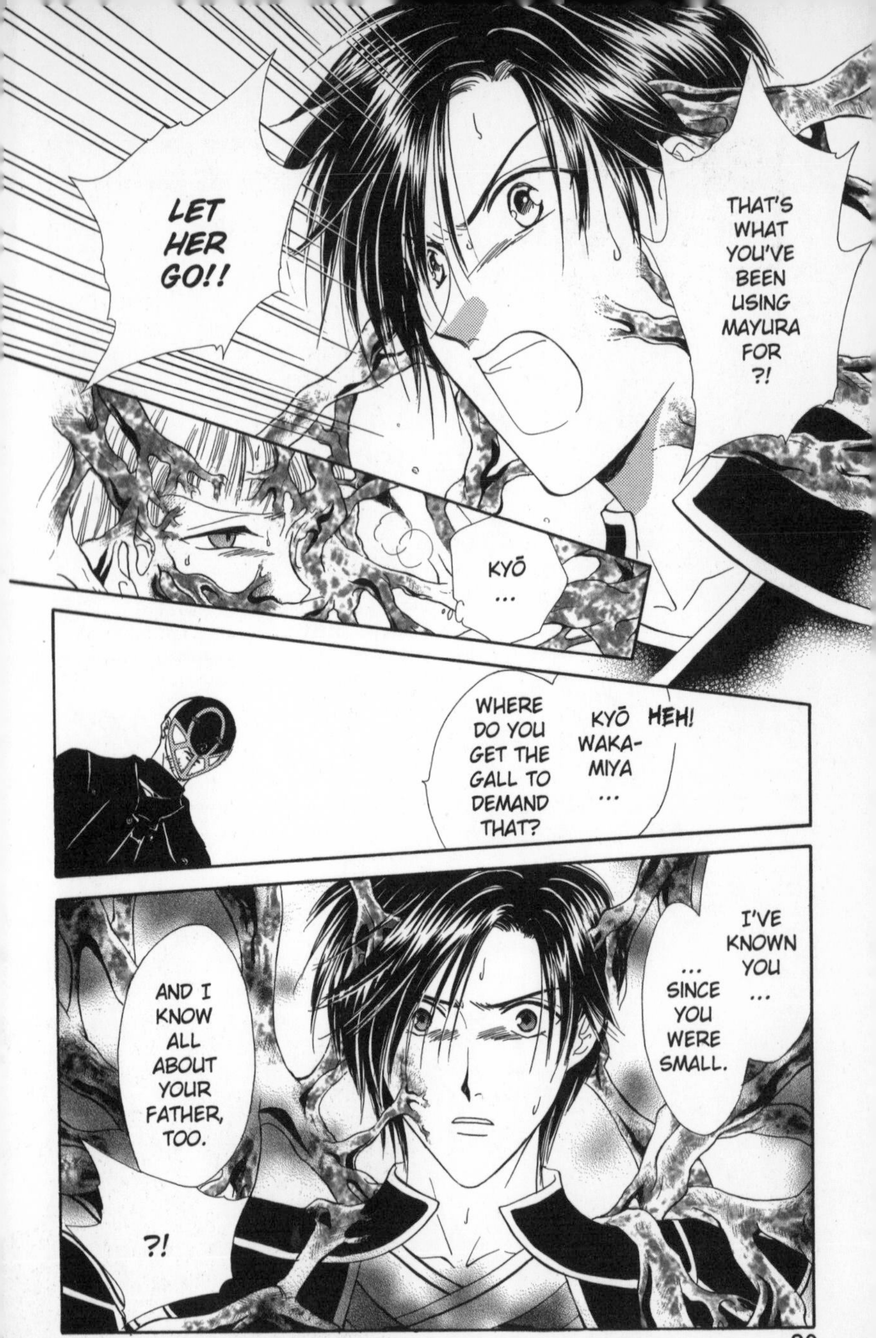
THAT'S WHAT YOU'VE BEEN USING MAYURA FOR ?!
LET HER GO!!
KYŌ ...
HEH!
KYŌ WAKA-MIYA ...
WHERE DO YOU GET THE GALL TO DEMAND THAT?
I'VE KNOWN YOU ... ... SINCE YOU WERE SMALL.
AND I KNOW ALL ABOUT YOUR FATHER, TOO.
?!

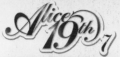

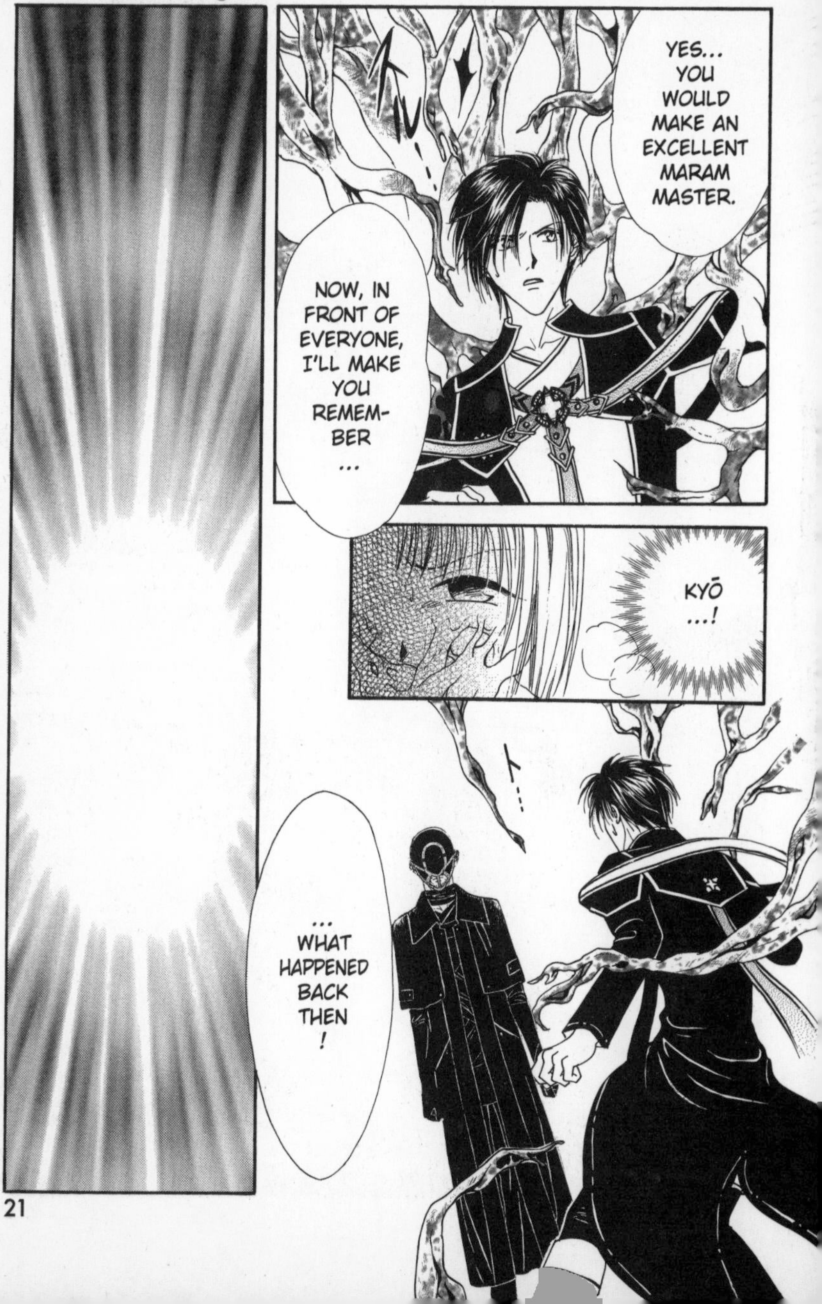
YES... YOU WOULD MAKE AN EXCELLENT MARAM MASTER.
NOW, IN FRONT OF EVERYONE, I'LL MAKE YOU REMEMBER ...
KYŌ ...!
... WHAT HAPPENED BACK THEN !

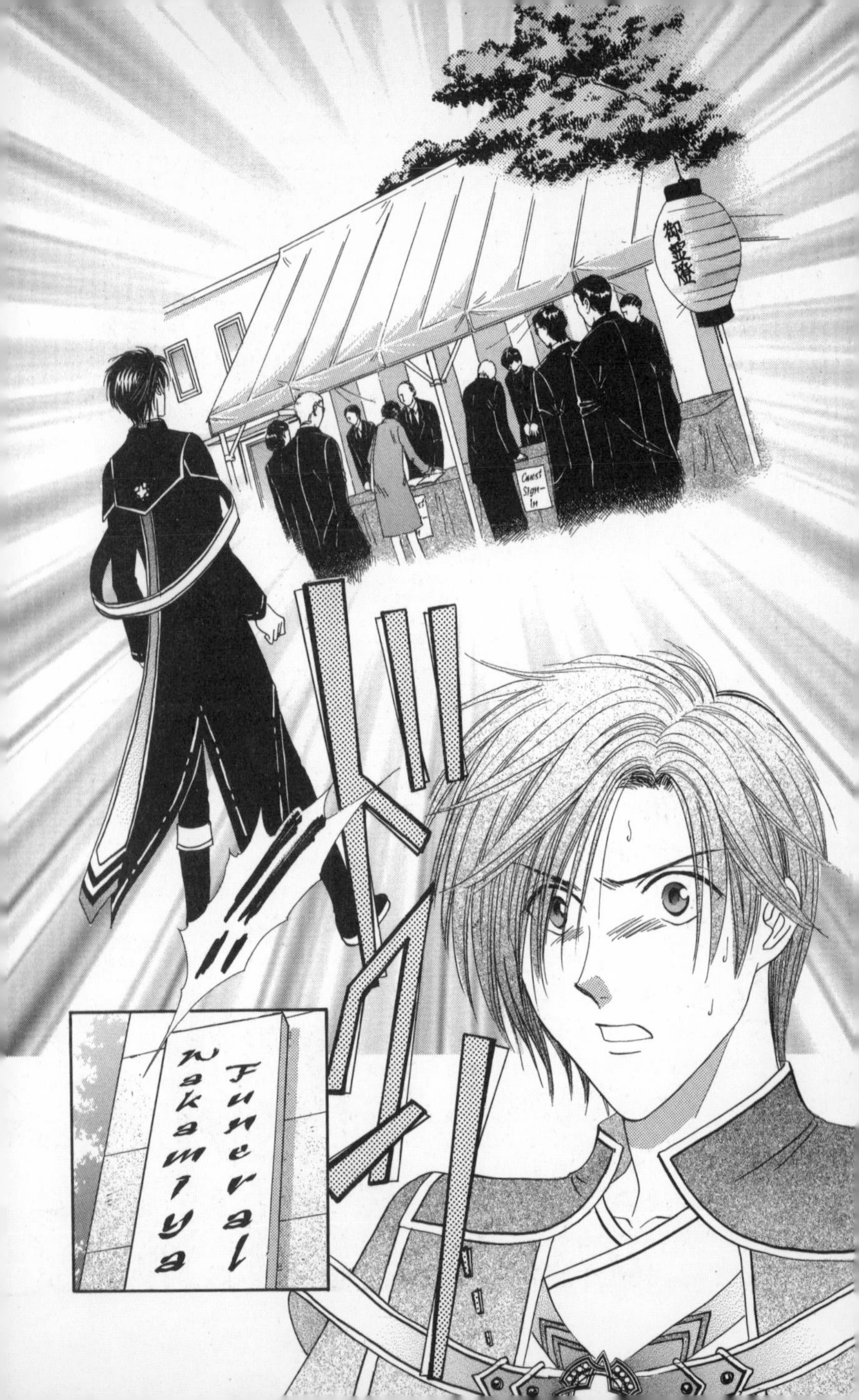
御霊燈
Guest Sign-In
Wakamiya Funeral

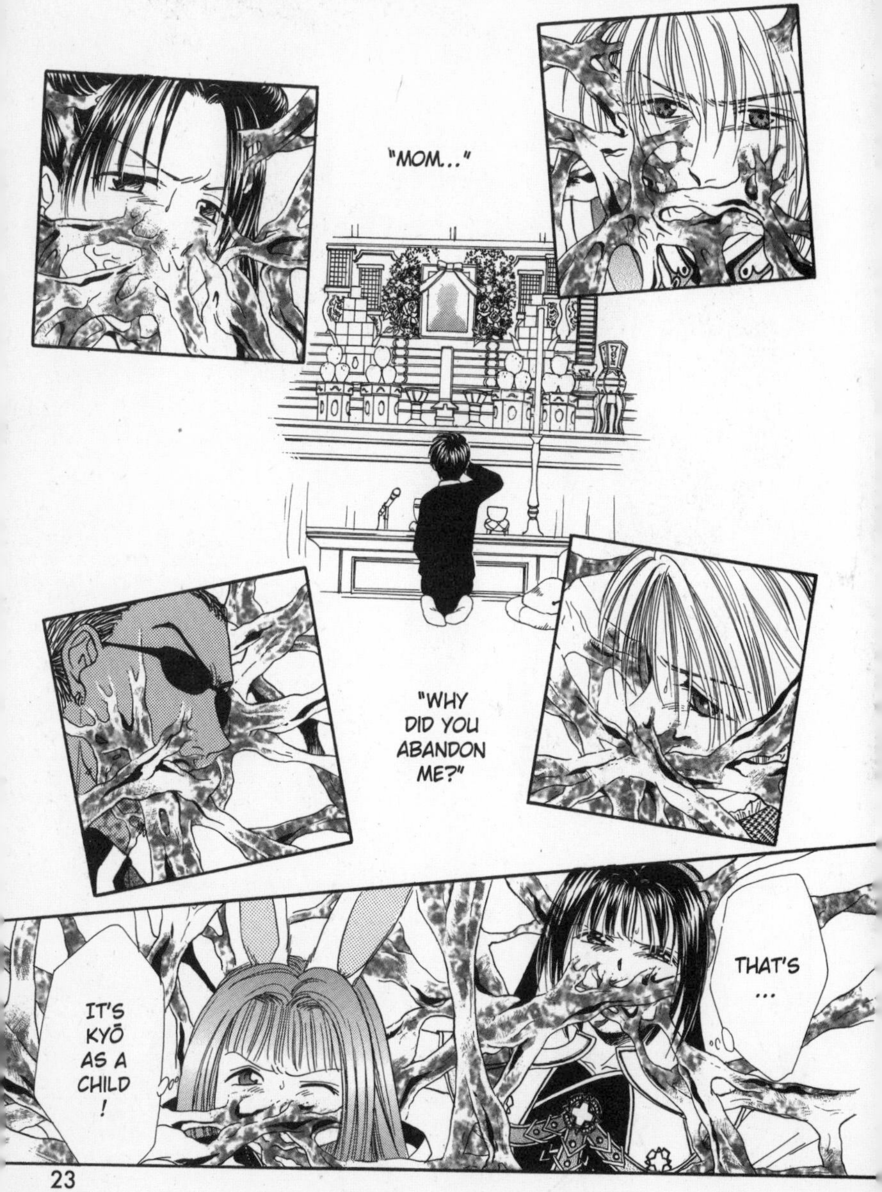
"MOM.."
"WHY DID YOU ABANDON ME?"
THAT'S ...
IT'S KYŌ AS A CHILD!

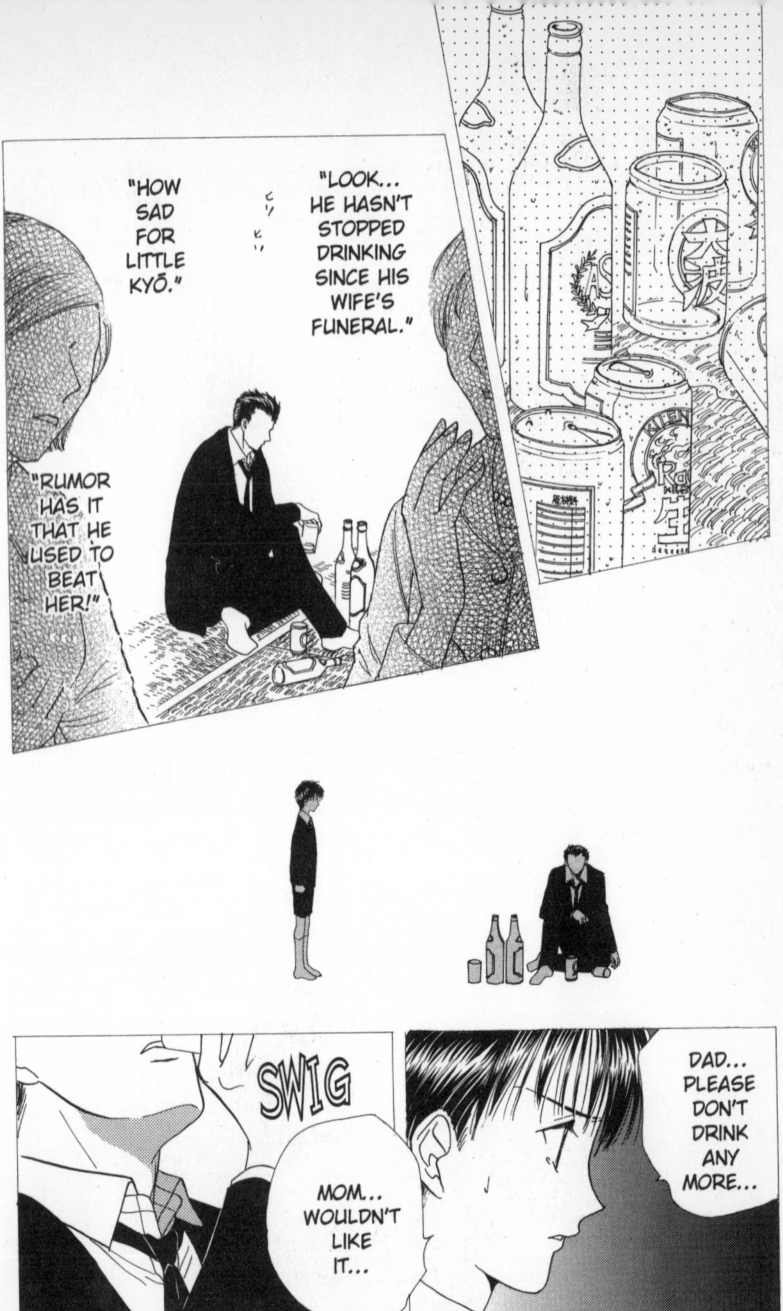
"LOOK... HE HASN'T STOPPED DRINKING SINCE HIS WIFE'S FUNERAL."
"HOW SAD FOR LITTLE KYŌ."
"RUMOR HAS IT THAT HE USED TO BEAT HER!"
DAD... PLEASE DON'T DRINK ANY MORE...
MOM... WOULDN'T LIKE IT...
SWIG

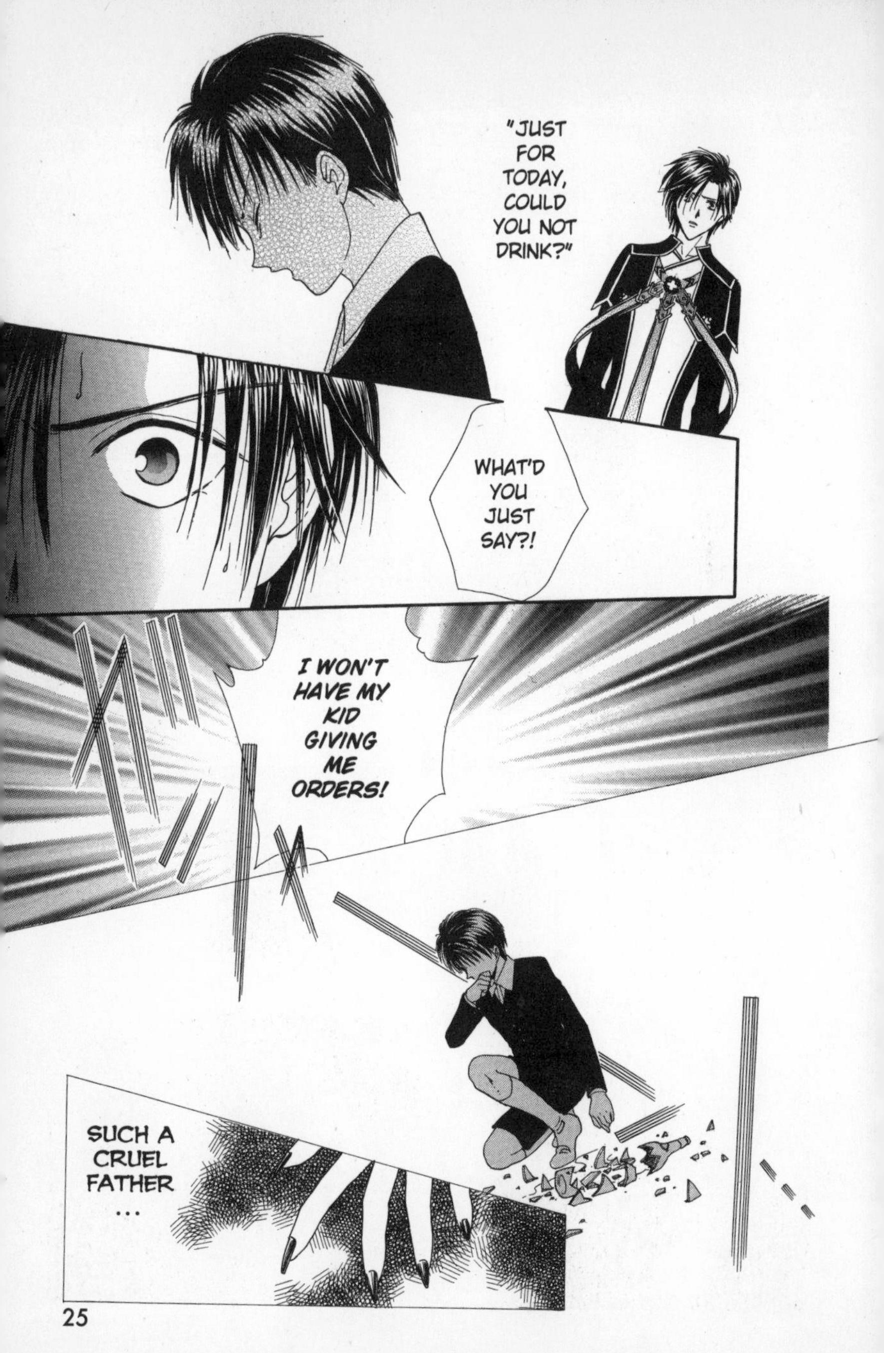
"JUST FOR TODAY, COULD YOU NOT DRINK?"
WHAT'D YOU JUST SAY?!
I WON'T HAVE MY KID GIVING ME ORDERS!
SUCH A CRUEL FATHER ...

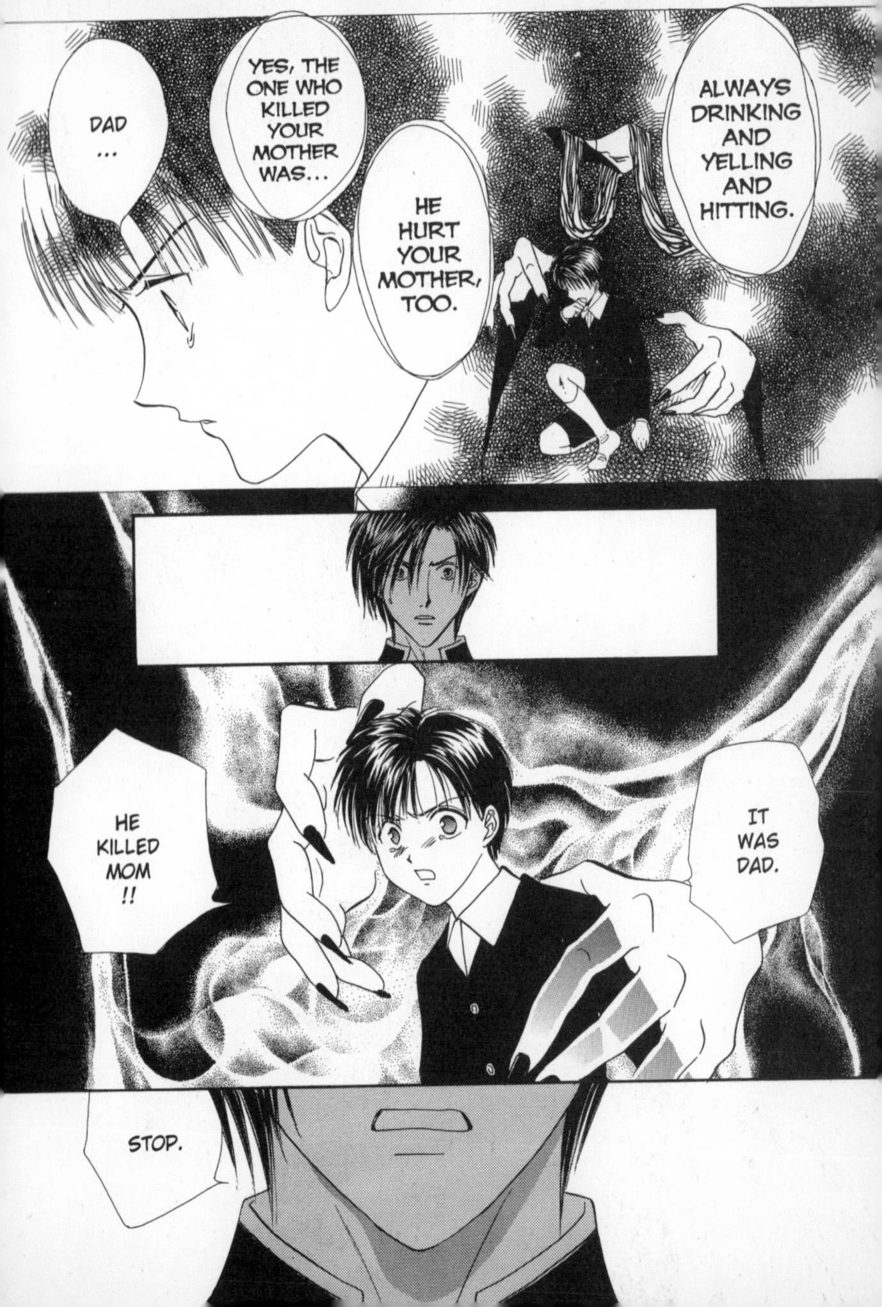
ALWAYS DRINKING AND YELLING AND HITTING.
HE HURT YOUR MOTHER, TOO.
YES, THE ONE WHO KILLED YOUR MOTHER WAS...
DAD ...
IT WAS DAD.
HE KILLED MOM !!
STOP.

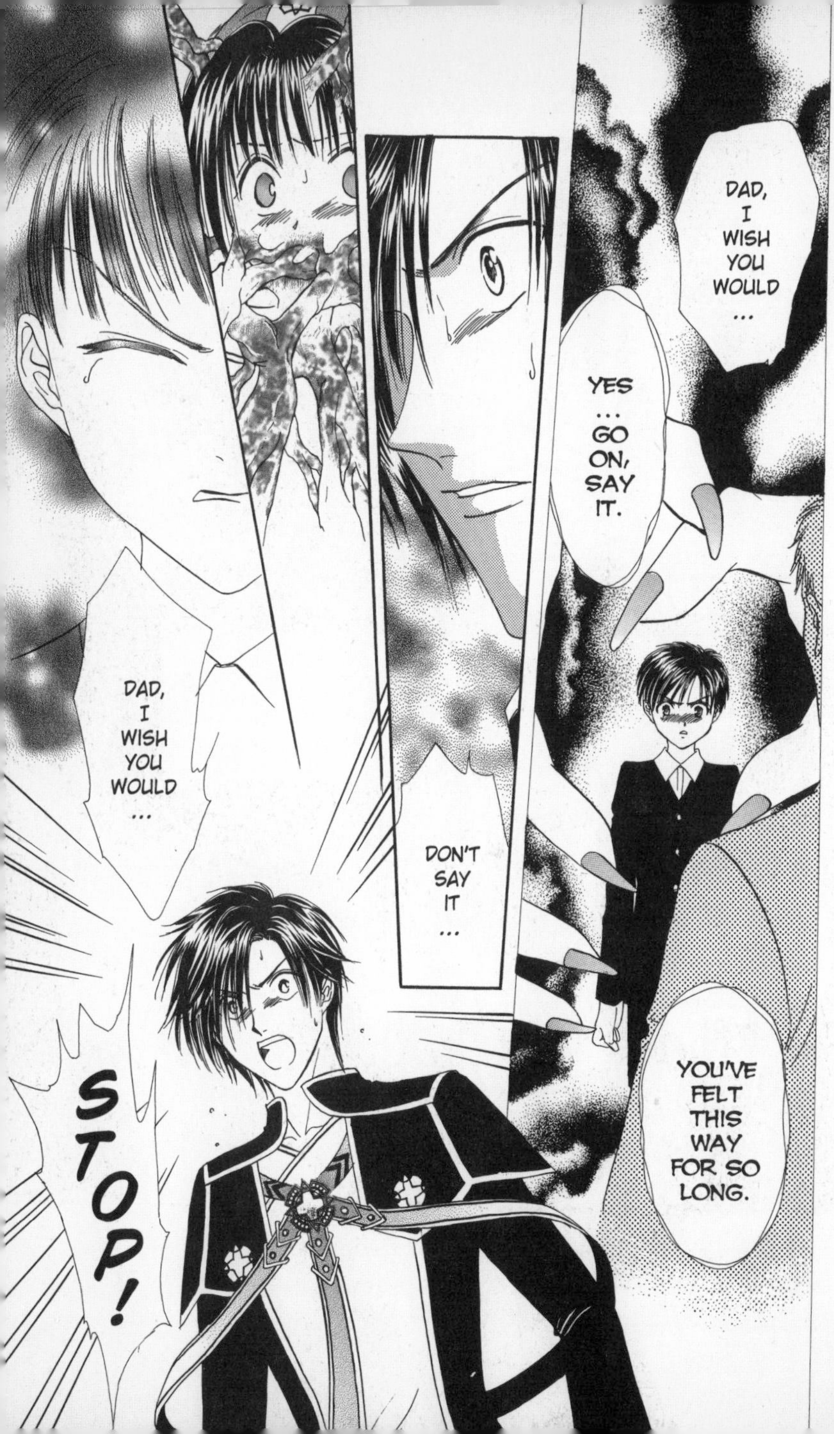
DAD, I WISH YOU WOULD ...
YES ... GO ON, SAY IT.
YOU'VE FELT THIS WAY FOR SO LONG.
DON'T SAY IT ...
DAD, I WISH YOU WOULD ...
STOP!

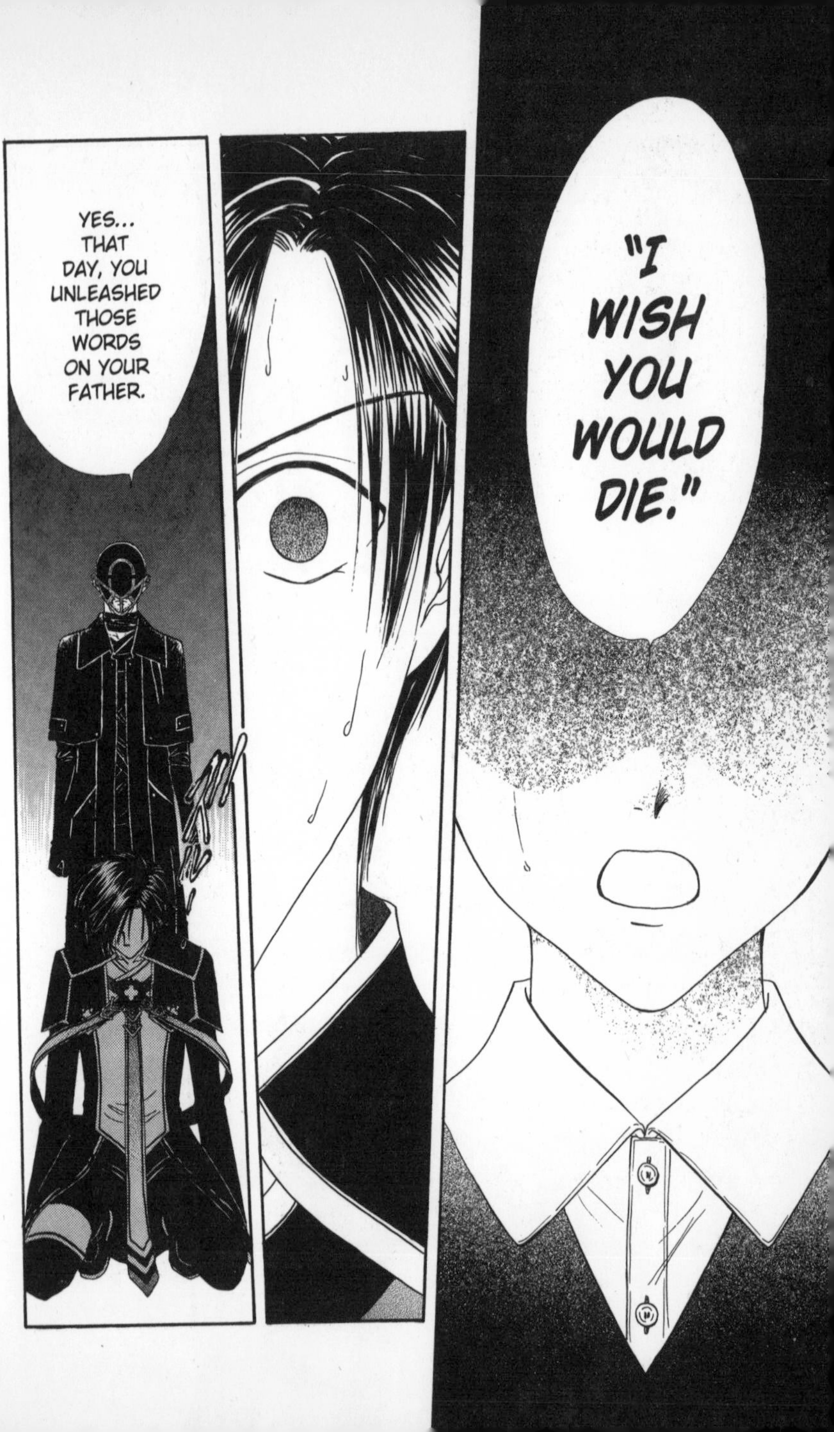
"I WISH YOU WOULD DIE."
YES... THAT DAY, YOU UNLEASHED THOSE WORDS ON YOUR FATHER.

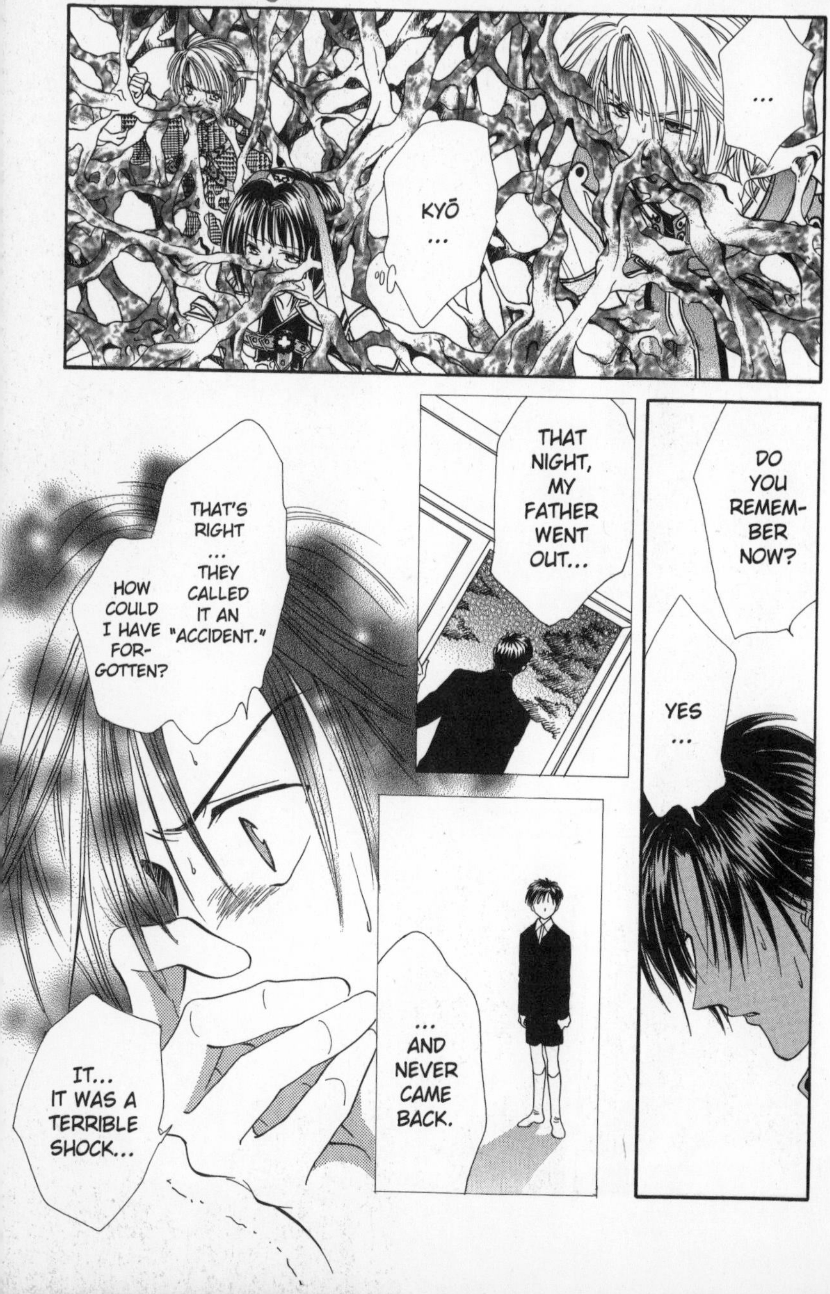
...
KYŌ ...
DO YOU REMEMBER NOW?
YES ...
THAT NIGHT, MY FATHER WENT OUT...
... AND NEVER CAME BACK.
THAT'S RIGHT ... THEY CALLED IT AN "ACCIDENT."
HOW COULD I HAVE FORGOTTEN?
IT... IT WAS A TERRIBLE SHOCK...

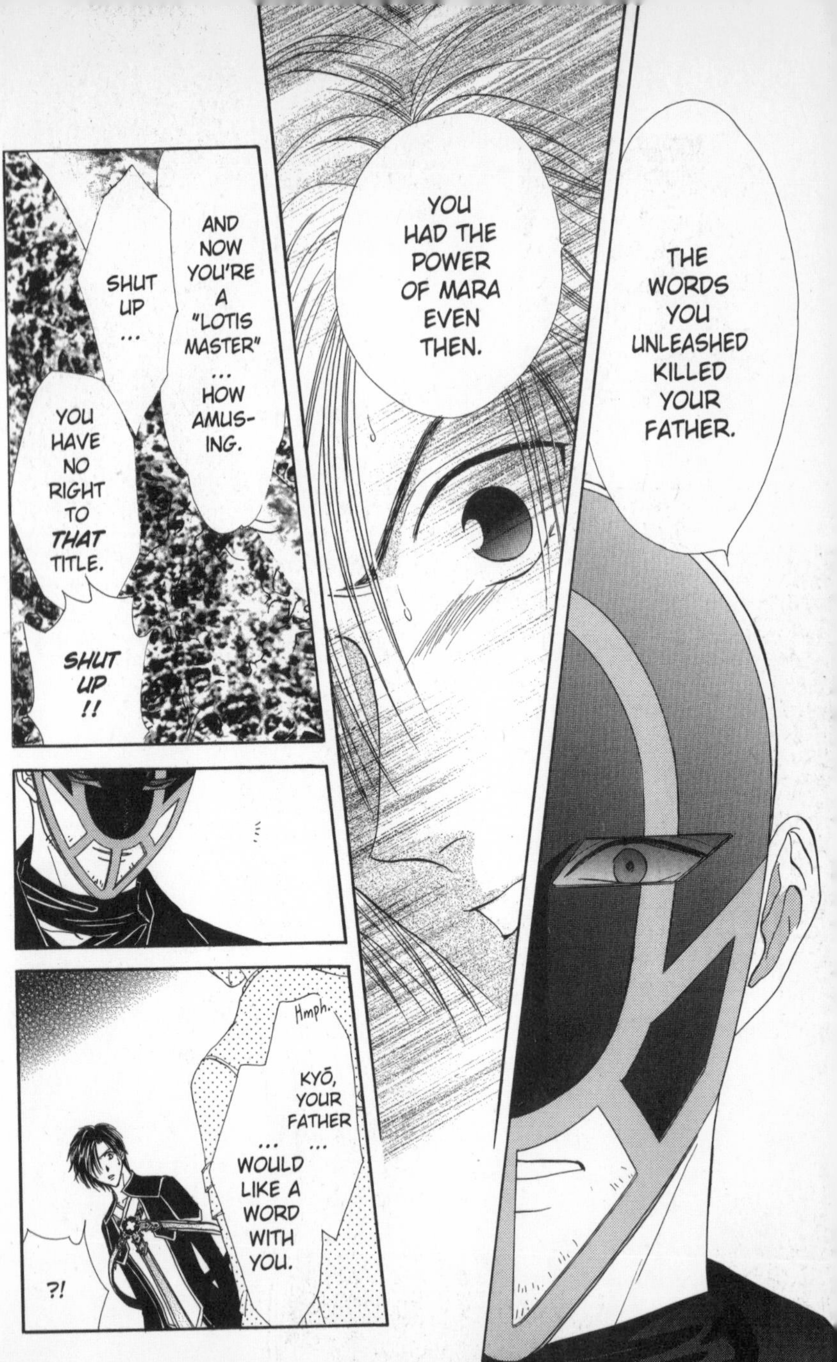
THE WORDS YOU UNLEASHED KILLED YOUR FATHER.
YOU HAD THE POWER OF MARA EVEN THEN.
AND NOW YOU'RE A "LOTIS MASTER" ... HOW AMUSING.
SHUT UP ...
YOU HAVE NO RIGHT TO *THAT* TITLE.
SHUT UP !!
...
Hmph..
KYŌ, YOUR FATHER ... ... WOULD LIKE A WORD WITH YOU.
?!

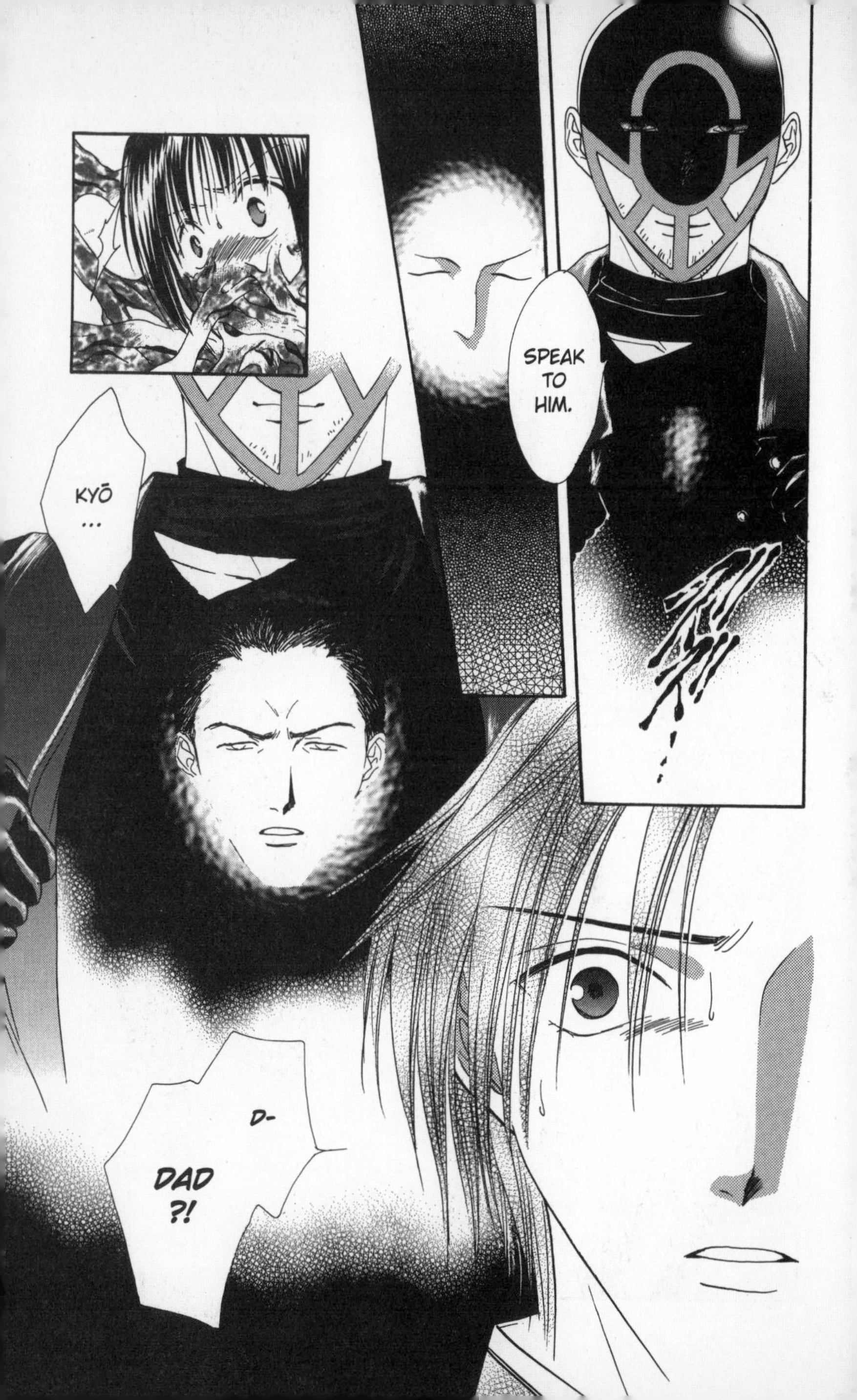
SPEAK TO HIM.
KYŌ ...
D- DAD ?!

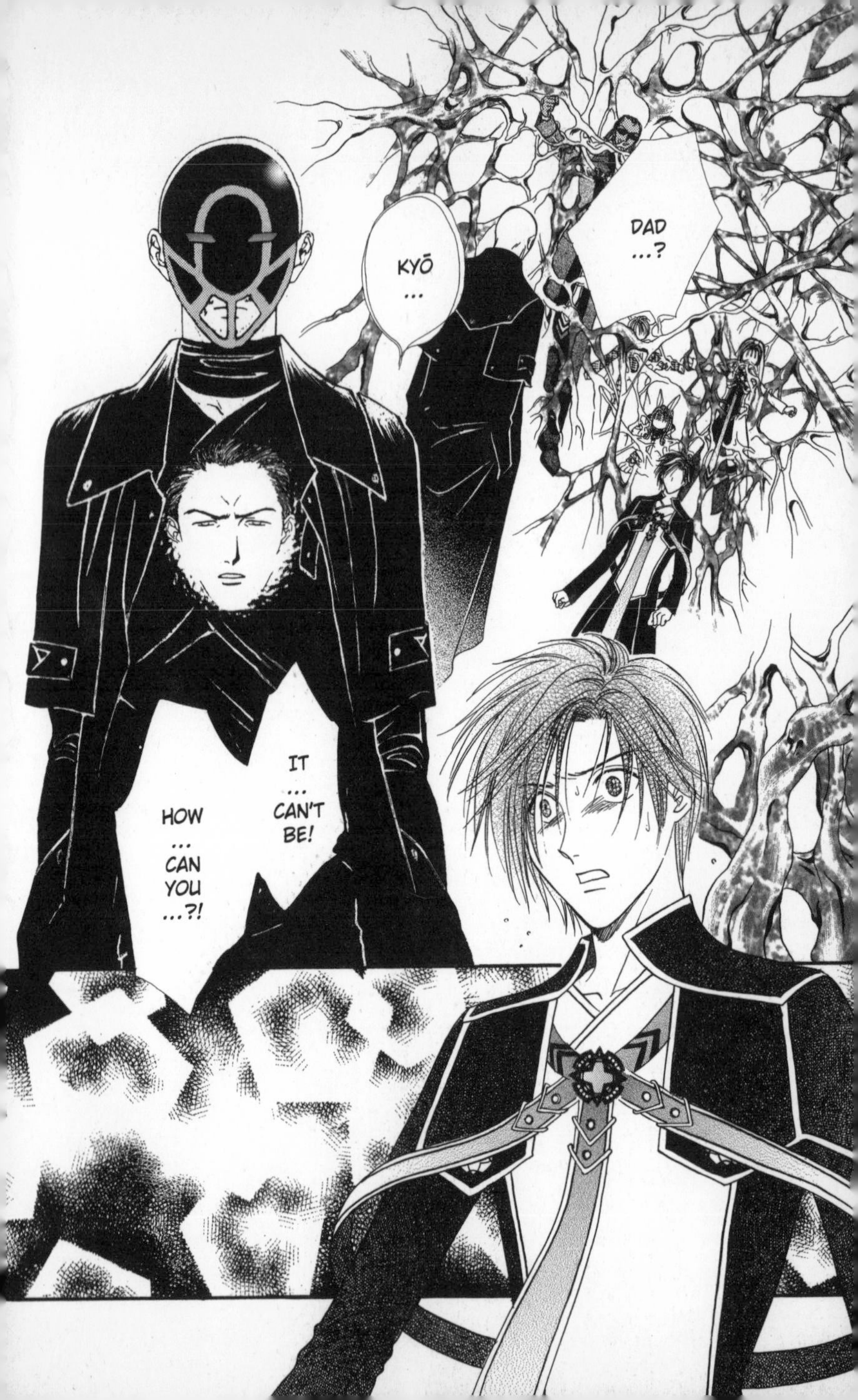
DAD ...?
KYŌ ...
IT ... CAN'T BE!
HOW ... CAN YOU ...?!

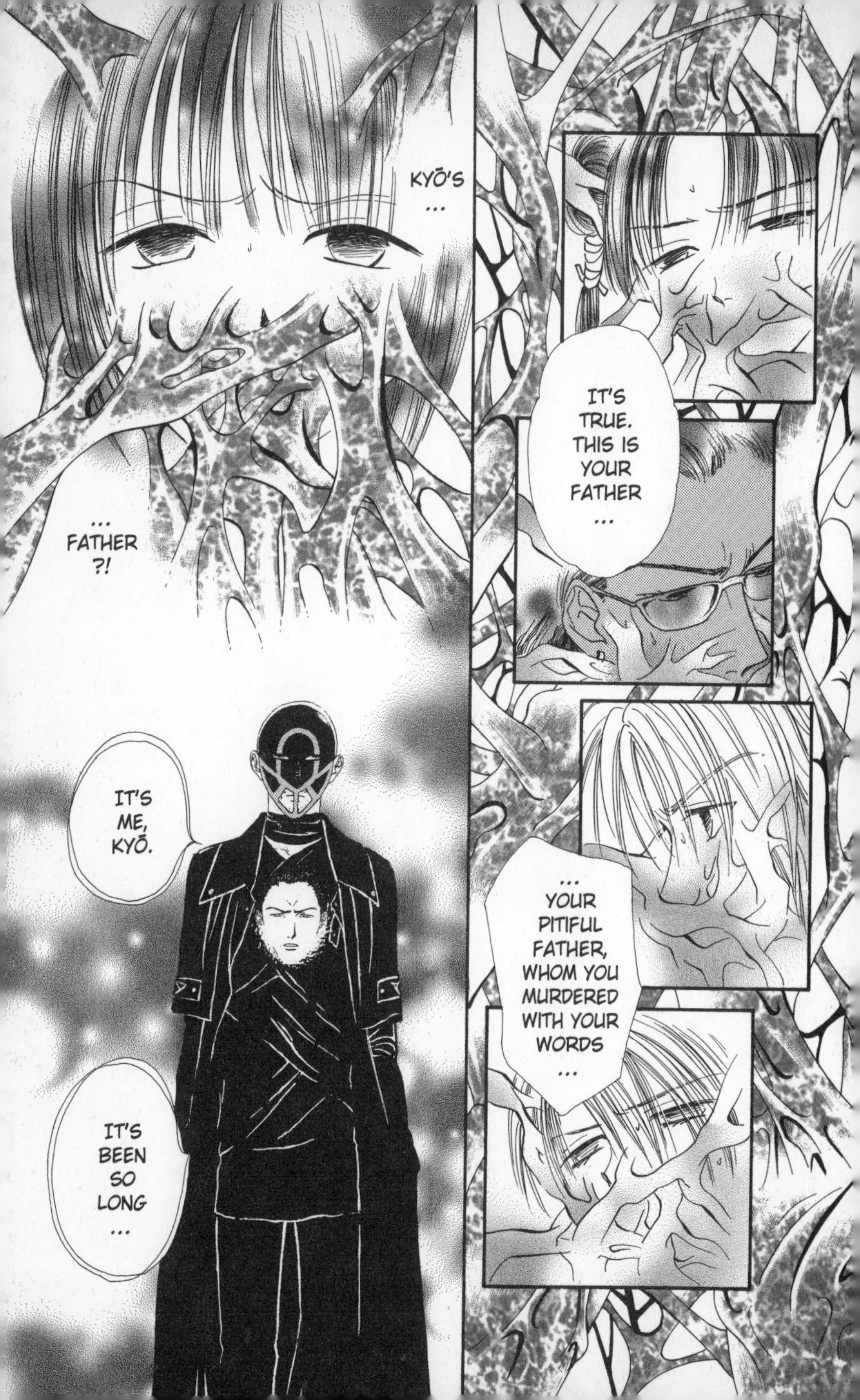
IT'S TRUE. THIS IS YOUR FATHER ...
... YOUR PITIFUL FATHER, WHOM YOU MURDERED WITH YOUR WORDS ...
KYŌ'S ...
... FATHER ?!
IT'S ME, KYŌ.
IT'S BEEN SO LONG ...

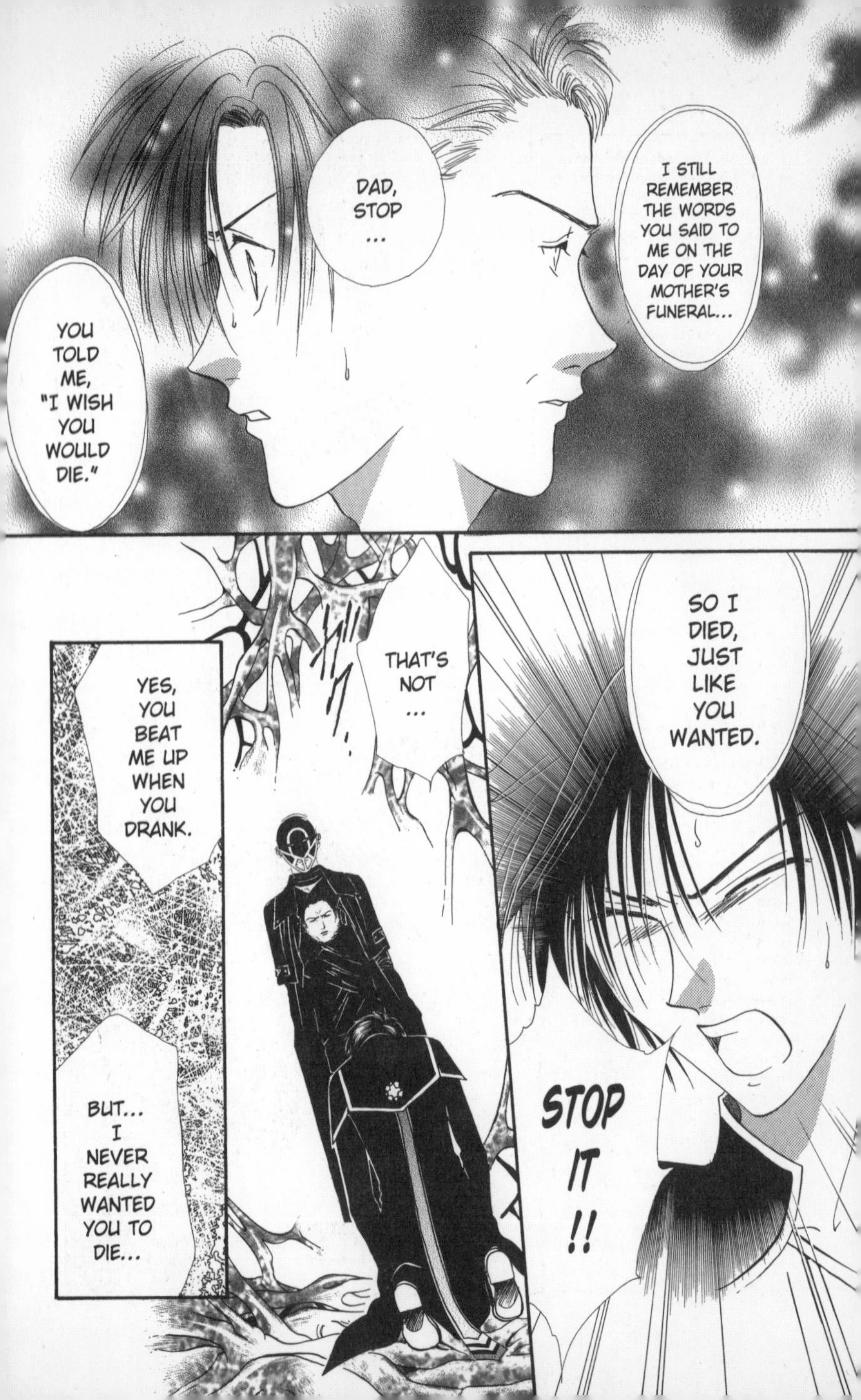
I STILL REMEMBER THE WORDS YOU SAID TO ME ON THE DAY OF YOUR MOTHER'S FUNERAL...
DAD, STOP ...
YOU TOLD ME, "I WISH YOU WOULD DIE."
SO I DIED, JUST LIKE YOU WANTED.
STOP IT !!
THAT'S NOT ...
YES, YOU BEAT ME UP WHEN YOU DRANK.
BUT... I NEVER REALLY WANTED YOU TO DIE...

THAT'S NOT TRUE! YOU *DID* WANT YOUR FATHER TO DIE.
YOU USED THE POWER OF MARAM TO ELIMINATE HIM.
ELIMINATE...
"DISAPPEAR."
SIS...

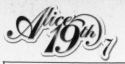

It's over! (Once and for all!) Finally, Alice 19th is completed. Not that it matters, but there's sleet falling outside. Uh-oh, the snow has made my hands numb. Brrr. But I like winter. Actually, I can take it or leave it. Now that you've read all seven volumes, did you enjoy Alice, dear readers? I'm not sure if I satisfactorily expressed what I wanted to say, but it'll be good if each of you realizes, even a little, that "the power of words" is very important. In my line of work, I draw encouragement from the kind words in my readers' letters. Although there are those who'd say they don't think writers are human beings. (Ha ha!) That's cold!
Oh, I just realized that even the inside of my wallet is cold! (But that's got nothing to do with anything, does it?)
I'd like to write about the same subject again sometime in a different way. Anyway, thank you for your support.
Now then, about my new work, a new series will start in Shôjo Comics issue 12, due out on 5/20. It's going to be a modern romantic comedy, but in the style of the old Shishunki Miman Okotowari-era Watase. Yep, it's that kind of story! I'm usually associated with fantasy stories, but romantic high school comedies are my trademark, too. I think maybe the first volume will be out around autumn?
Also, Fushigi Yûgi: Genbu Kaiden has started in the special issue of Shôjo Comics out on 3/15. After seven years, Fushigi Yûgi has been revived in manga form. The time has finally come to answer the impassioned requests of my fans from Japan and abroad! However, even fans who've never read Fushigi Yûgi will enjoy it. It comes out on odd-numbered months (May, July, etc.), so I'll be counting on your support again. Does this mean that volume 1 of the book will be out next winter?
Well...anyway, I'll be counting on your patronage again.
(Appare Jipangu 3 will be out soon so... Please buy it!)

Until my next story, then...

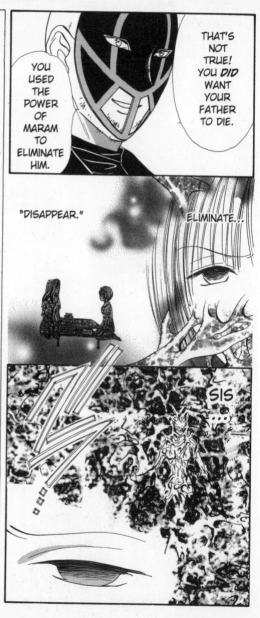

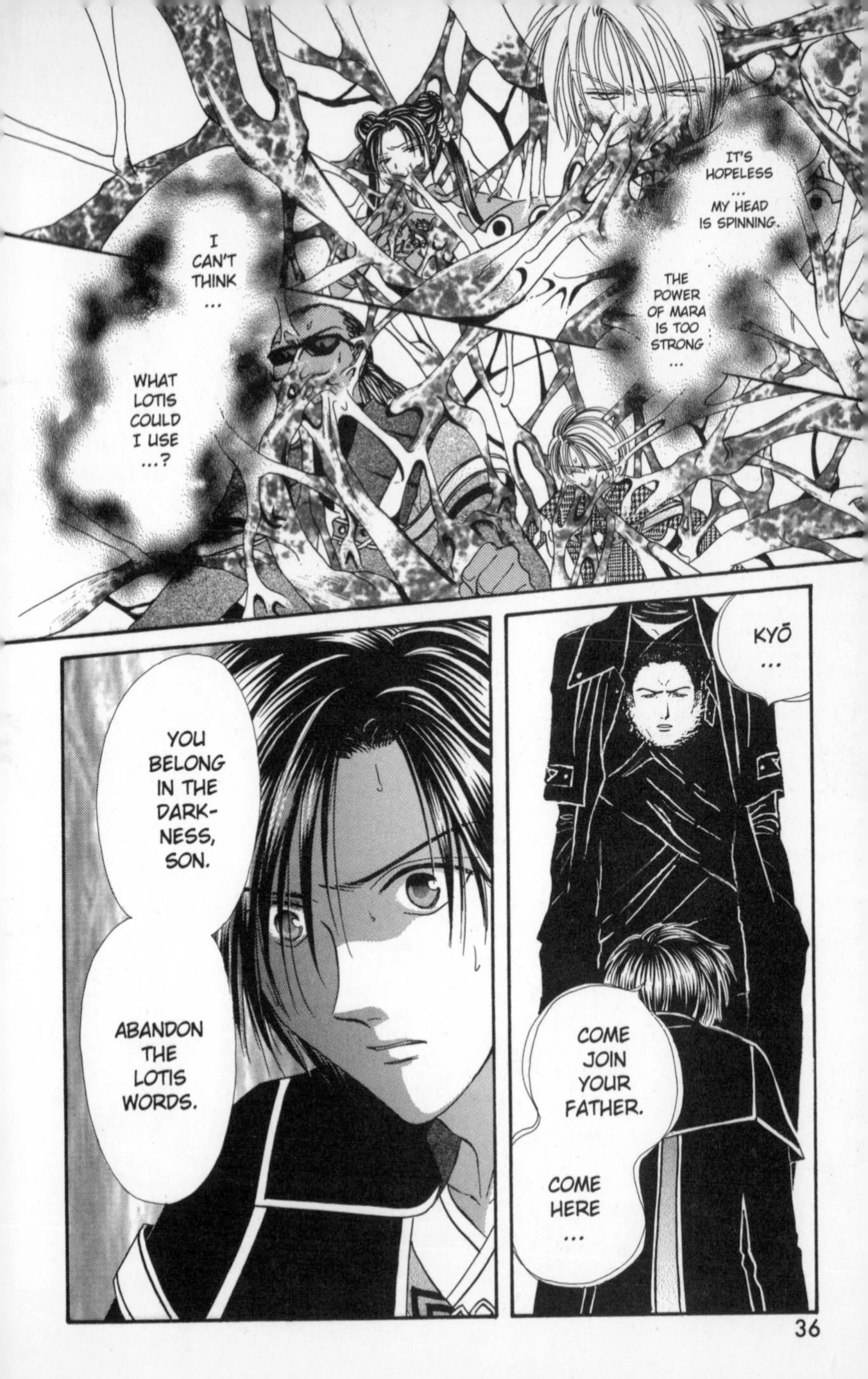
IT'S HOPELESS ... MY HEAD IS SPINNING.
THE POWER OF MARA IS TOO STRONG ...
I CAN'T THINK ...
WHAT LOTIS COULD I USE ...?
KYŌ ...
COME JOIN YOUR FATHER.
COME HERE ...
YOU BELONG IN THE DARK-NESS, SON.
ABANDON THE LOTIS WORDS.

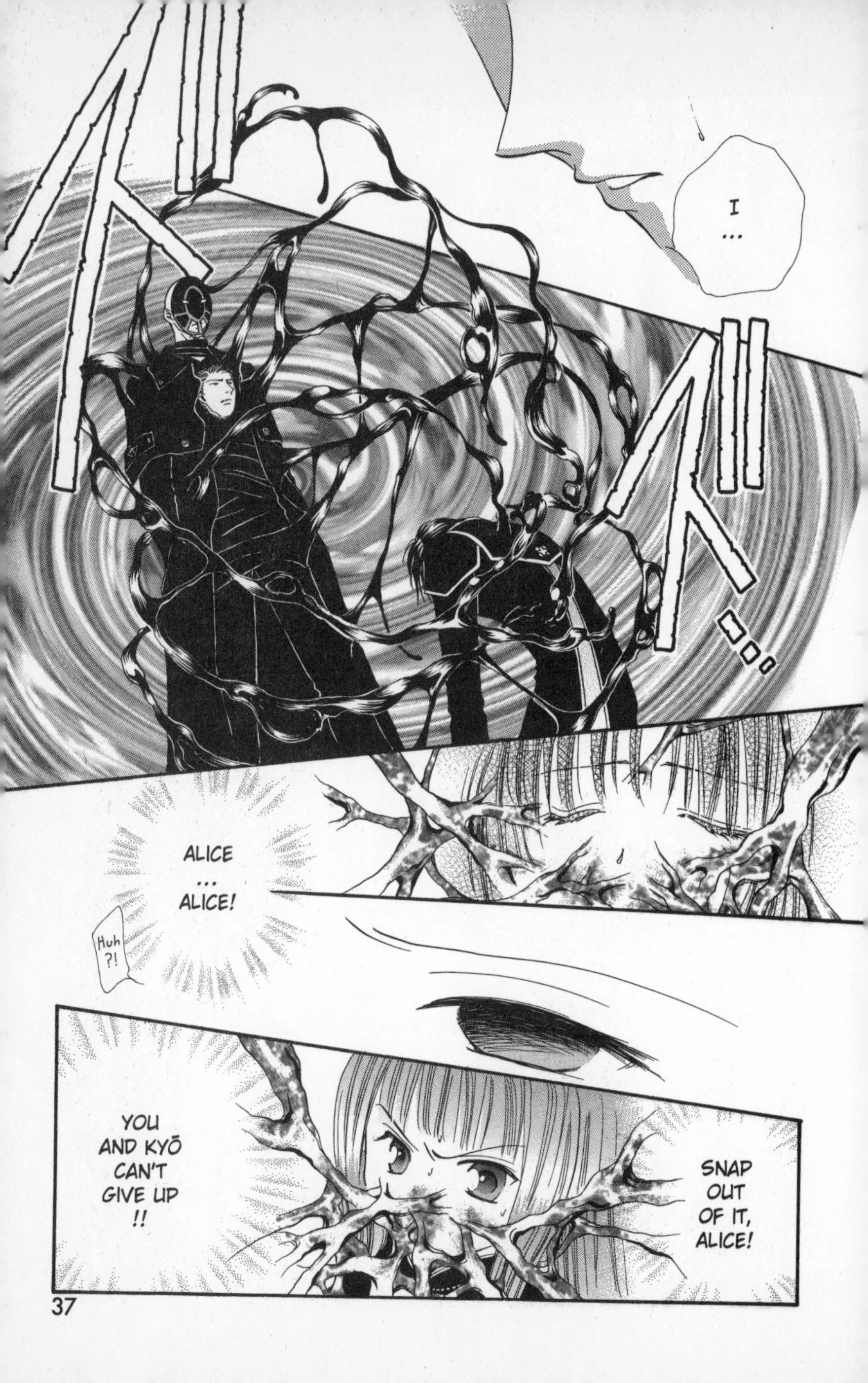
I...
ALICE... ALICE!
Huh?!
SNAP OUT OF IT, ALICE!
YOU AND KYŌ CAN'T GIVE UP!!

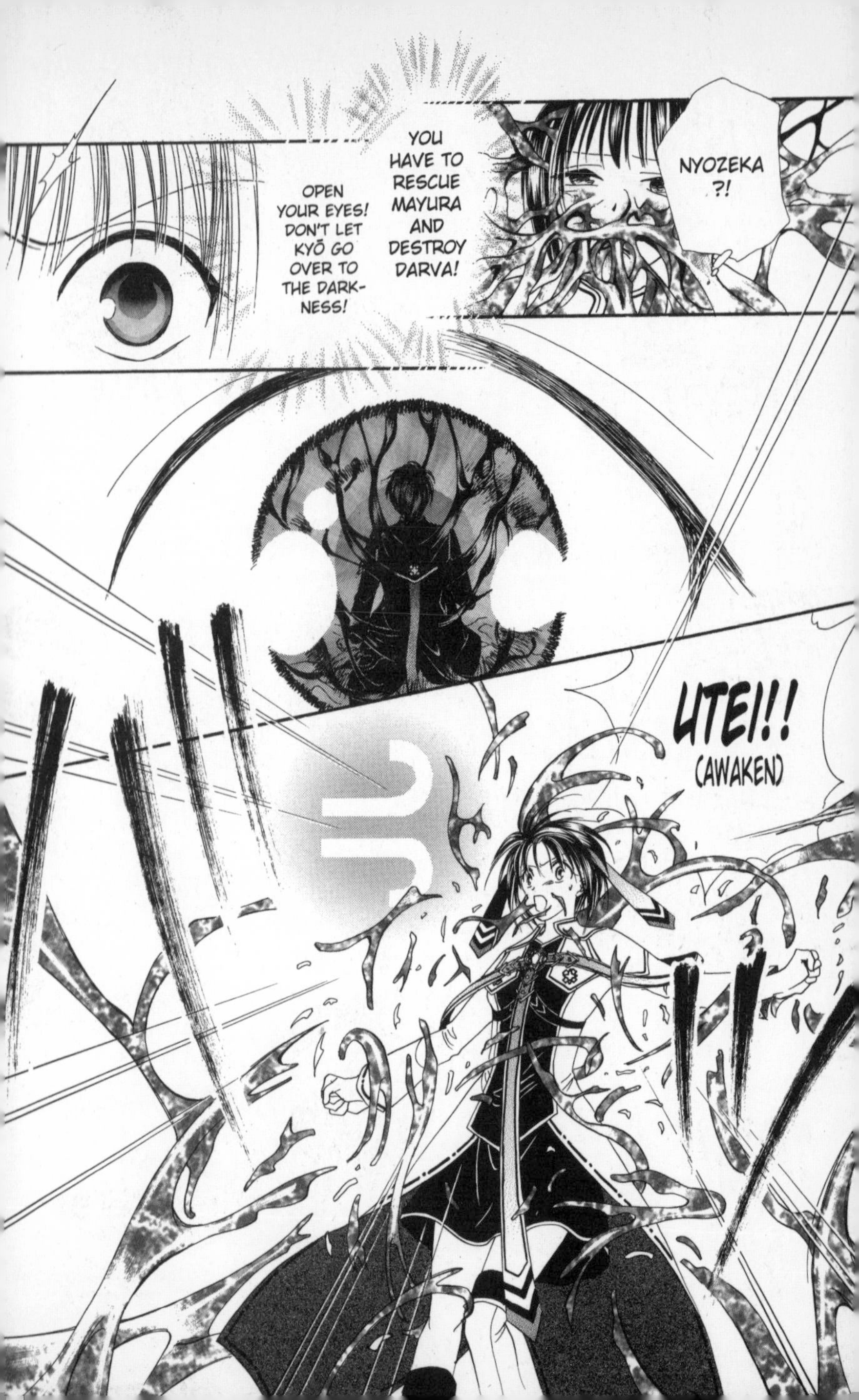
NYOZEKA ?!
YOU HAVE TO RESCUE MAYURA AND DESTROY DARVA!
OPEN YOUR EYES! DON'T LET KYŌ GO OVER TO THE DARKNESS!
UTEI!!
(AWAKEN)

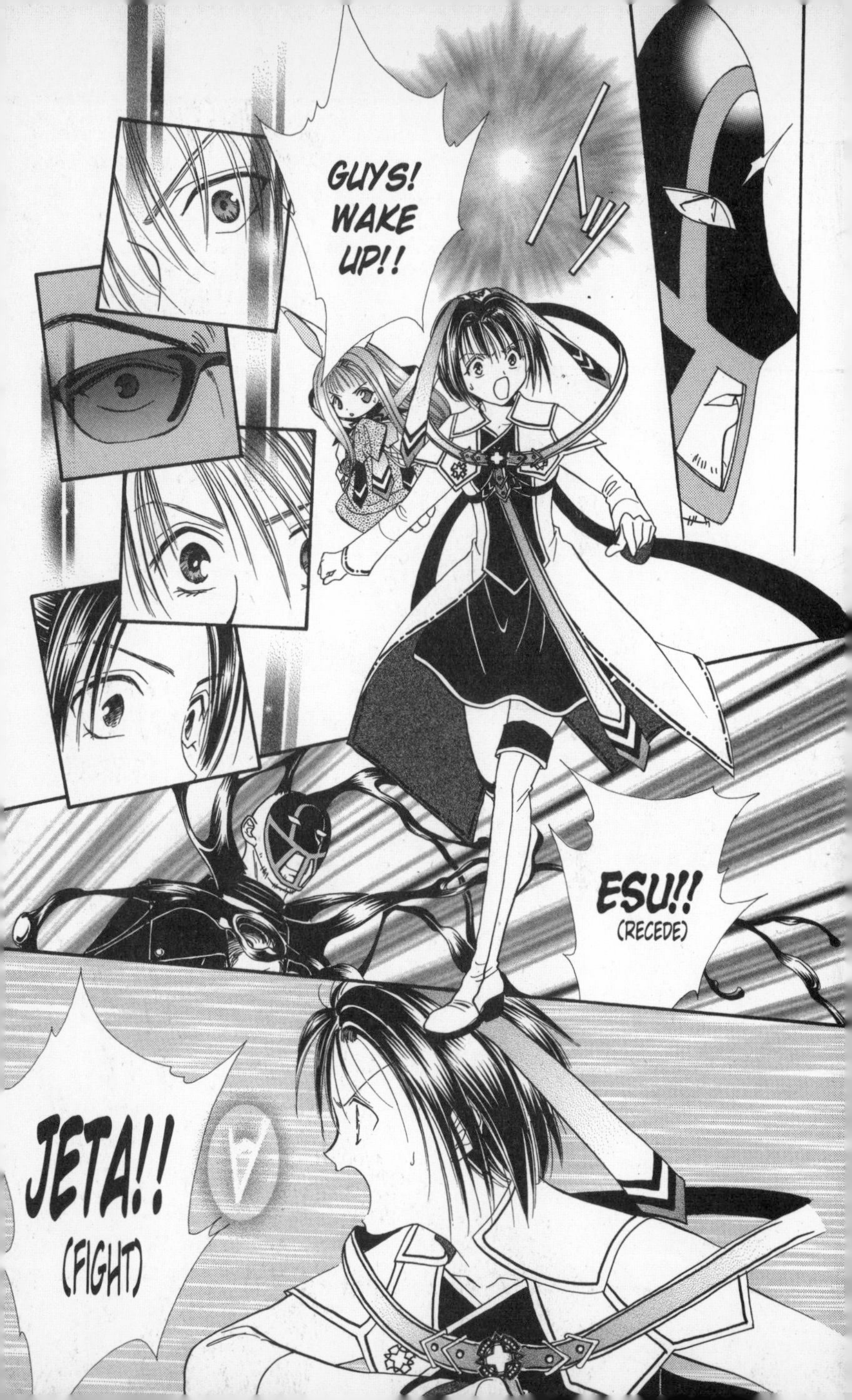
GUYS! WAKE UP!!
ESU!!
(RECEDE)
JETA!!
(FIGHT)

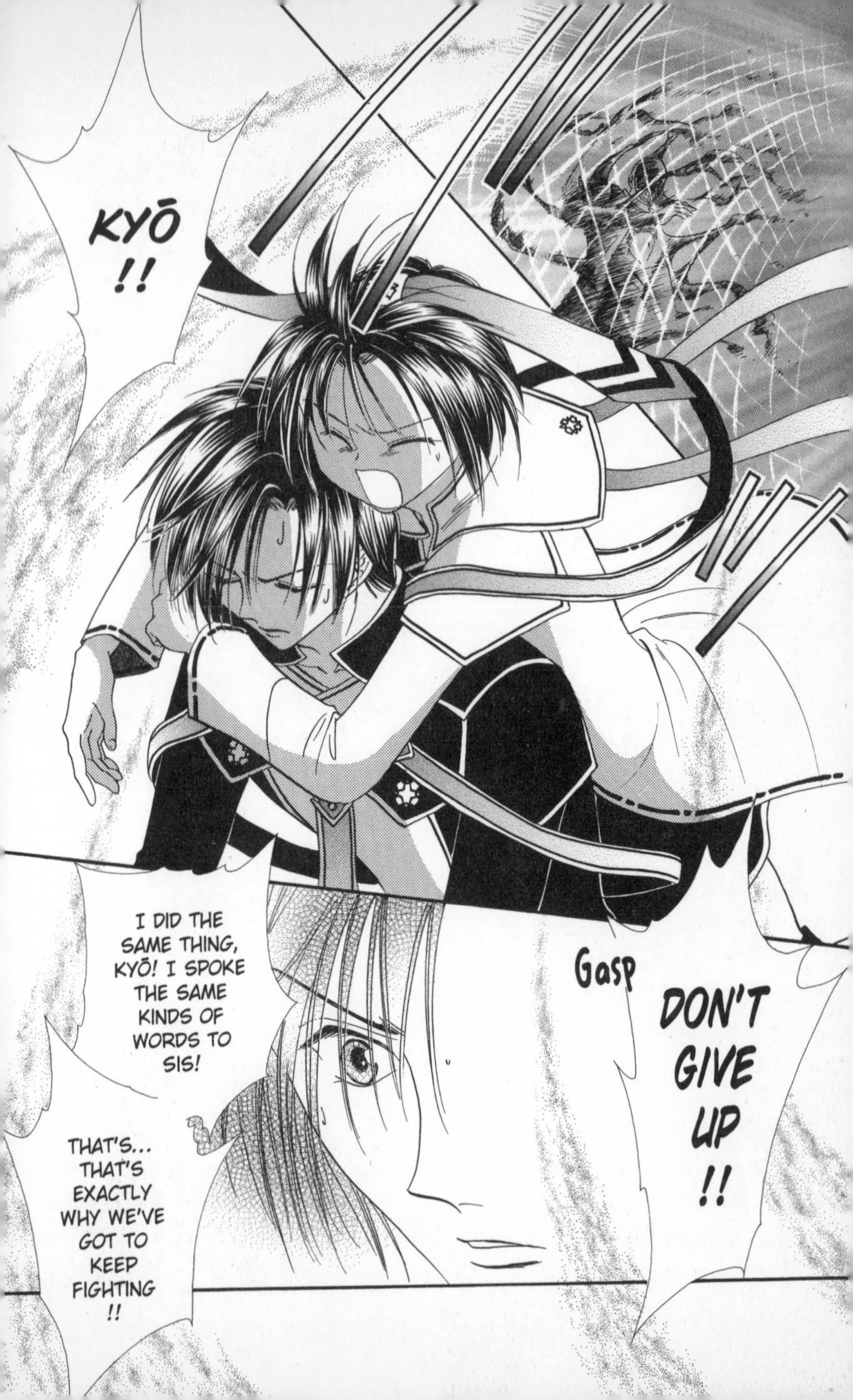
KYŌ !!
DON'T GIVE UP !!
Gasp
I DID THE SAME THING, KYŌ! I SPOKE THE SAME KINDS OF WORDS TO SIS!
THAT'S... THAT'S EXACTLY WHY WE'VE GOT TO KEEP FIGHTING !!

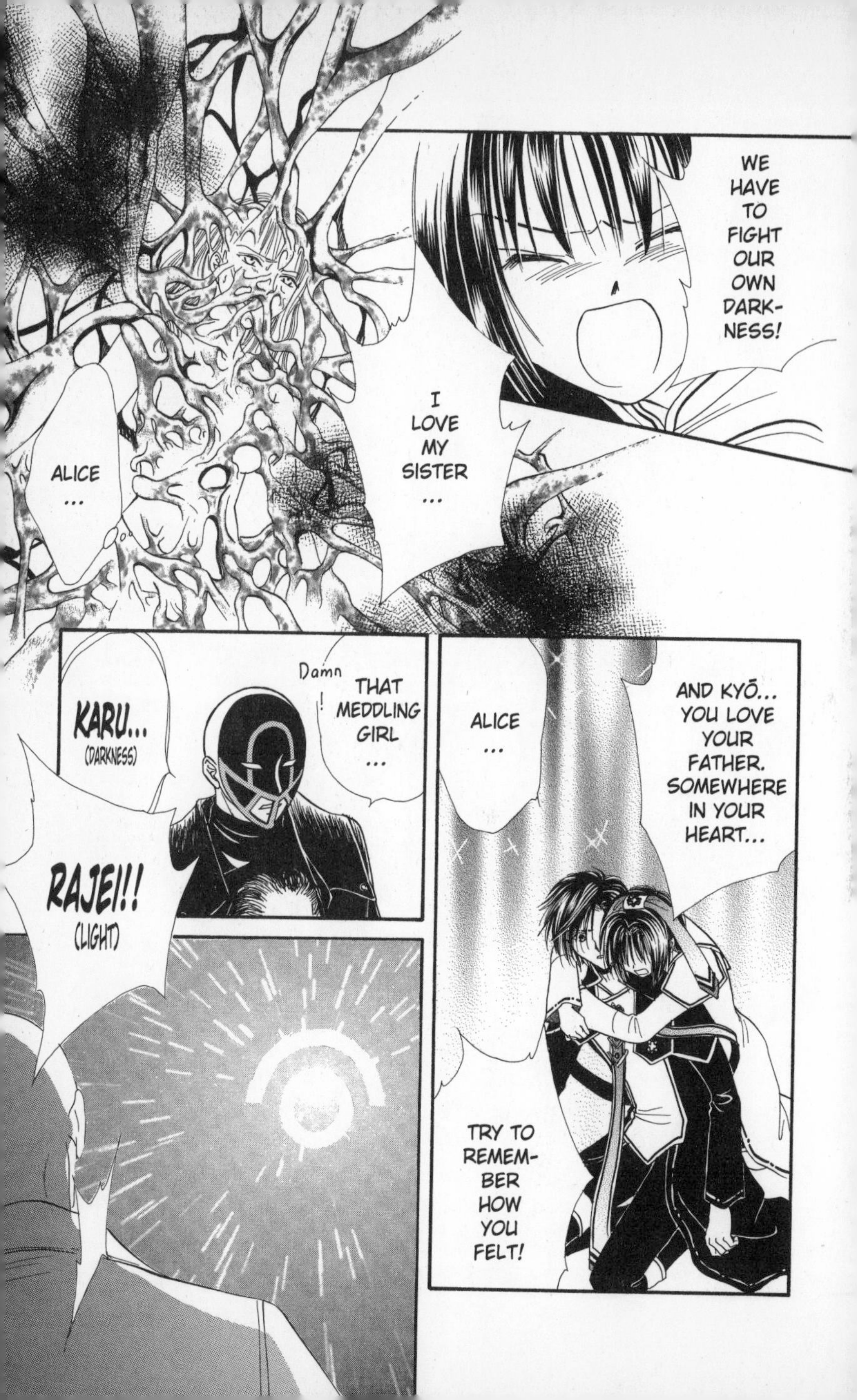
WE HAVE TO FIGHT OUR OWN DARK-NESS!
I LOVE MY SISTER ...
ALICE ...
AND KYŌ... YOU LOVE YOUR FATHER. SOMEWHERE IN YOUR HEART...
ALICE ...
TRY TO REMEM-BER HOW YOU FELT!
THAT MEDDLING GIRL ...
Damn !
KARU... (DARKNESS)
RAJEI!! (LIGHT)

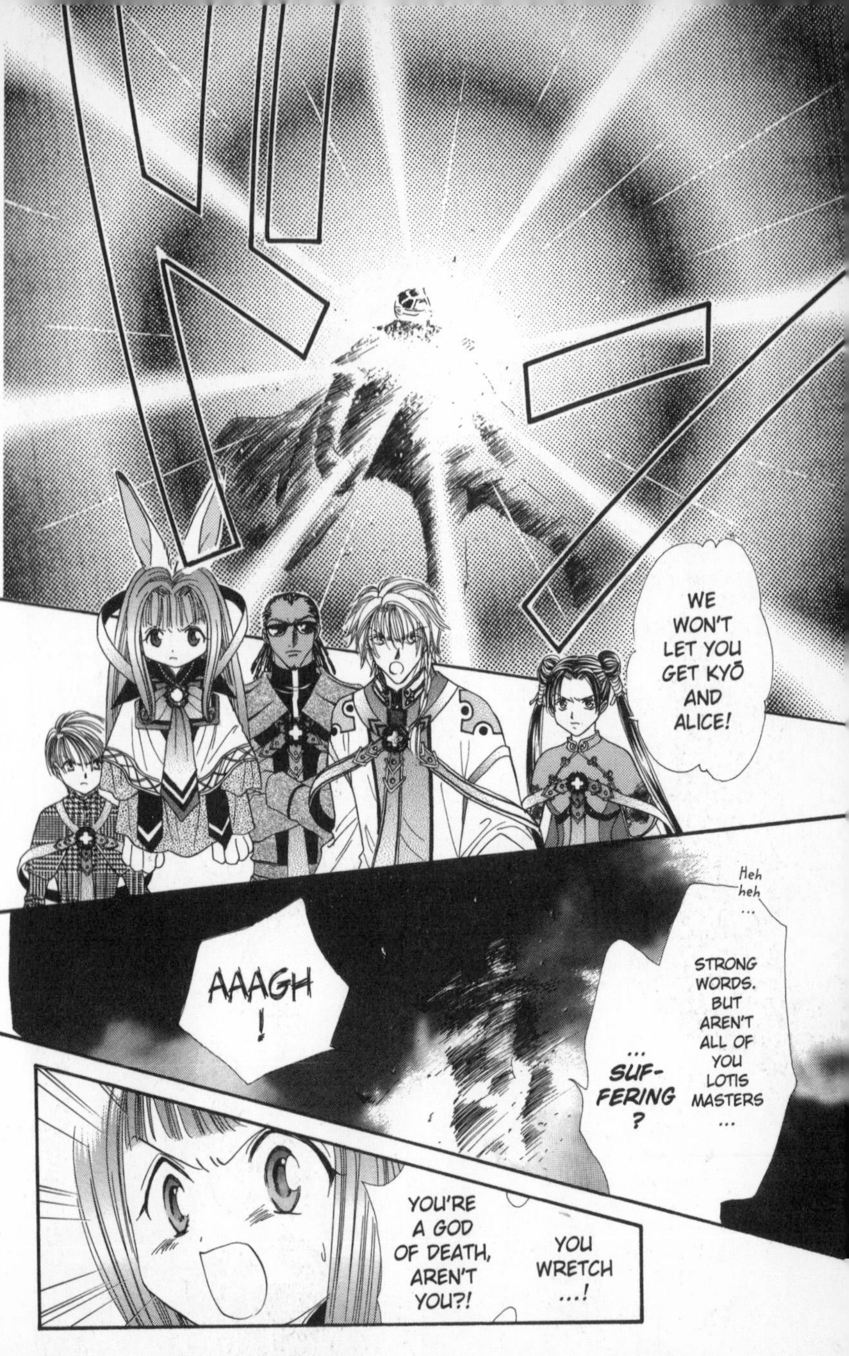
WE WON'T LET YOU GET KYŌ AND ALICE!
Heh heh ...
STRONG WORDS. BUT AREN'T ALL OF YOU LOTIS MASTERS ...
... SUF-FERING?
AAAGH!
YOU WRETCH ...!
YOU'RE A GOD OF DEATH, AREN'T YOU?!

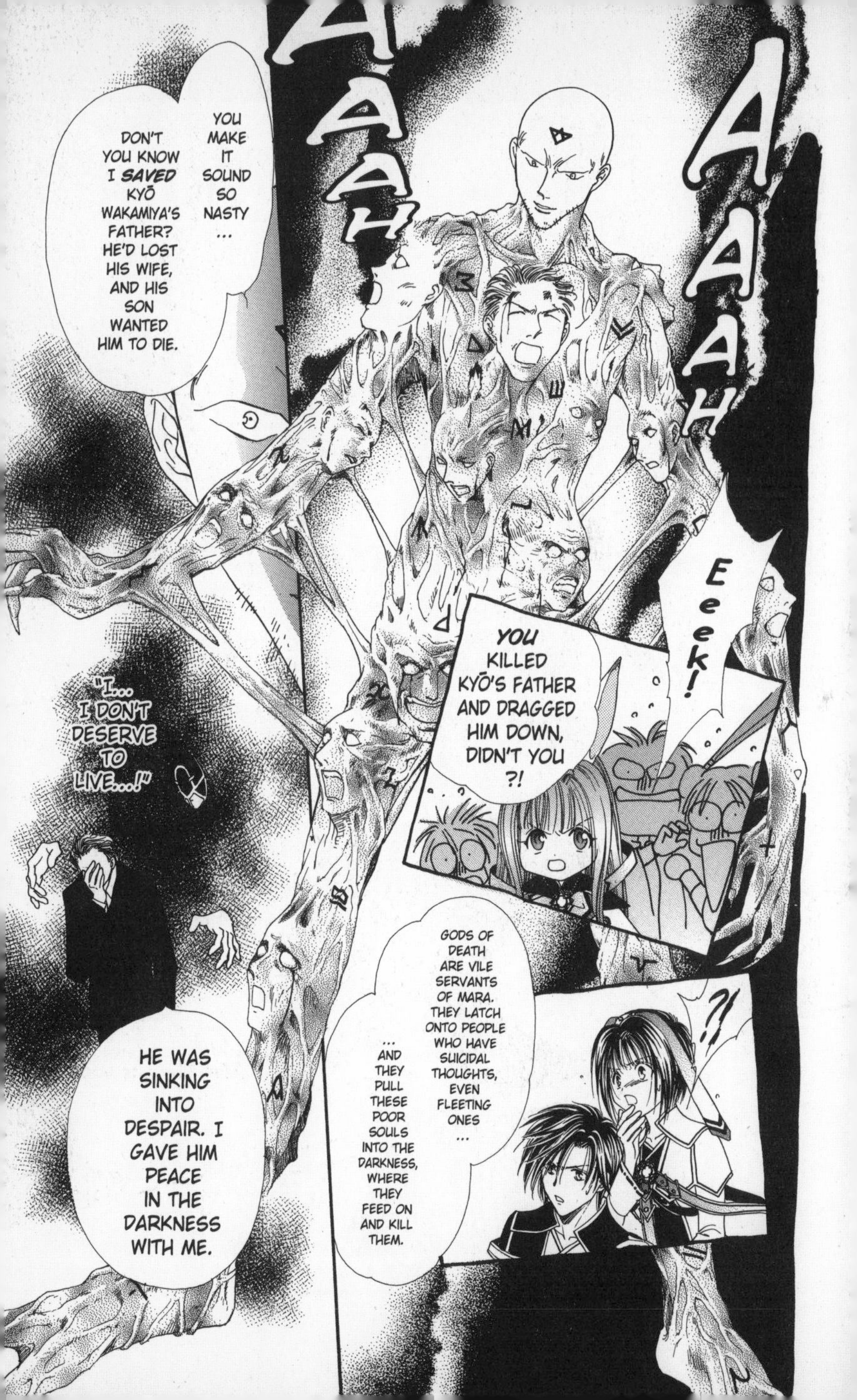
AAAAH
AAAH
YOU MAKE IT SOUND SO NASTY ...
DON'T YOU KNOW I SAVED KYŌ WAKAMIYA'S FATHER? HE'D LOST HIS WIFE, AND HIS SON WANTED HIM TO DIE.
"I... I DON'T DESERVE TO LIVE...!"
HE WAS SINKING INTO DESPAIR. I GAVE HIM PEACE IN THE DARKNESS WITH ME.
Eeek!
YOU KILLED KYŌ'S FATHER AND DRAGGED HIM DOWN, DIDN'T YOU ?!
?!
GODS OF DEATH ARE VILE SERVANTS OF MARA. THEY LATCH ONTO PEOPLE WHO HAVE SUICIDAL THOUGHTS, EVEN FLEETING ONES ...
... AND THEY PULL THESE POOR SOULS INTO THE DARKNESS, WHERE THEY FEED ON AND KILL THEM.

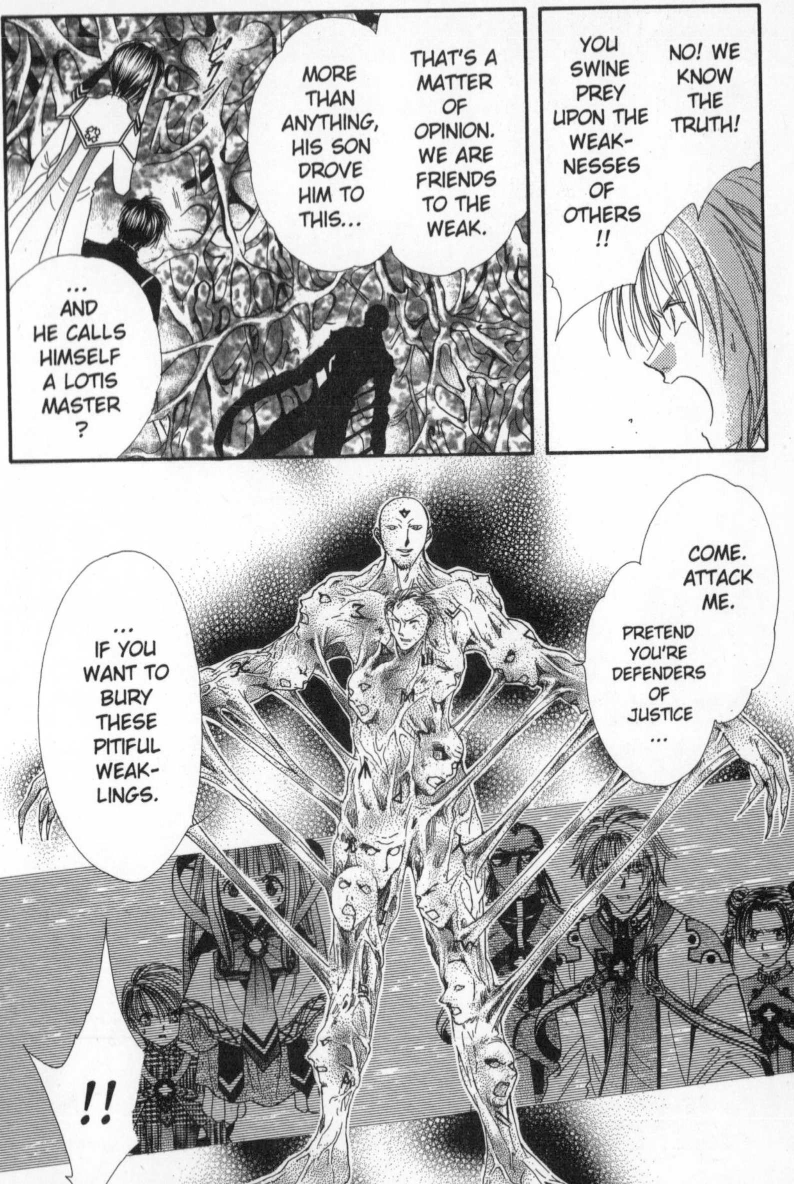
NO! WE KNOW THE TRUTH!
YOU SWINE PREY UPON THE WEAK-NESSES OF OTHERS !!
THAT'S A MATTER OF OPINION. WE ARE FRIENDS TO THE WEAK.
MORE THAN ANYTHING, HIS SON DROVE HIM TO THIS...
... AND HE CALLS HIMSELF A LOTIS MASTER ?
COME. ATTACK ME.
PRETEND YOU'RE DEFENDERS OF JUSTICE ...
... IF YOU WANT TO BURY THESE PITIFUL WEAK-LINGS.
!!

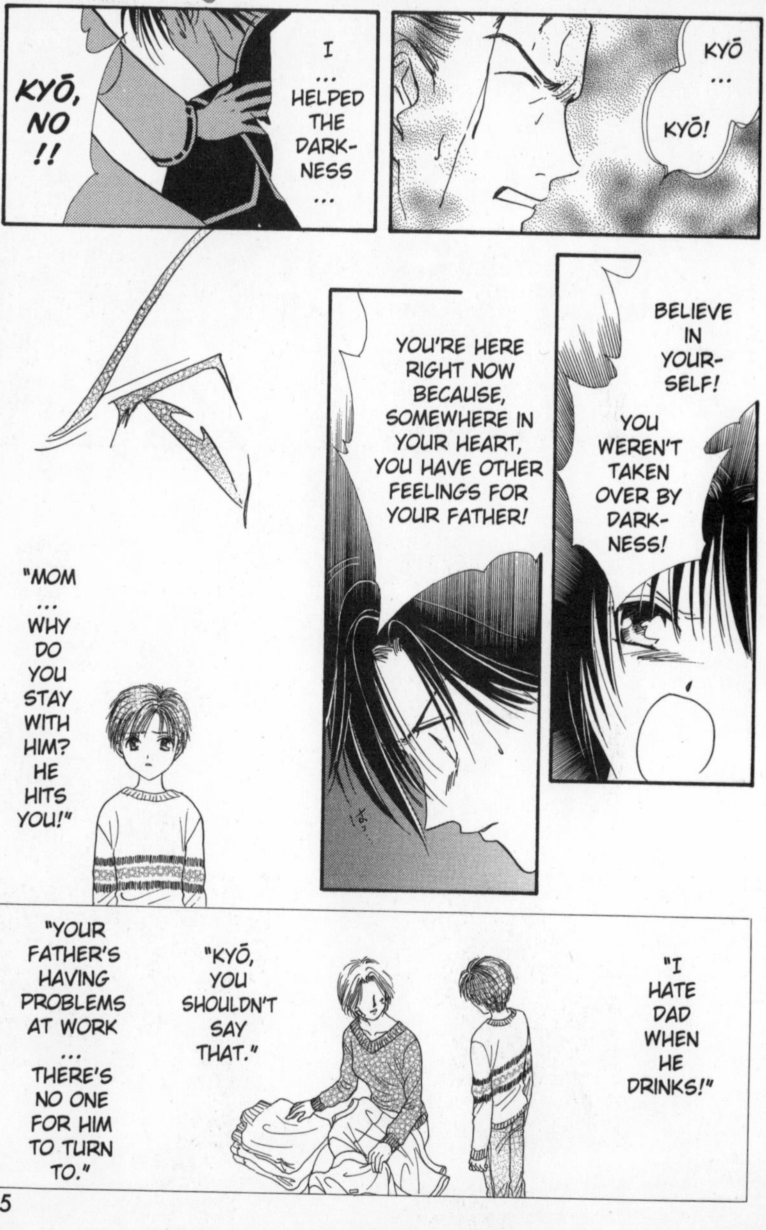
KYŌ ... KYŌ!
I ... HELPED THE DARKNESS ...
KYŌ, NO!!
BELIEVE IN YOURSELF!
YOU WEREN'T TAKEN OVER BY DARKNESS!
YOU'RE HERE RIGHT NOW BECAUSE, SOMEWHERE IN YOUR HEART, YOU HAVE OTHER FEELINGS FOR YOUR FATHER!
"MOM ... WHY DO YOU STAY WITH HIM? HE HITS YOU!"
"I HATE DAD WHEN HE DRINKS!"
"KYŌ, YOU SHOULDN'T SAY THAT."
"YOUR FATHER'S HAVING PROBLEMS AT WORK ... THERE'S NO ONE FOR HIM TO TURN TO."

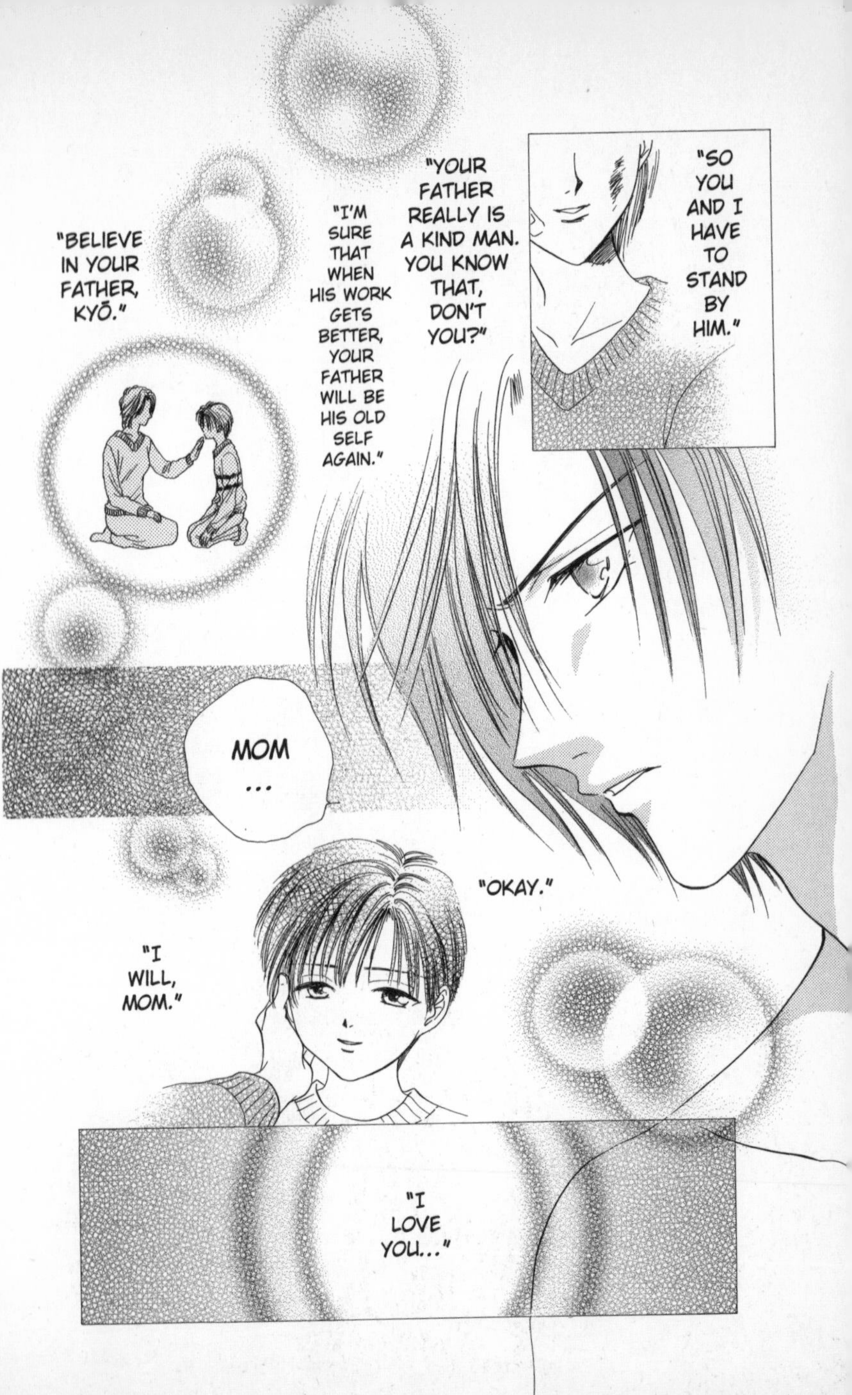
"SO YOU AND I HAVE TO STAND BY HIM."
"YOUR FATHER REALLY IS A KIND MAN. YOU KNOW THAT, DON'T YOU?"
"I'M SURE THAT WHEN HIS WORK GETS BETTER, YOUR FATHER WILL BE HIS OLD SELF AGAIN."
"BELIEVE IN YOUR FATHER, KYŌ."
MOM ...
"OKAY."
"I WILL, MOM."
"I LOVE YOU..."

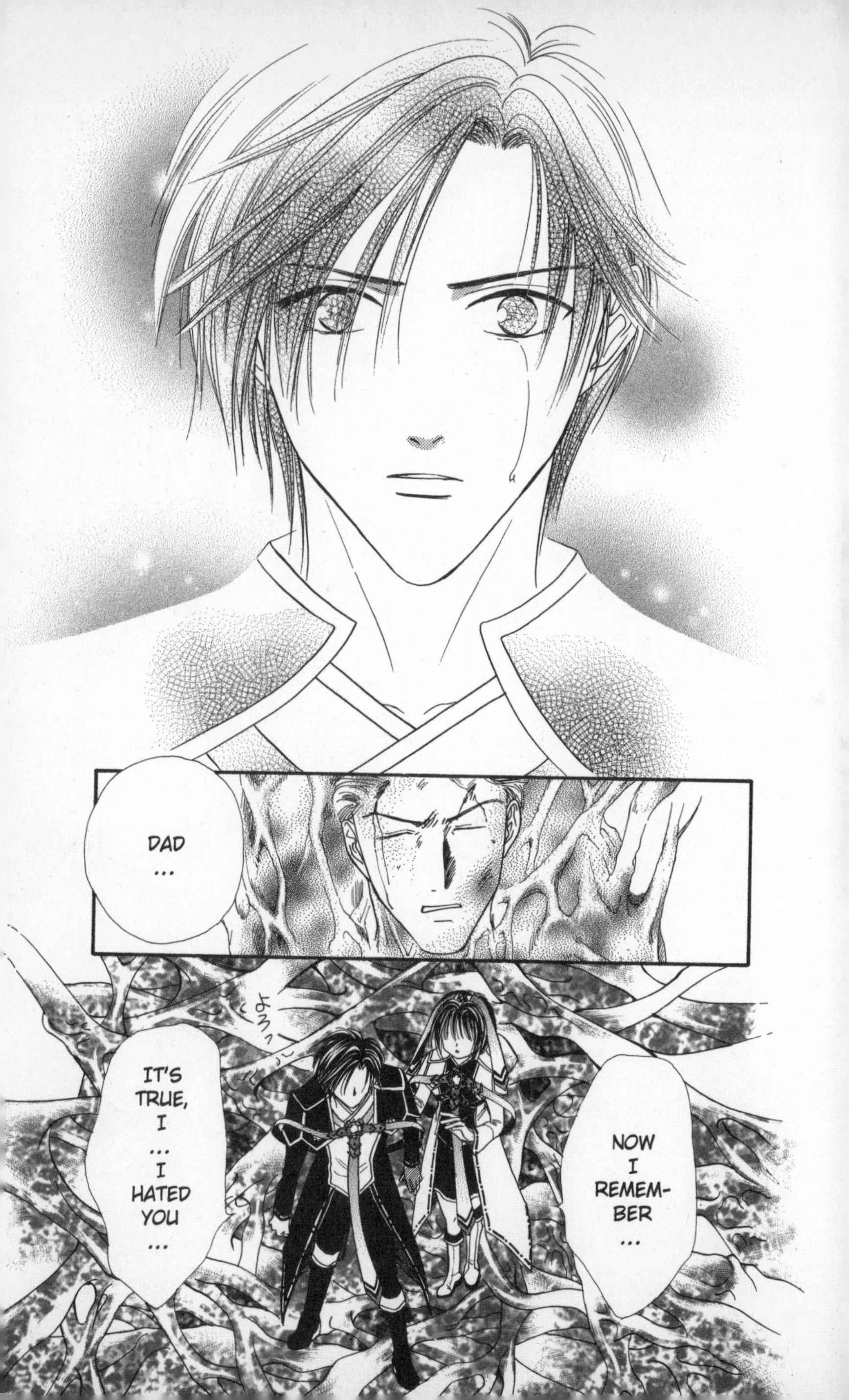
DAD ...
NOW I REMEM-BER ...
IT'S TRUE, I ... I HATED YOU ...

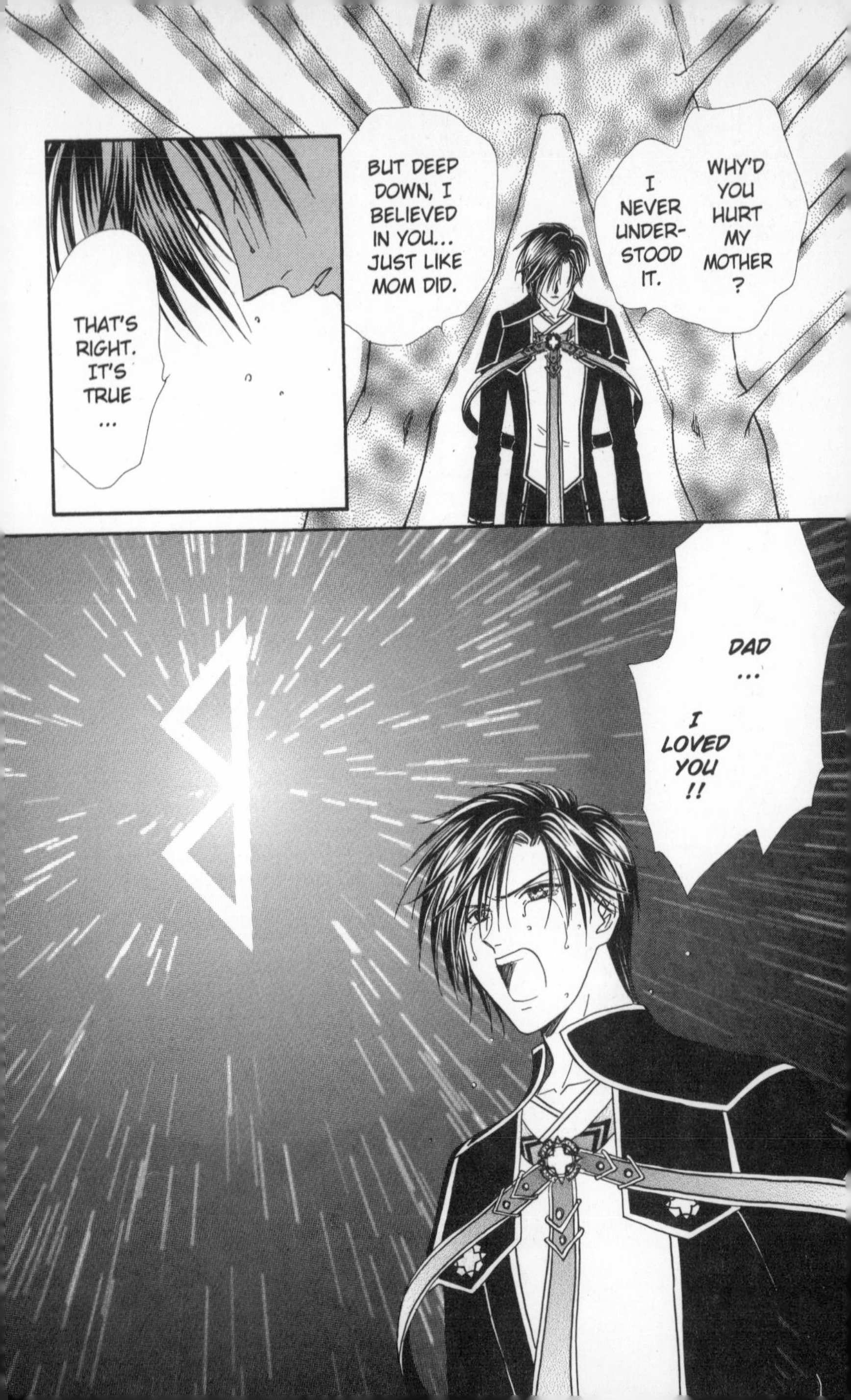
WHY'D YOU HURT MY MOTHER?
I NEVER UNDERSTOOD IT.
BUT DEEP DOWN, I BELIEVED IN YOU... JUST LIKE MOM DID.
THAT'S RIGHT. IT'S TRUE...
DAD...
I LOVED YOU!!

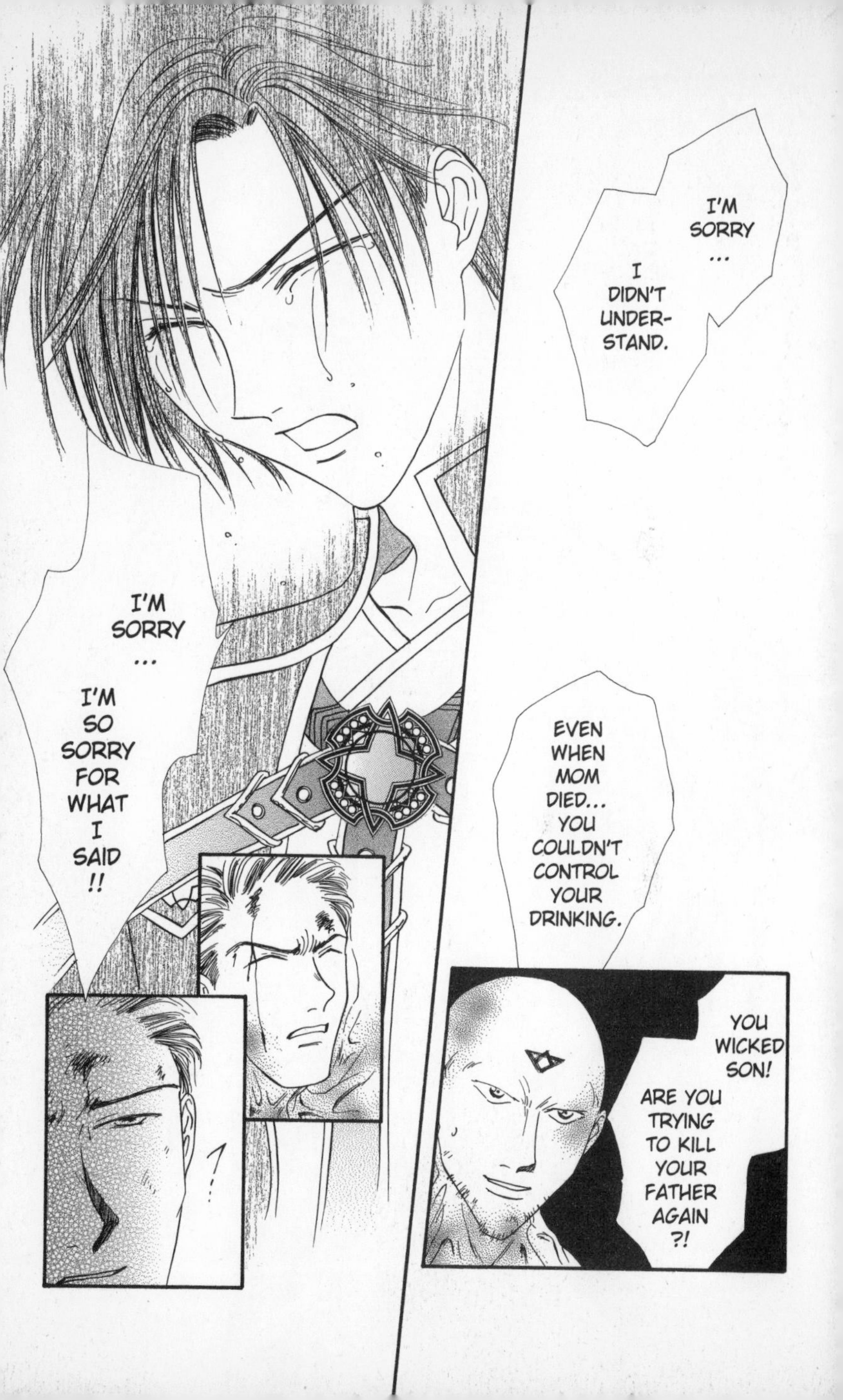
I'M SORRY...
I DIDN'T UNDERSTAND.
EVEN WHEN MOM DIED... YOU COULDN'T CONTROL YOUR DRINKING.
YOU WICKED SON!
ARE YOU TRYING TO KILL YOUR FATHER AGAIN?!
I'M SORRY...
I'M SO SORRY FOR WHAT I SAID!!

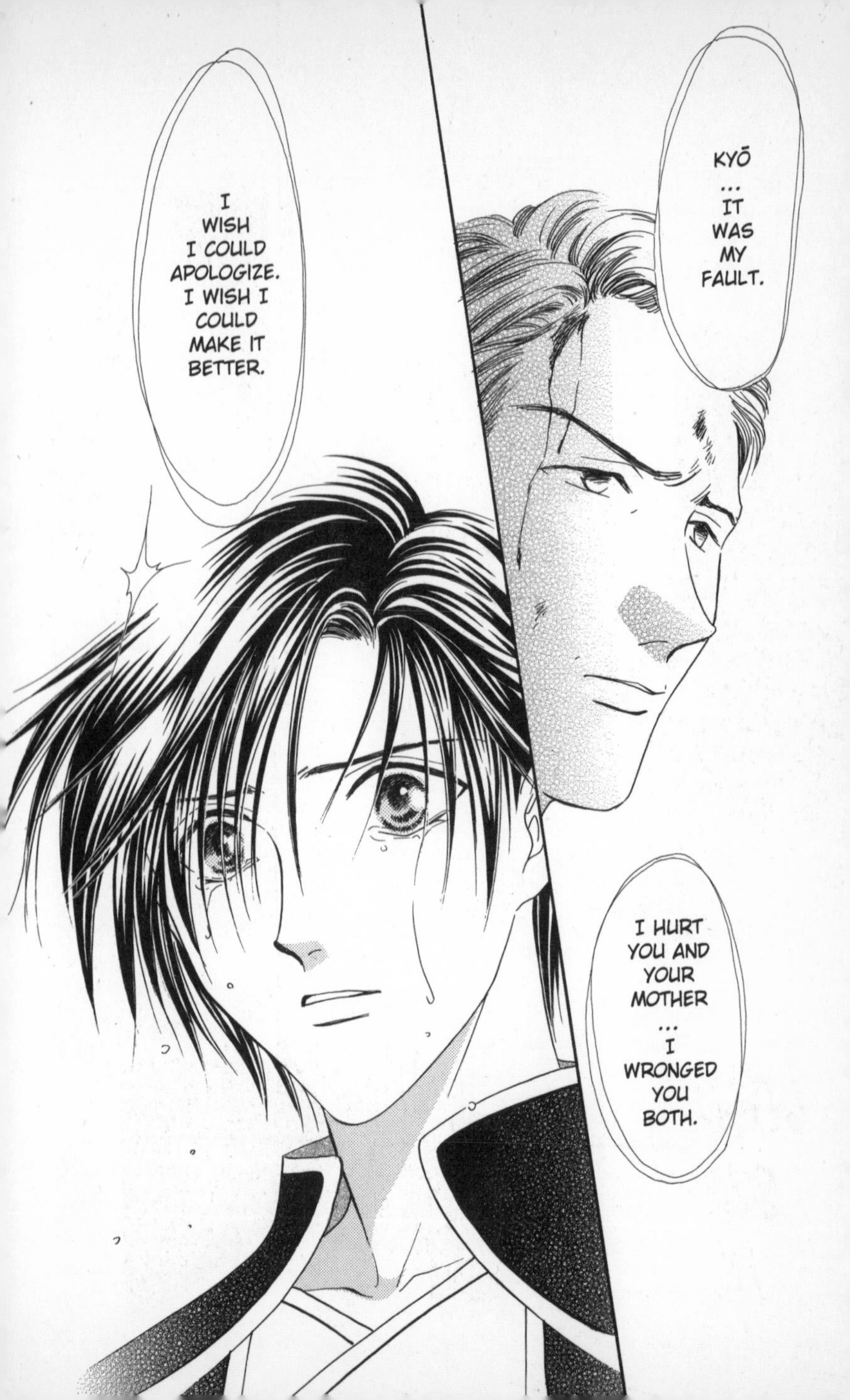
KYŌ ... IT WAS MY FAULT.
I WISH I COULD APOLOGIZE. I WISH I COULD MAKE IT BETTER.
I HURT YOU AND YOUR MOTHER ... I WRONGED YOU BOTH.

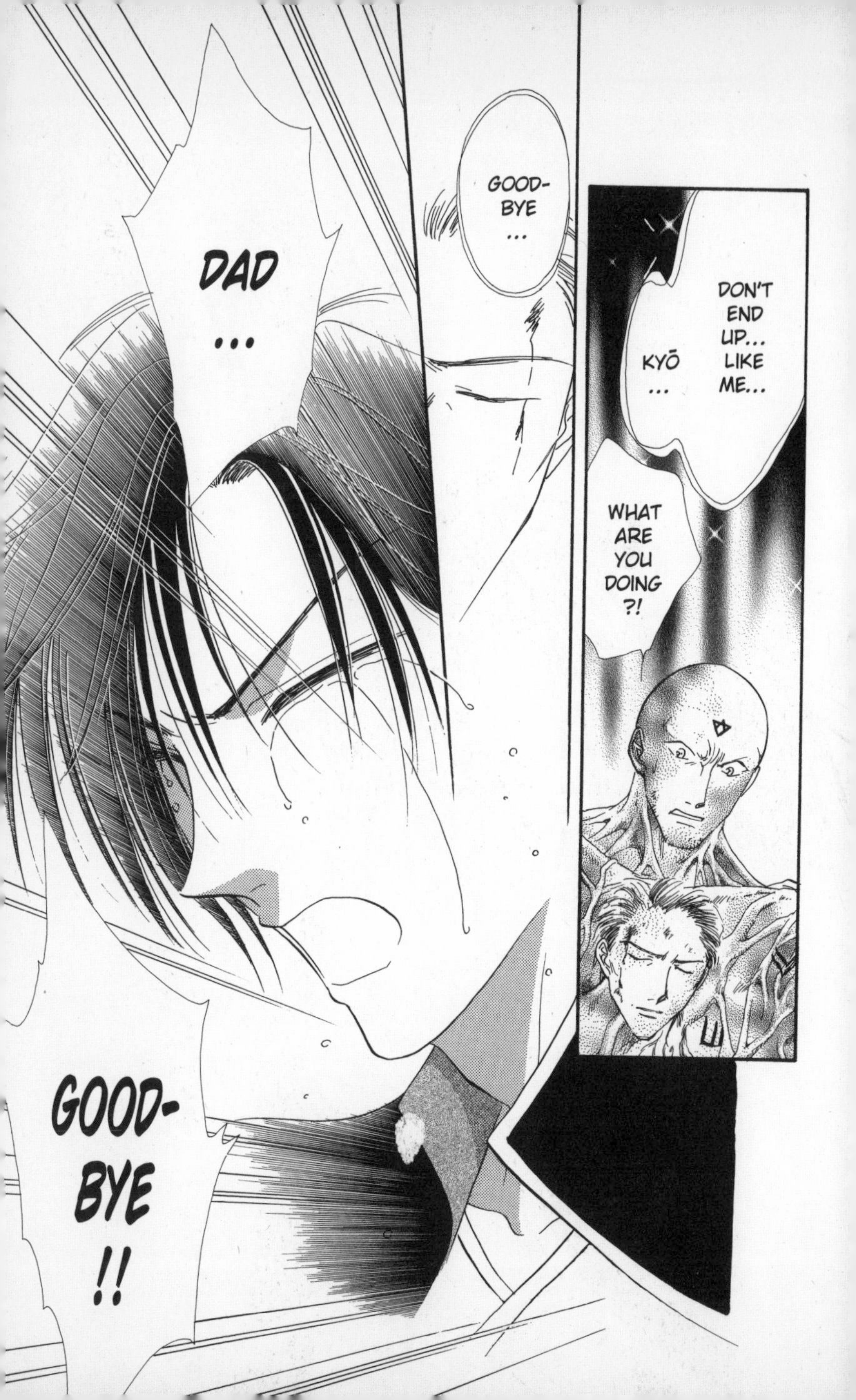
KYŌ ... DON'T END UP... LIKE ME...
WHAT ARE YOU DOING ?!
GOOD-BYE ...
DAD ...
GOOD-BYE !!

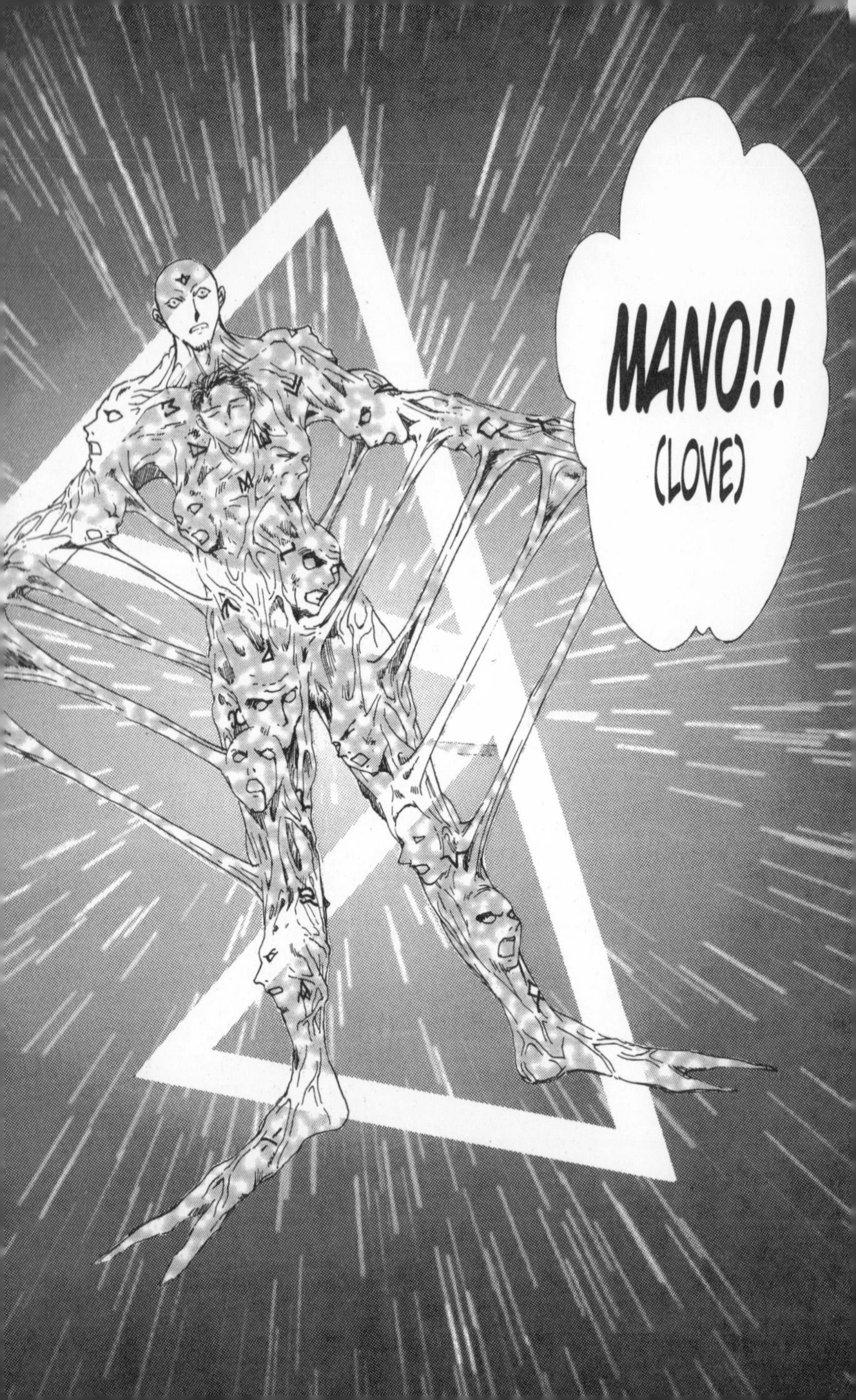
MANO!!
(LOVE)

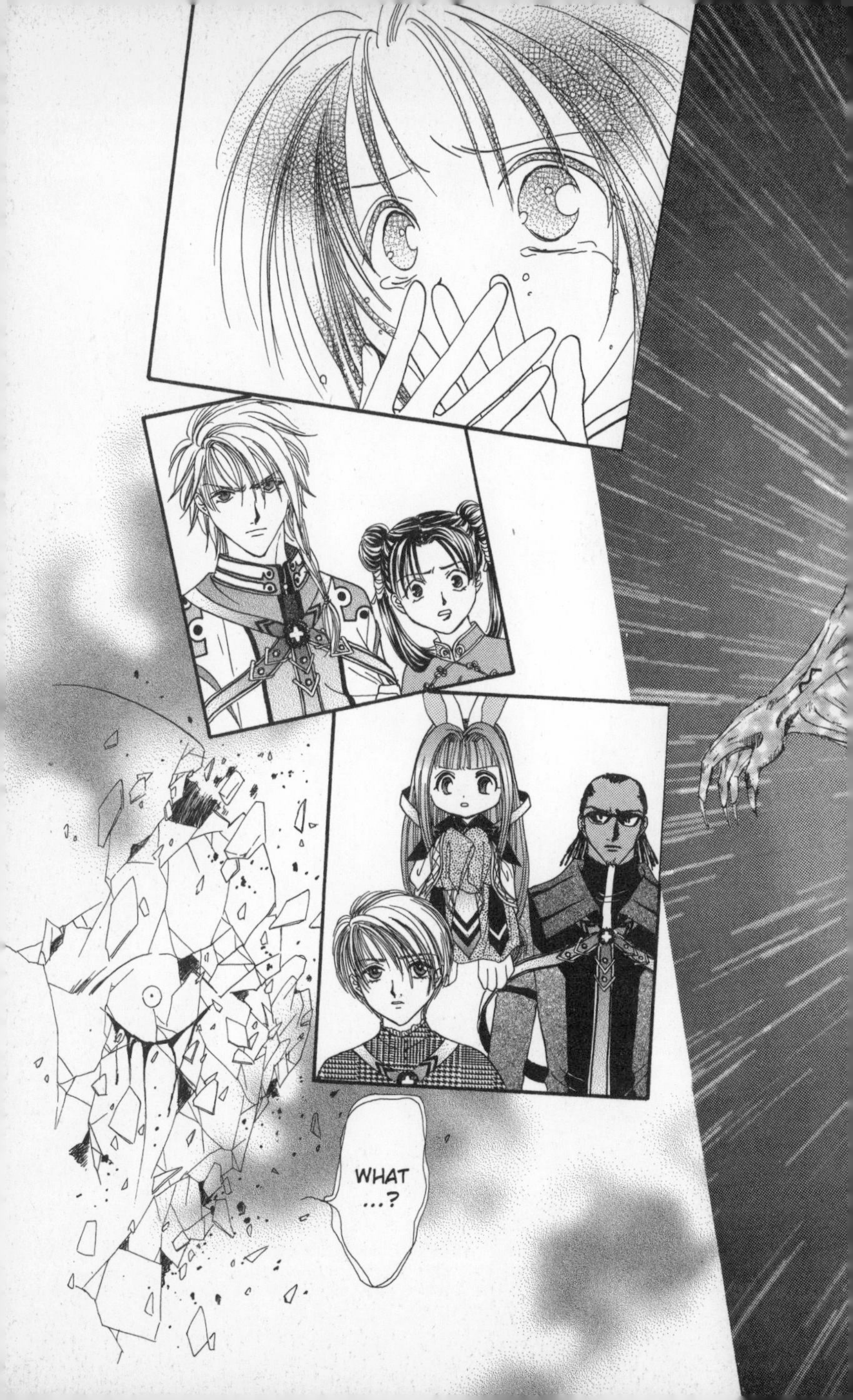
WHAT ...?

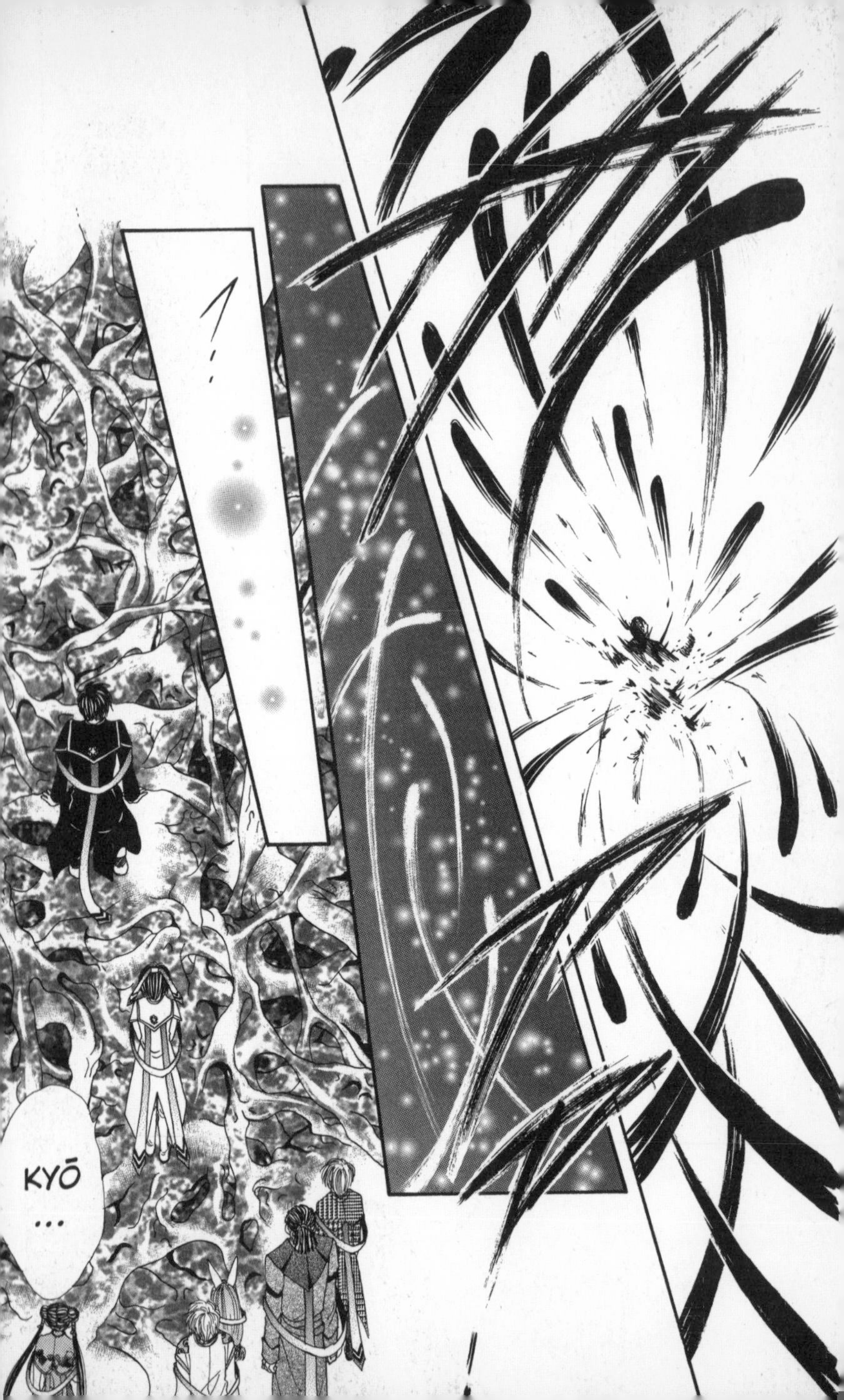

KYŌ ...

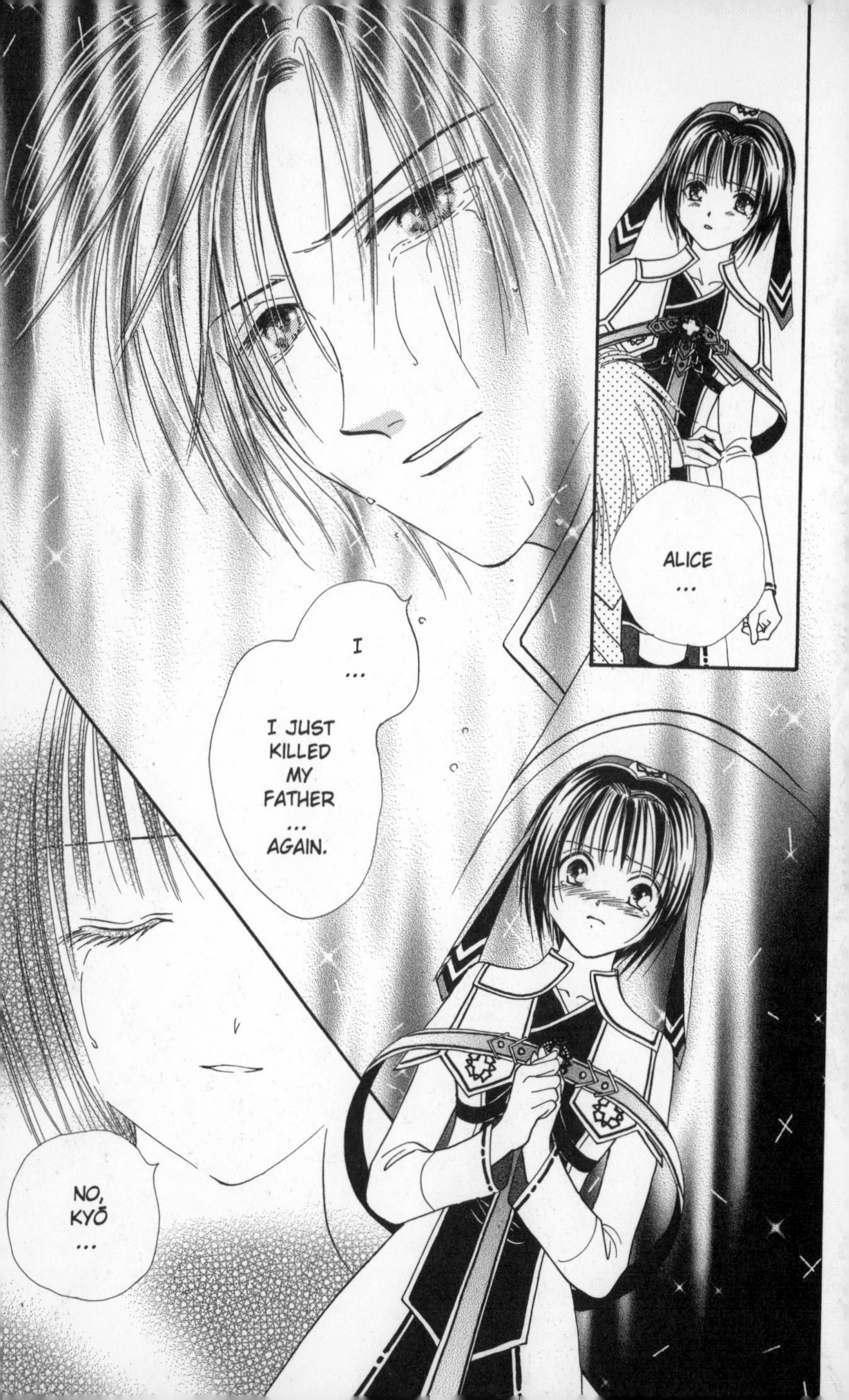
ALICE ...
I ...
I JUST KILLED MY FATHER ... AGAIN.
NO, KYŌ ...

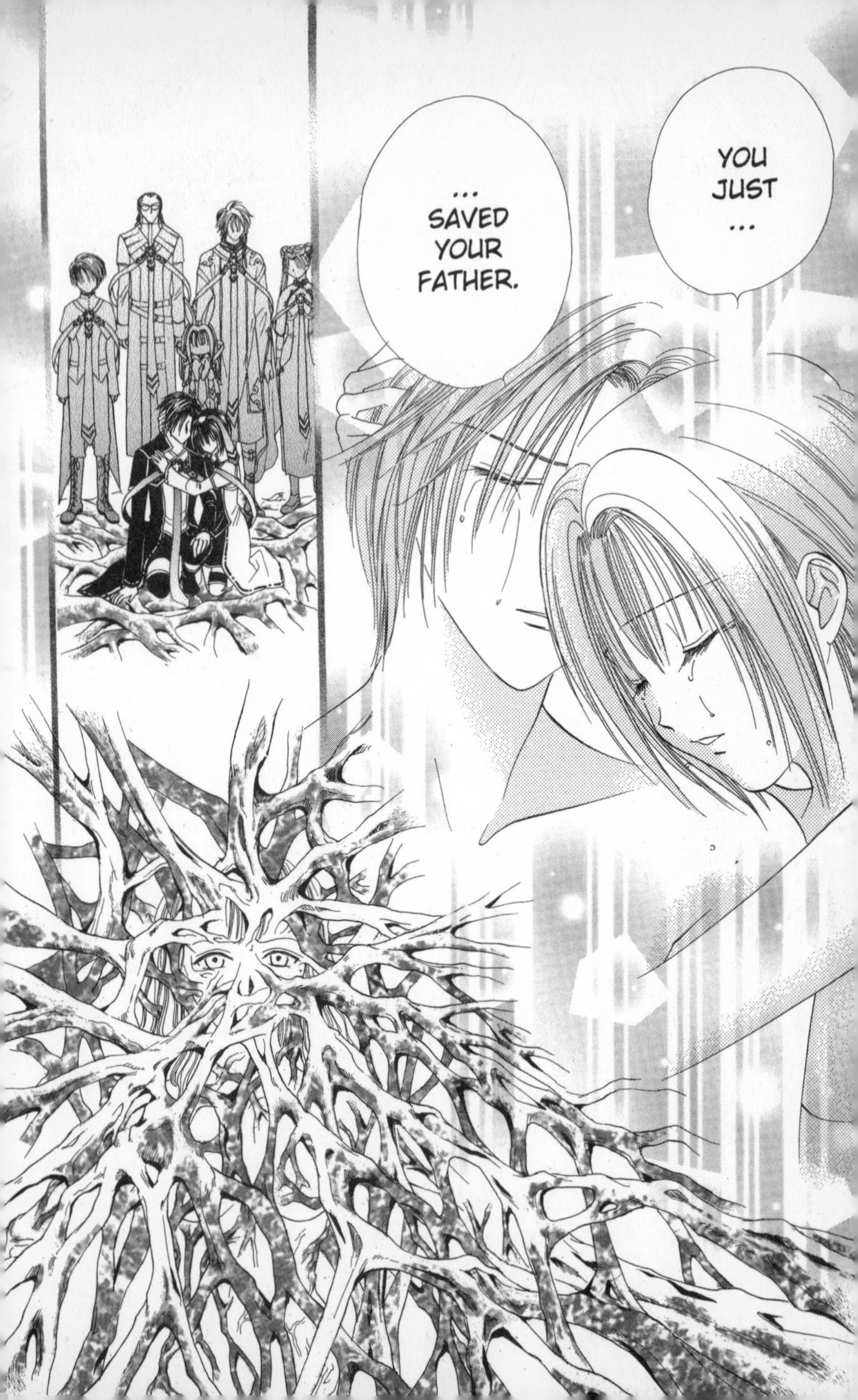
YOU JUST ...
... SAVED YOUR FATHER.

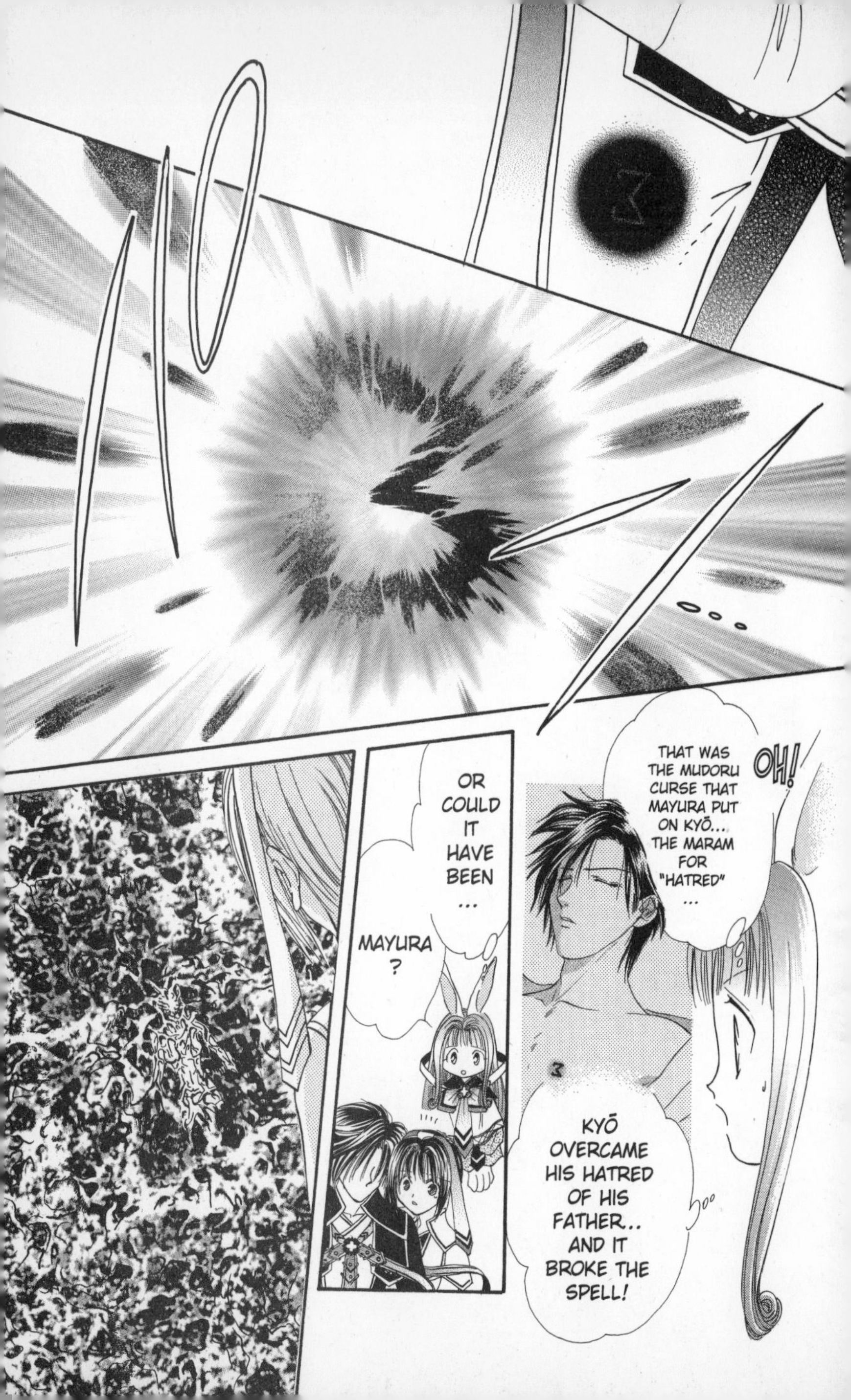
OH!
THAT WAS THE MUDORU CURSE THAT MAYURA PUT ON KYŌ... THE MARAM FOR "HATRED"...
KYŌ OVERCAME HIS HATRED OF HIS FATHER.. AND IT BROKE THE SPELL!
OR COULD IT HAVE BEEN ...
MAYURA ?

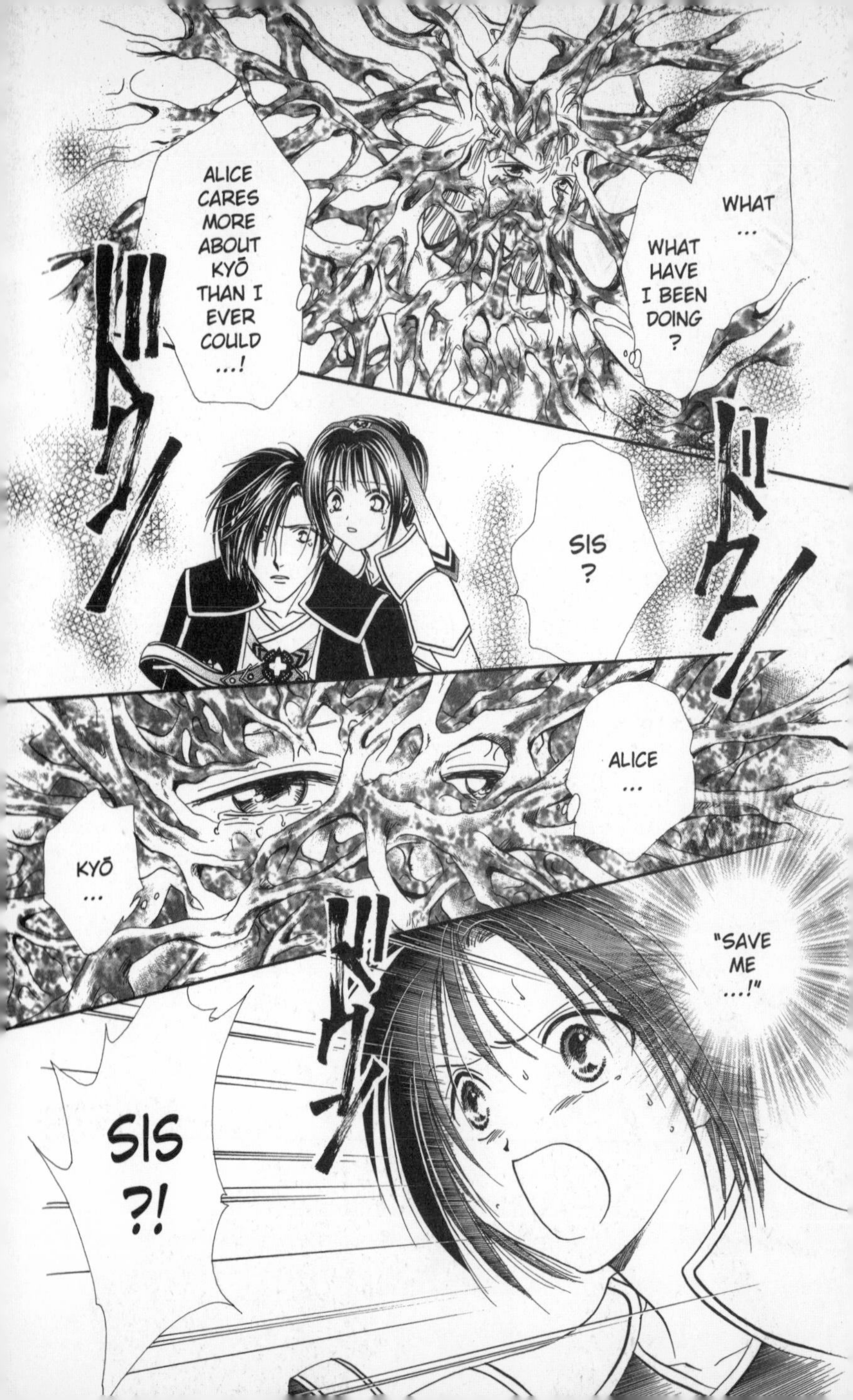
WHAT ... WHAT HAVE I BEEN DOING ?
ALICE CARES MORE ABOUT KYŌ THAN I EVER COULD ...!
SIS ?
ALICE ...
KYŌ ...
"SAVE ME ...!"
SIS ?!

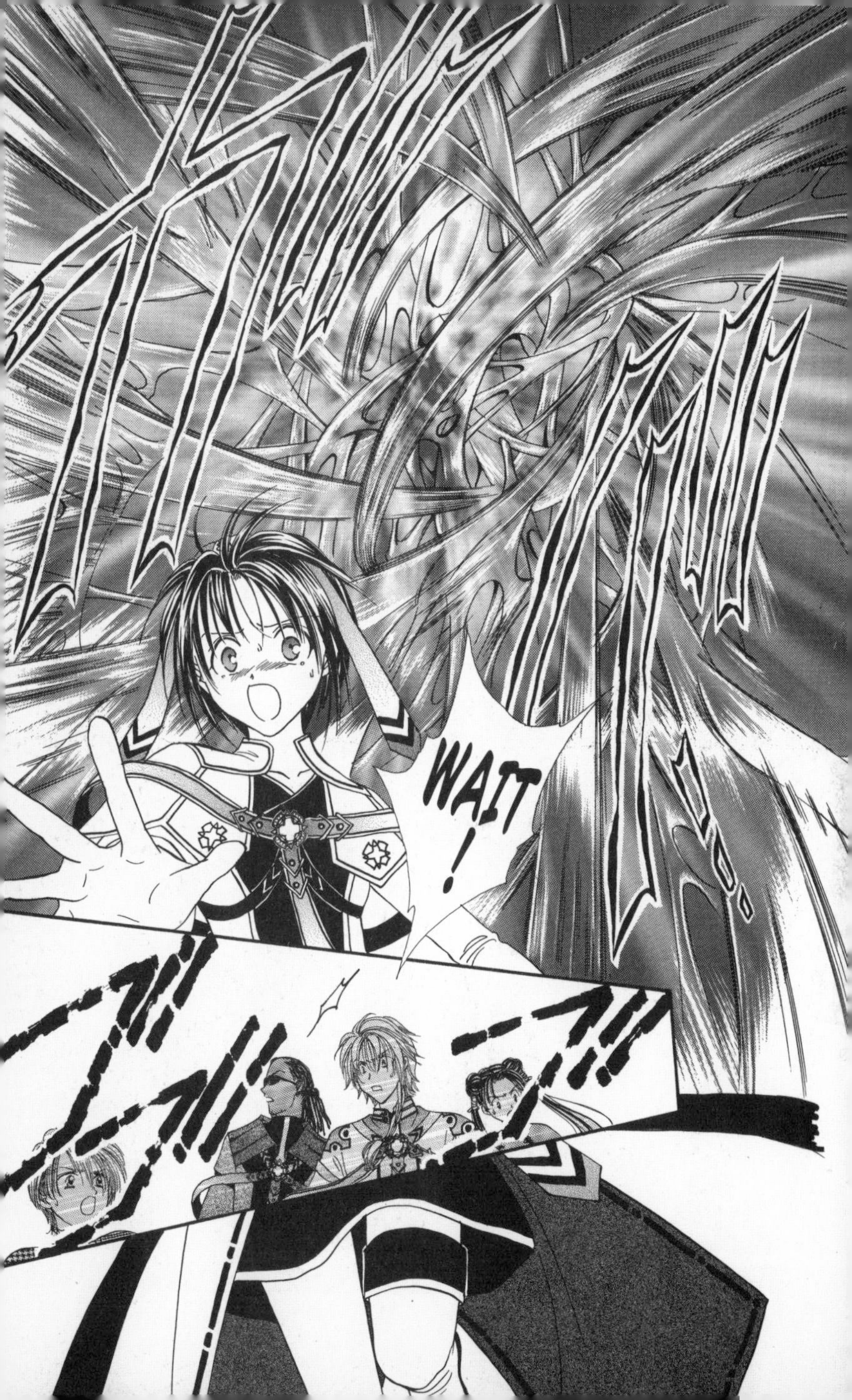
WAIT!

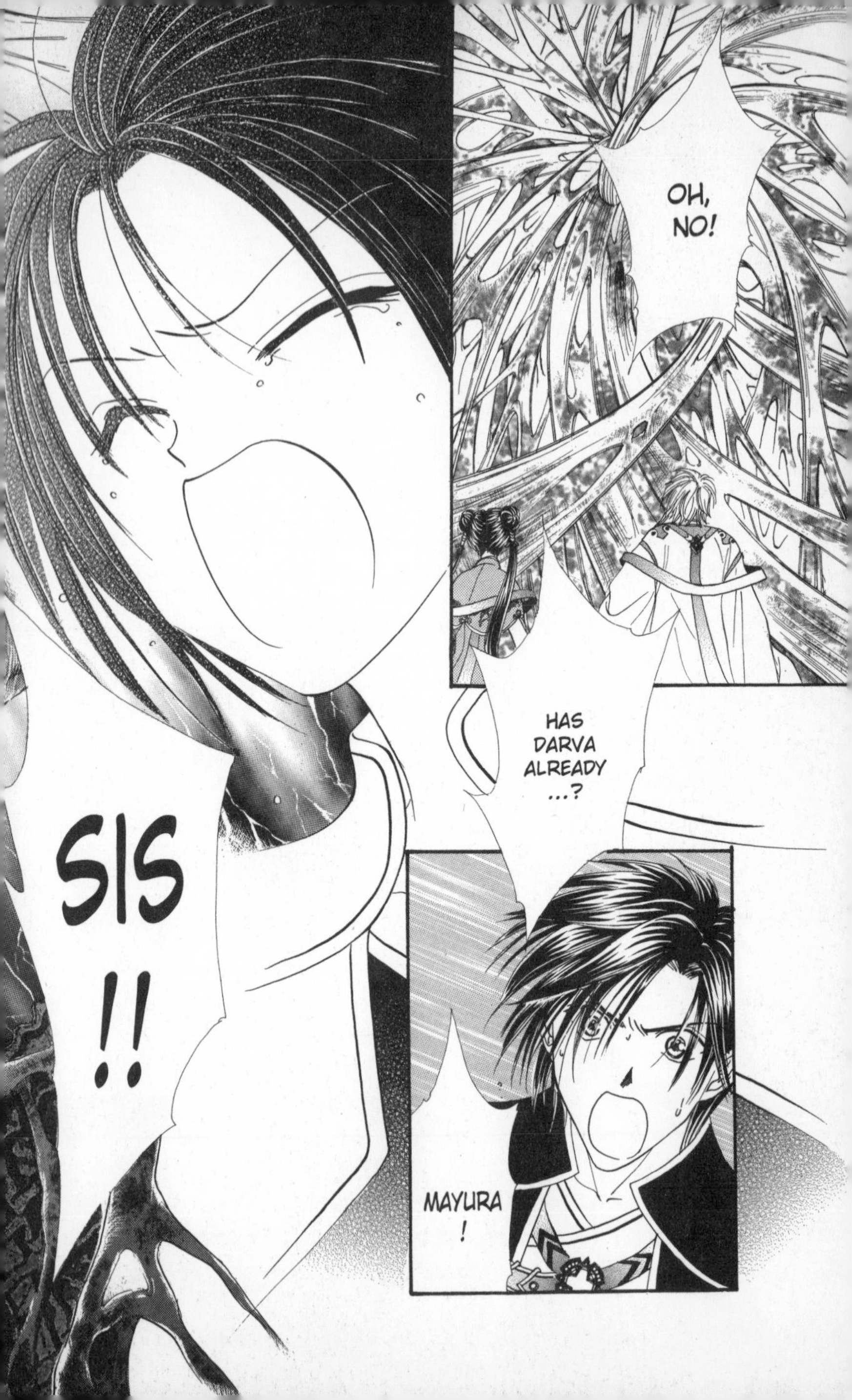
OH, NO!
HAS DARVA ALREADY ...?
MAYURA!
SIS!!

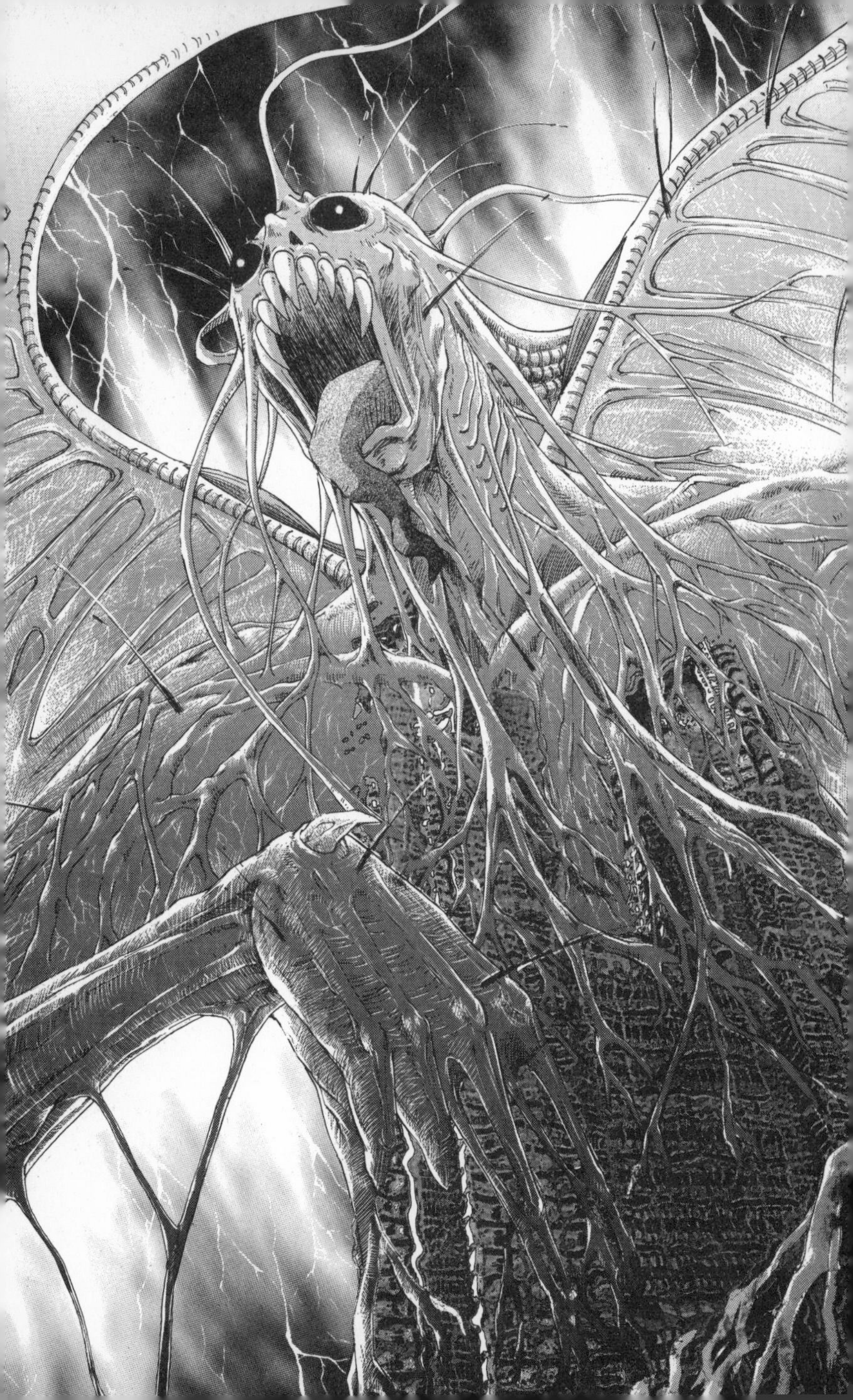

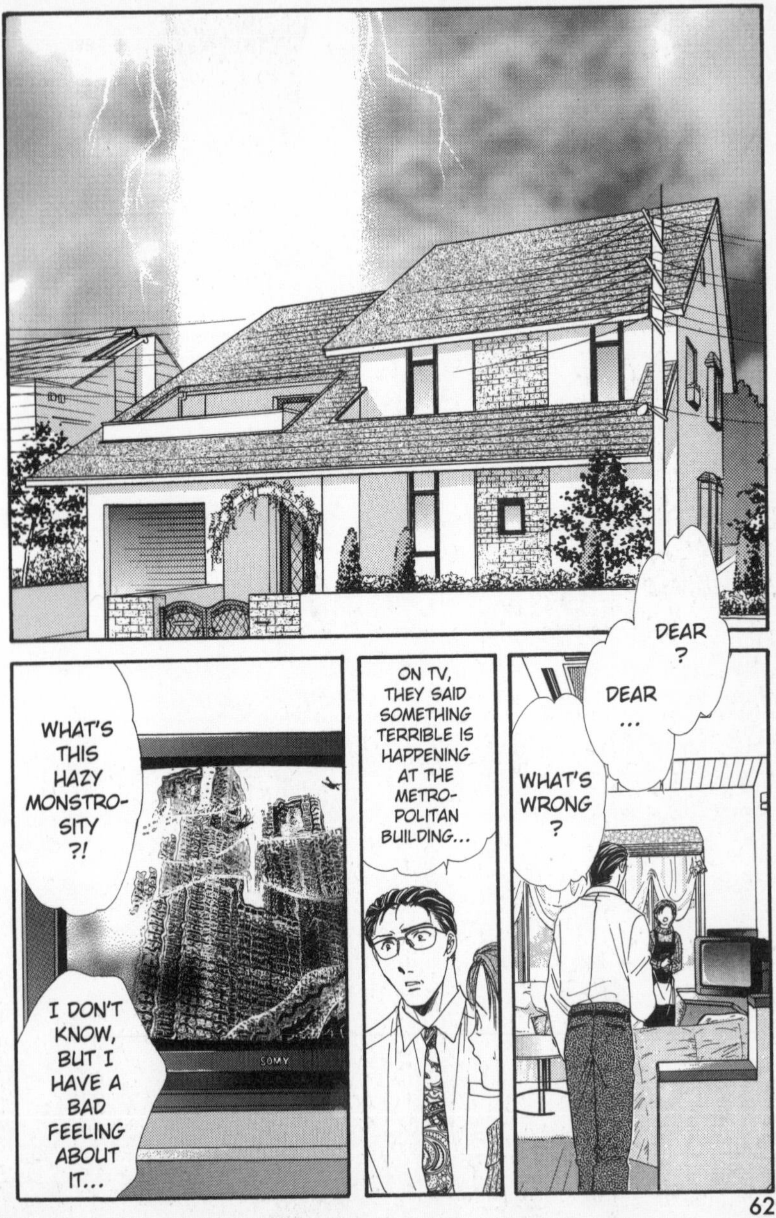
DEAR?
DEAR...
WHAT'S WRONG?
ON TV, THEY SAID SOMETHING TERRIBLE IS HAPPENING AT THE METRO-POLITAN BUILDING...
WHAT'S THIS HAZY MONSTRO-SITY?!
SOMY
I DON'T KNOW, BUT I HAVE A BAD FEELING ABOUT IT...

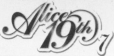

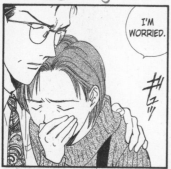

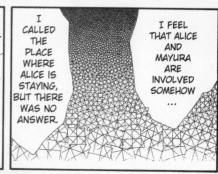

I FEEL THAT ALICE AND MAYURA ARE INVOLVED SOMEHOW ...
I CALLED THE PLACE WHERE ALICE IS STAYING, BUT THERE WAS NO ANSWER.
I'M WORRIED.
I'M SURE THEY'RE ALL RIGHT.
WE DECIDED TO HAVE FAITH IN THEM, RIGHT?
THEY'RE GOING TO COME HOME SAFE AND SOUND ...

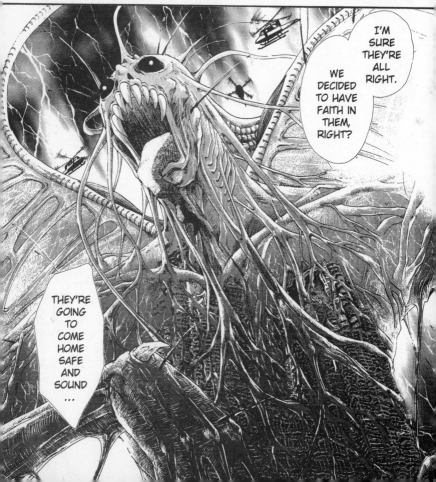

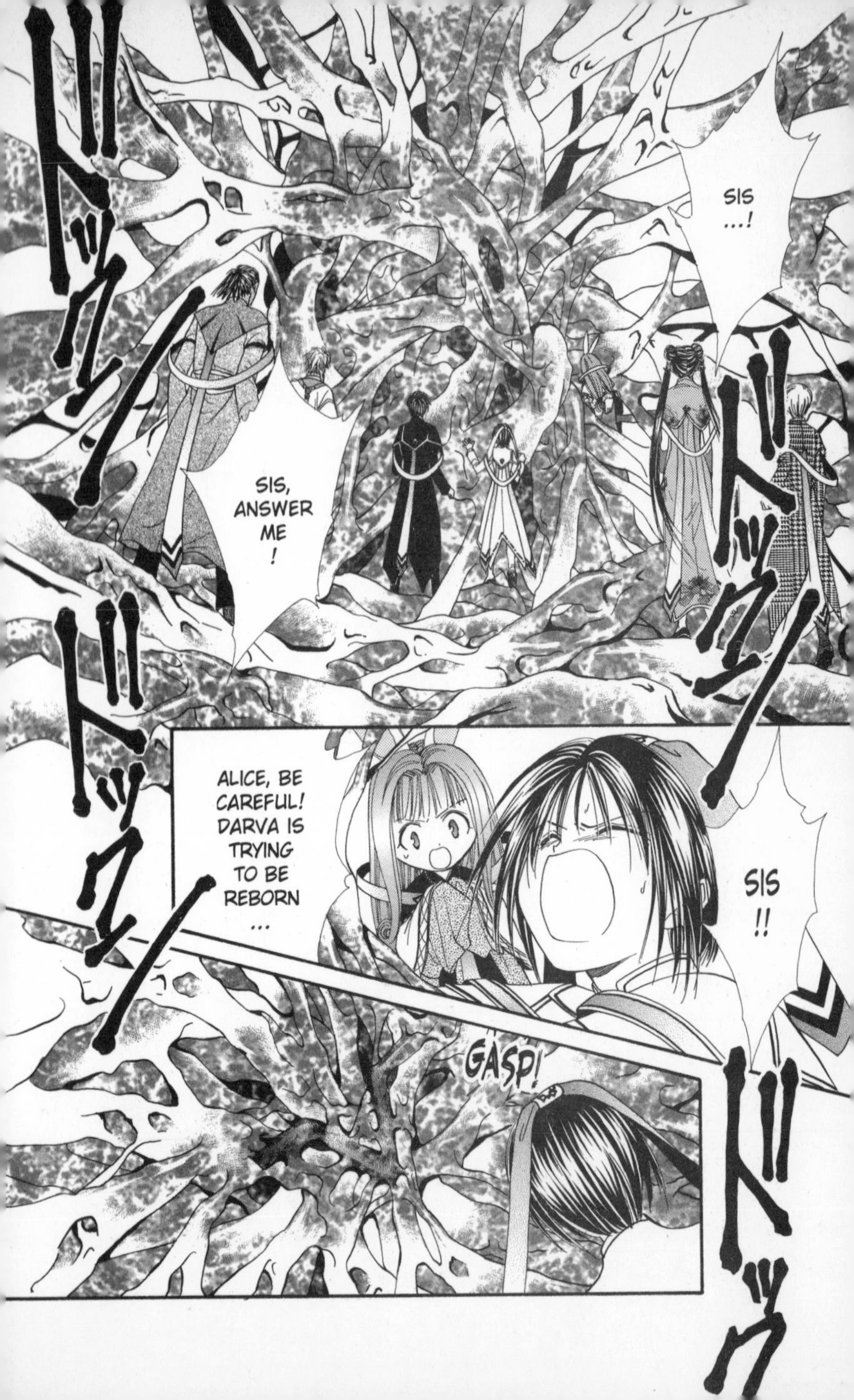
SIS ...!
SIS, ANSWER ME !
SIS !!
ALICE, BE CAREFUL! DARVA IS TRYING TO BE REBORN ...
GASP!

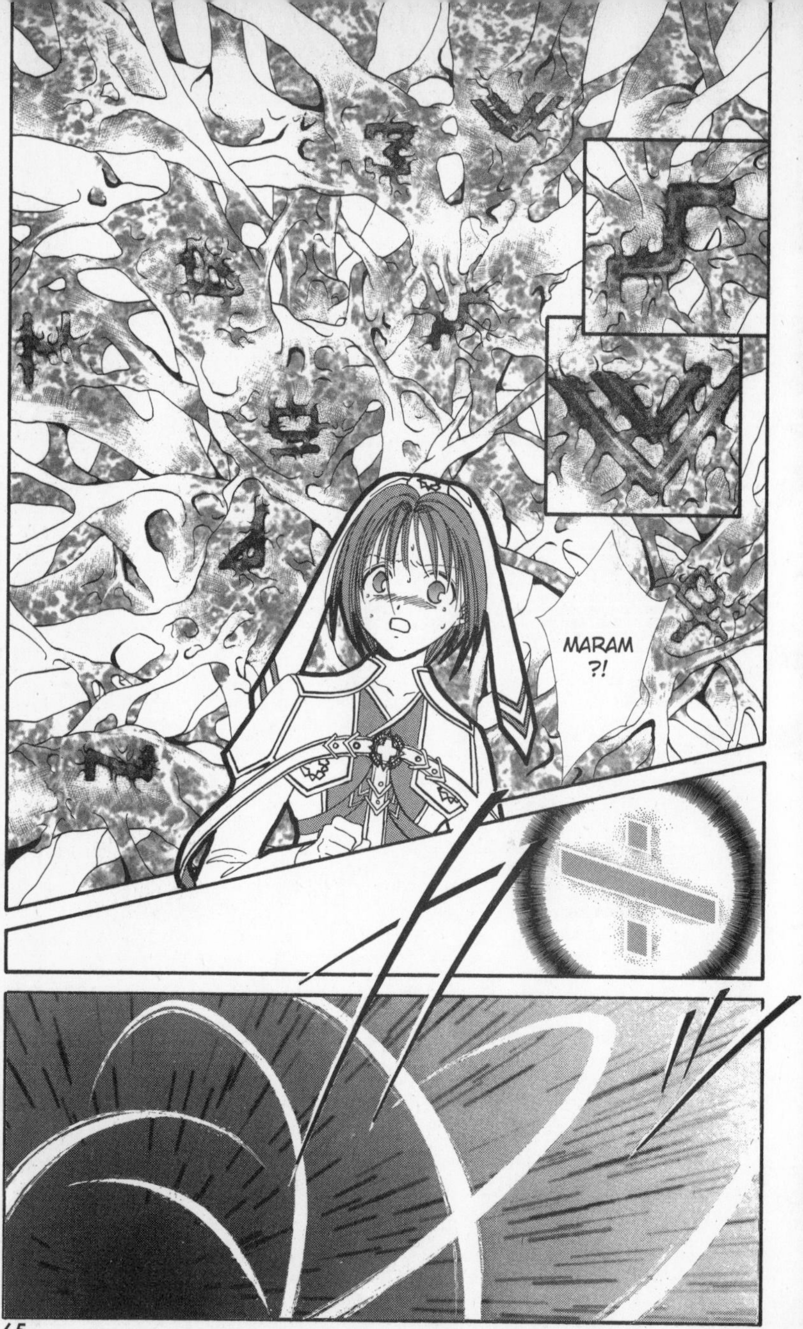
MARAM ?!

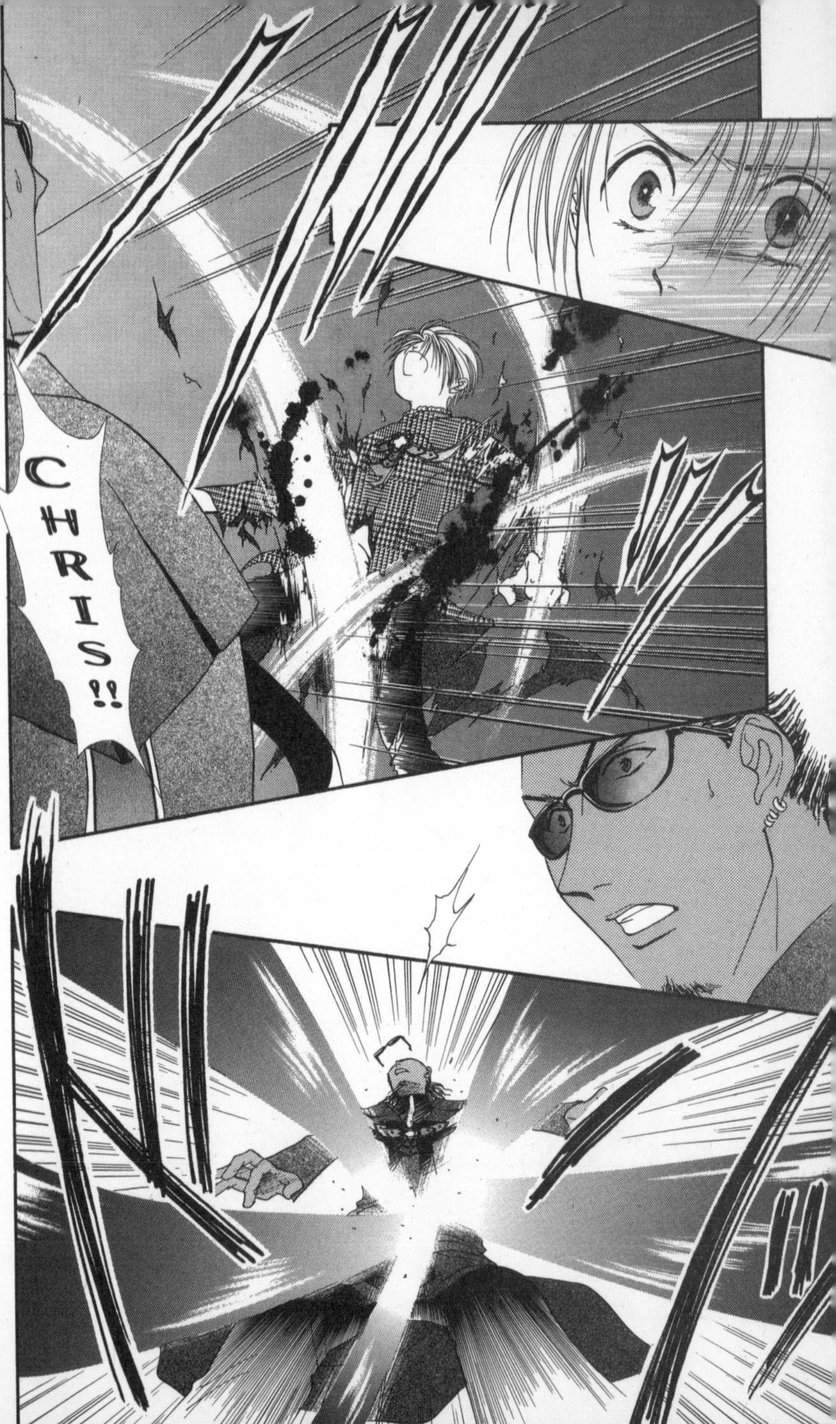
CHRIS!!

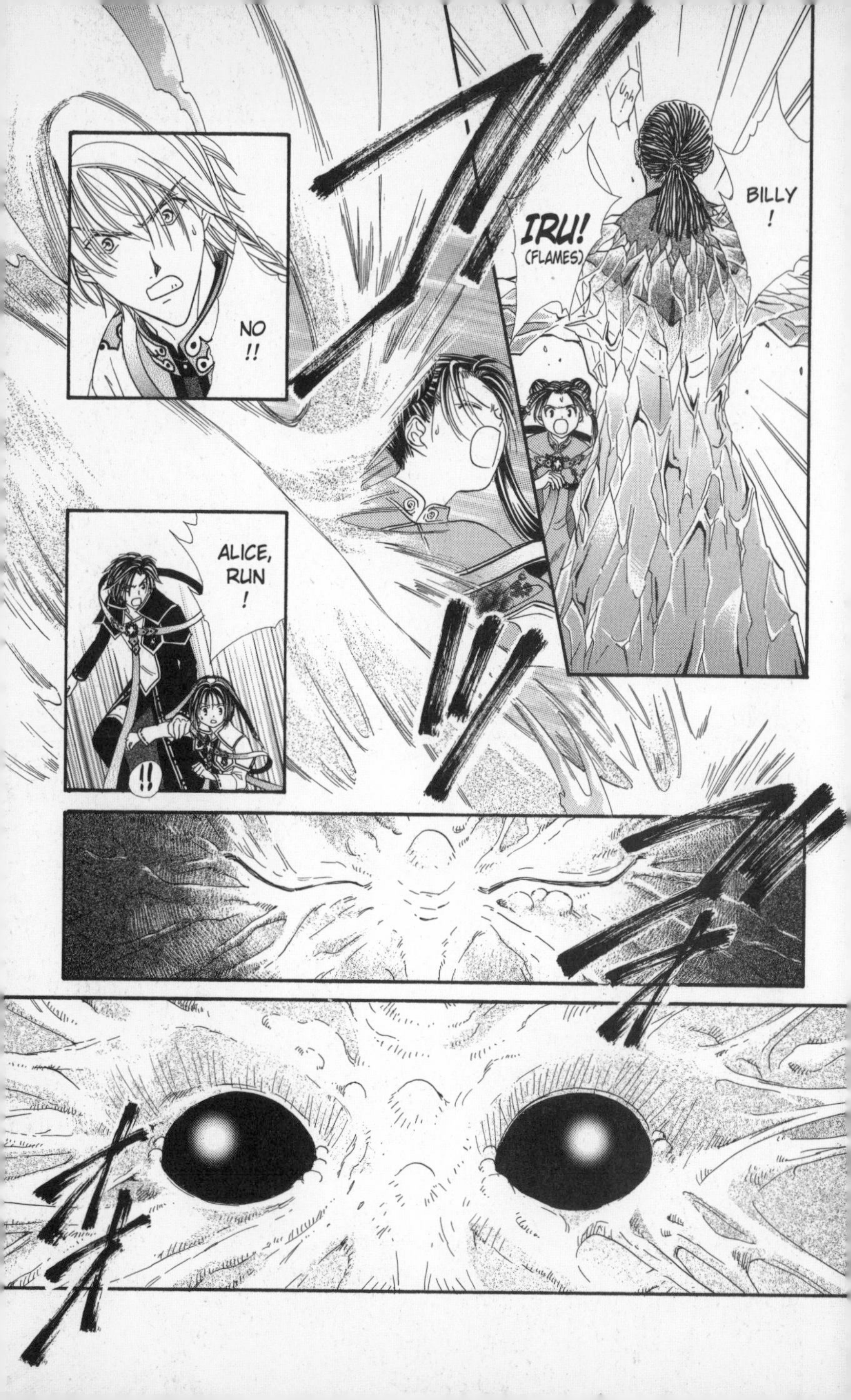
Unh!
BILLY !
IRU!
(FLAMES)
NO !!
ALICE, RUN !
!!

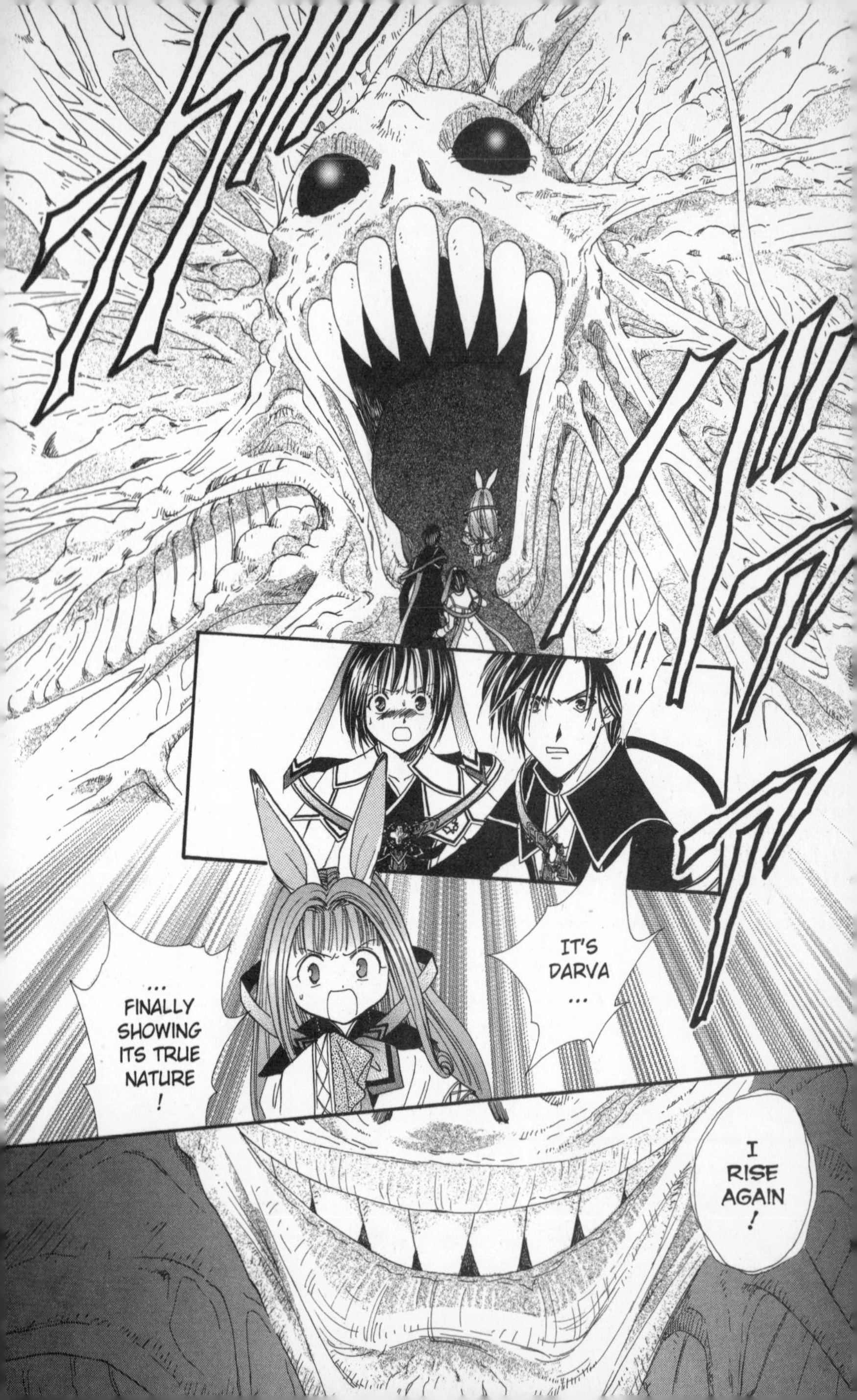
IT'S DARVA ...
... FINALLY SHOWING ITS TRUE NATURE !
I RISE AGAIN !

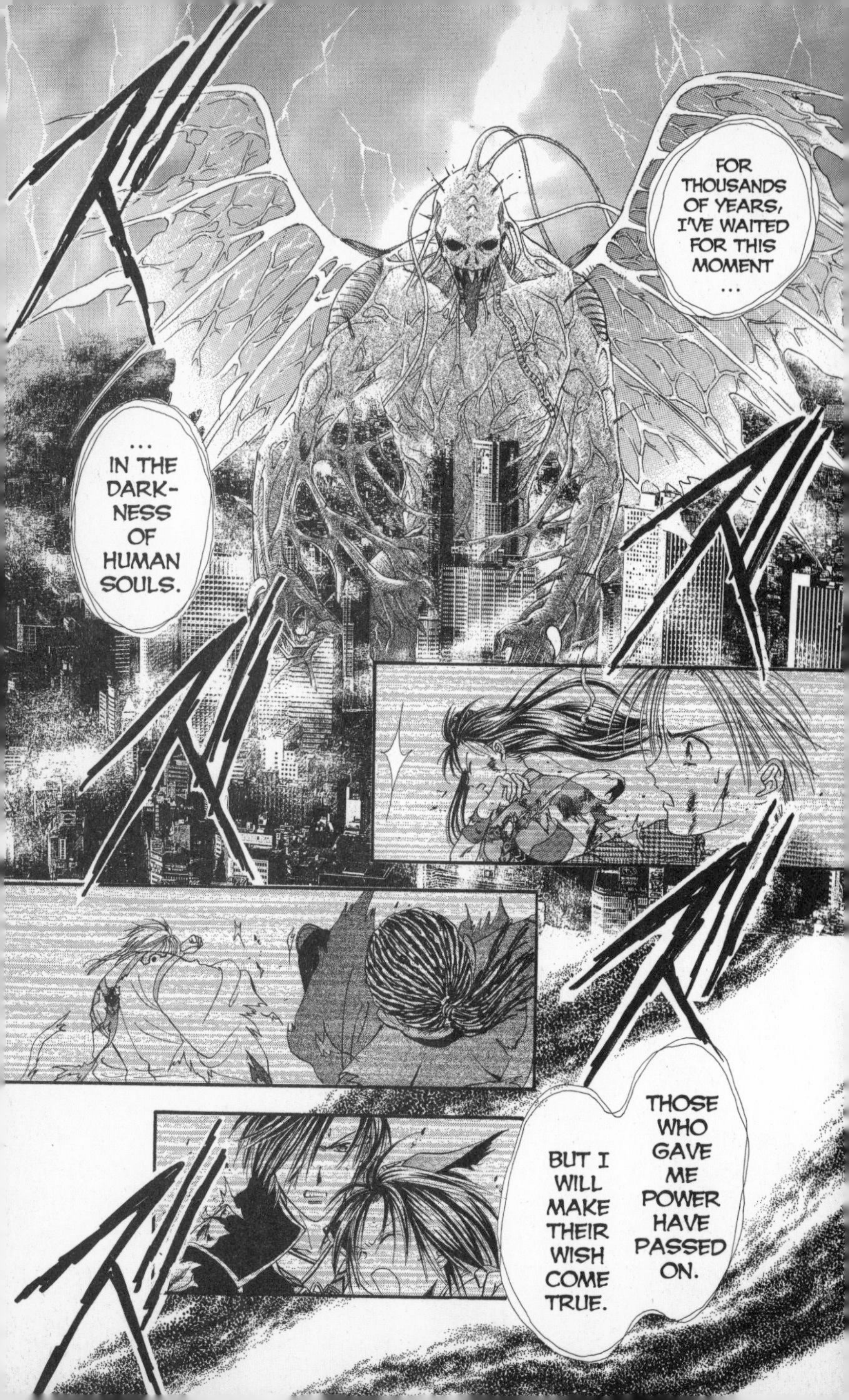
FOR THOUSANDS OF YEARS, I'VE WAITED FOR THIS MOMENT ...
... IN THE DARK-NESS OF HUMAN SOULS.
THOSE WHO GAVE ME POWER HAVE PASSED ON.
BUT I WILL MAKE THEIR WISH COME TRUE.

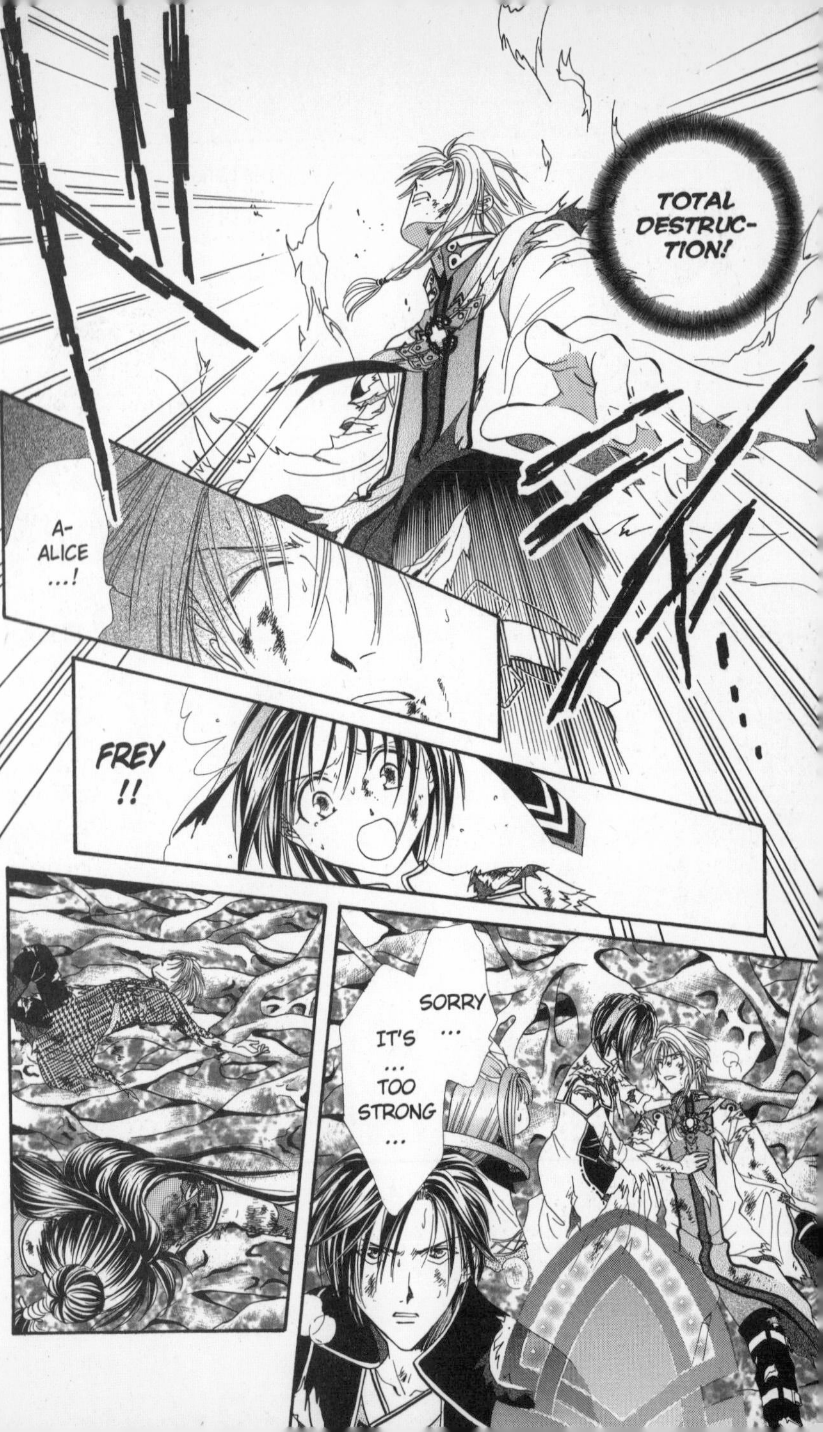
TOTAL DESTRUC-TION!
A-ALICE ...!
FREY !!
SORRY ...
IT'S ... TOO STRONG ...

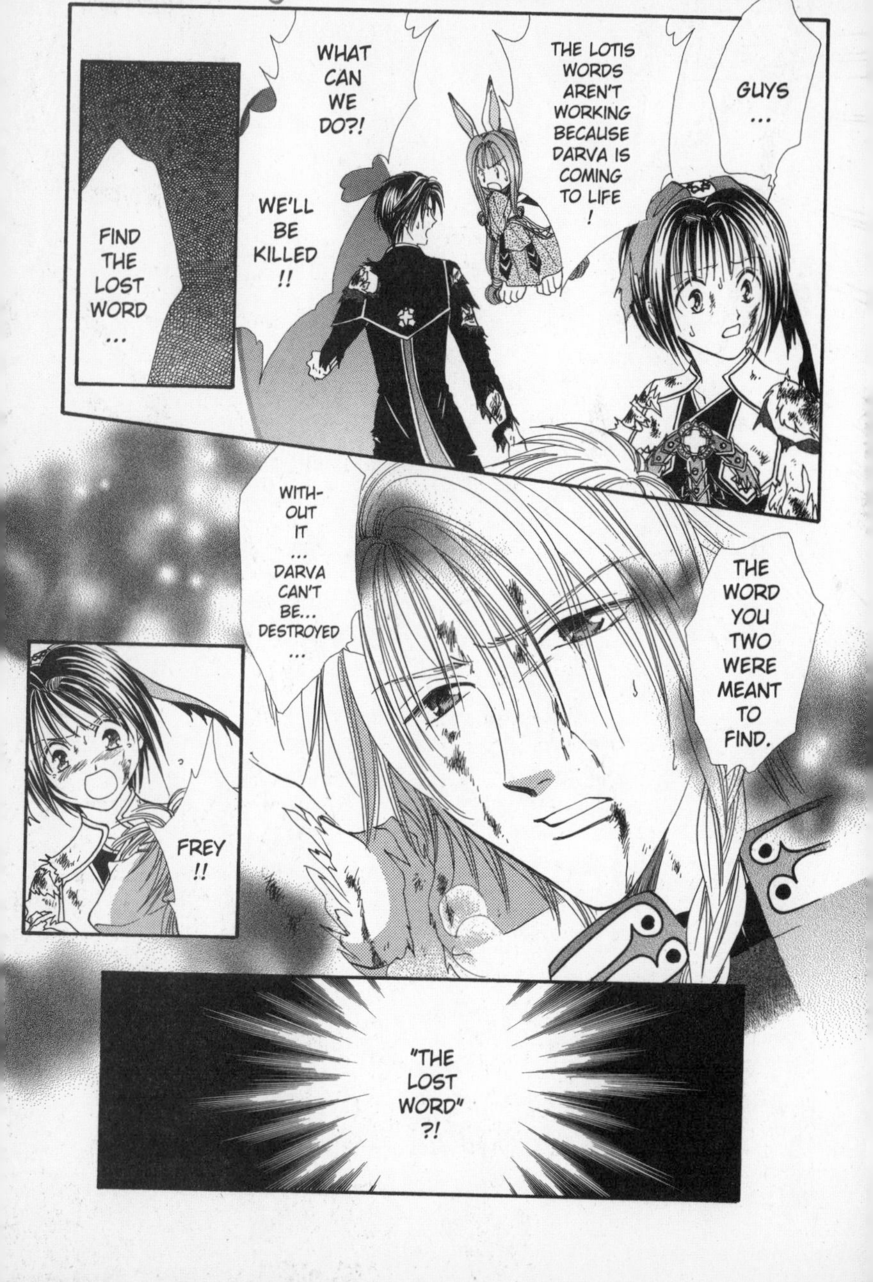
GUYS ...
THE LOTIS WORDS AREN'T WORKING BECAUSE DARVA IS COMING TO LIFE !
WHAT CAN WE DO?!
WE'LL BE KILLED !!
FIND THE LOST WORD ...
THE WORD YOU TWO WERE MEANT TO FIND.
WITH-OUT IT ... DARVA CAN'T BE... DESTROYED ...
FREY !!
"THE LOST WORD" ?!

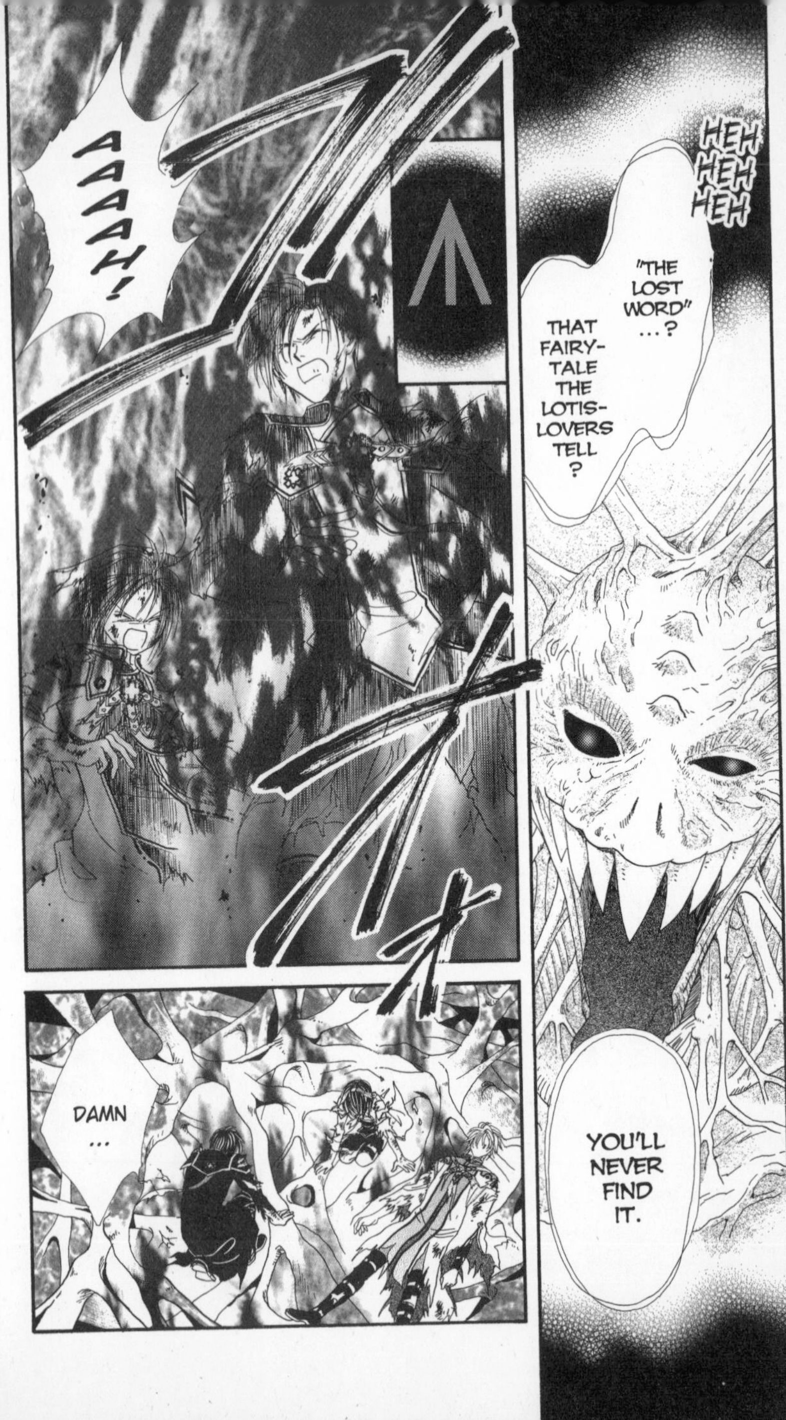
HEH HEH HEH
"THE LOST WORD" ...? THAT FAIRY-TALE THE LOTIS-LOVERS TELL?
YOU'LL NEVER FIND IT.
AAAAAH!
DAMN ...

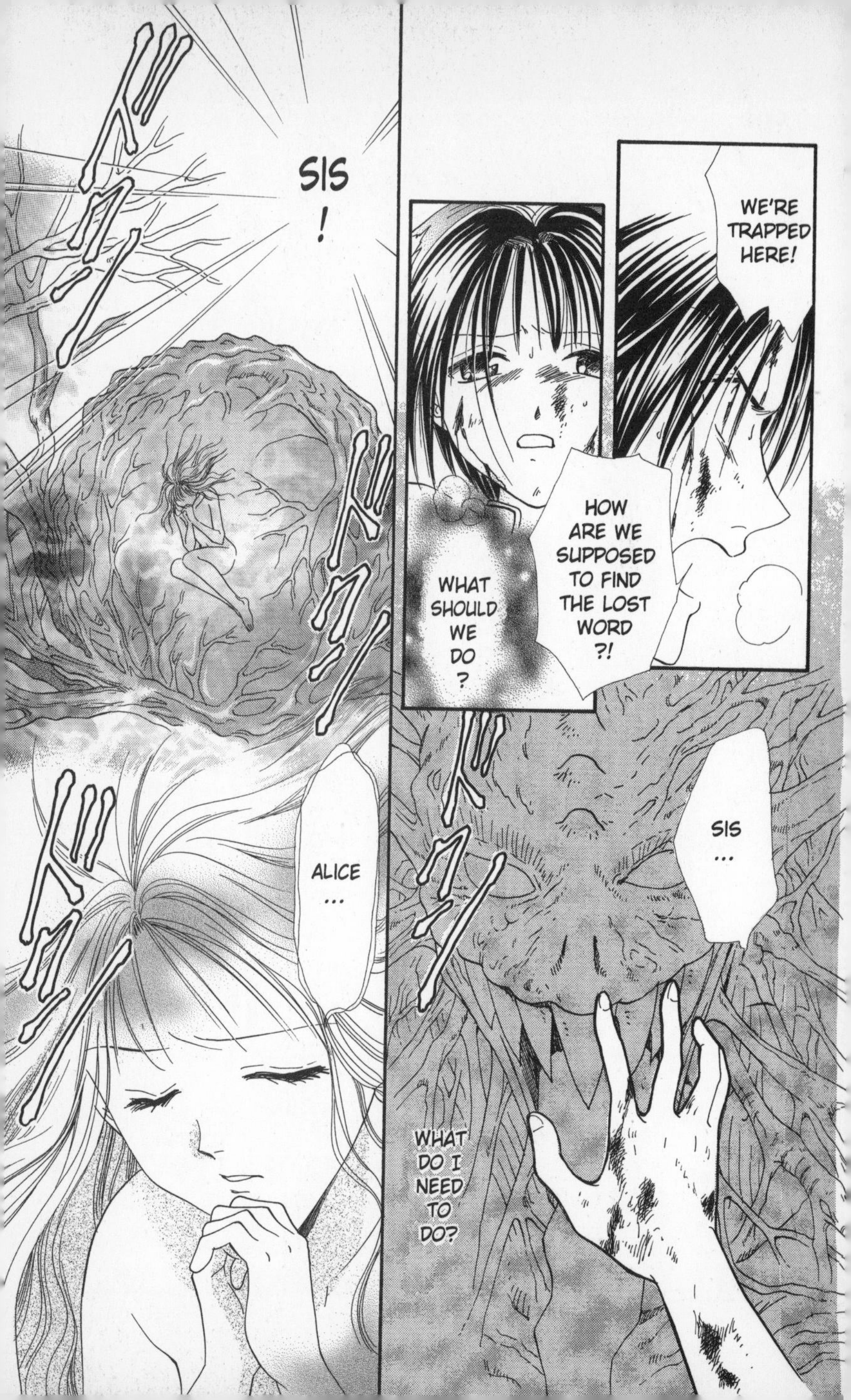
WE'RE TRAPPED HERE!
HOW ARE WE SUPPOSED TO FIND THE LOST WORD ?!
WHAT SHOULD WE DO ?
SIS ...
WHAT DO I NEED TO DO?
SIS !
ALICE ...

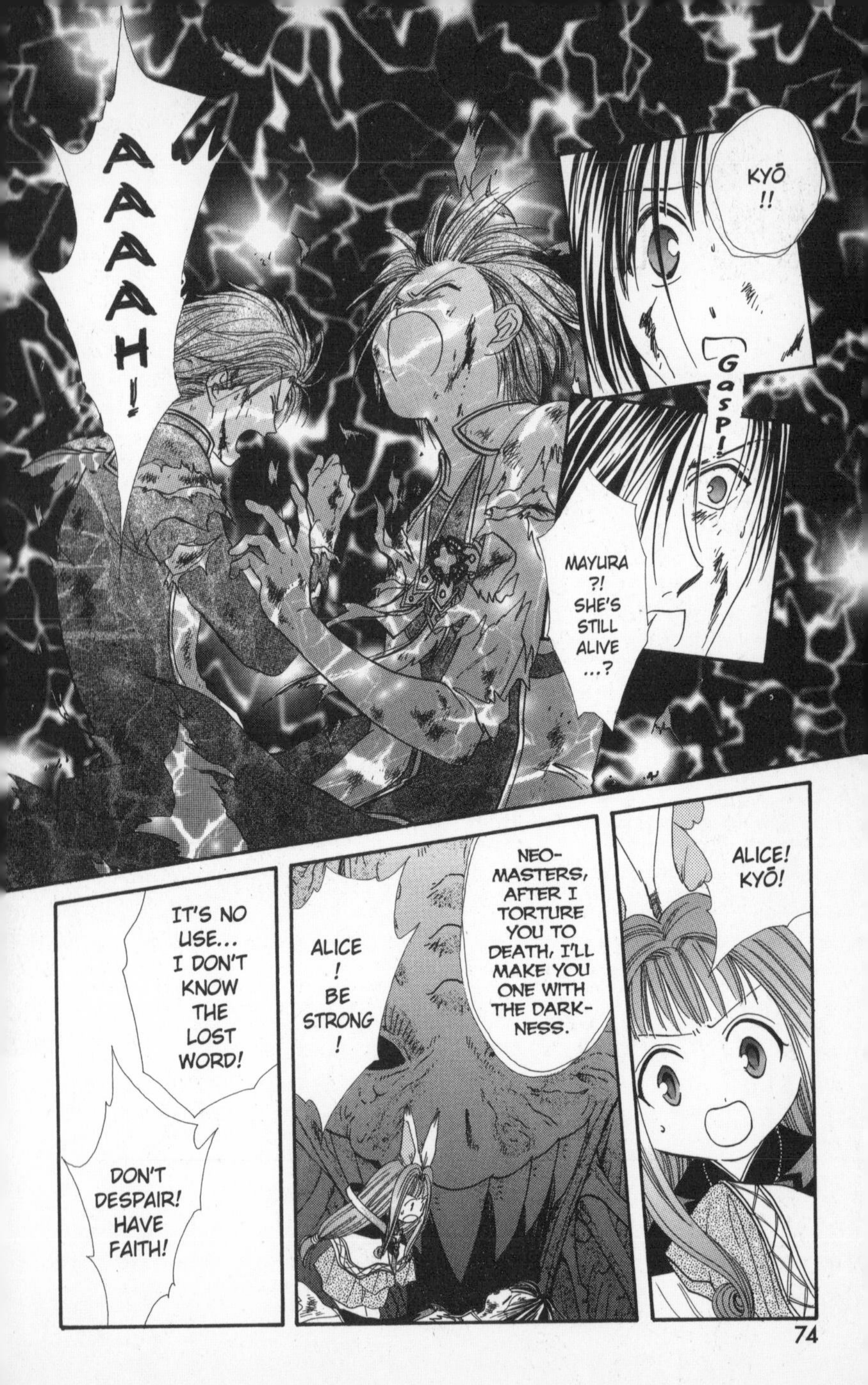
KYŌ !!
GASP!
MAYURA ?! SHE'S STILL ALIVE ...?
AAAAH!
ALICE! KYŌ!
NEO-MASTERS, AFTER I TORTURE YOU TO DEATH, I'LL MAKE YOU ONE WITH THE DARKNESS.
ALICE ! BE STRONG !
IT'S NO USE... I DON'T KNOW THE LOST WORD!
DON'T DESPAIR! HAVE FAITH!

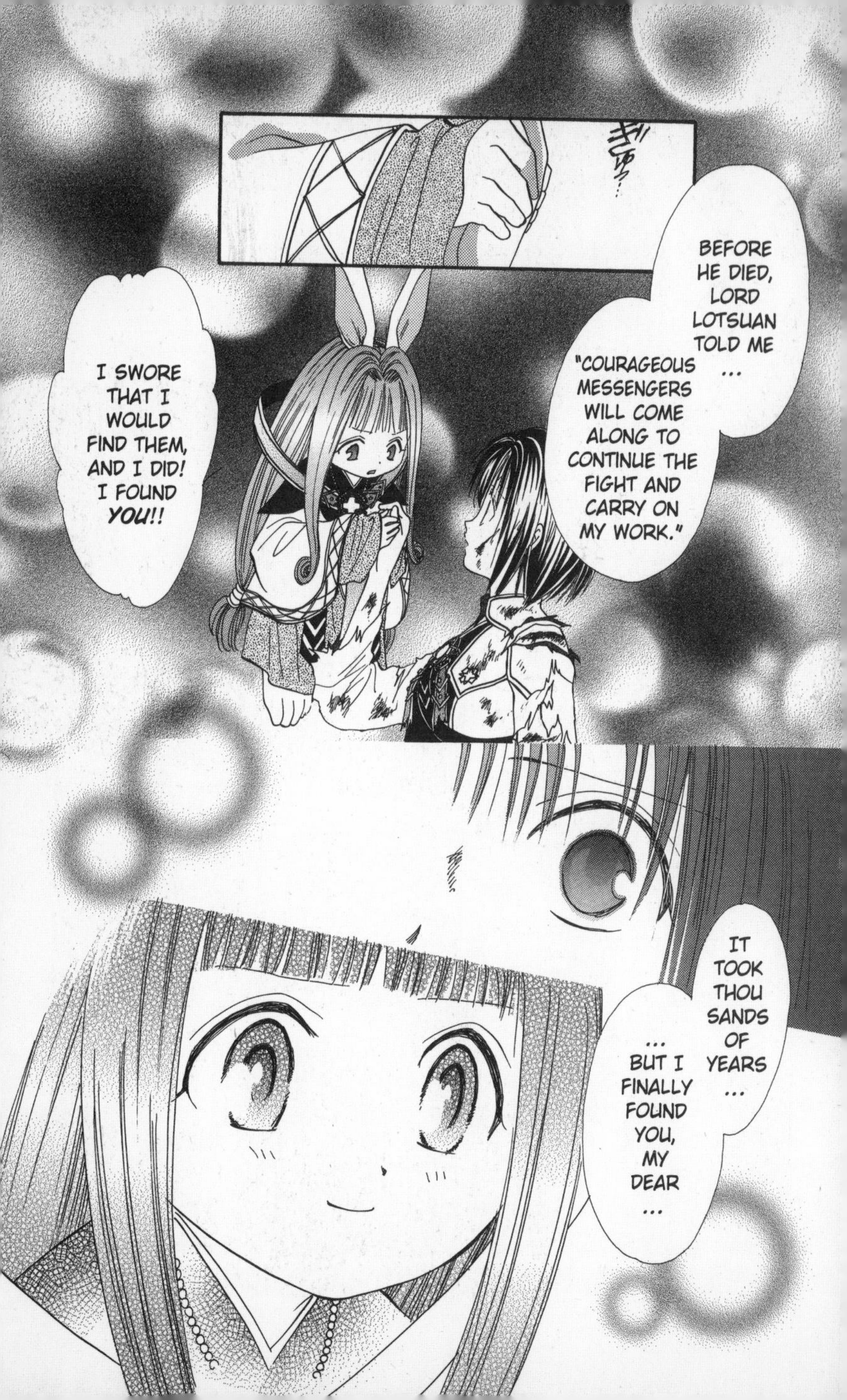

BEFORE HE DIED, LORD LOTSUAN TOLD ME ...
"COURAGEOUS MESSENGERS WILL COME ALONG TO CONTINUE THE FIGHT AND CARRY ON MY WORK."
I SWORE THAT I WOULD FIND THEM, AND I DID! I FOUND *YOU*!!
IT TOOK THOUSANDS OF YEARS ...
... BUT I FINALLY FOUND YOU, MY DEAR ...

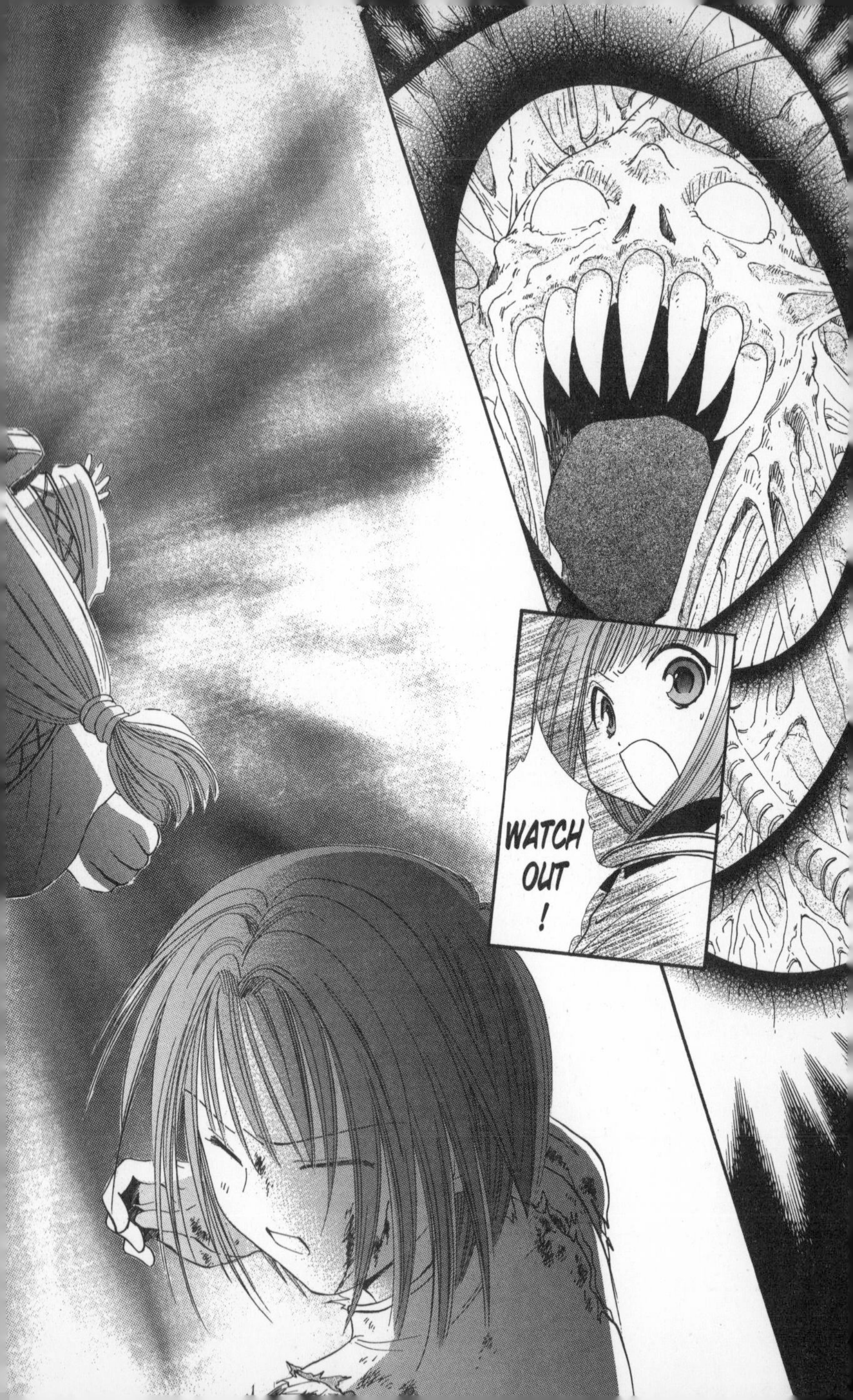
WATCH OUT !

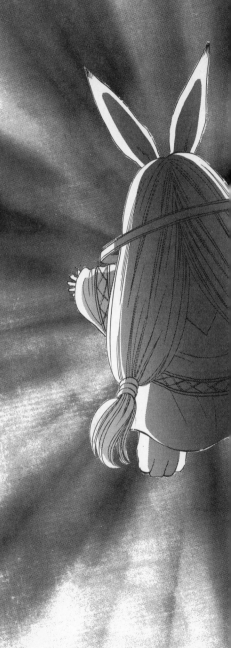

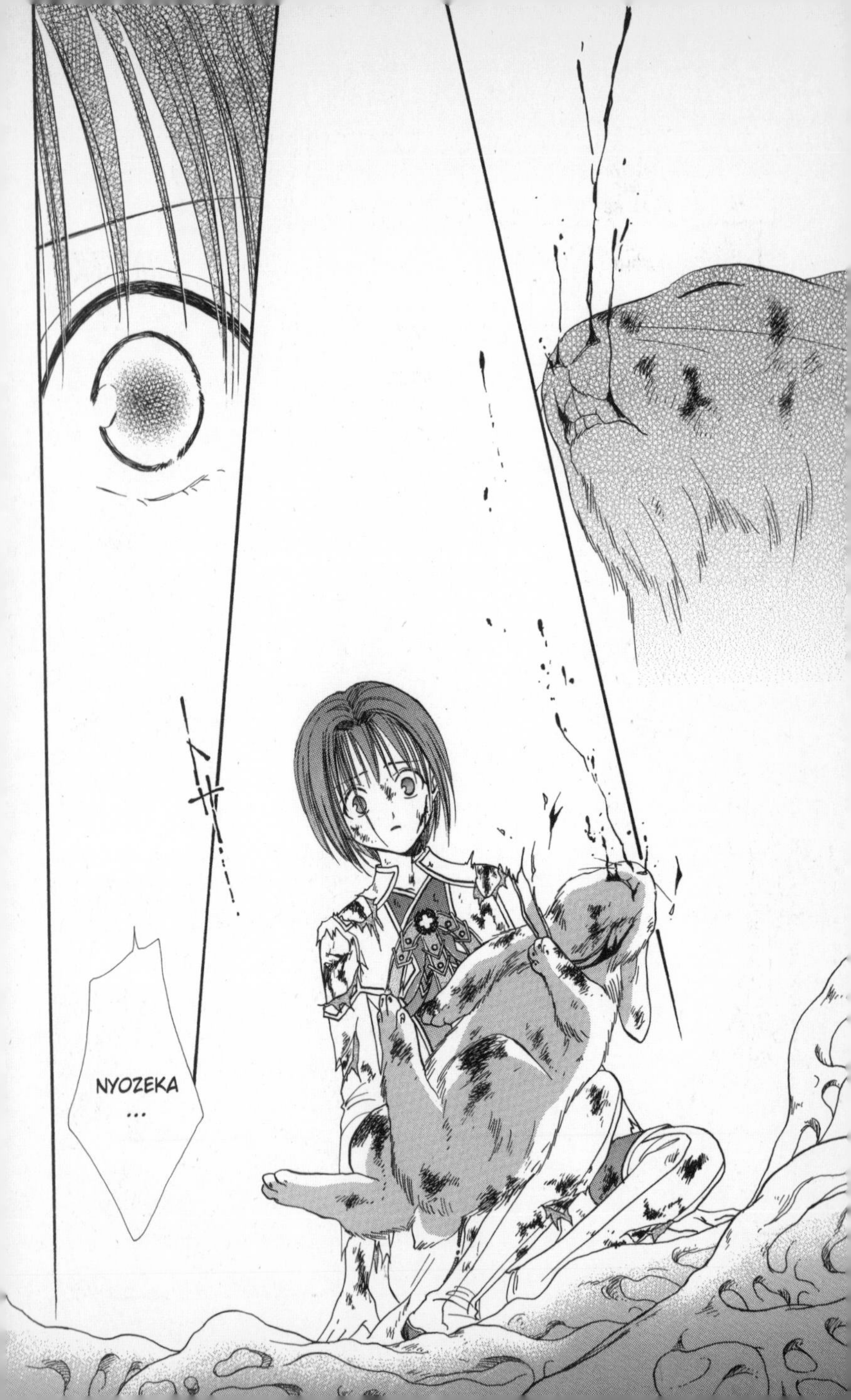
NYOZEKA
...

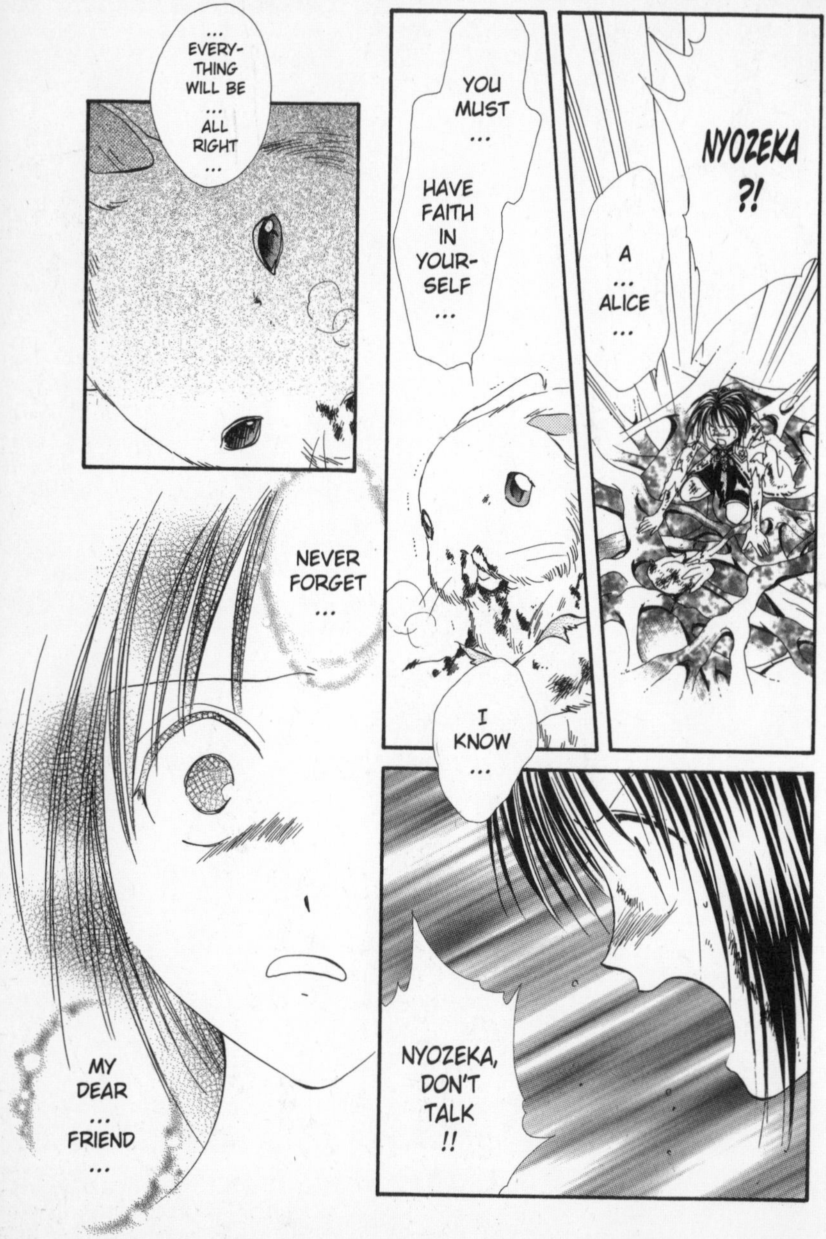
NYOZEKA ?!
A ... ALICE ...
YOU MUST ... HAVE FAITH IN YOURSELF ...
I KNOW ...
... EVERYTHING WILL BE ... ALL RIGHT ...
NYOZEKA, DON'T TALK !!
NEVER FORGET ...
MY DEAR ... FRIEND ...

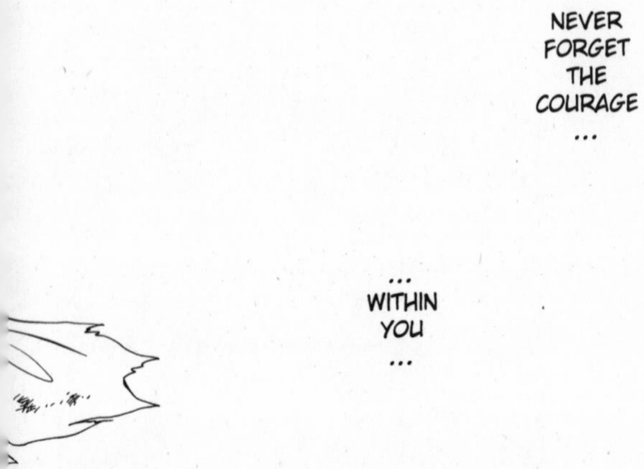
NEVER FORGET THE COURAGE ...
... WITHIN YOU ...

...NYO-
ZEKA
?

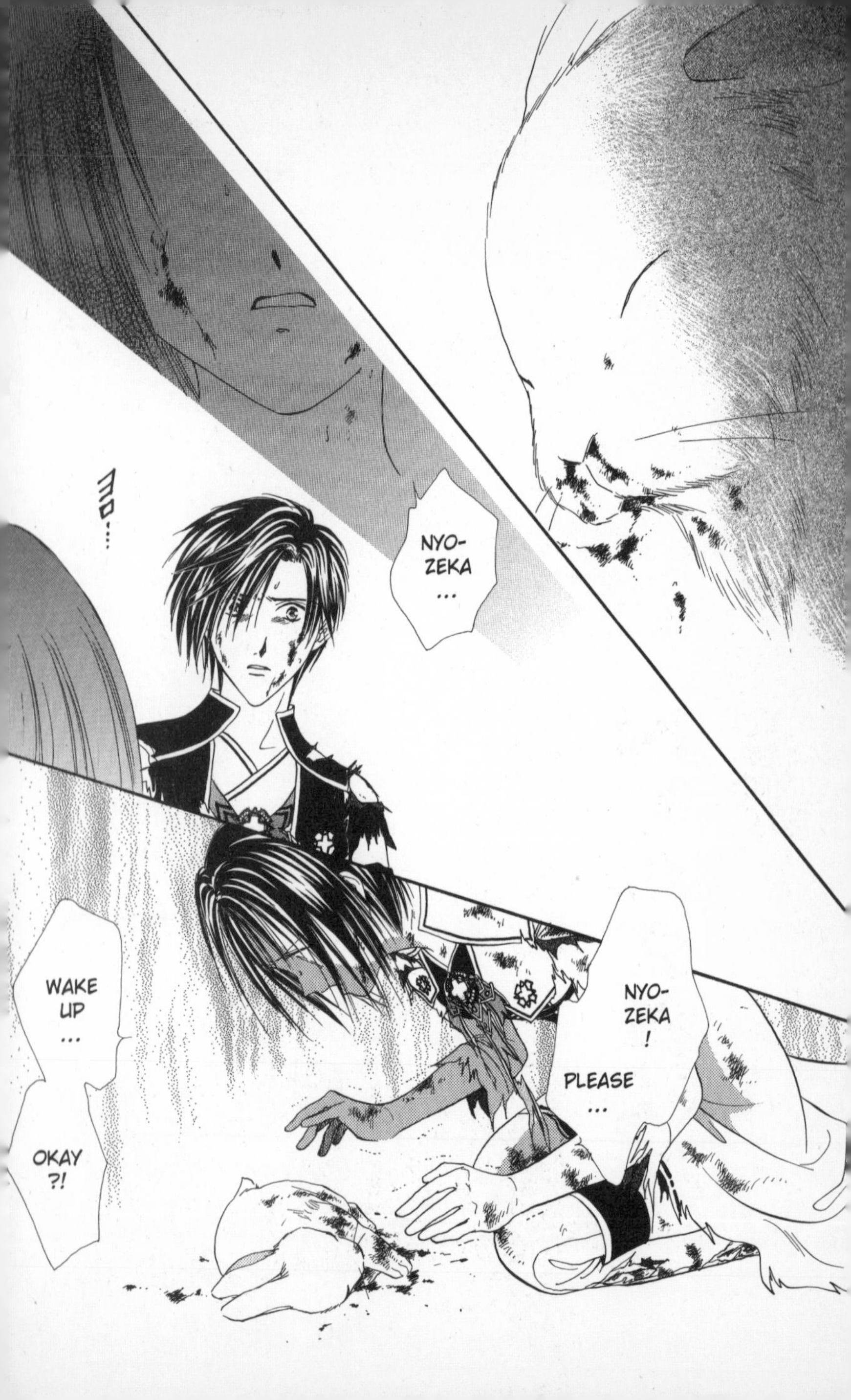
NYO-ZEKA ...
ヨロ…
NYO-ZEKA!
PLEASE ...
WAKE UP ...
OKAY?!

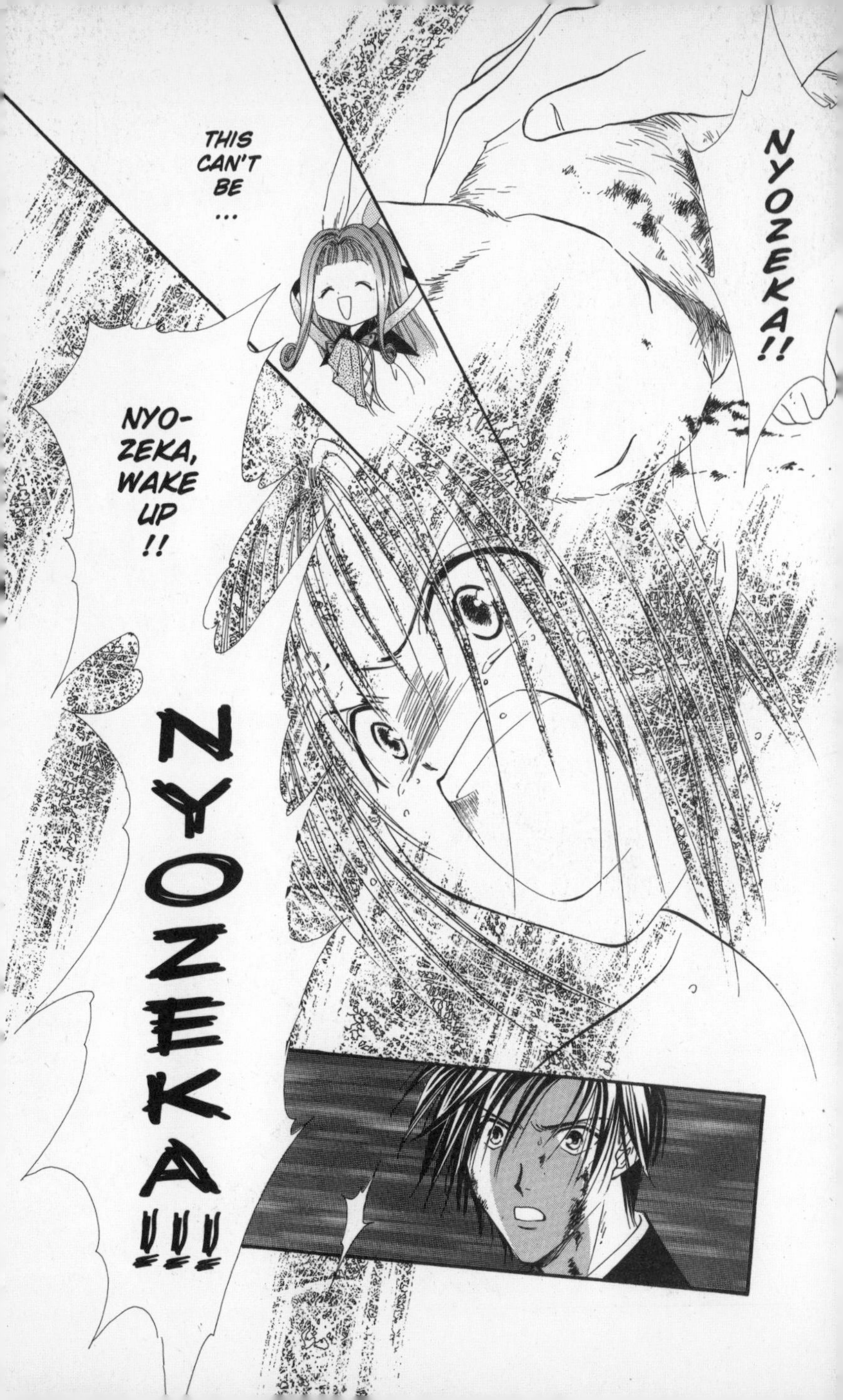
NYOZEKA!!
THIS CAN'T BE ...
NYO-ZEKA, WAKE UP !!
NYOZEKA!!!

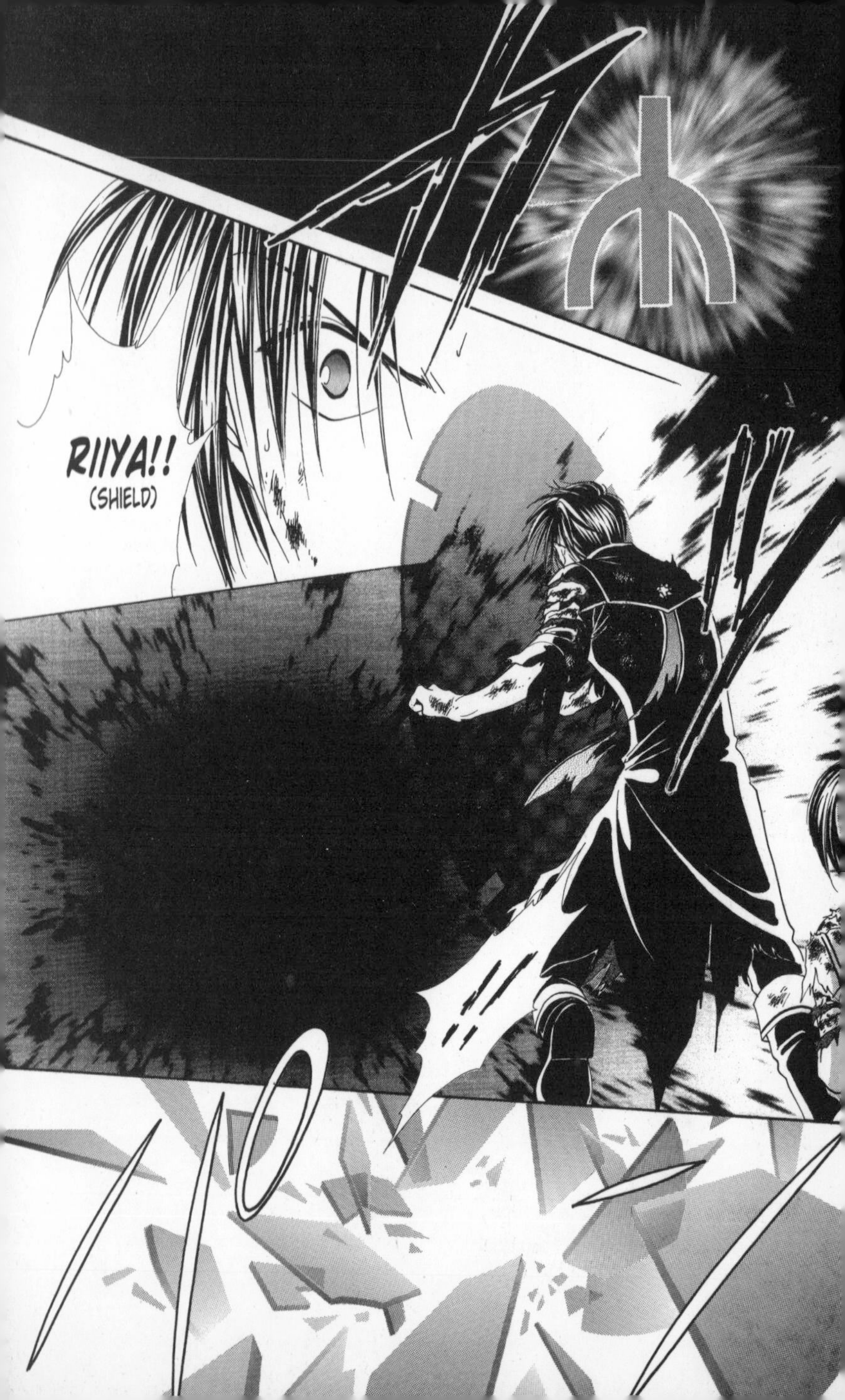
RIIYA!!
(SHIELD)

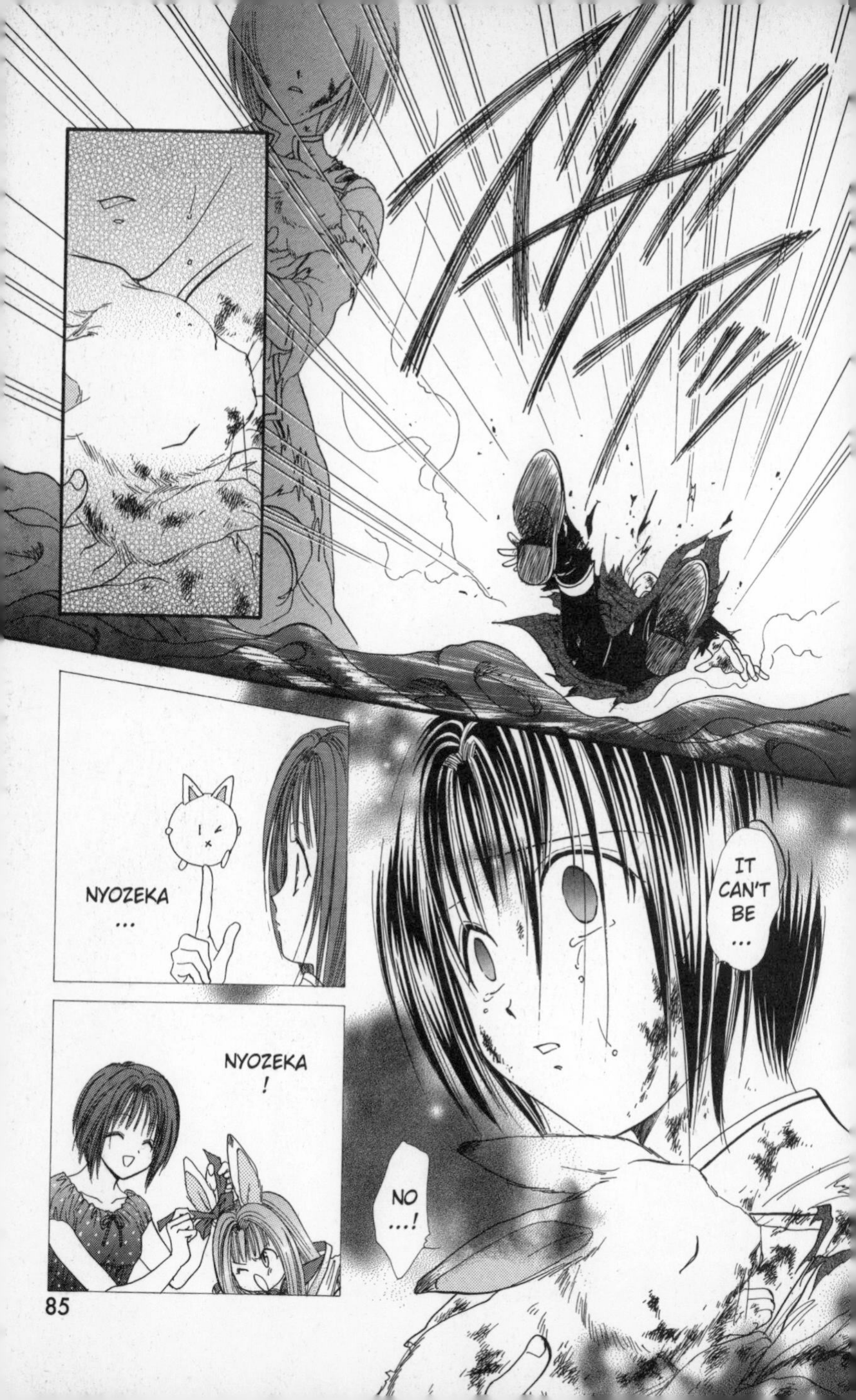
IT CAN'T BE ...
NO ...!
NYOZEKA ...
NYOZEKA !

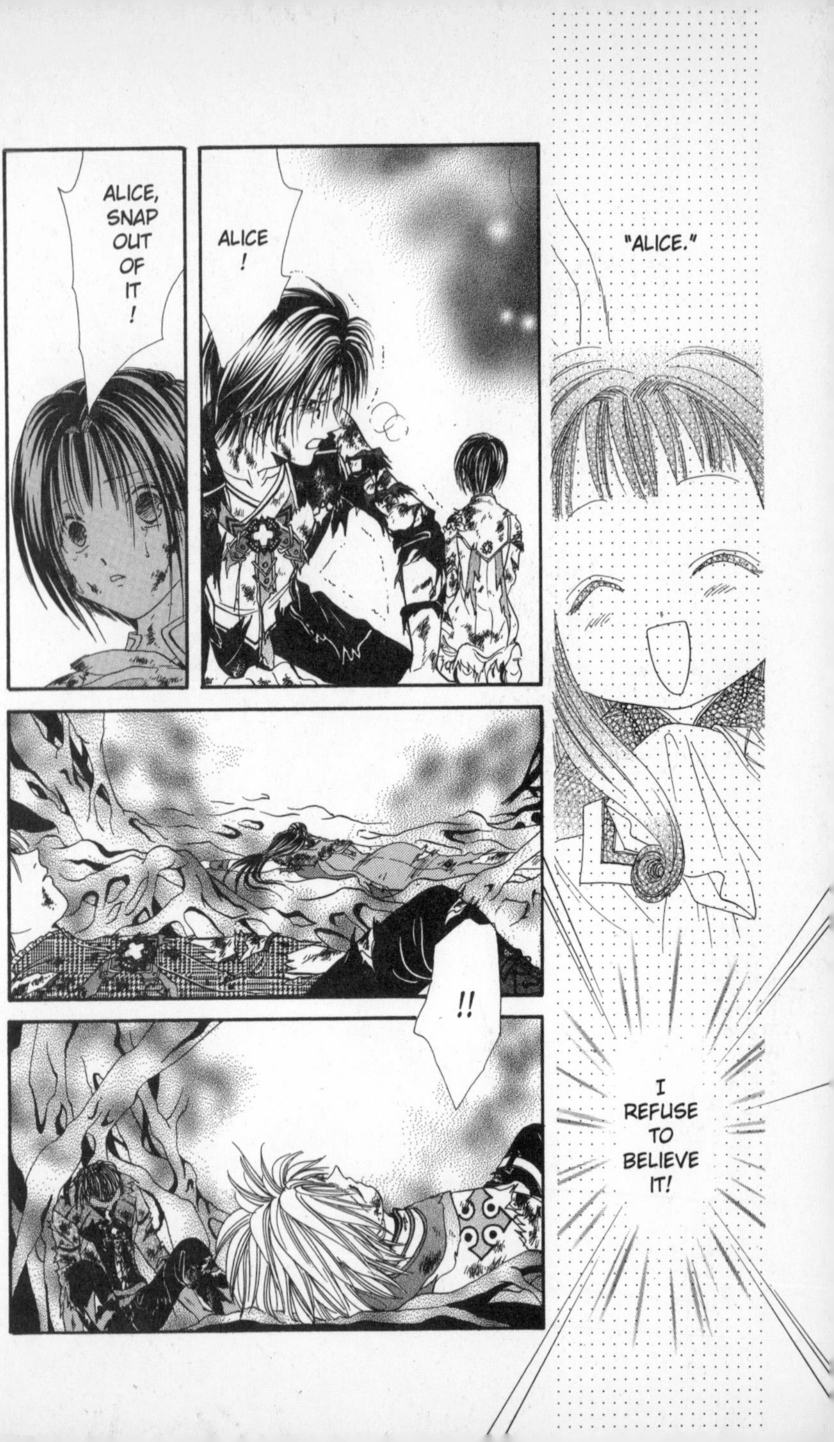
"ALICE."
I REFUSE TO BELIEVE IT!
ALICE!
ALICE, SNAP OUT OF IT!
!!

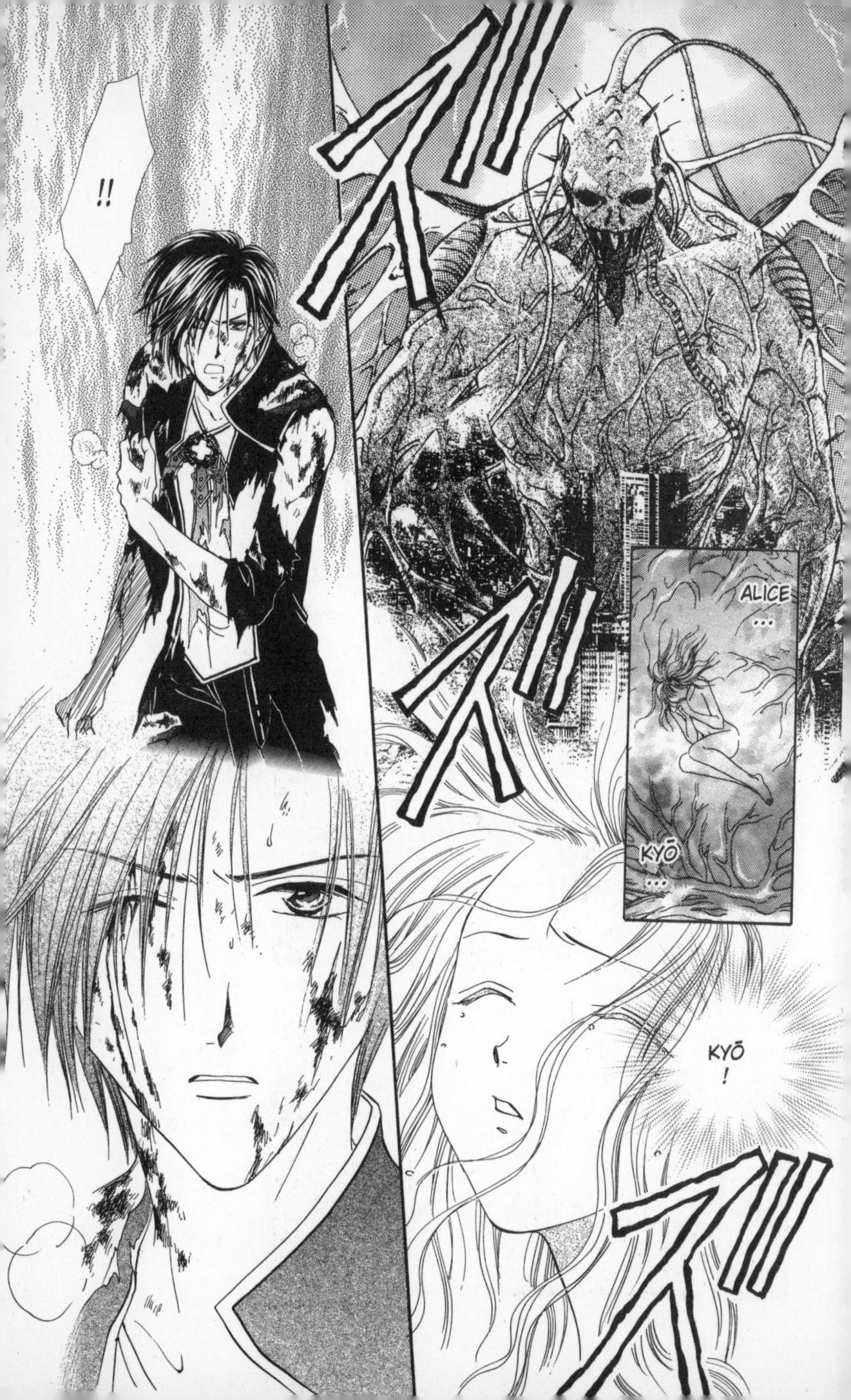
ALICE ...
KYŌ ...
KYŌ !
!!

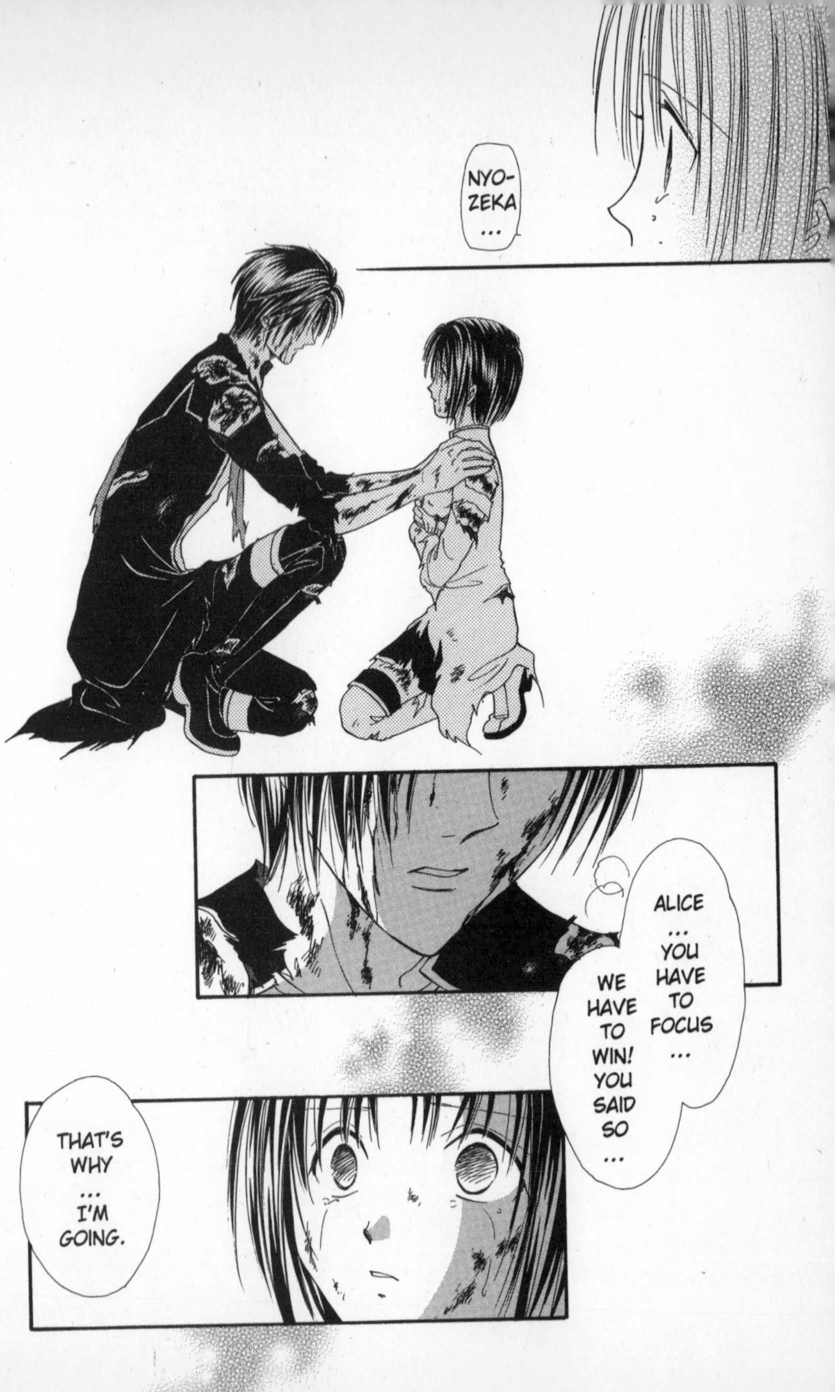
NYO-ZEKA ...
ALICE ... YOU HAVE TO FOCUS ...
WE HAVE TO WIN! YOU SAID SO ...
THAT'S WHY ... I'M GOING.

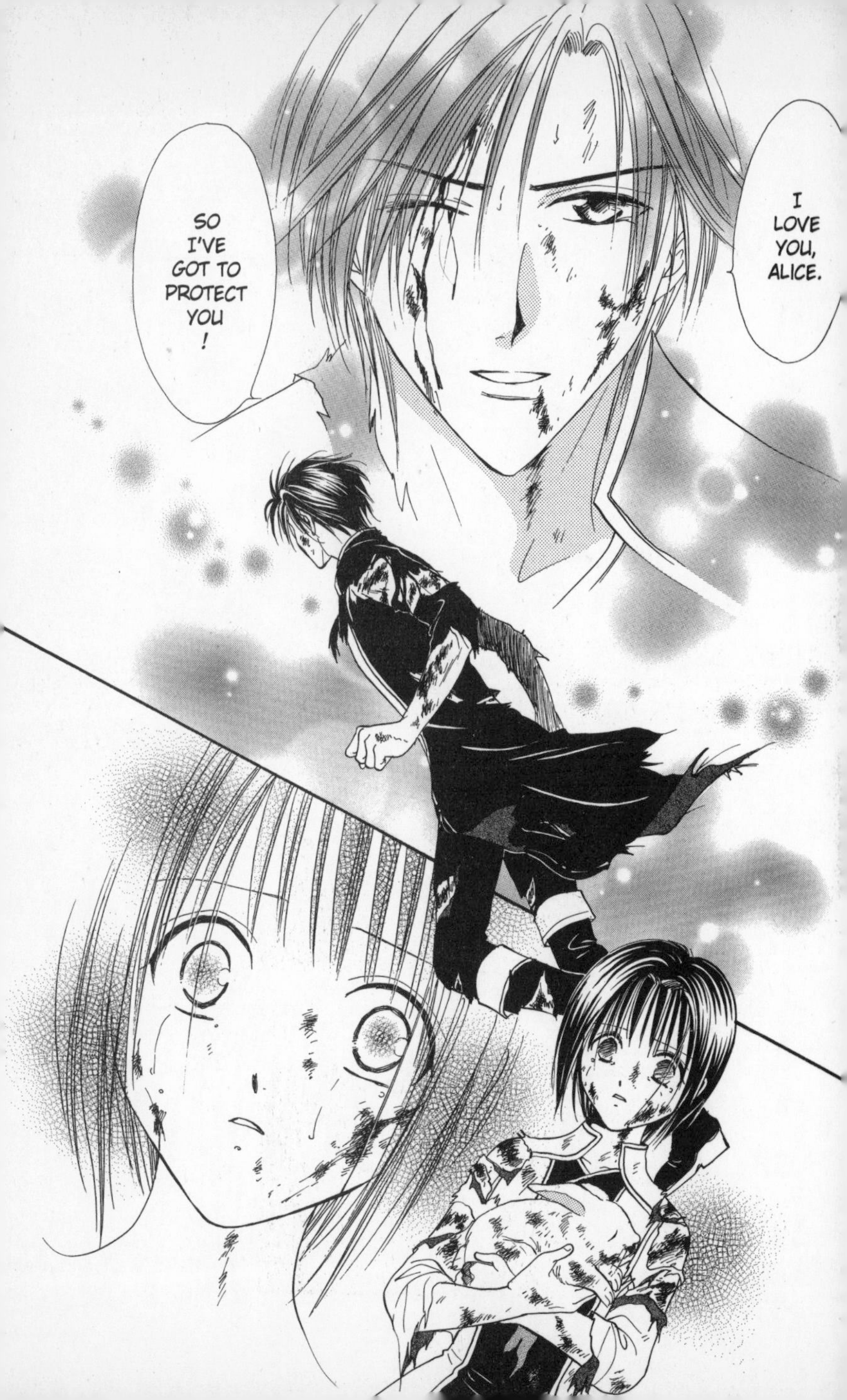
I LOVE YOU, ALICE.
SO I'VE GOT TO PROTECT YOU!

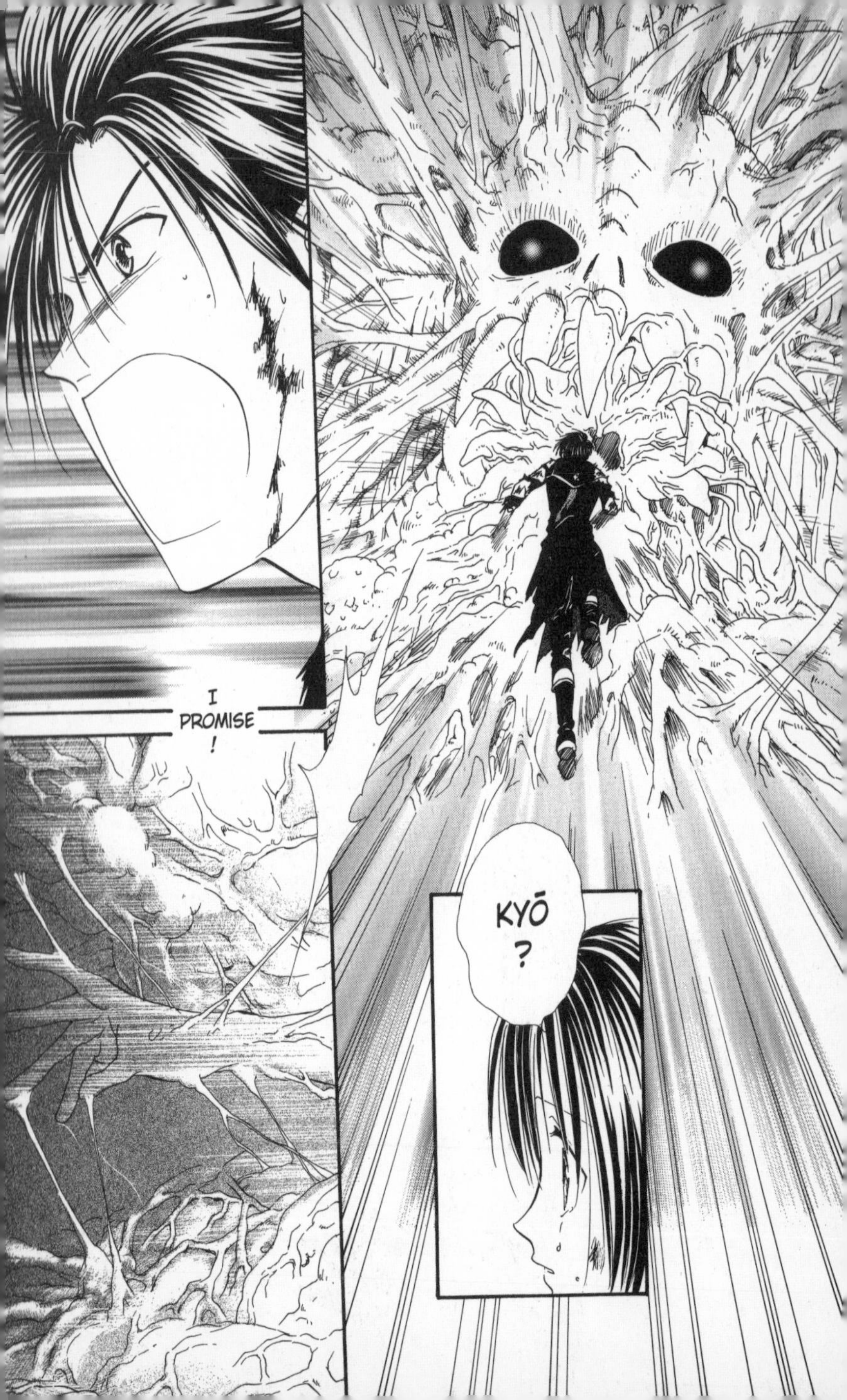
I PROMISE!
KYŌ?

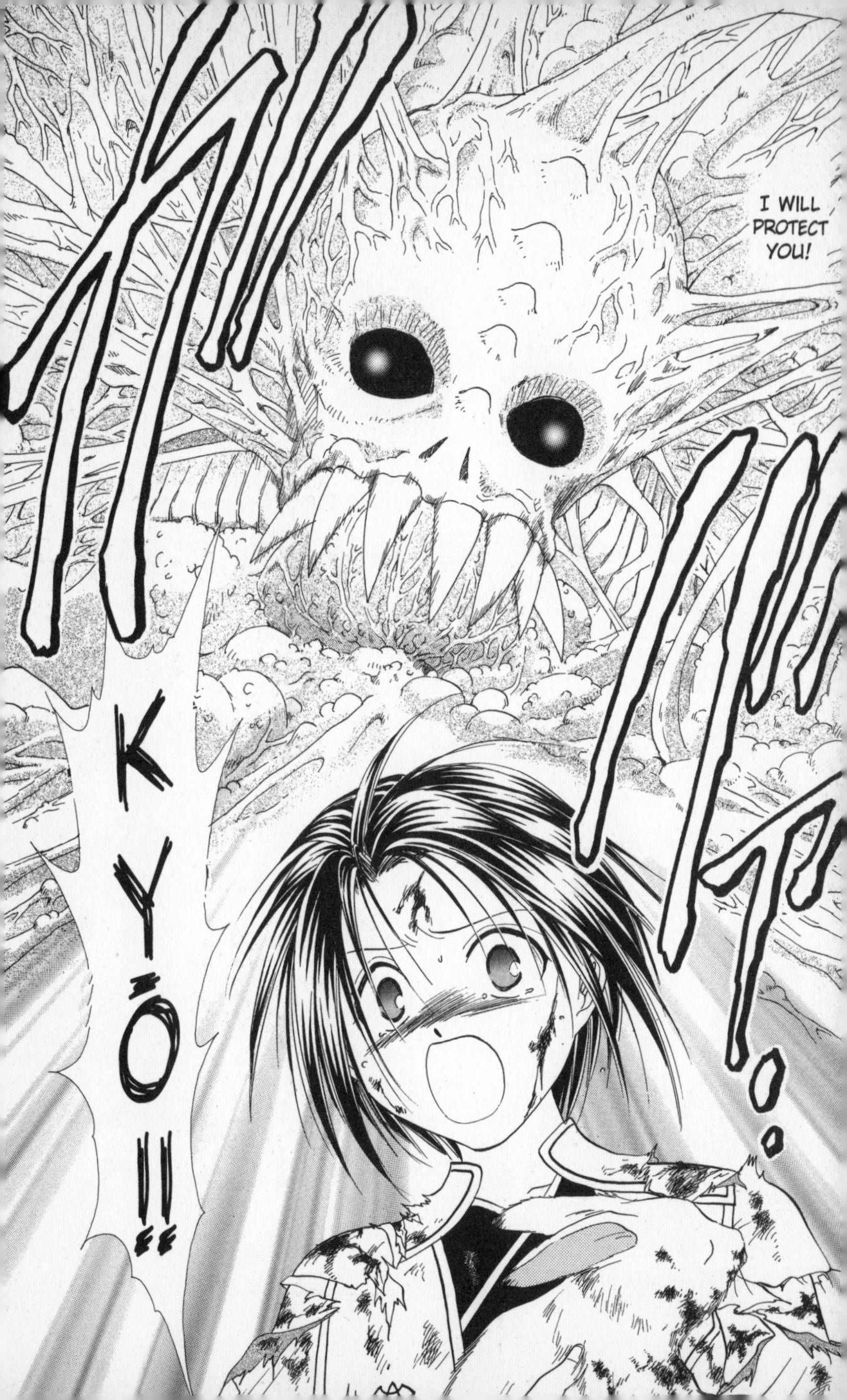
I WILL PROTECT YOU!
KYŌ!!

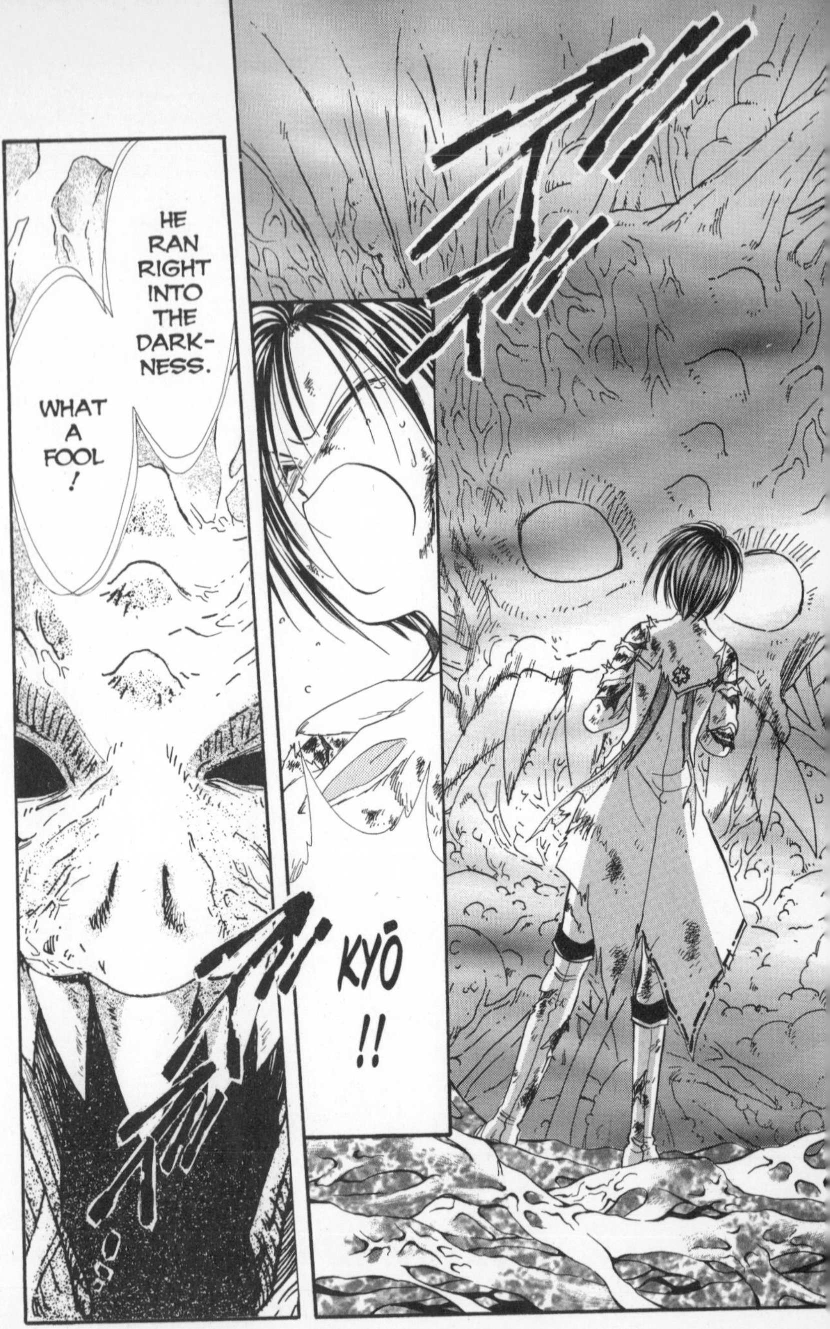
KYŌ !!
HE RAN RIGHT INTO THE DARKNESS.
WHAT A FOOL!

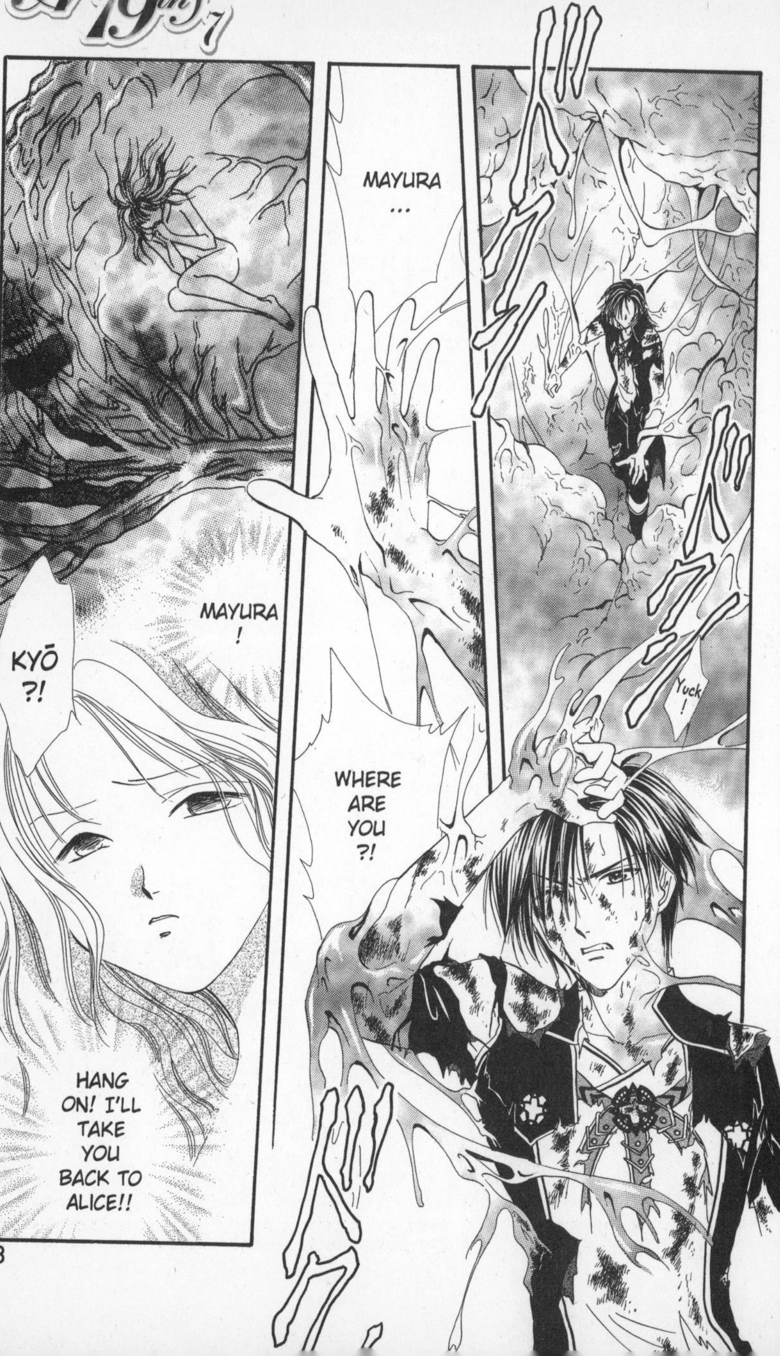
Yuck!
MAYURA ...
WHERE ARE YOU ?!
MAYURA !
KYŌ ?!
HANG ON! I'LL TAKE YOU BACK TO ALICE!!

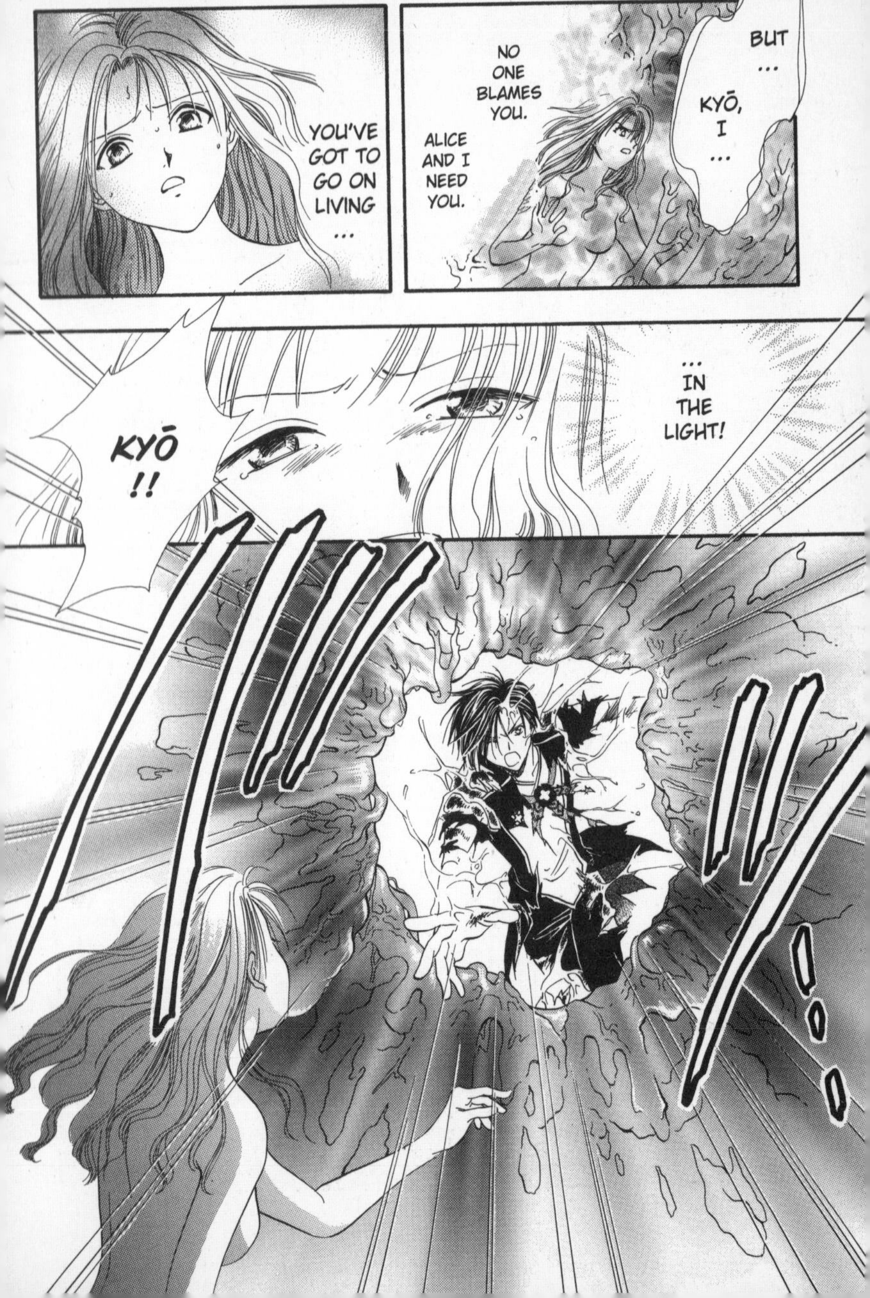
BUT ... KYŌ, I ...
NO ONE BLAMES YOU.
ALICE AND I NEED YOU.
YOU'VE GOT TO GO ON LIVING ...
... IN THE LIGHT!
KYŌ !!

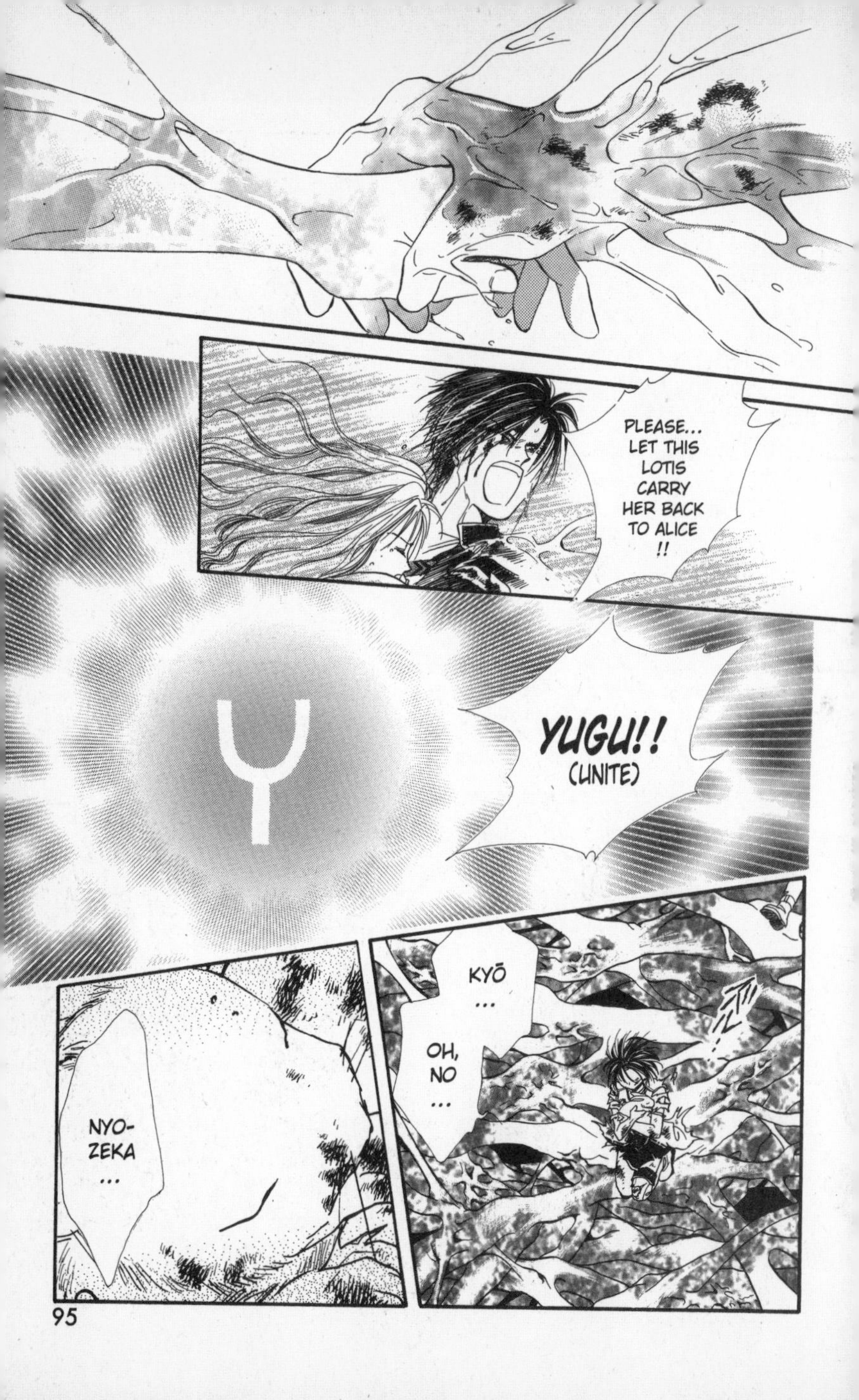
PLEASE... LET THIS LOTIS CARRY HER BACK TO ALICE !!
YUGU!! (UNITE)
KYŌ ...
OH, NO ...
NYO-ZEKA ...

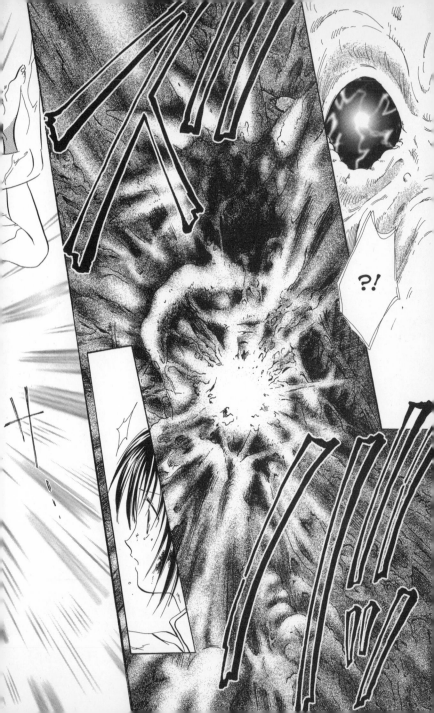

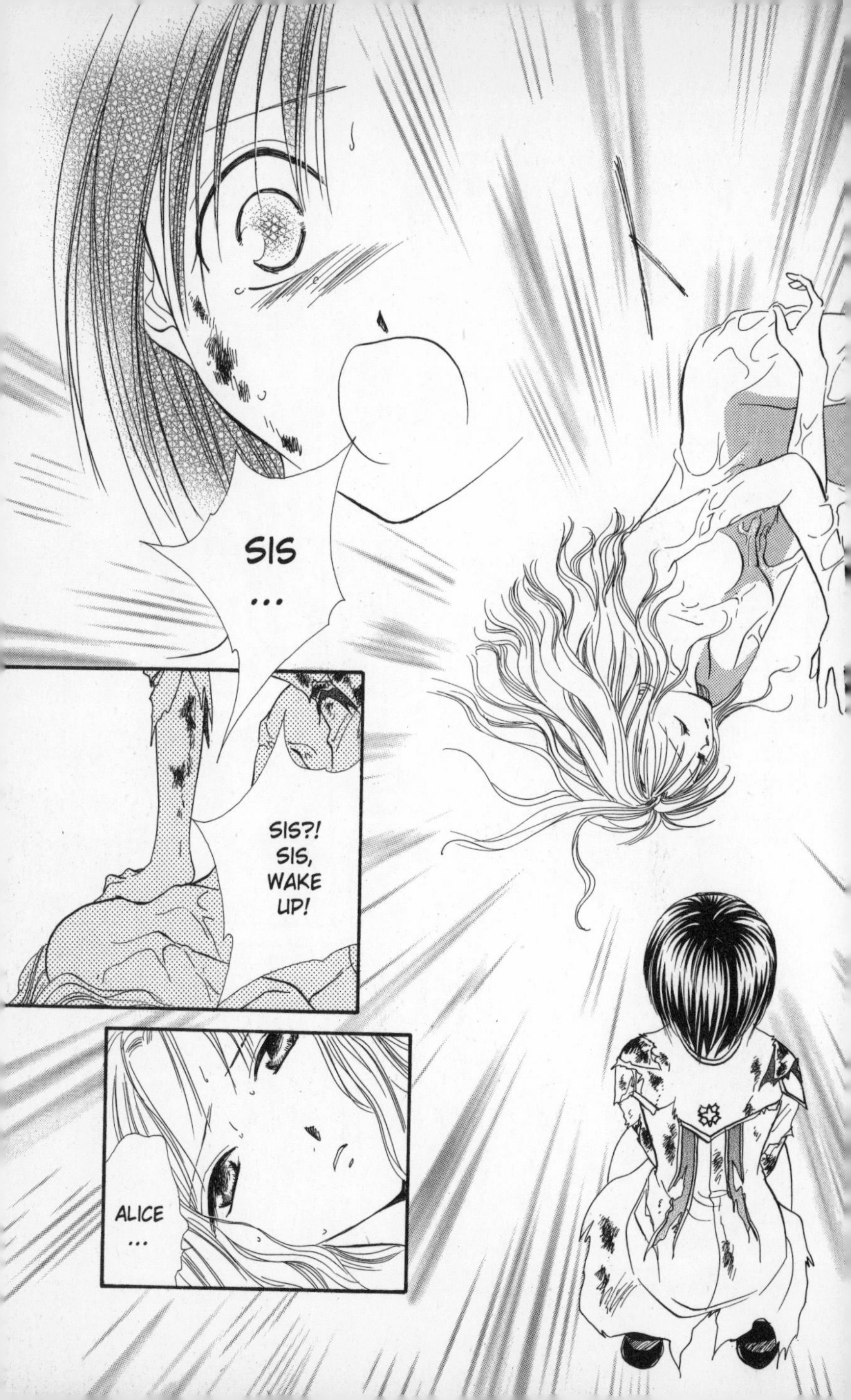
SIS ...
SIS?! SIS, WAKE UP!
ALICE ...

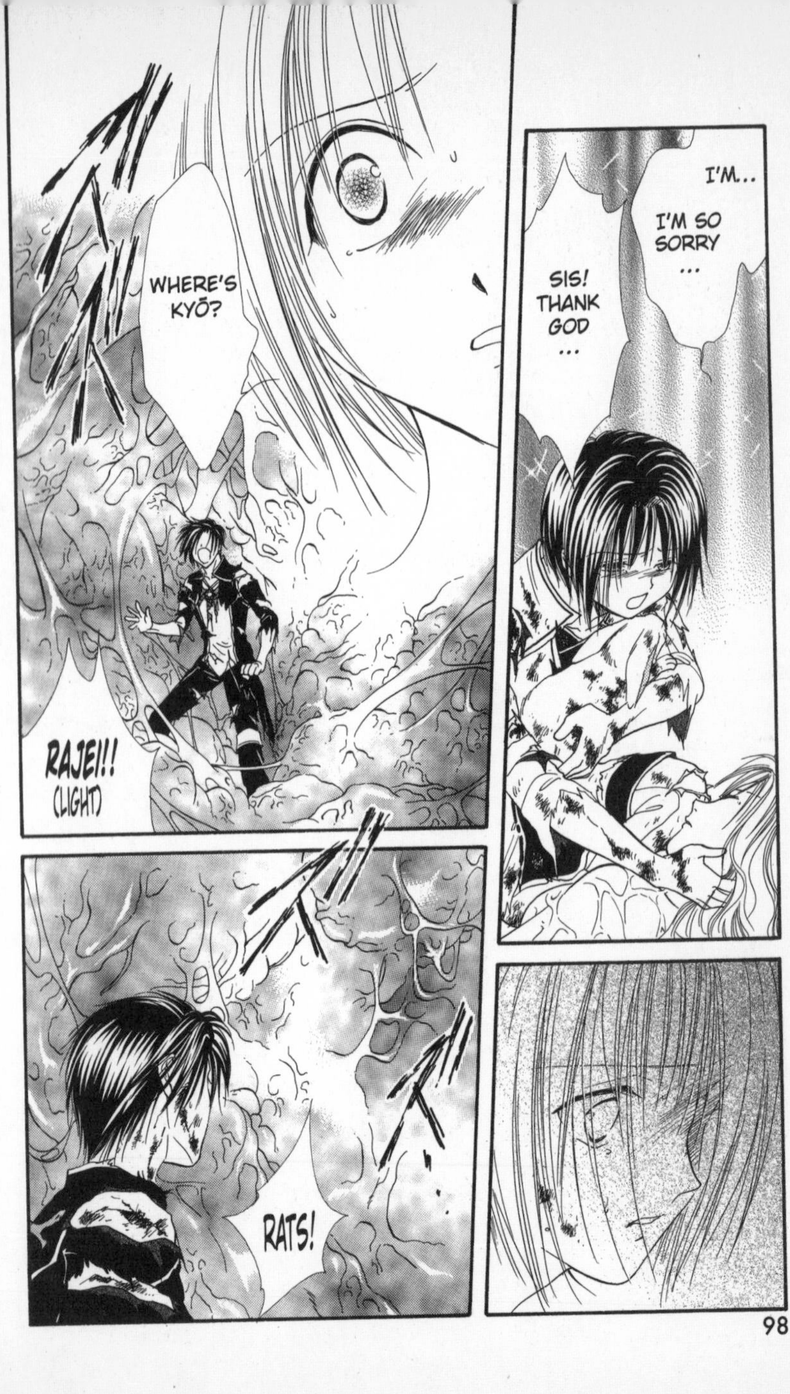
I'M...
I'M SO SORRY ...
SIS! THANK GOD ...
WHERE'S KYŌ?
RAJEI!!! (LIGHT)
RATS!

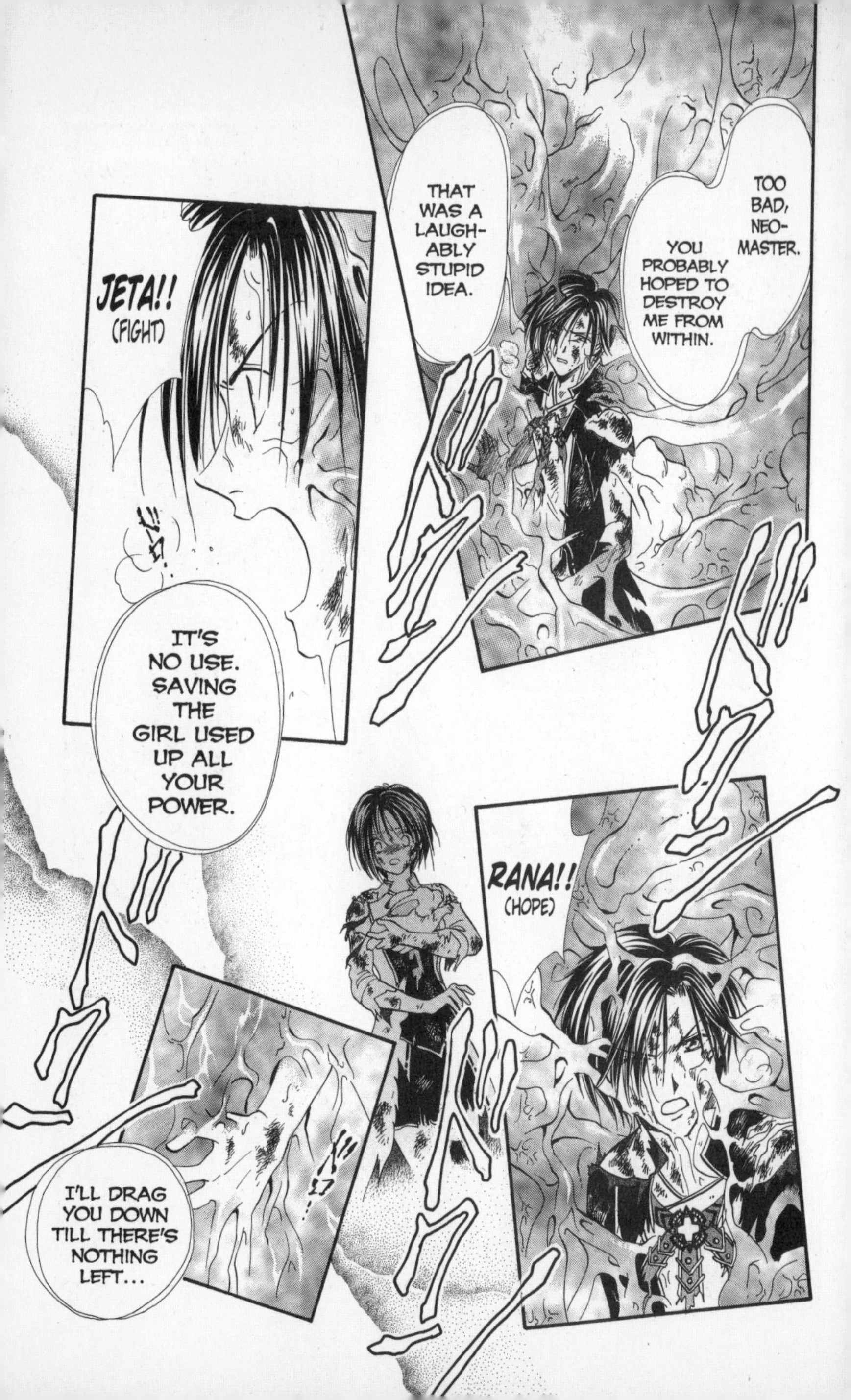
TOO BAD, NEO-MASTER.
YOU PROBABLY HOPED TO DESTROY ME FROM WITHIN.
THAT WAS A LAUGHABLY STUPID IDEA.
JETA!! (FIGHT)
IT'S NO USE. SAVING THE GIRL USED UP ALL YOUR POWER.
RANA!! (HOPE)
I'LL DRAG YOU DOWN TILL THERE'S NOTHING LEFT...

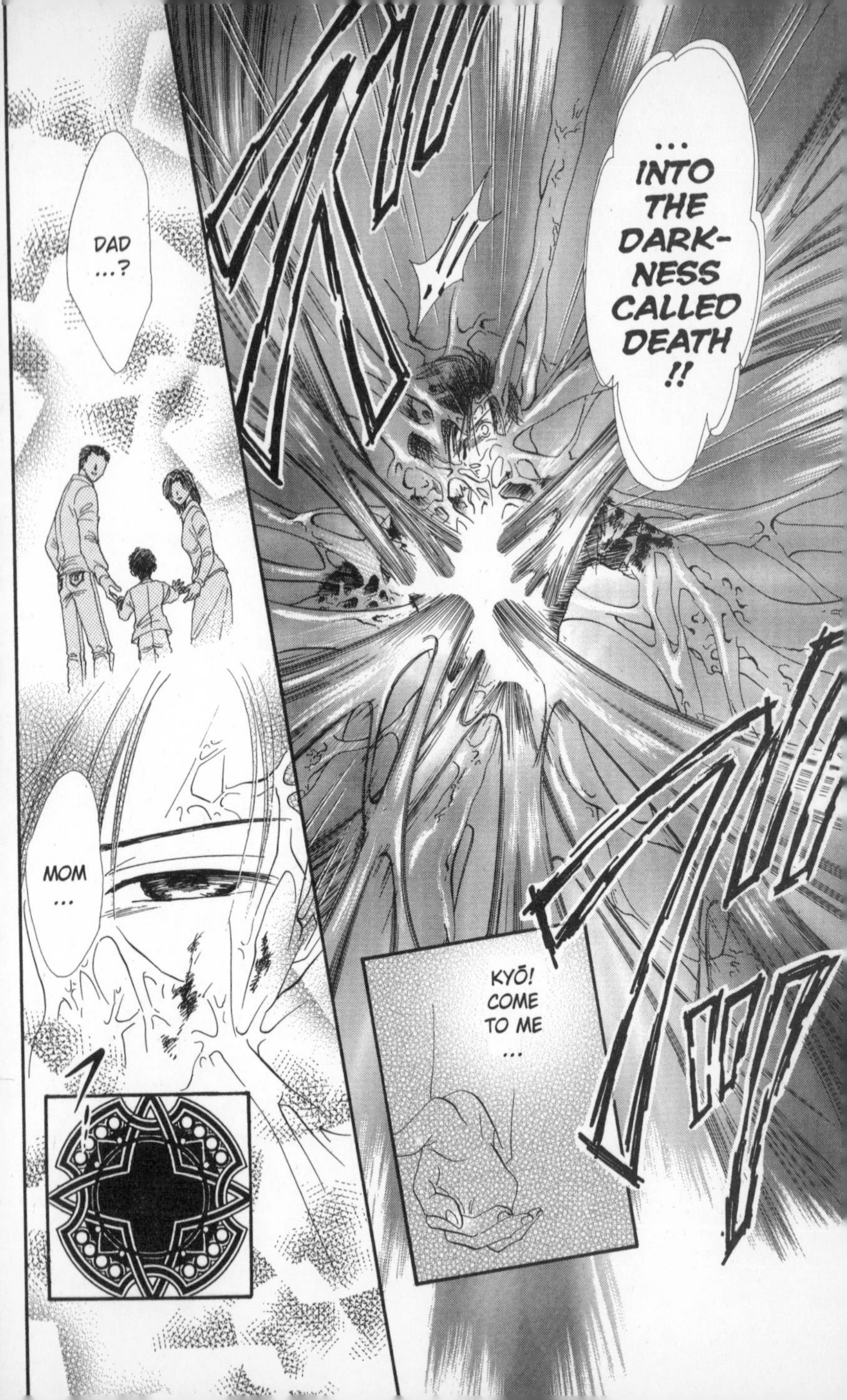
...INTO THE DARKNESS CALLED DEATH!!
KYŌ! COME TO ME...
DAD...?
MOM...

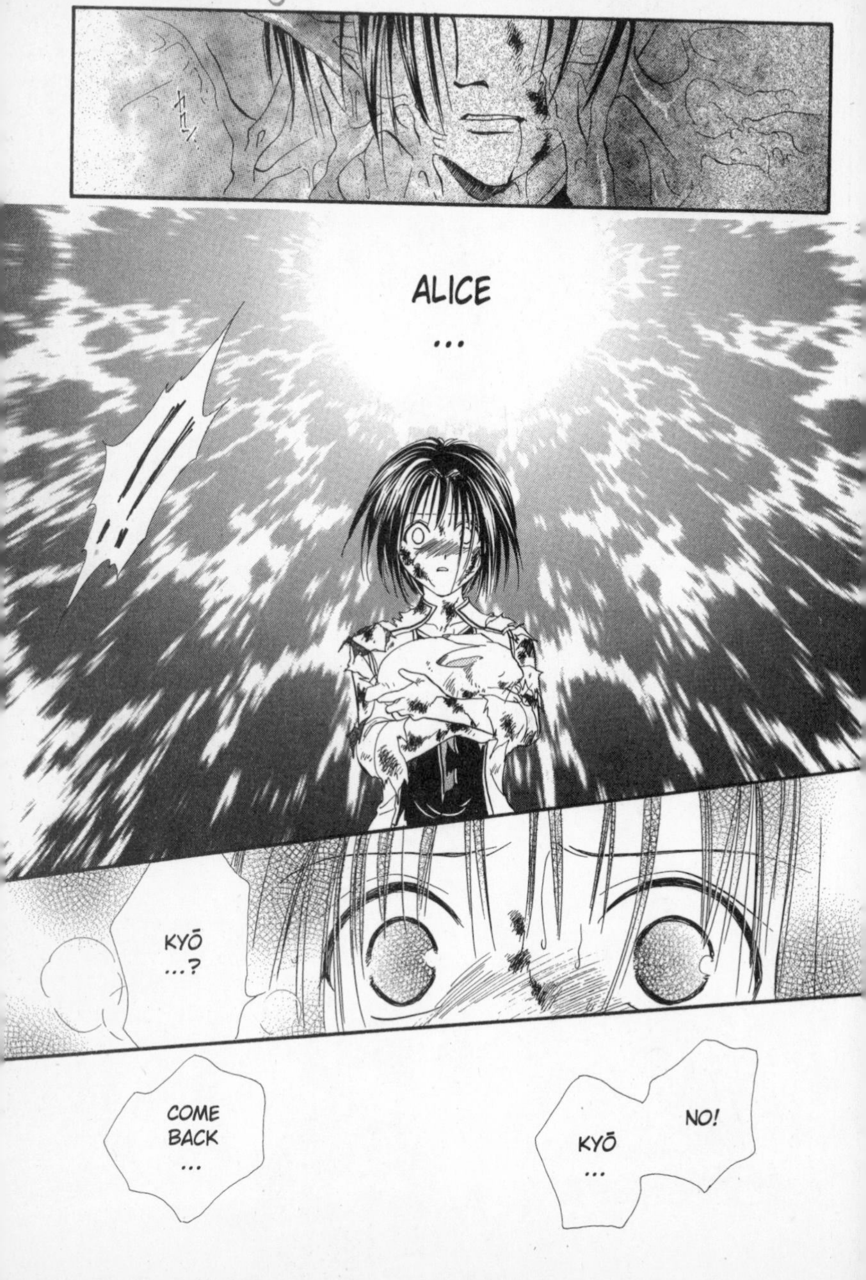
ALICE
...
KYŌ
...?
NO!
KYŌ
...
COME BACK
...

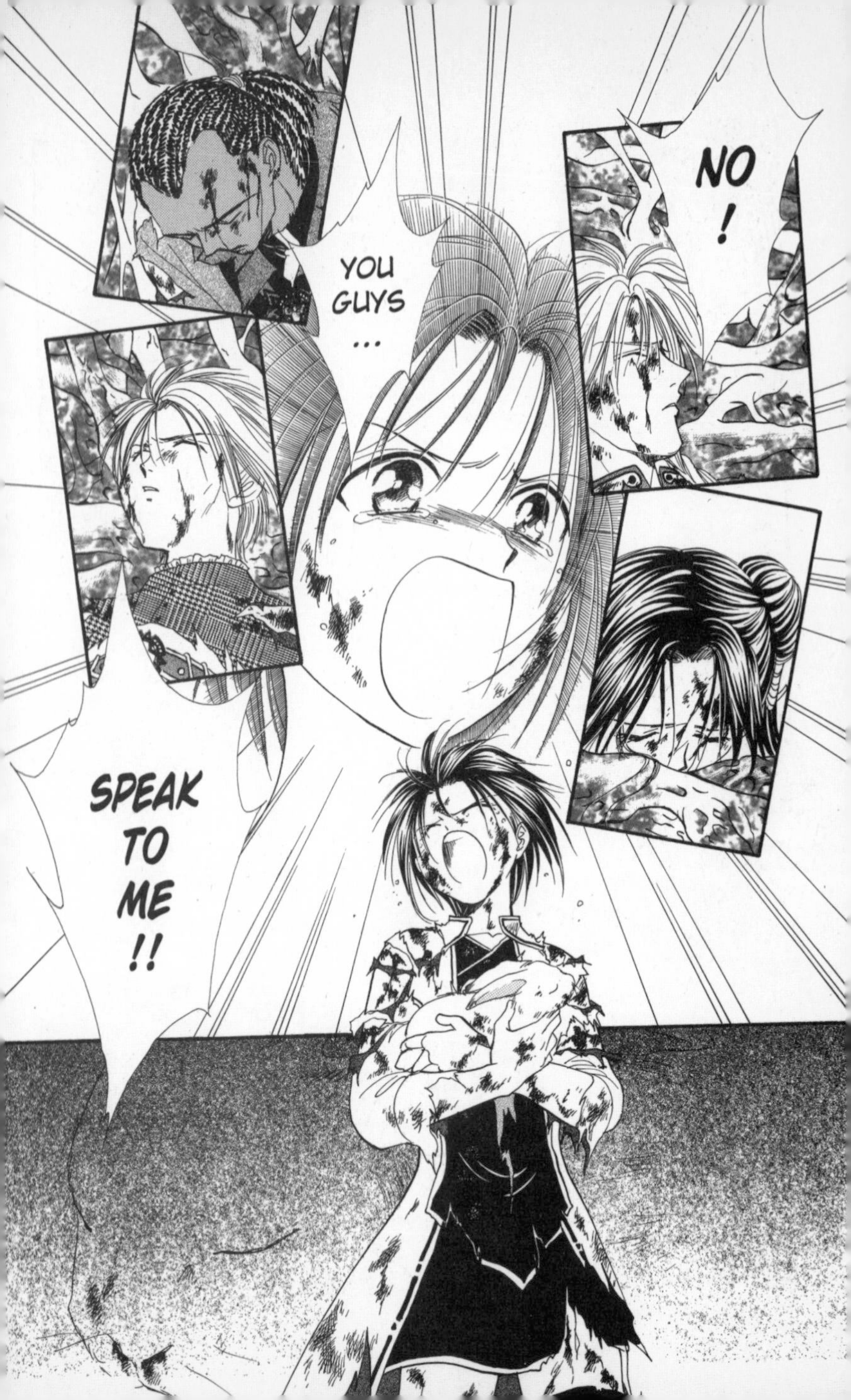
NO !
YOU GUYS ...
SPEAK TO ME !!

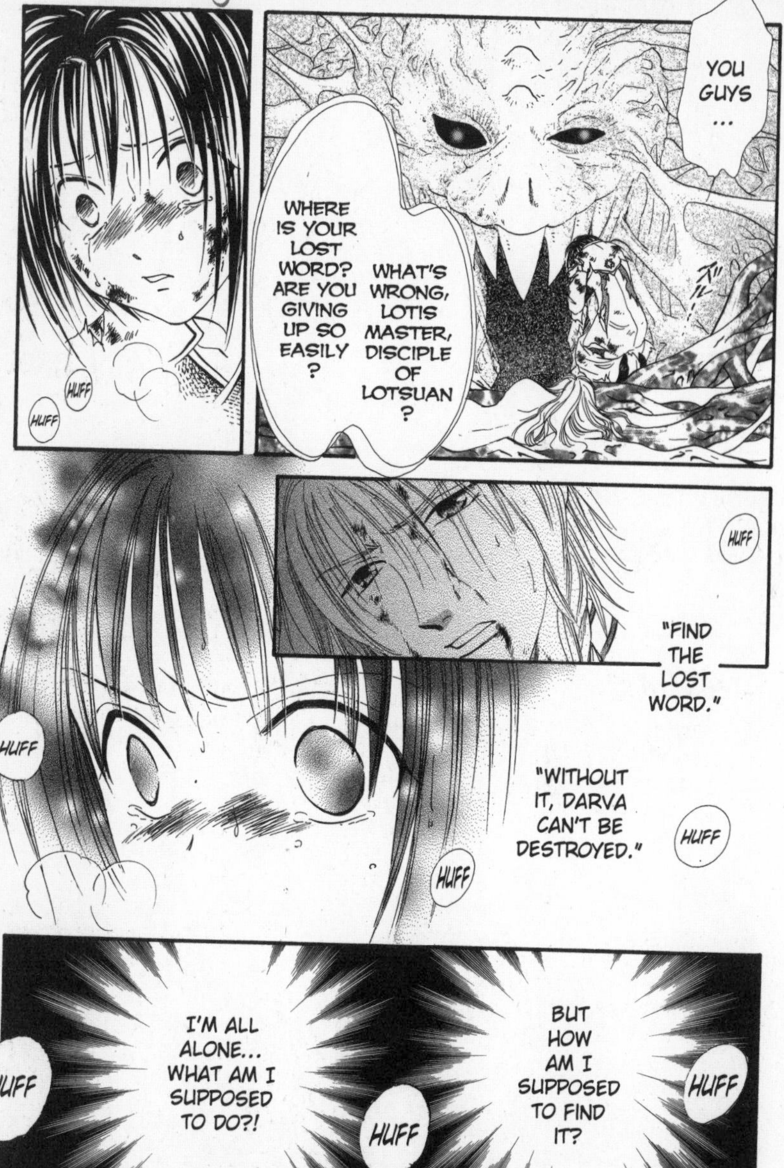
YOU GUYS ...
WHAT'S WRONG, LOTIS MASTER, DISCIPLE OF LOTSUAN?
WHERE IS YOUR LOST WORD? ARE YOU GIVING UP SO EASILY?
HUFF
HUFF
HUFF
HUFF
"FIND THE LOST WORD."
"WITHOUT IT, DARVA CAN'T BE DESTROYED."
HUFF
HUFF
HUFF
HUFF
BUT HOW AM I SUPPOSED TO FIND IT?
HUFF
I'M ALL ALONE... WHAT AM I SUPPOSED TO DO?!
HUFF

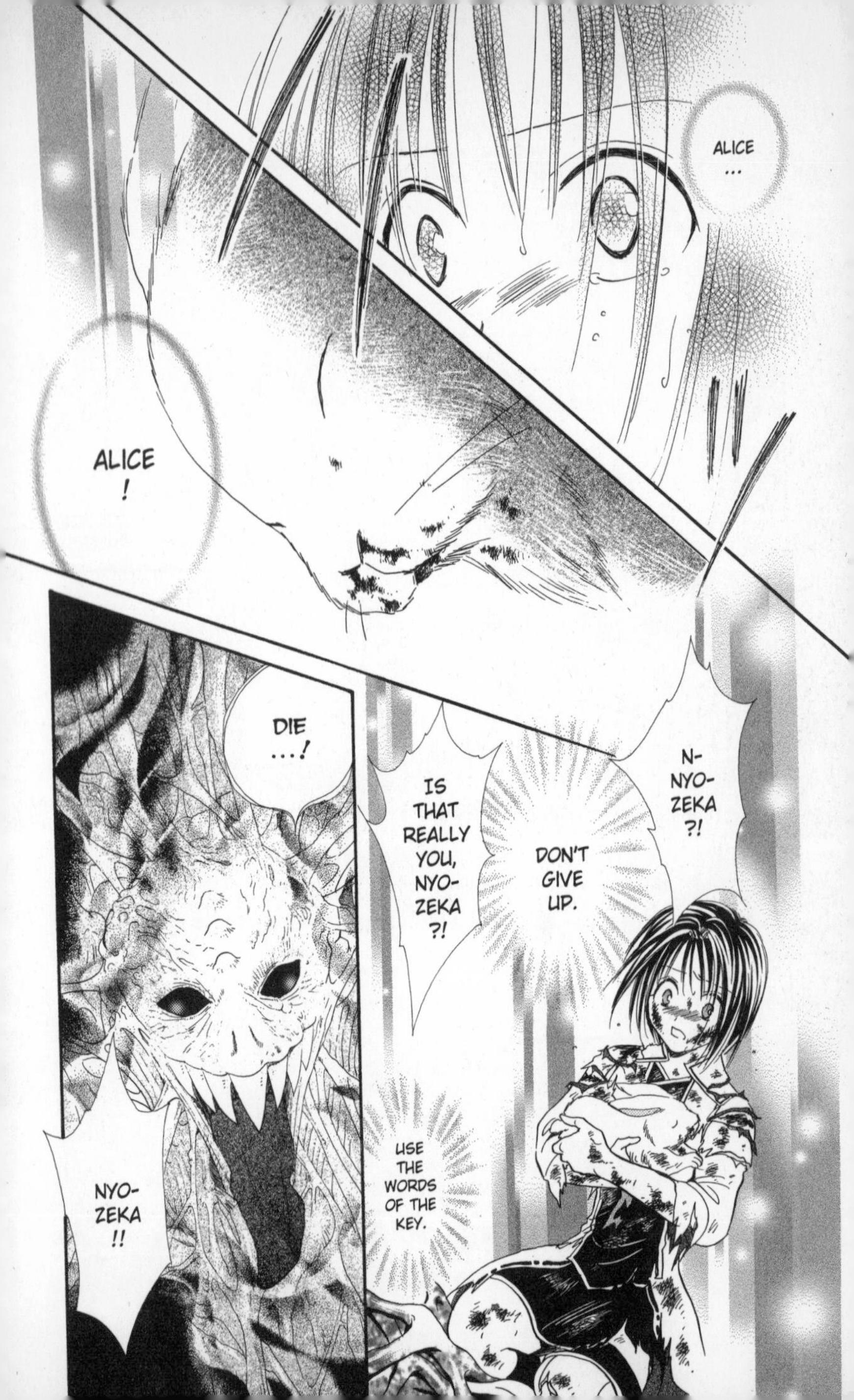
ALICE ...
ALICE !
N-NYO-ZEKA?!
DON'T GIVE UP.
IS THAT REALLY YOU, NYO-ZEKA?!
USE THE WORDS OF THE KEY.
DIE ...!
NYO-ZEKA !!

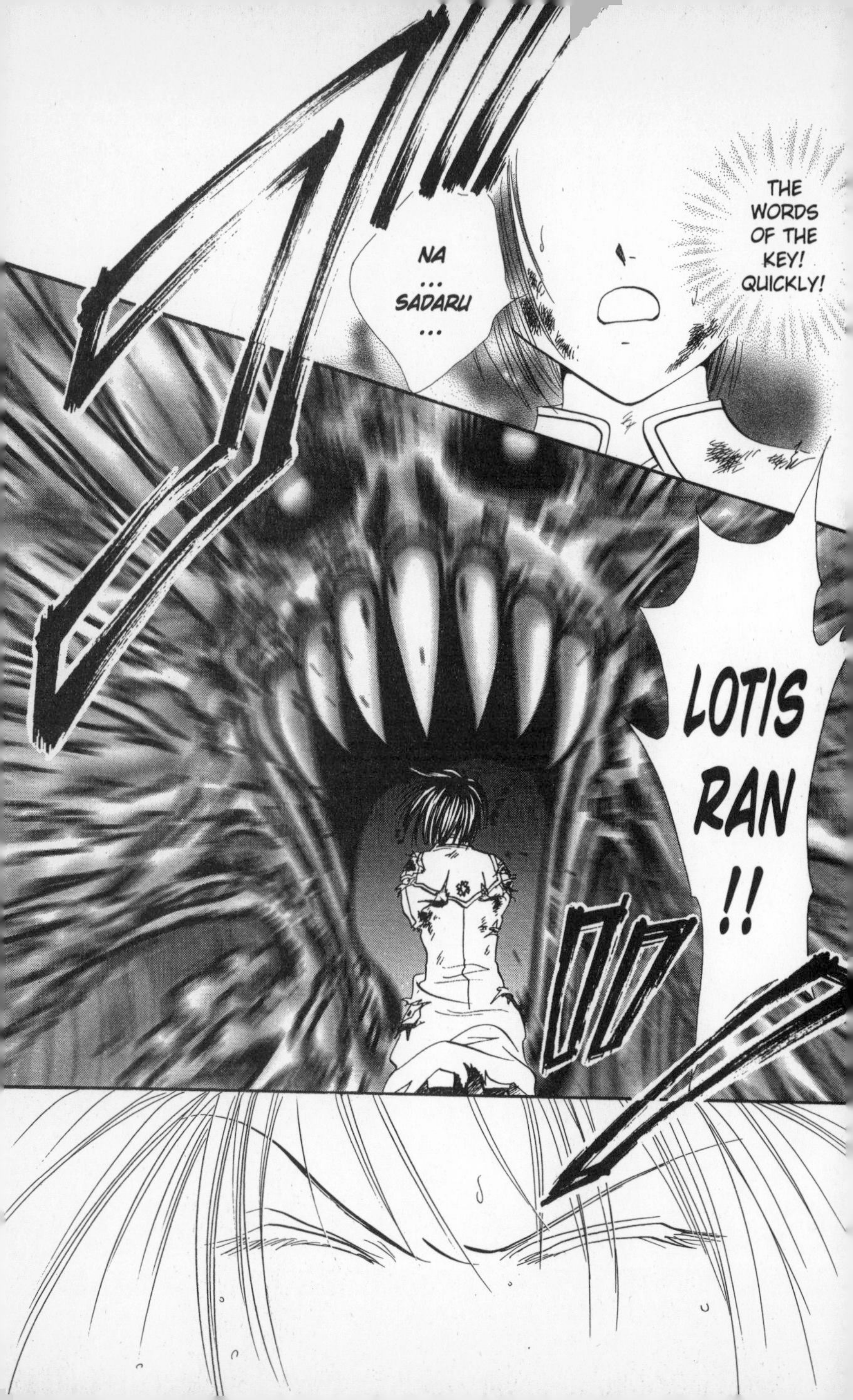
THE WORDS OF THE KEY! QUICKLY!
NA ... SADARU ...
LOTIS RAN !!

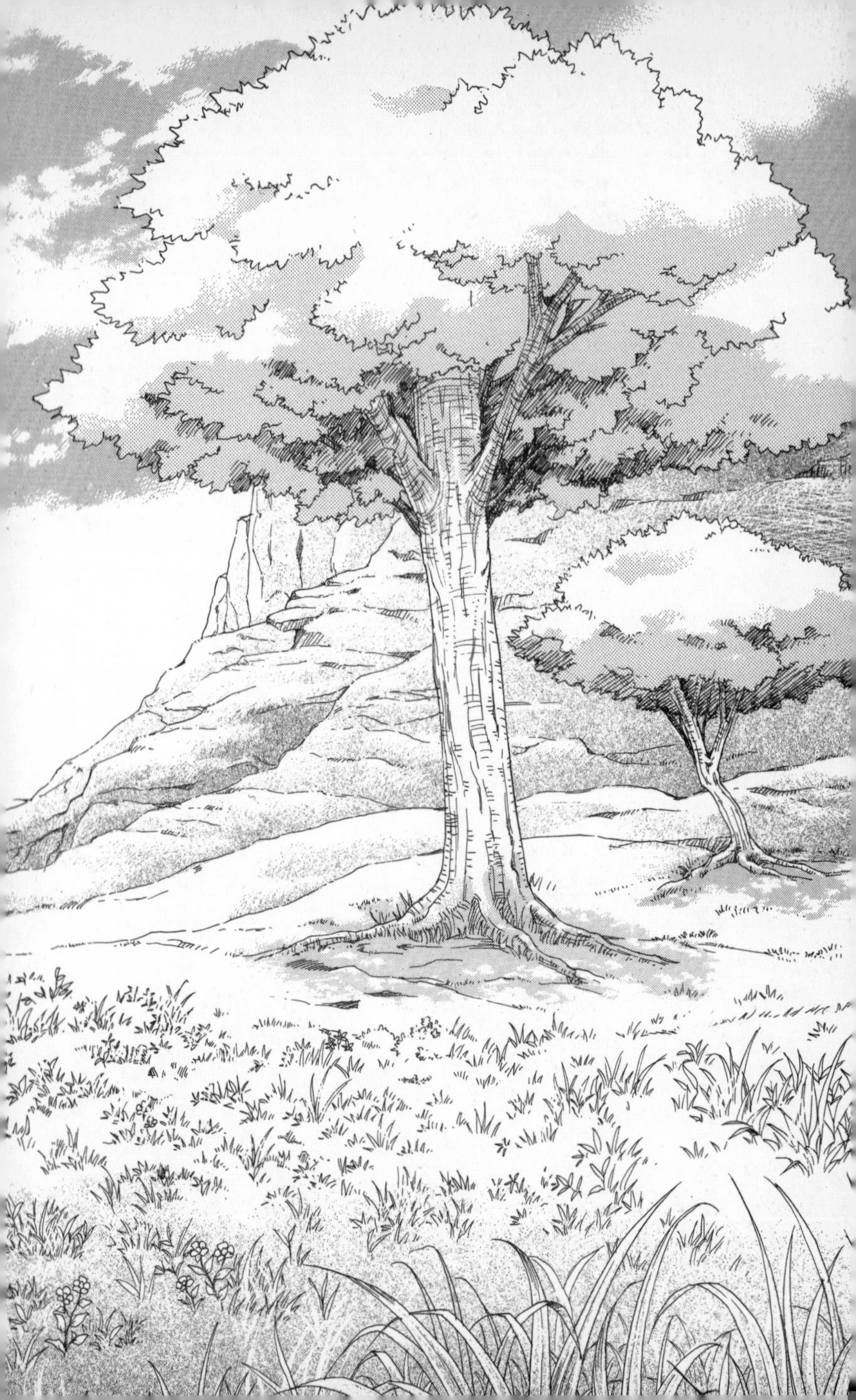

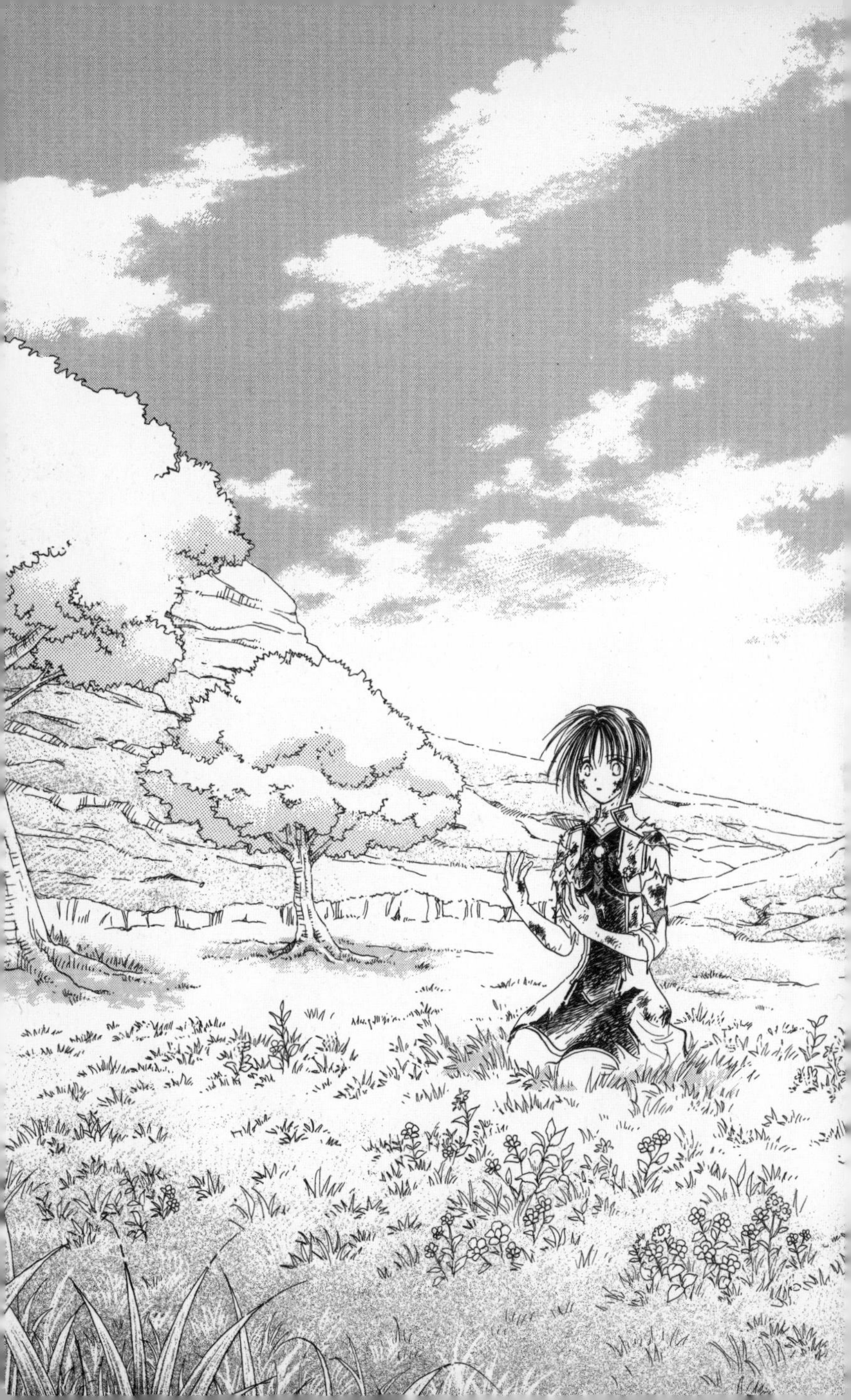

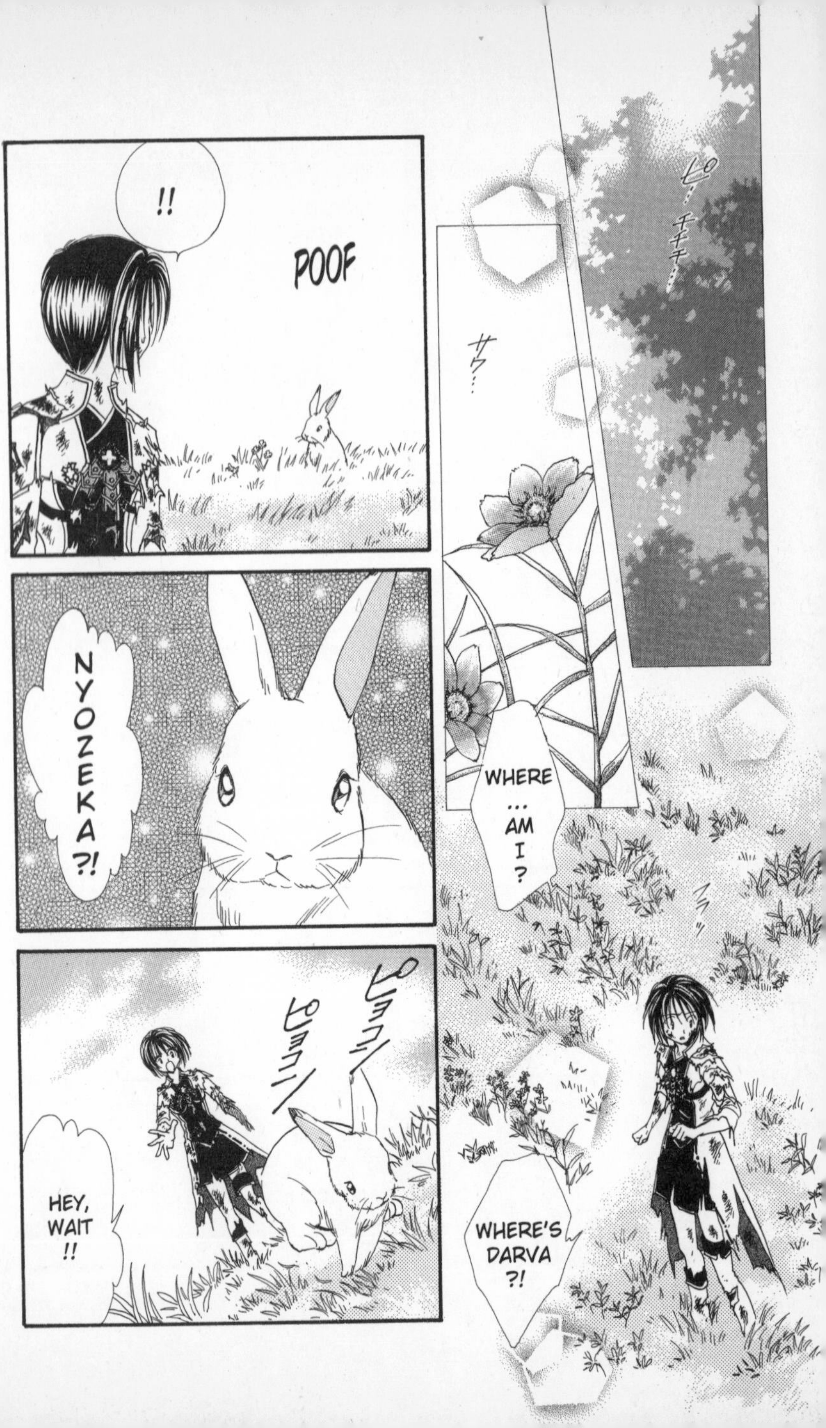
ピピ…チチチ…
サク…
WHERE ... AM I?
フラッ
WHERE'S DARVA?!
!!
POOF
NYOZEKA?!
ピョコン
ピョコン
HEY, WAIT!!

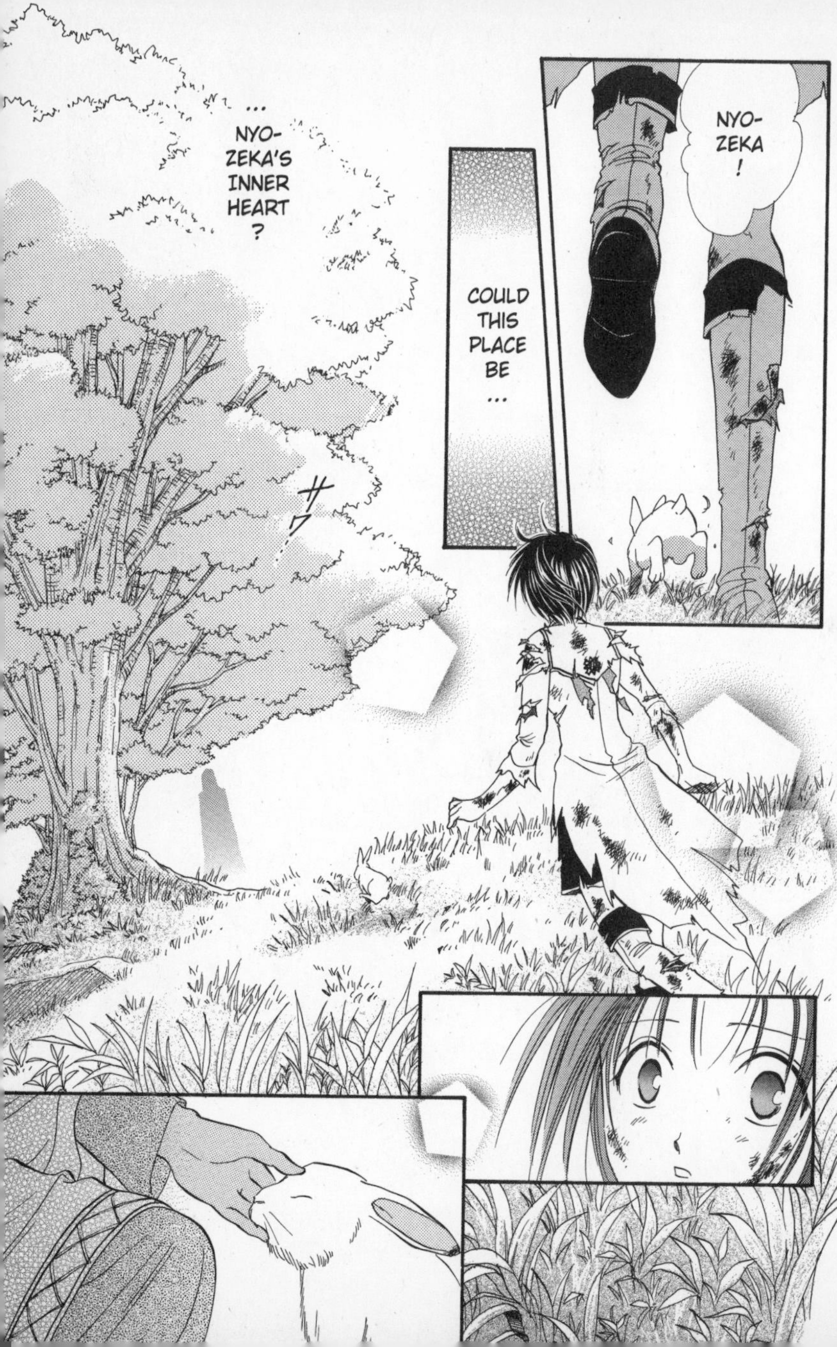
NYO-ZEKA!
COULD THIS PLACE BE ...
... NYO-ZEKA'S INNER HEART?
サワ...

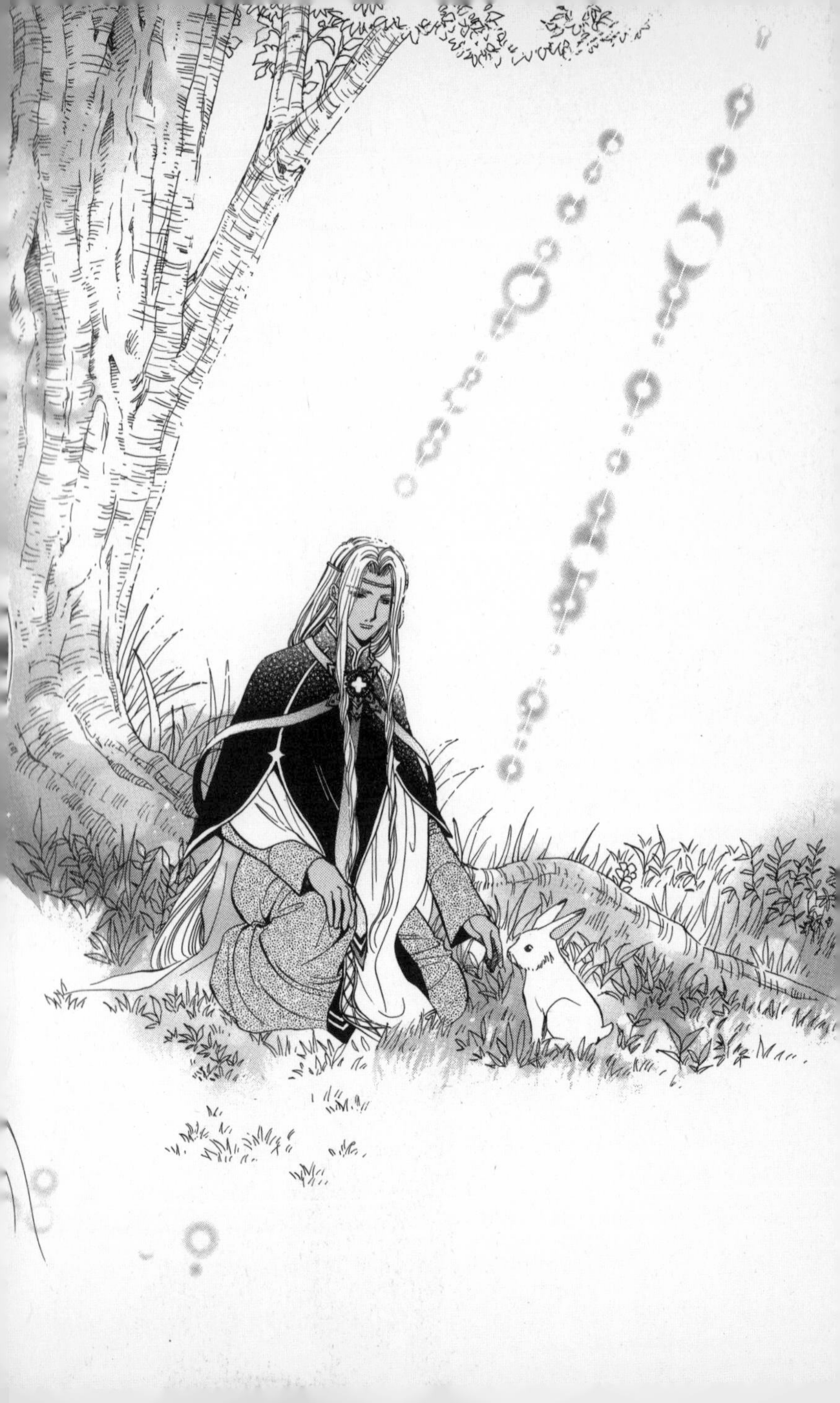

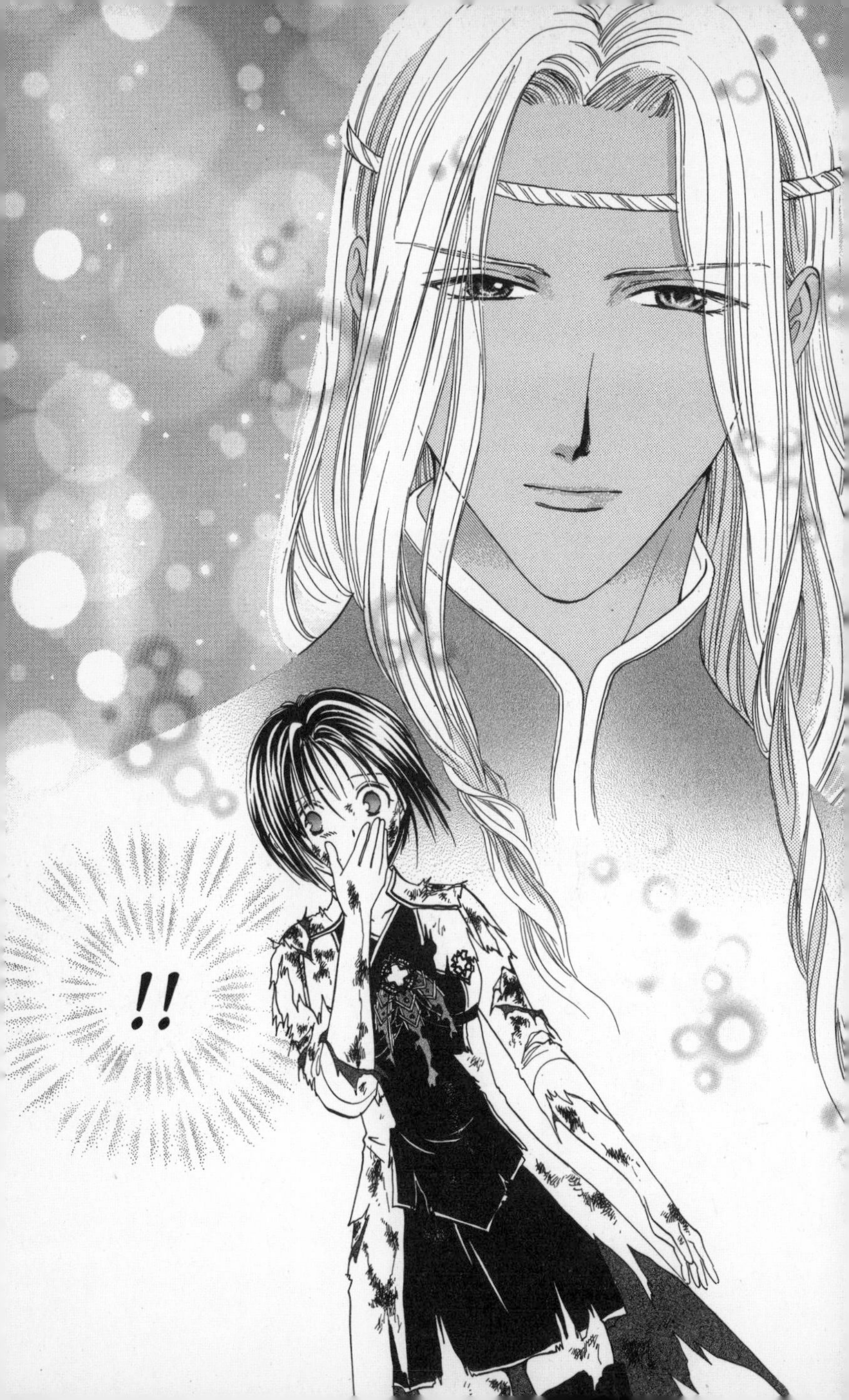
!!

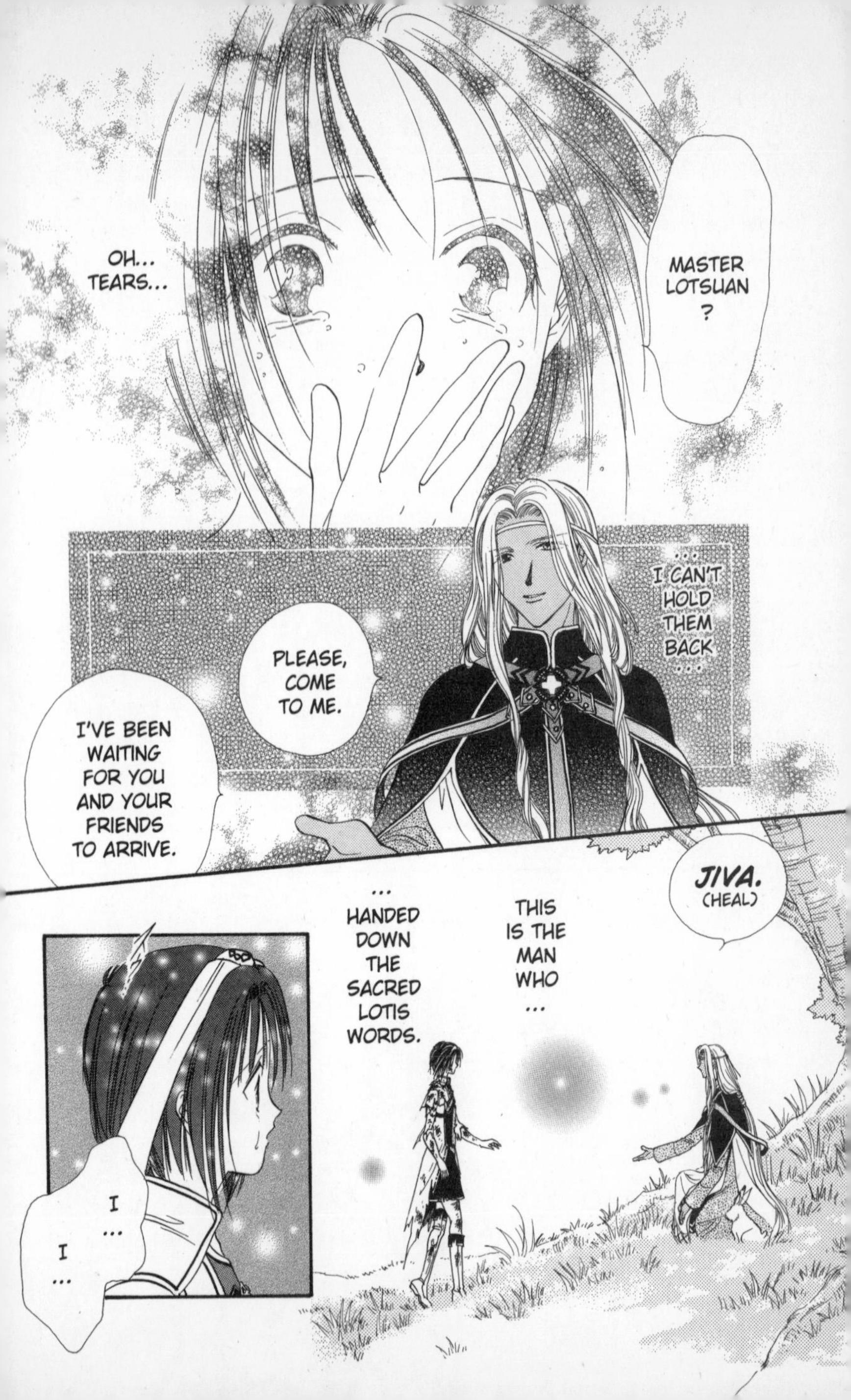
MASTER LOTSUAN?
OH... TEARS...
... I CAN'T HOLD THEM BACK ...
PLEASE, COME TO ME.
I'VE BEEN WAITING FOR YOU AND YOUR FRIENDS TO ARRIVE.
JIVA. (HEAL)
THIS IS THE MAN WHO ...
... HANDED DOWN THE SACRED LOTIS WORDS.
I ...
I ...

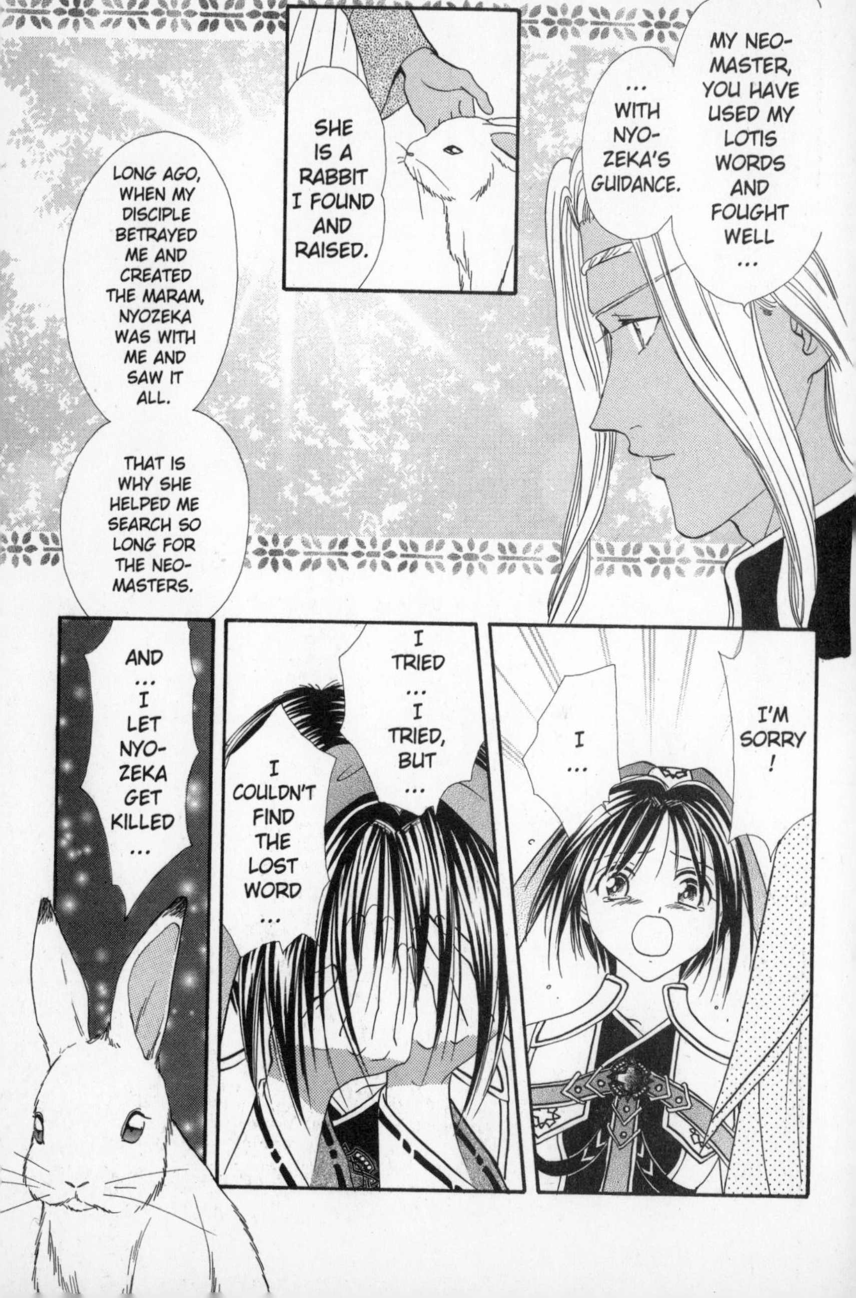
MY NEO-MASTER, YOU HAVE USED MY LOTIS WORDS AND FOUGHT WELL ...
... WITH NYOZEKA'S GUIDANCE.
SHE IS A RABBIT I FOUND AND RAISED.
LONG AGO, WHEN MY DISCIPLE BETRAYED ME AND CREATED THE MARAM, NYOZEKA WAS WITH ME AND SAW IT ALL.
THAT IS WHY SHE HELPED ME SEARCH SO LONG FOR THE NEO-MASTERS.
I'M SORRY!
I ...
I TRIED ... I TRIED, BUT ...
I COULDN'T FIND THE LOST WORD ...
AND ... I LET NYOZEKA GET KILLED ...

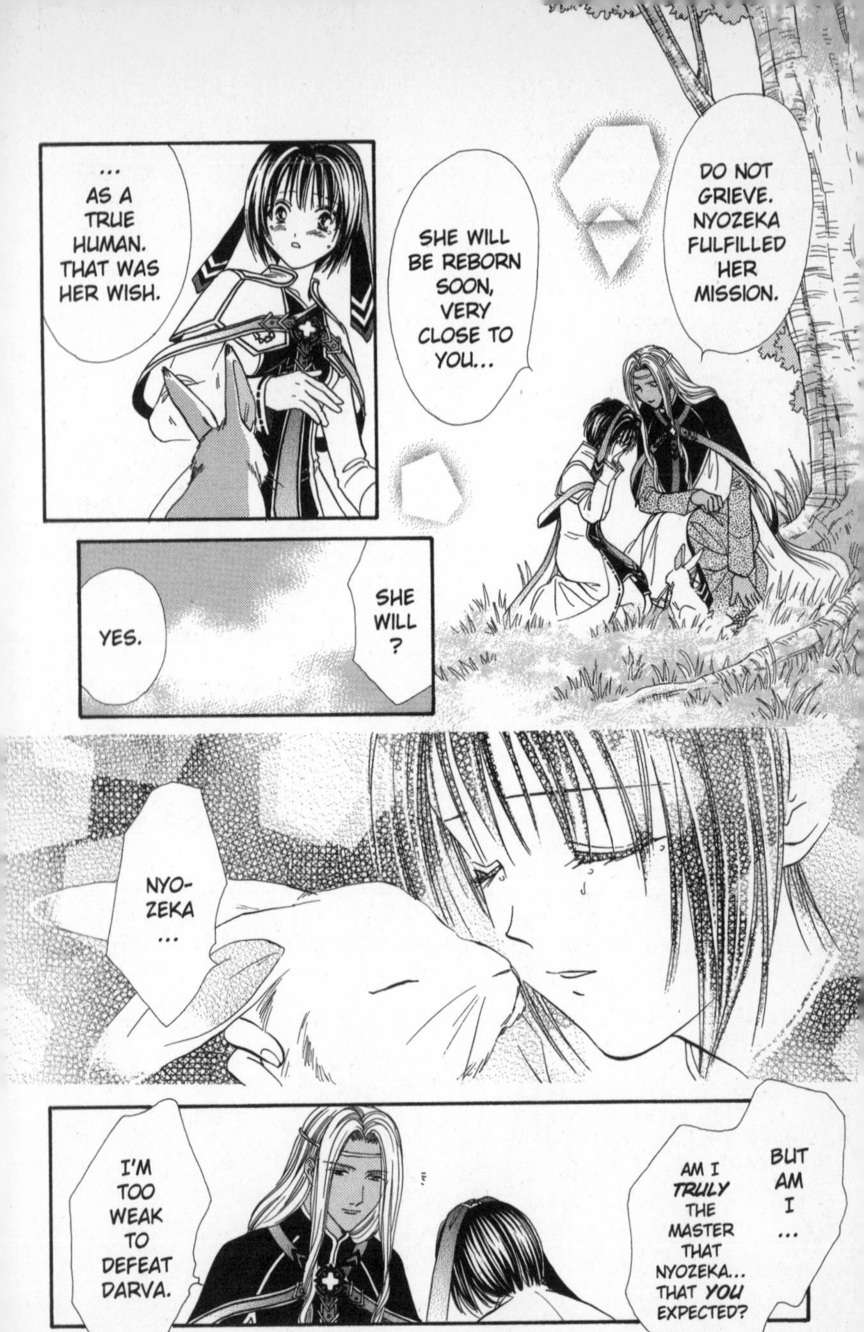
DO NOT GRIEVE. NYOZEKA FULFILLED HER MISSION.
SHE WILL BE REBORN SOON, VERY CLOSE TO YOU...
... AS A TRUE HUMAN. THAT WAS HER WISH.
SHE WILL ?
YES.
NYO-ZEKA ...
BUT AM I ...
AM I *TRULY* THE MASTER THAT NYOZEKA... THAT *YOU* EXPECTED?
I'M TOO WEAK TO DEFEAT DARVA.

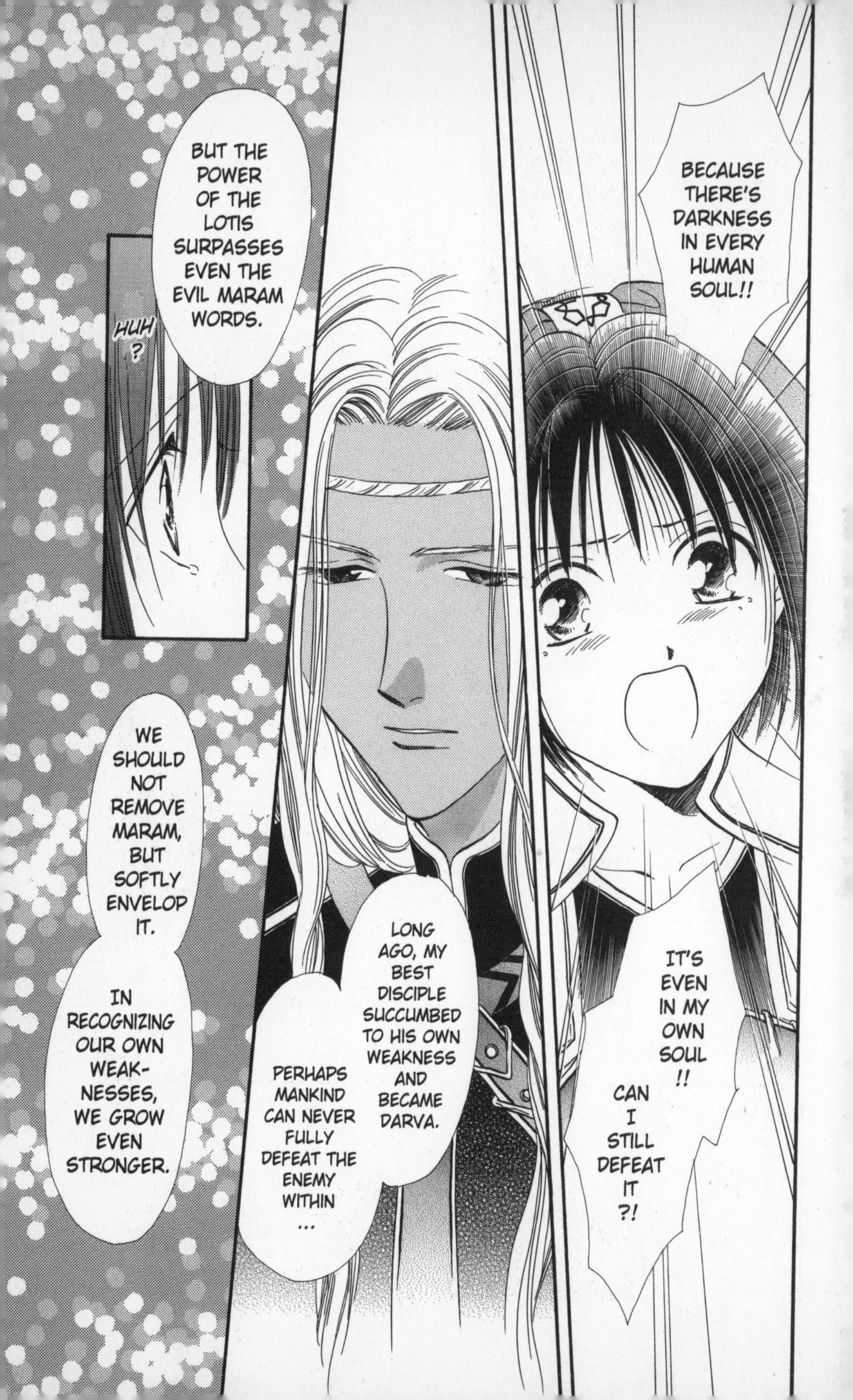
BECAUSE THERE'S DARKNESS IN EVERY HUMAN SOUL!!
IT'S EVEN IN MY OWN SOUL!!
CAN I STILL DEFEAT IT?!
LONG AGO, MY BEST DISCIPLE SUCCUMBED TO HIS OWN WEAKNESS AND BECAME DARVA.
PERHAPS MANKIND CAN NEVER FULLY DEFEAT THE ENEMY WITHIN...
BUT THE POWER OF THE LOTIS SURPASSES EVEN THE EVIL MARAM WORDS.
HUH?
WE SHOULD NOT REMOVE MARAM, BUT SOFTLY ENVELOP IT.
IN RECOGNIZING OUR OWN WEAK-NESSES, WE GROW EVEN STRONGER.

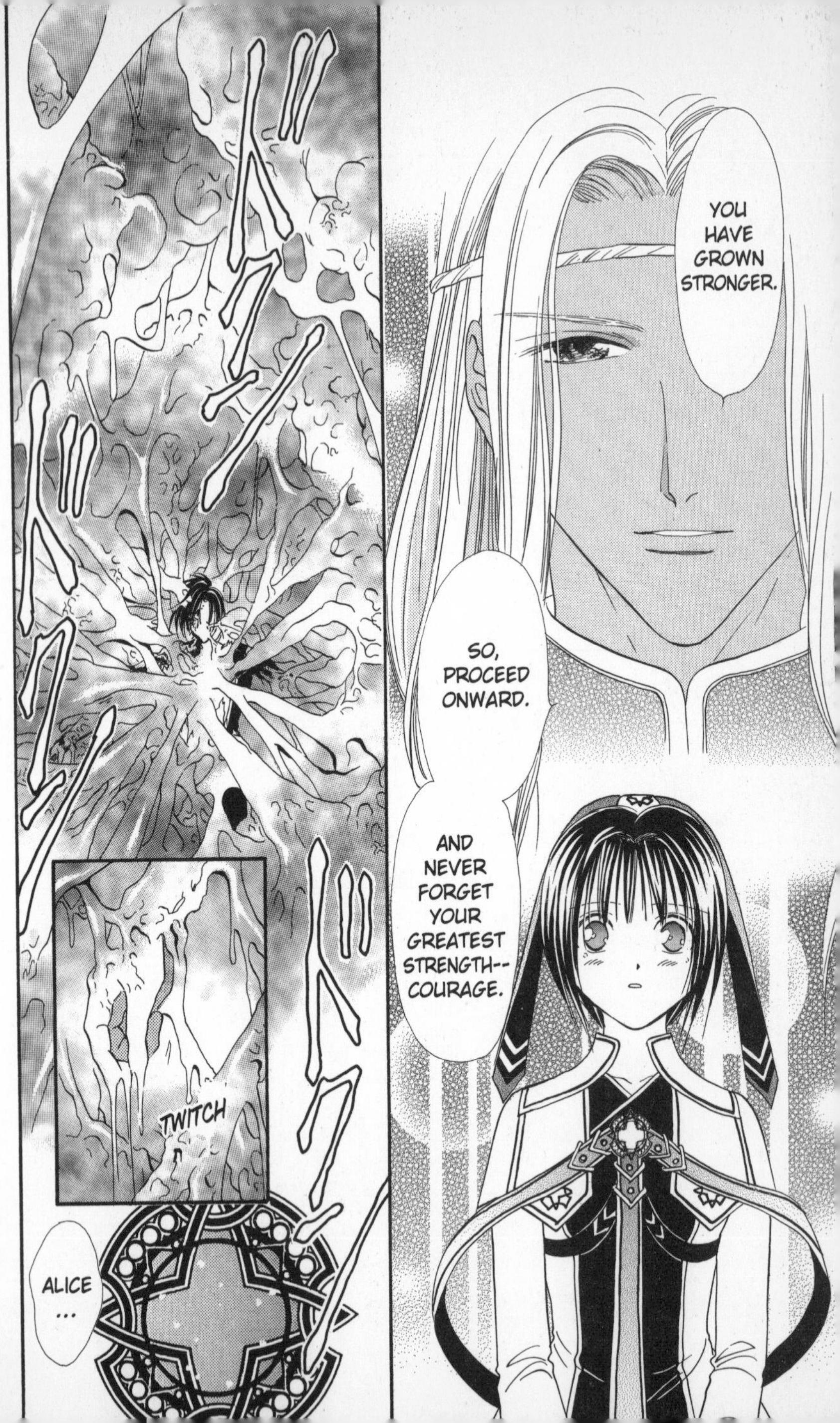
YOU HAVE GROWN STRONGER.
SO, PROCEED ONWARD.
AND NEVER FORGET YOUR GREATEST STRENGTH--COURAGE.
TWITCH
ALICE ...

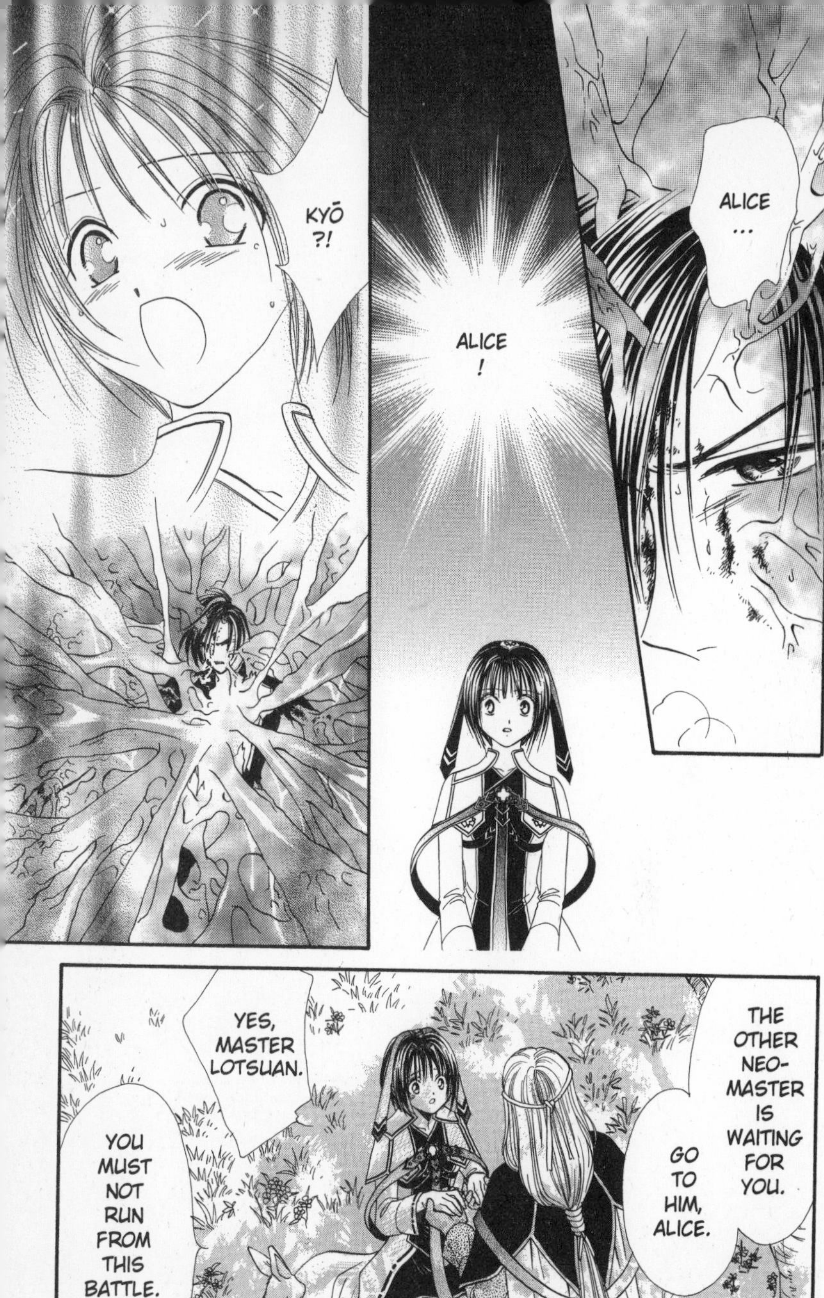
ALICE ...
ALICE !
KYŌ ?!
THE OTHER NEO-MASTER IS WAITING FOR YOU.
GO TO HIM, ALICE.
YOU MUST NOT RUN FROM THIS BATTLE.
YES, MASTER LOTSUAN.

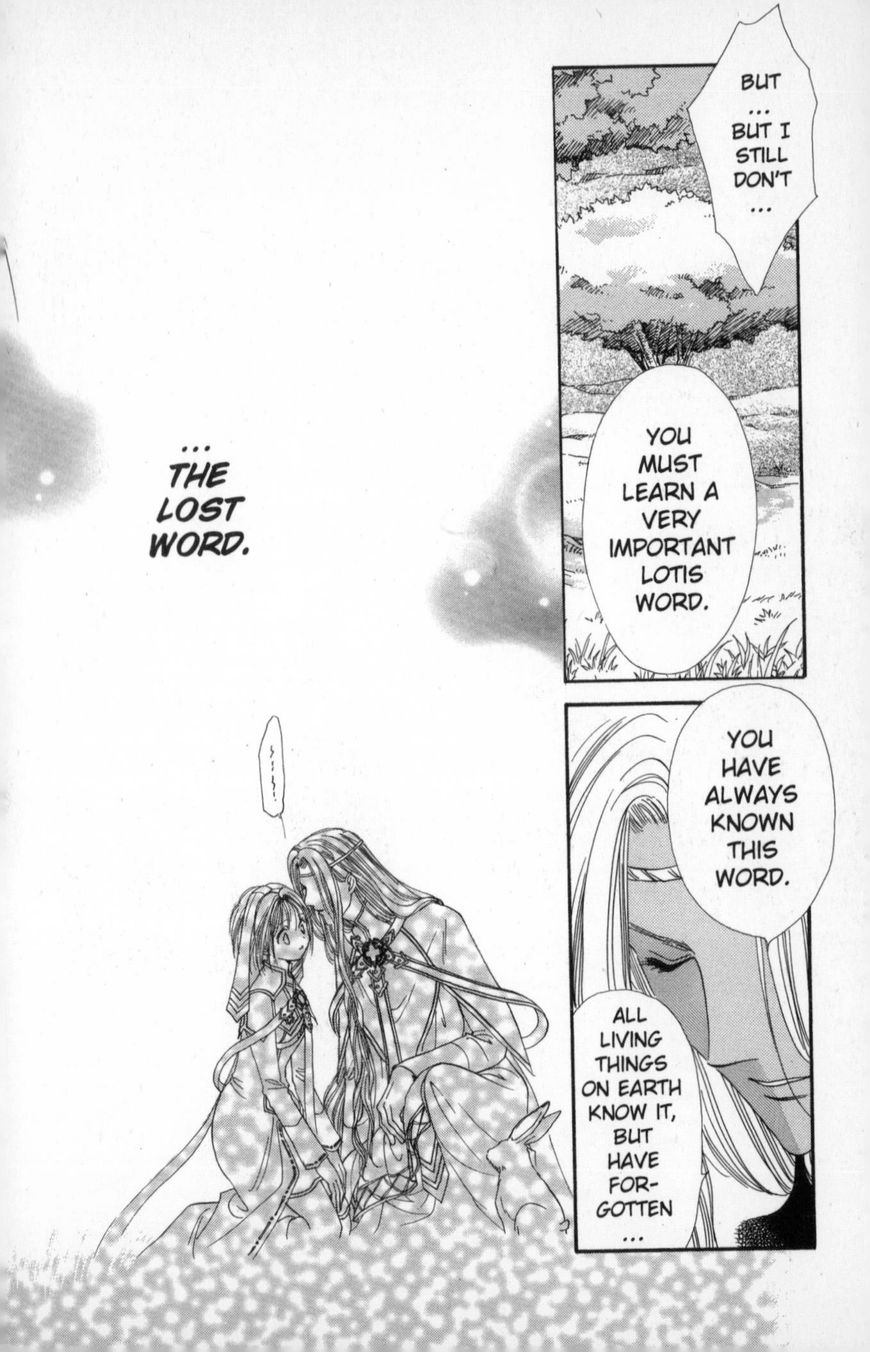
BUT ... BUT I STILL DON'T ...
YOU MUST LEARN A VERY IMPORTANT LOTIS WORD.
YOU HAVE ALWAYS KNOWN THIS WORD.
ALL LIVING THINGS ON EARTH KNOW IT, BUT HAVE FOR-GOTTEN ...
... THE LOST WORD.

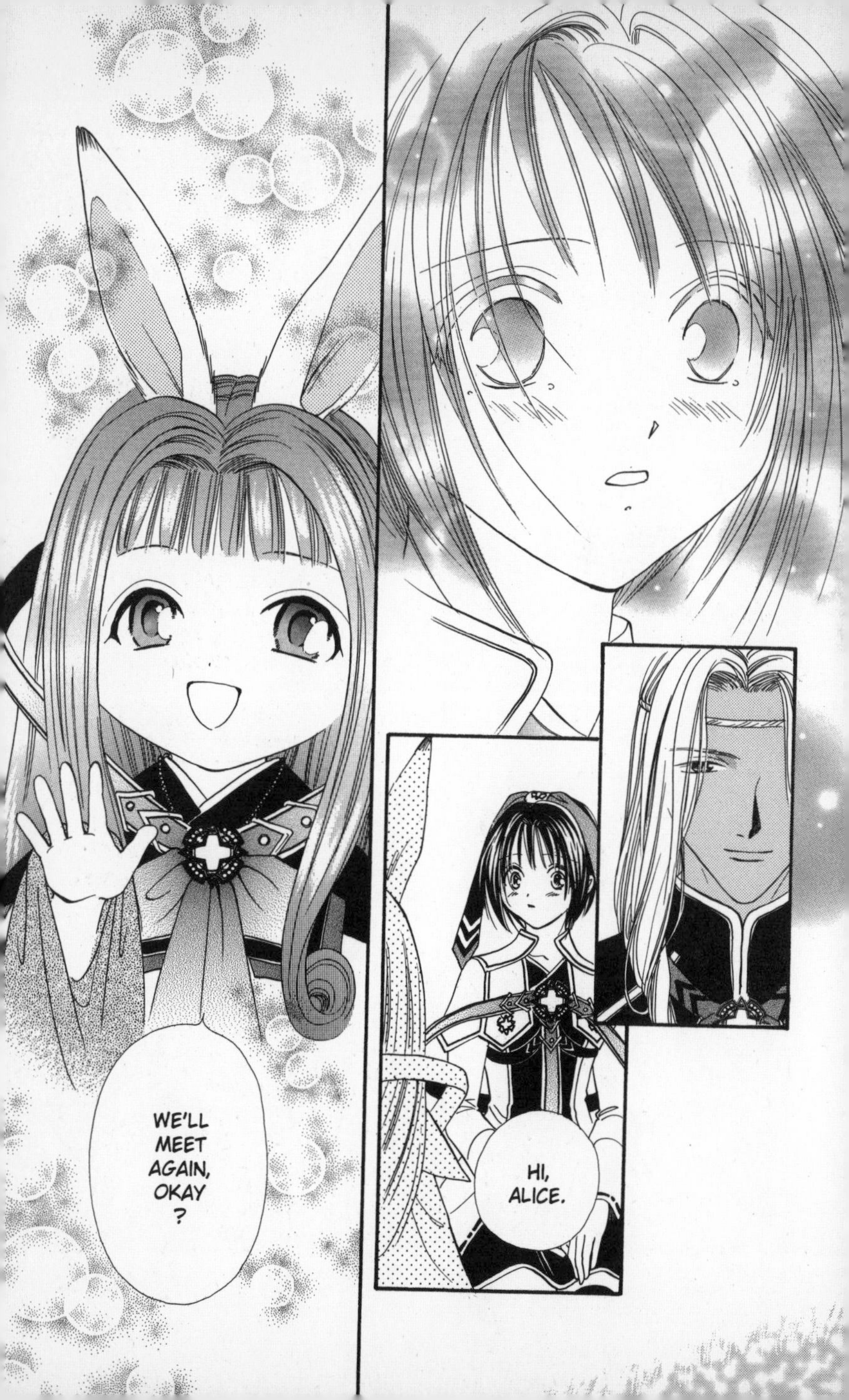
HI, ALICE.
WE'LL MEET AGAIN, OKAY ?

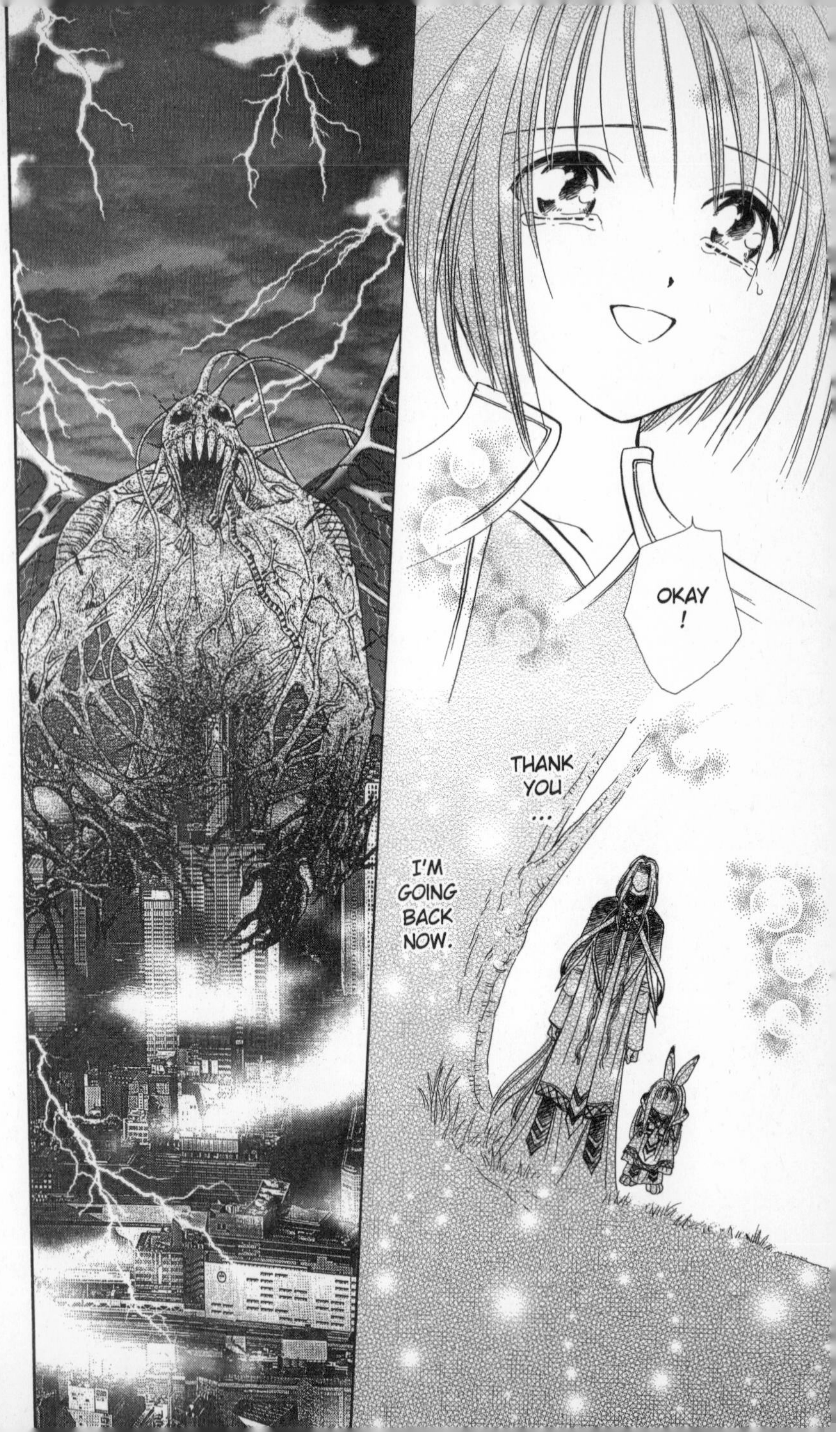
OKAY !
THANK YOU ...
I'M GOING BACK NOW.

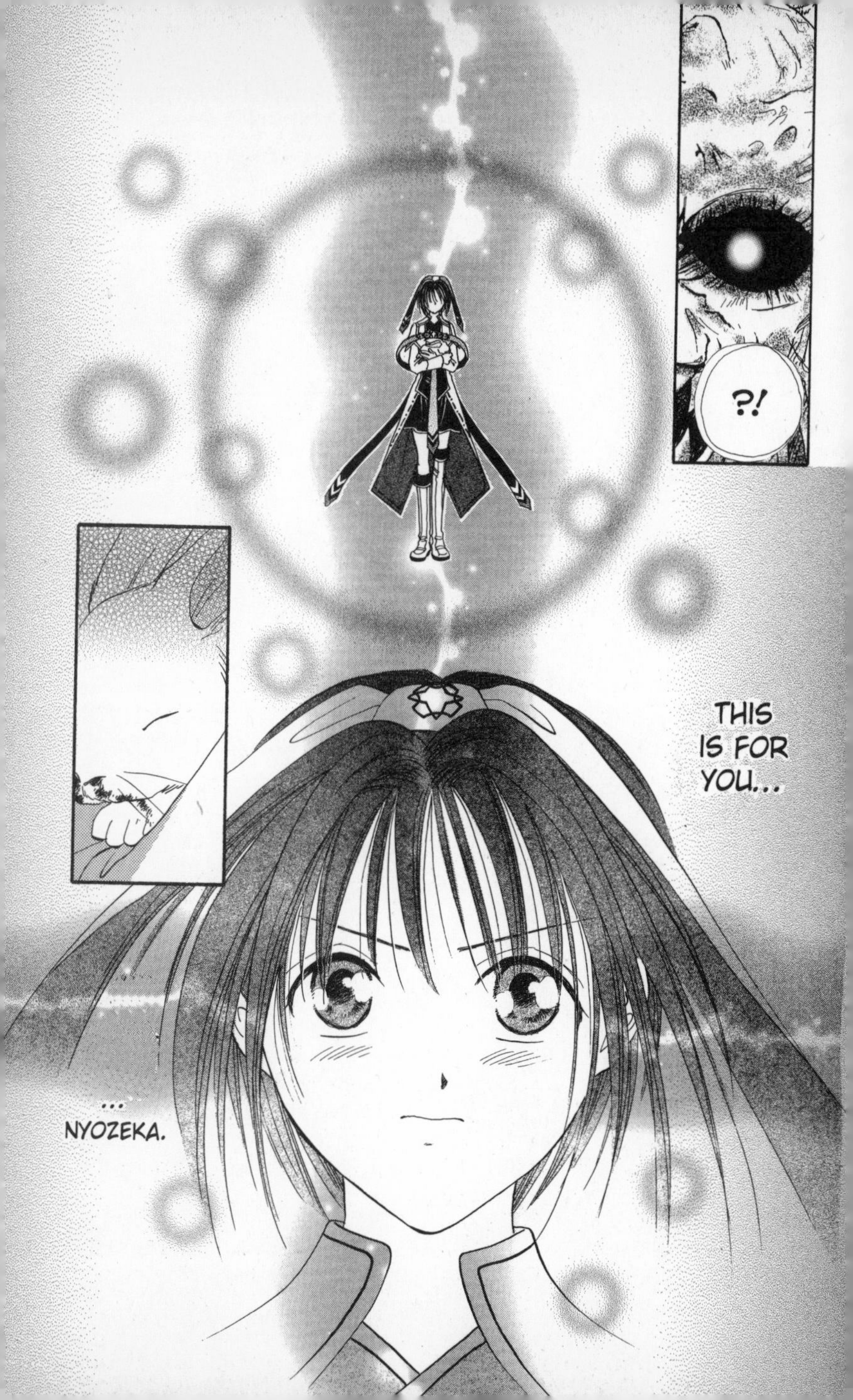
?!
THIS IS FOR YOU...
... NYOZEKA.

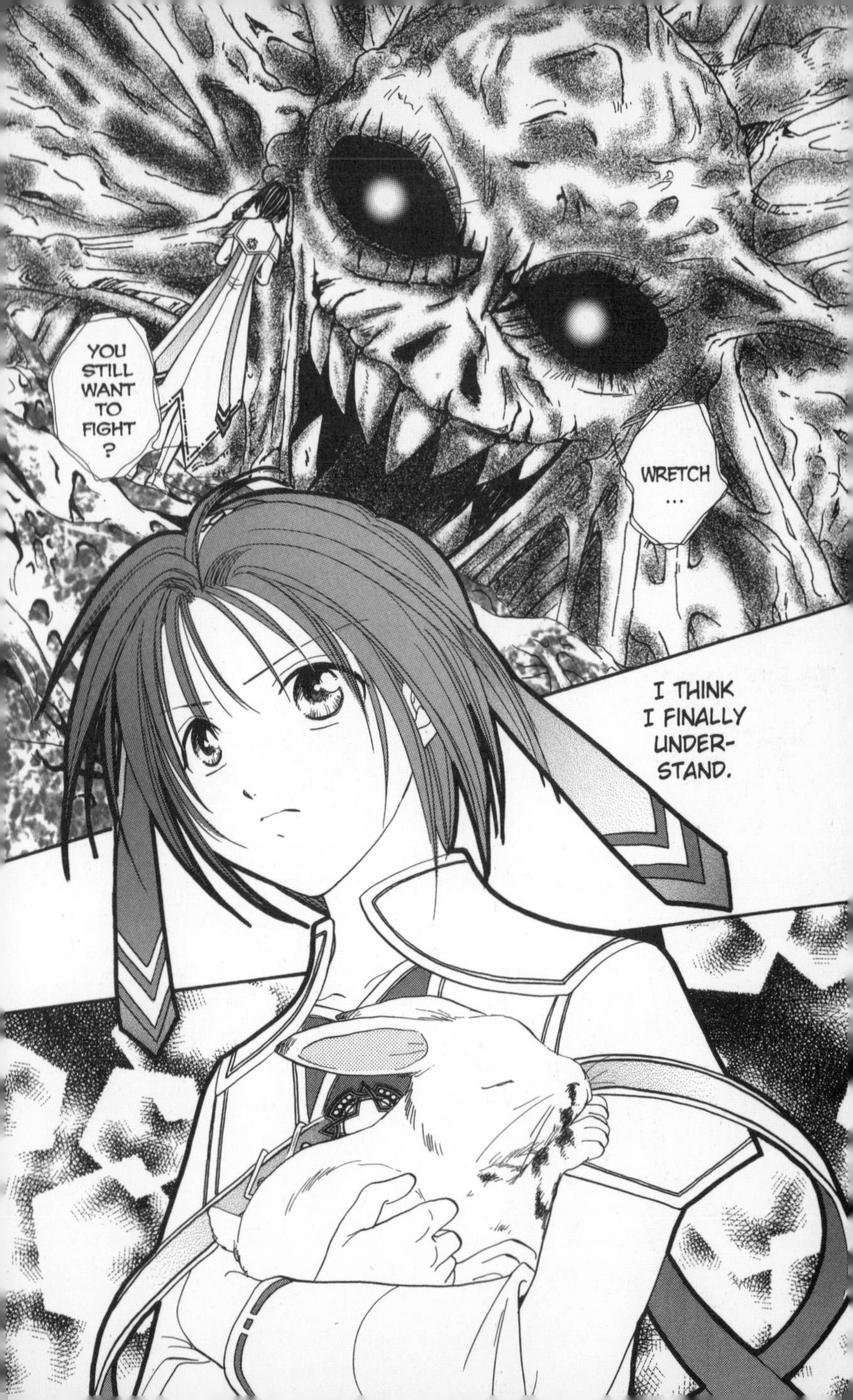
WRETCH ...
YOU STILL WANT TO FIGHT ?
I THINK I FINALLY UNDER-STAND.

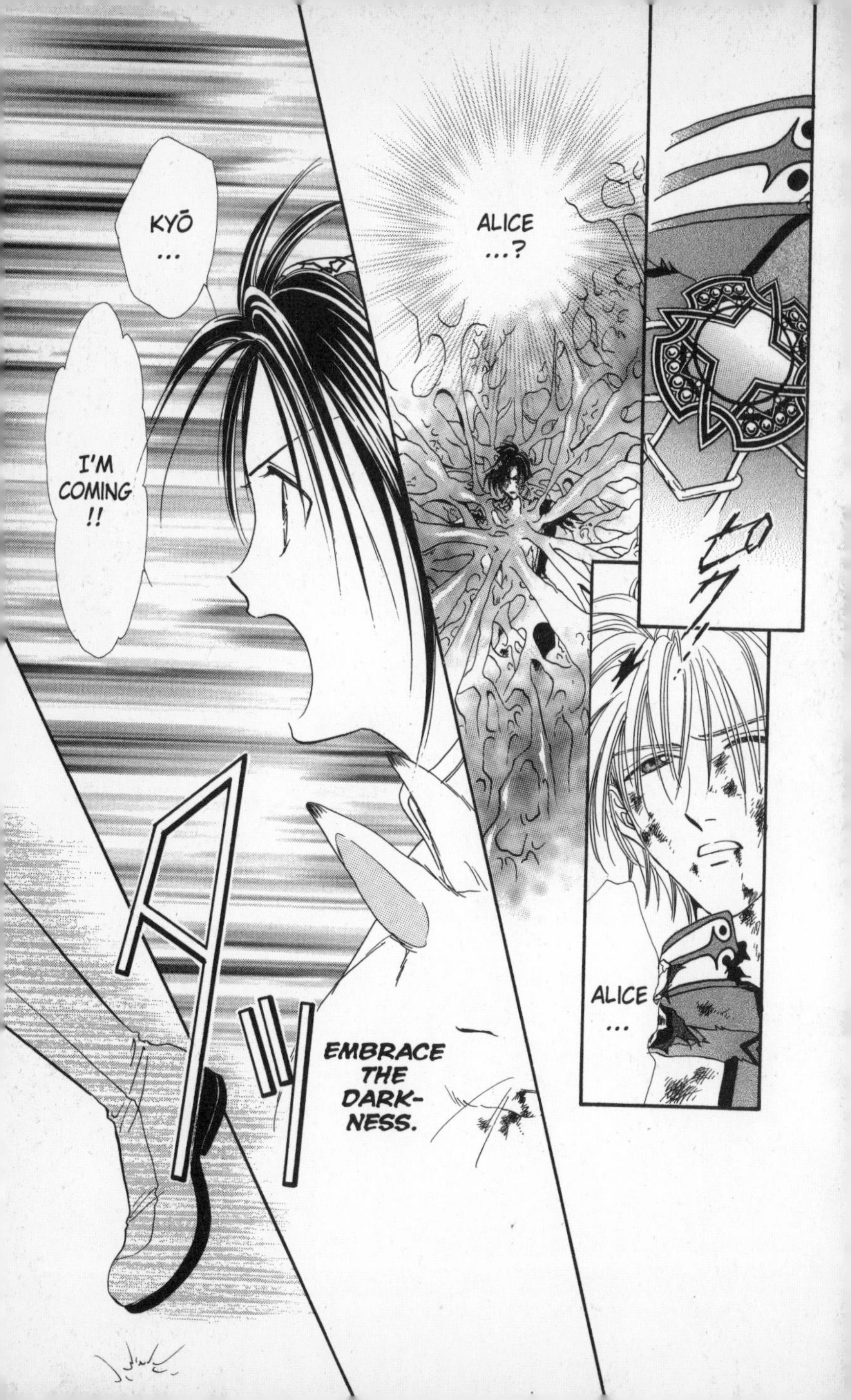
ALICE ...
ALICE ...?
KYŌ ...
I'M COMING !!
EMBRACE THE DARK-NESS.

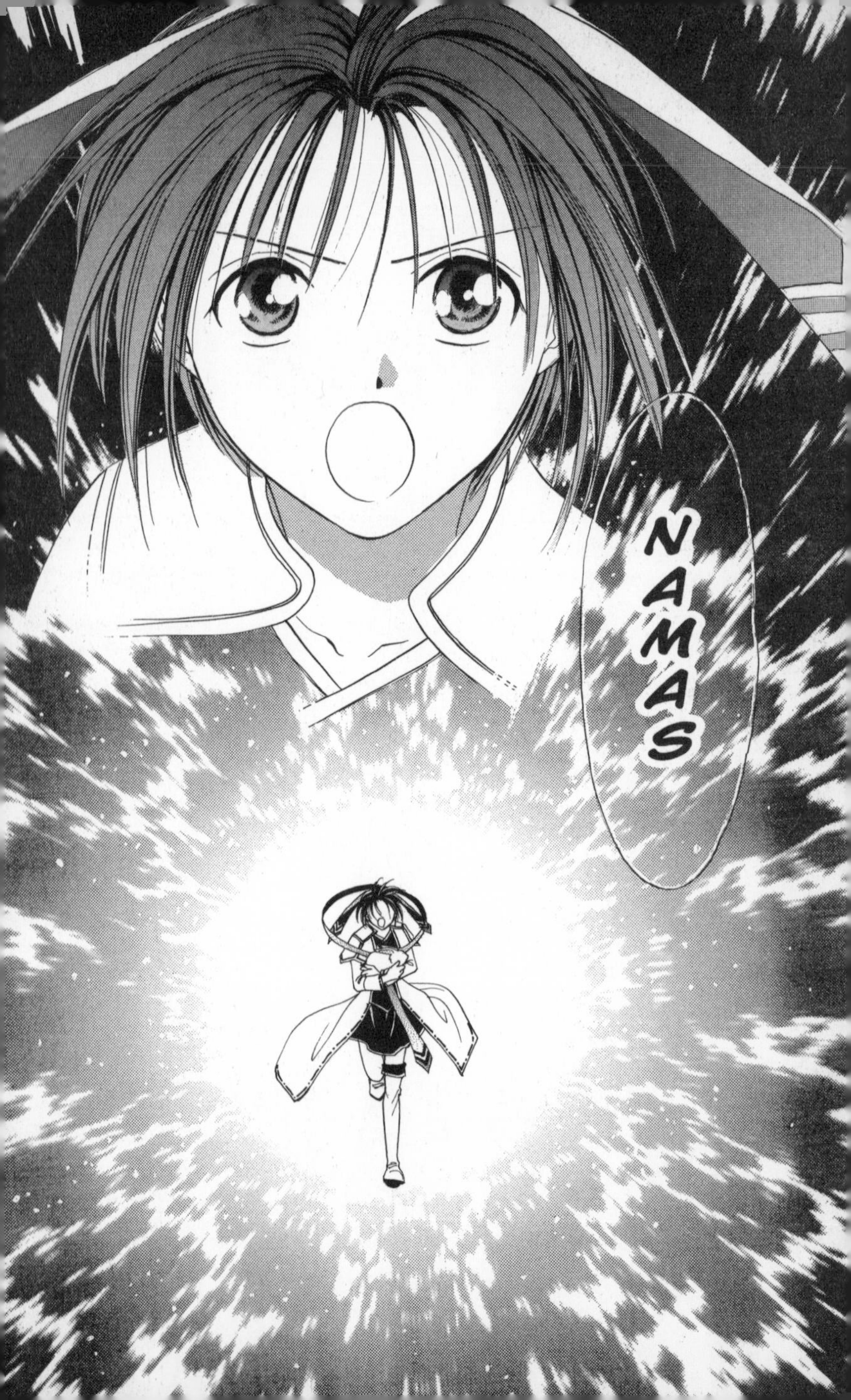
NAMAS

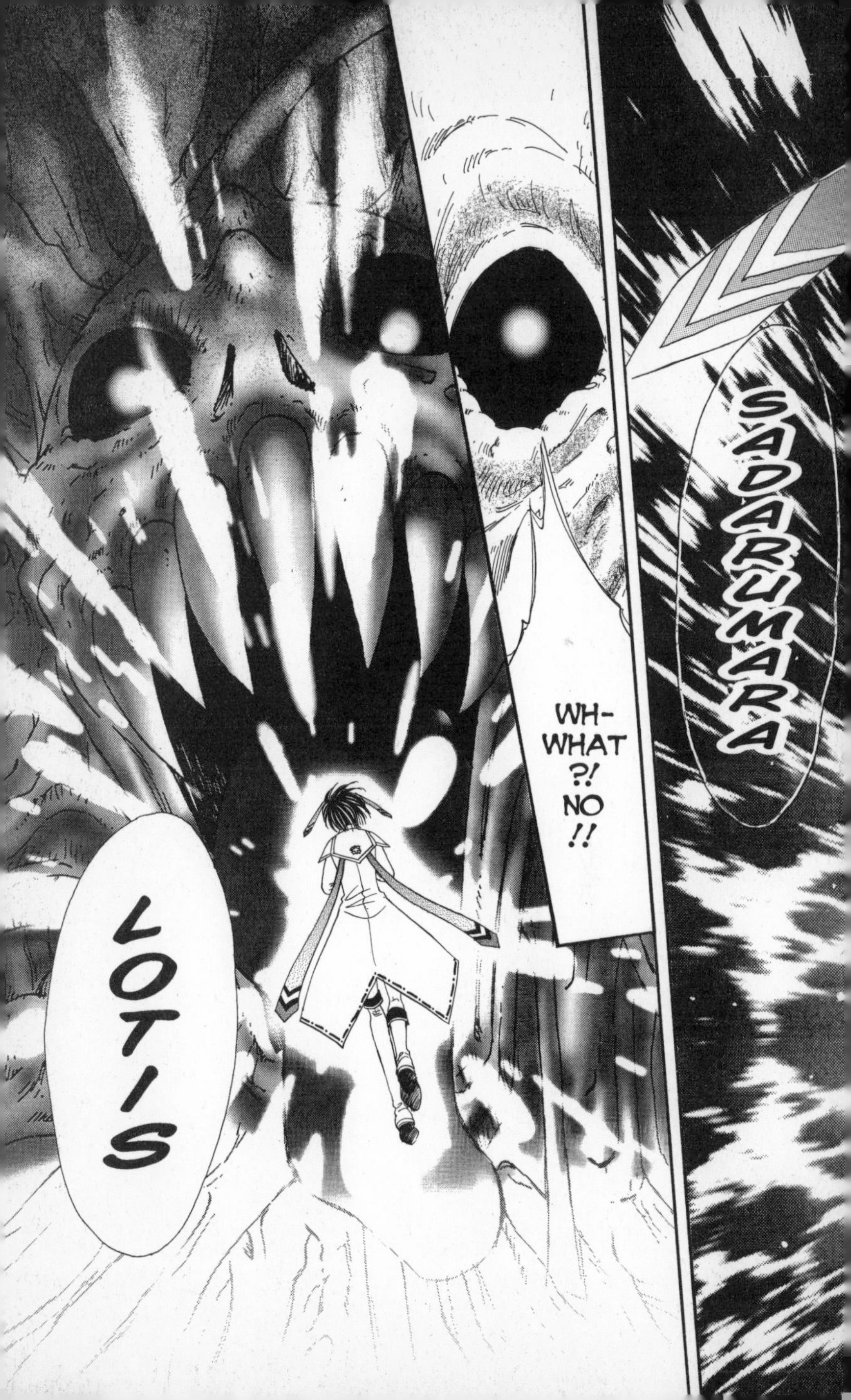
SADARUMARA
WH-WHAT?! NO!!
LOTIS

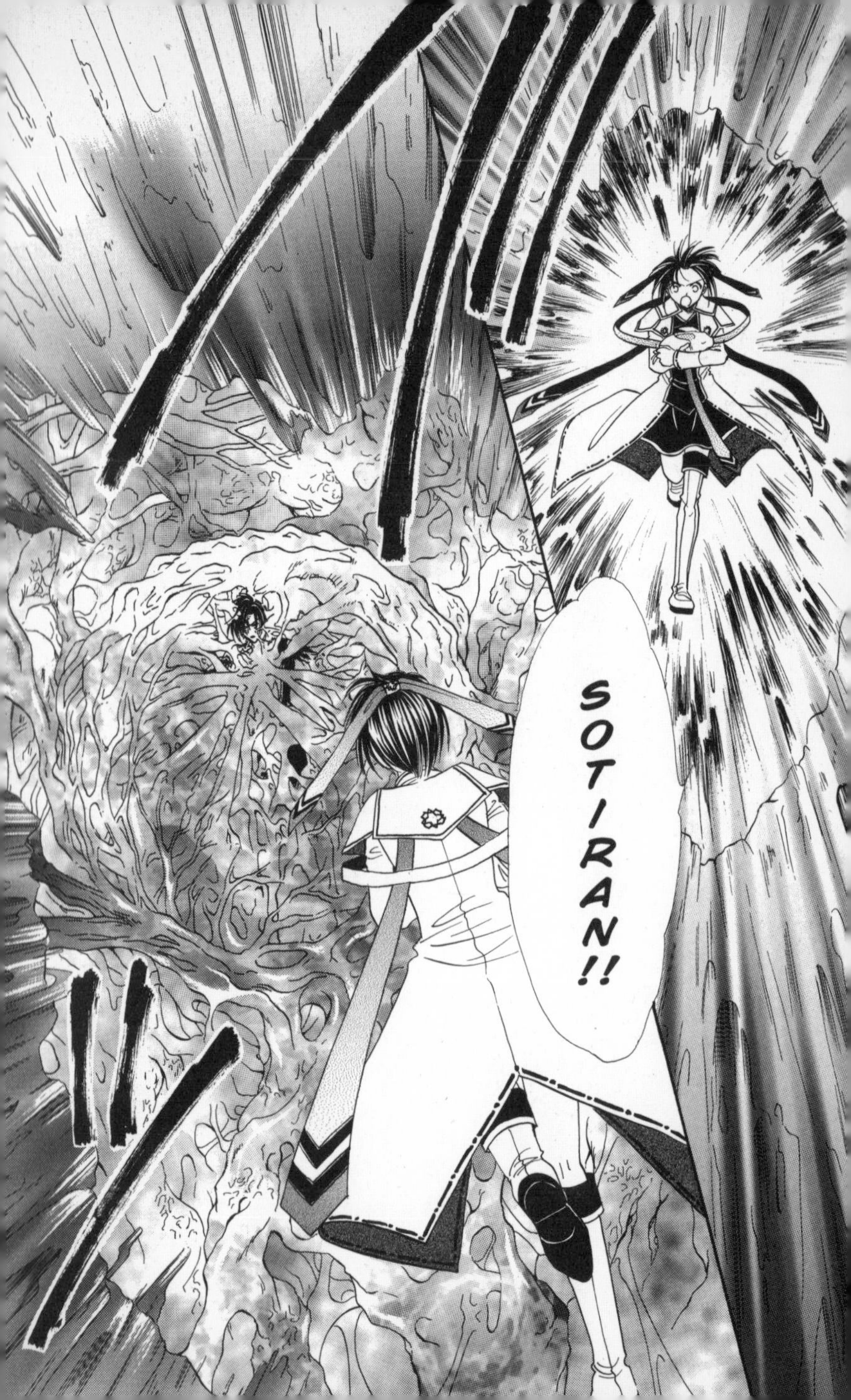
SOTIRAN!!

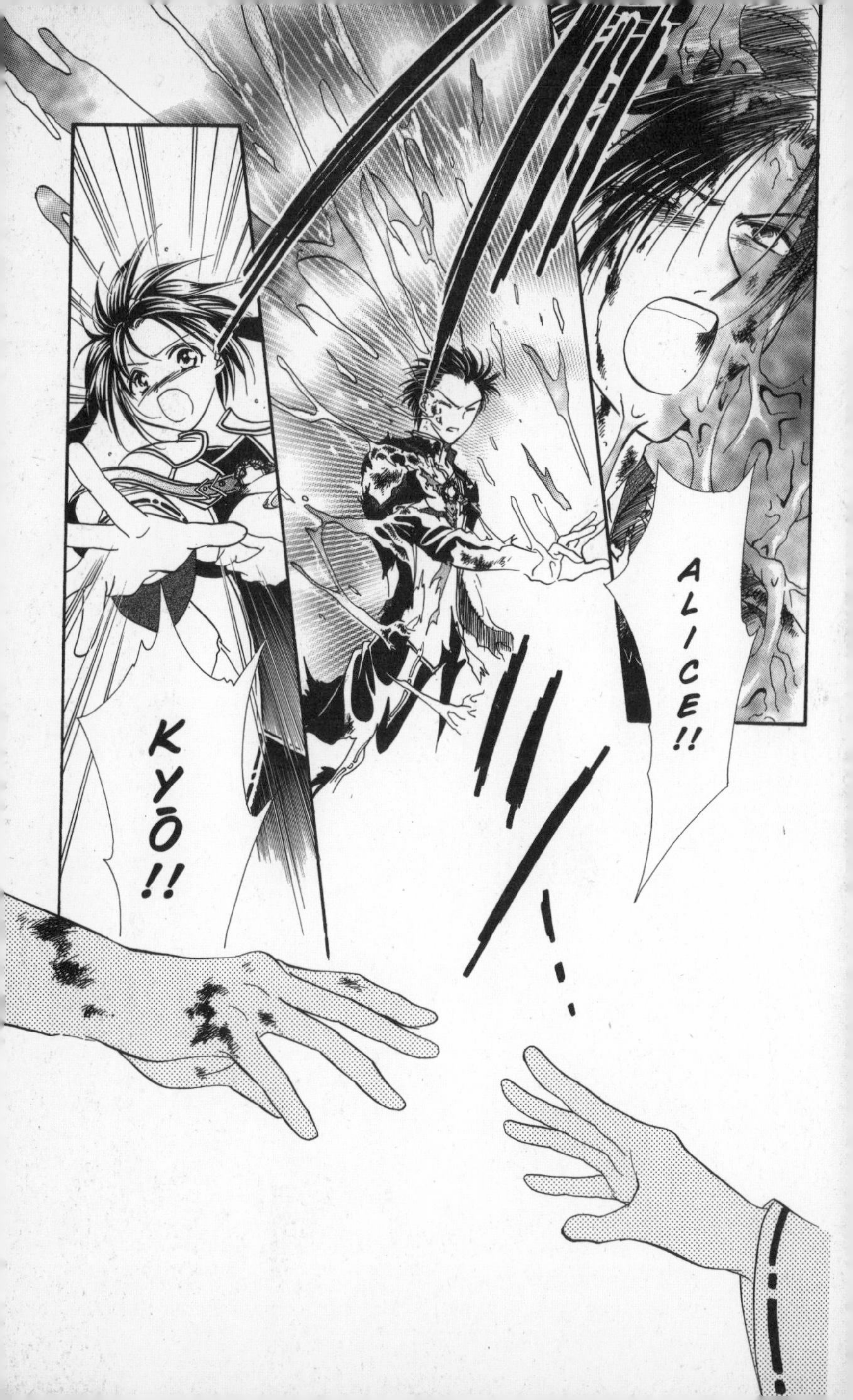
ALICE!!
KYŌ!!

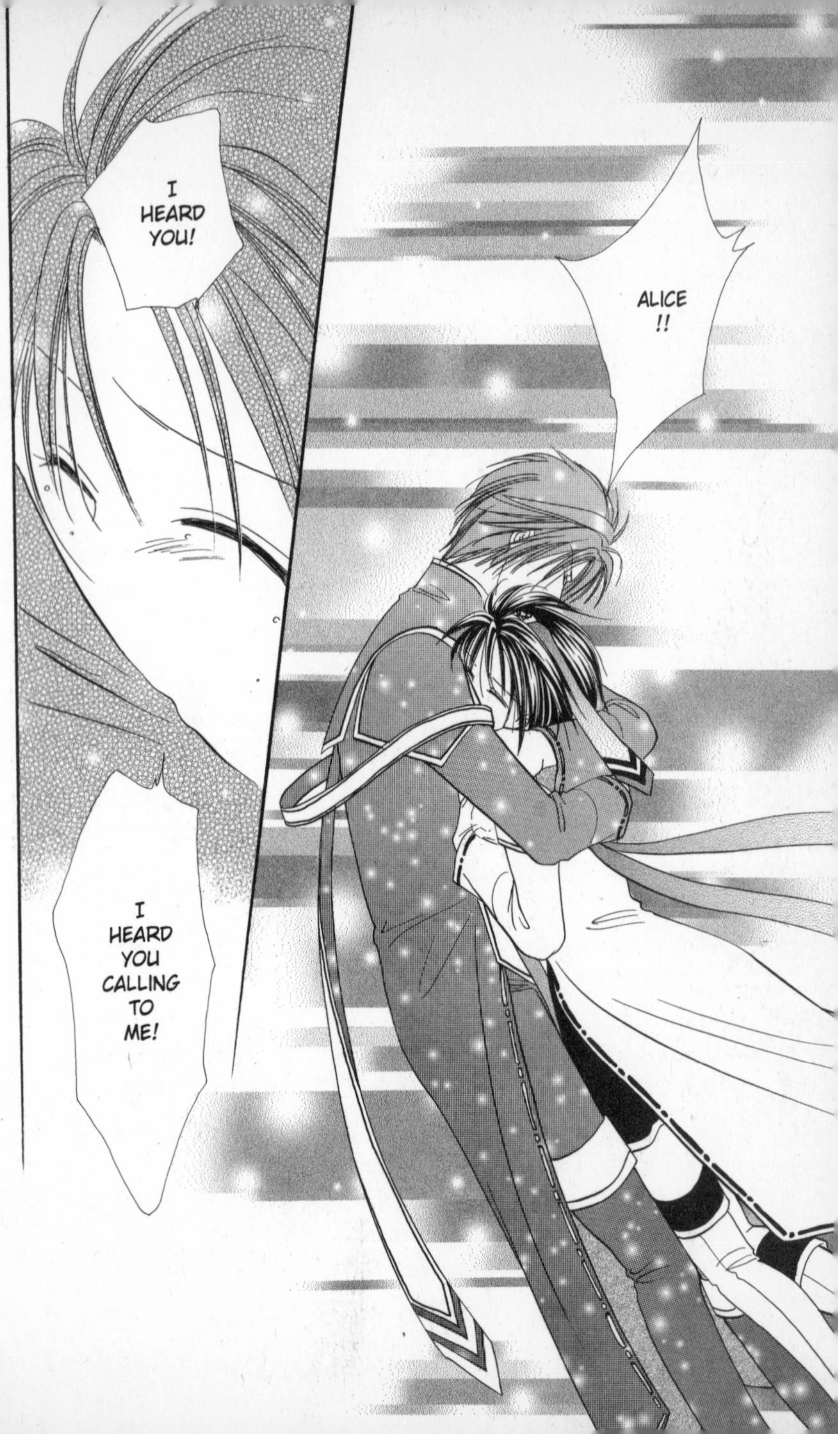
ALICE !!
I HEARD YOU!
I HEARD YOU CALLING TO ME!

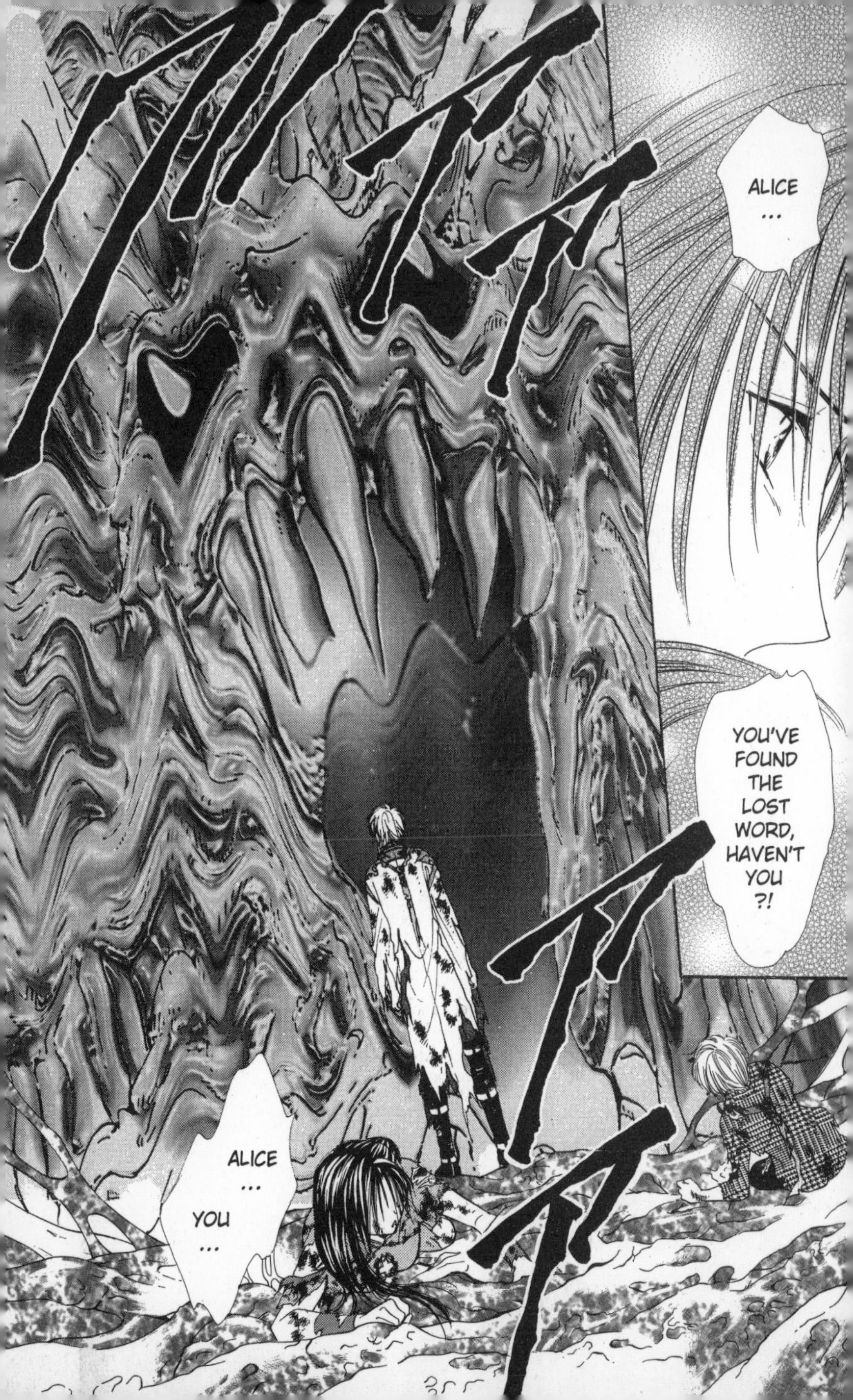
ALICE ...
YOU'VE FOUND THE LOST WORD, HAVEN'T YOU ?!
ALICE ... YOU ...

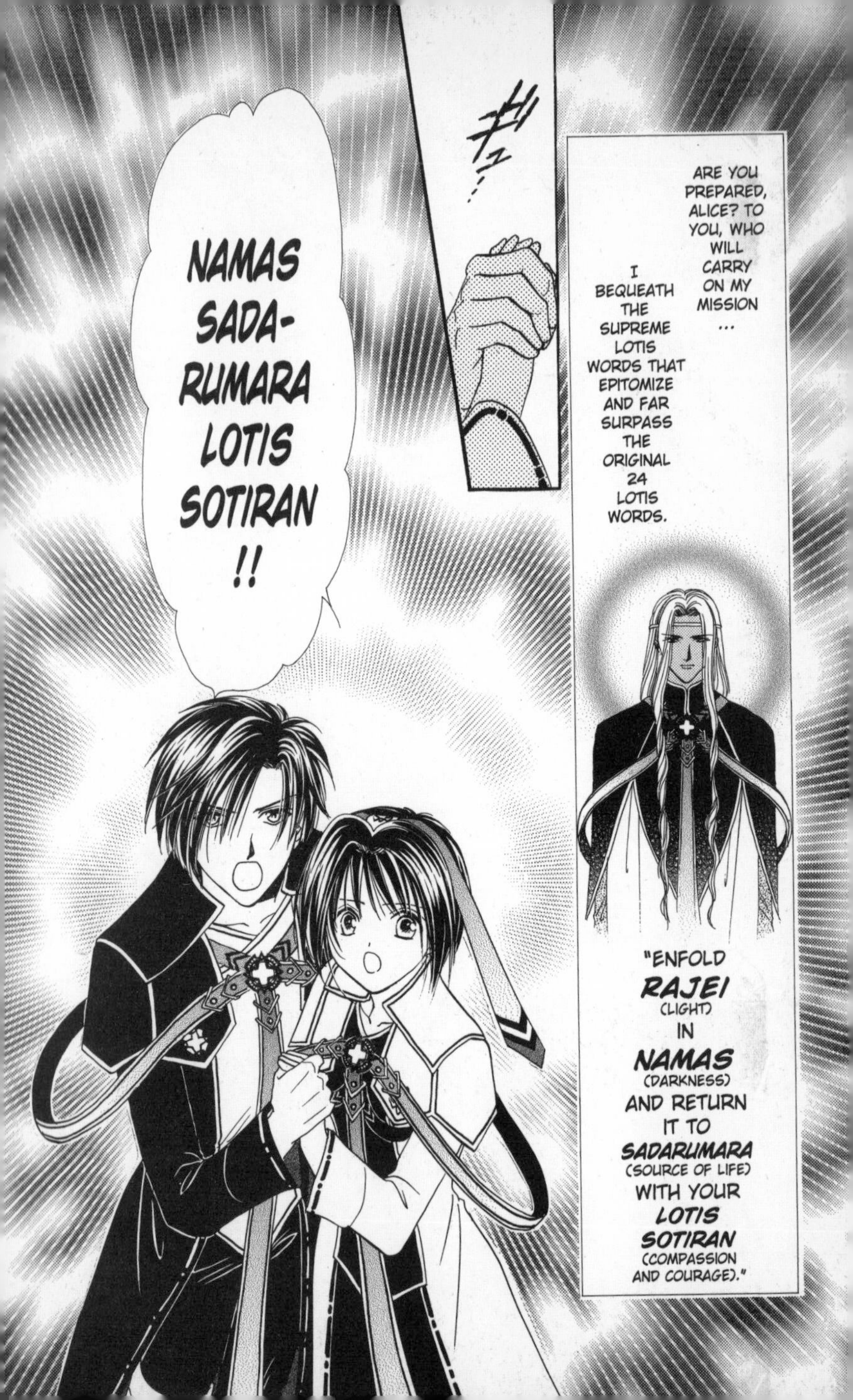
ARE YOU PREPARED, ALICE? TO YOU, WHO WILL CARRY ON MY MISSION ...
I BEQUEATH THE SUPREME LOTIS WORDS THAT EPITOMIZE AND FAR SURPASS THE ORIGINAL 24 LOTIS WORDS.
"ENFOLD RAJEI (LIGHT) IN NAMAS (DARKNESS) AND RETURN IT TO SADARUMARA (SOURCE OF LIFE) WITH YOUR LOTIS SOTIRAN (COMPASSION AND COURAGE)."
NAMAS SADA-RUMARA LOTIS SOTIRAN !!

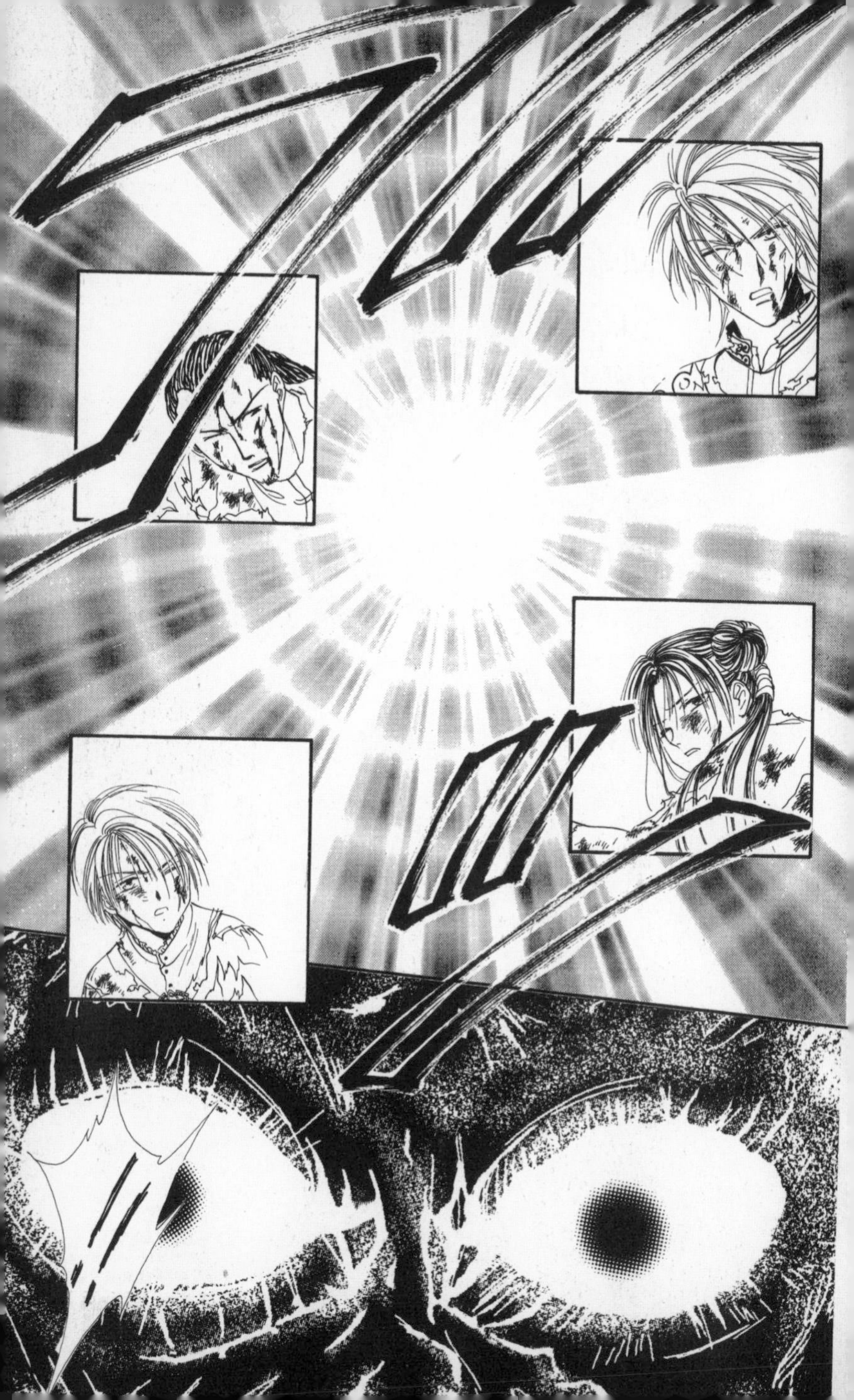

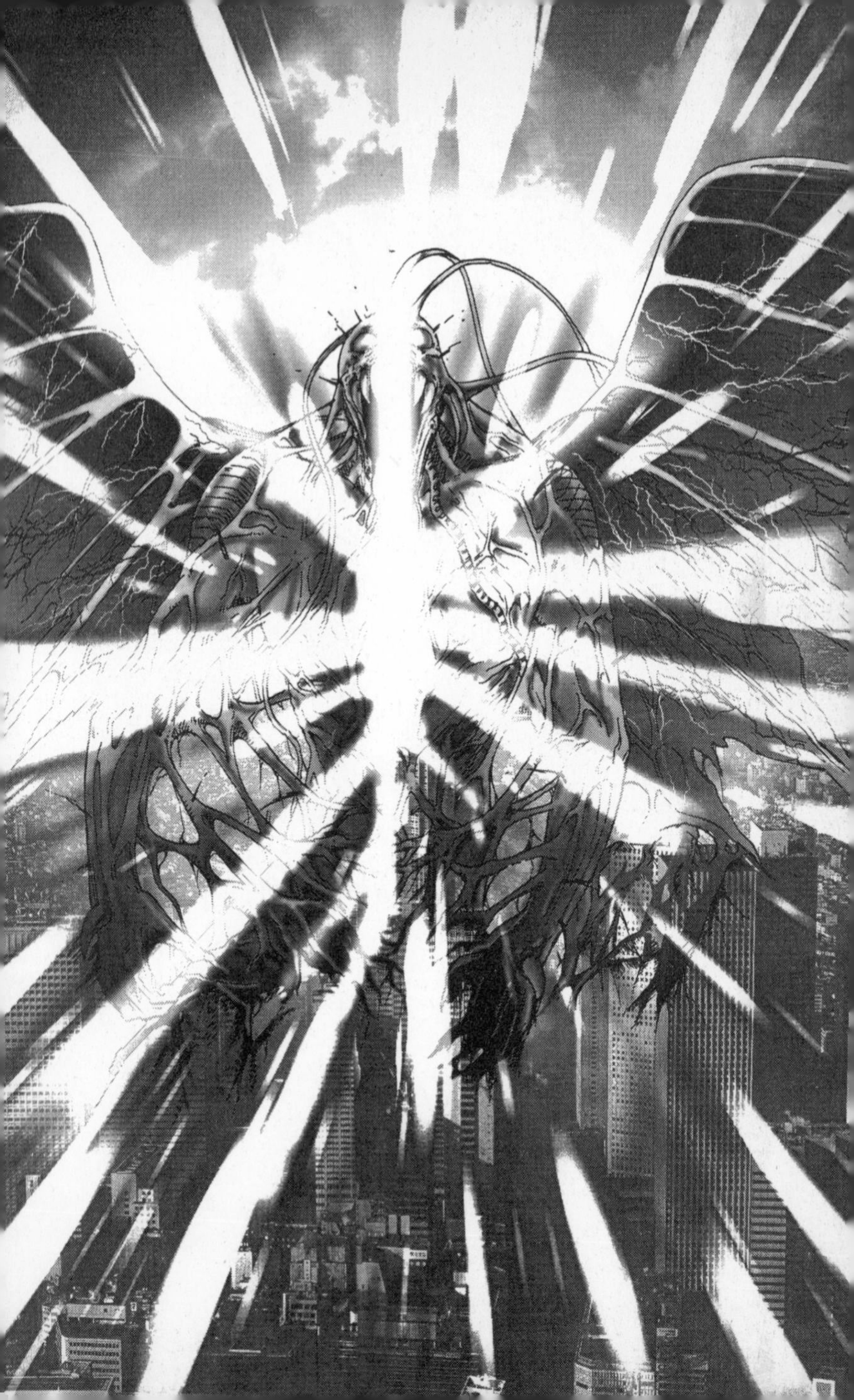

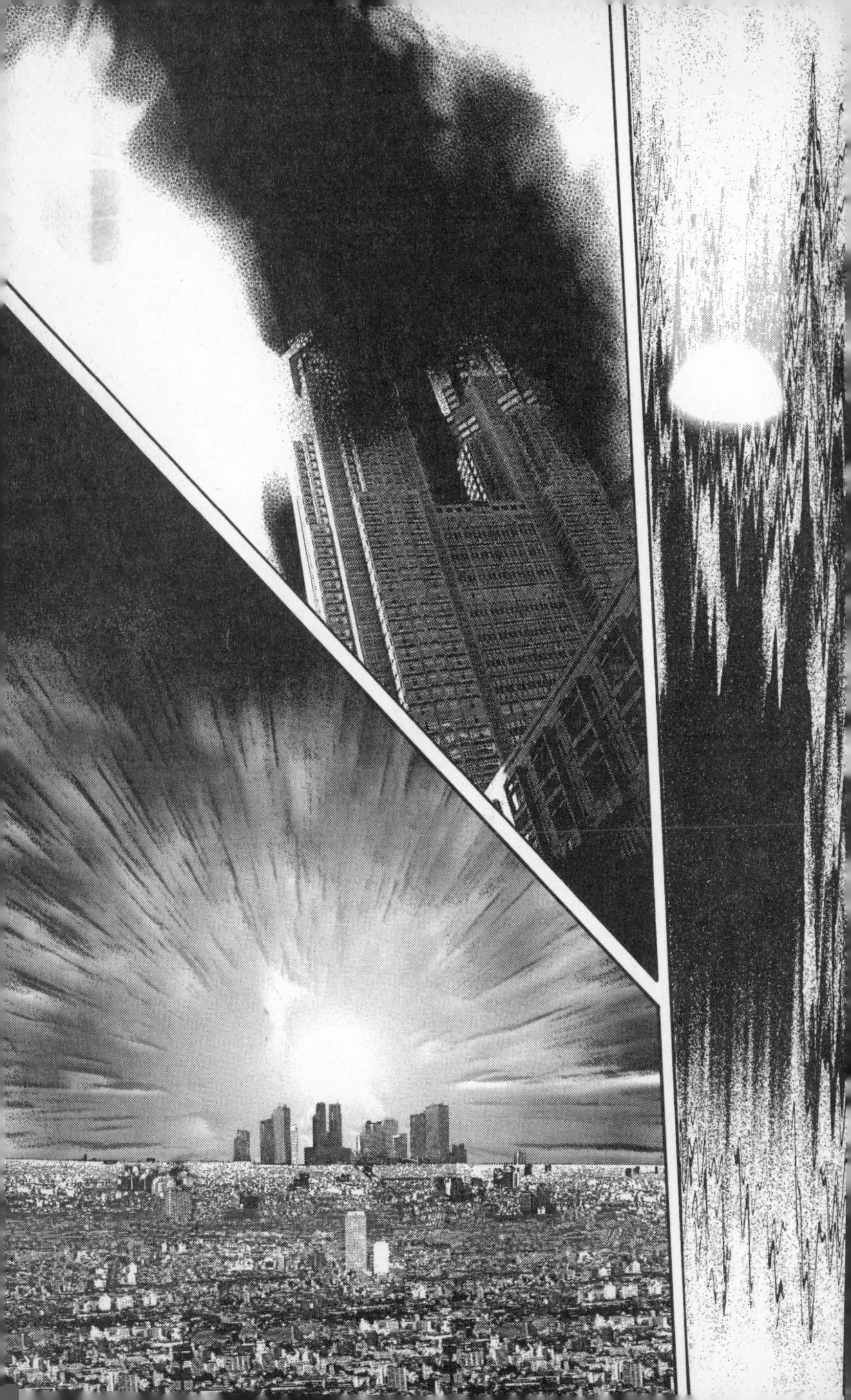

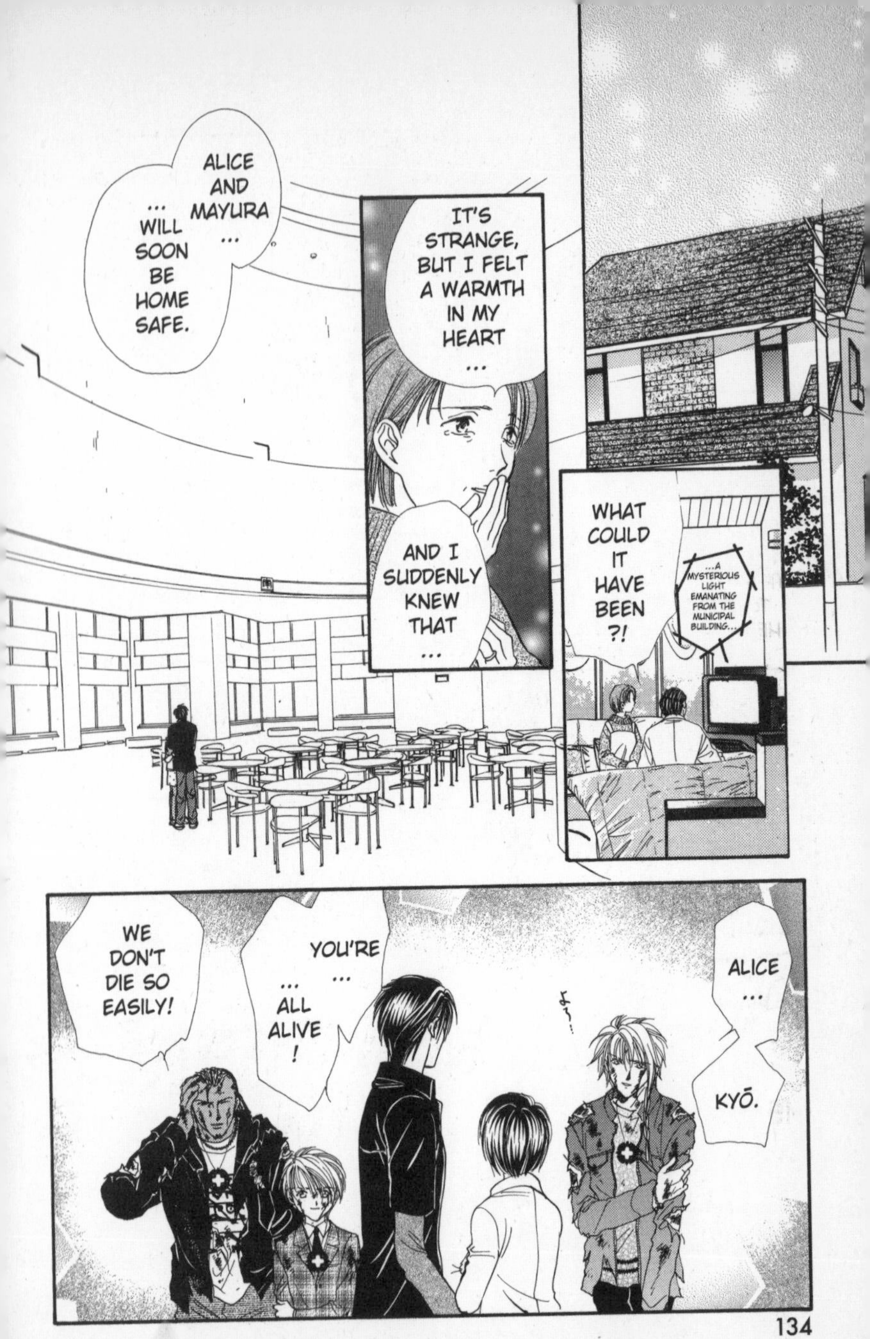
...A MYSTERIOUS LIGHT EMANATING FROM THE MUNICIPAL BUILDING...
WHAT COULD IT HAVE BEEN ?!
IT'S STRANGE, BUT I FELT A WARMTH IN MY HEART ...
AND I SUDDENLY KNEW THAT ...
ALICE AND MAYURA ...
... WILL SOON BE HOME SAFE.
ALICE ...
KYŌ.
YOU'RE ...
... ALL ALIVE !
WE DON'T DIE SO EASILY!

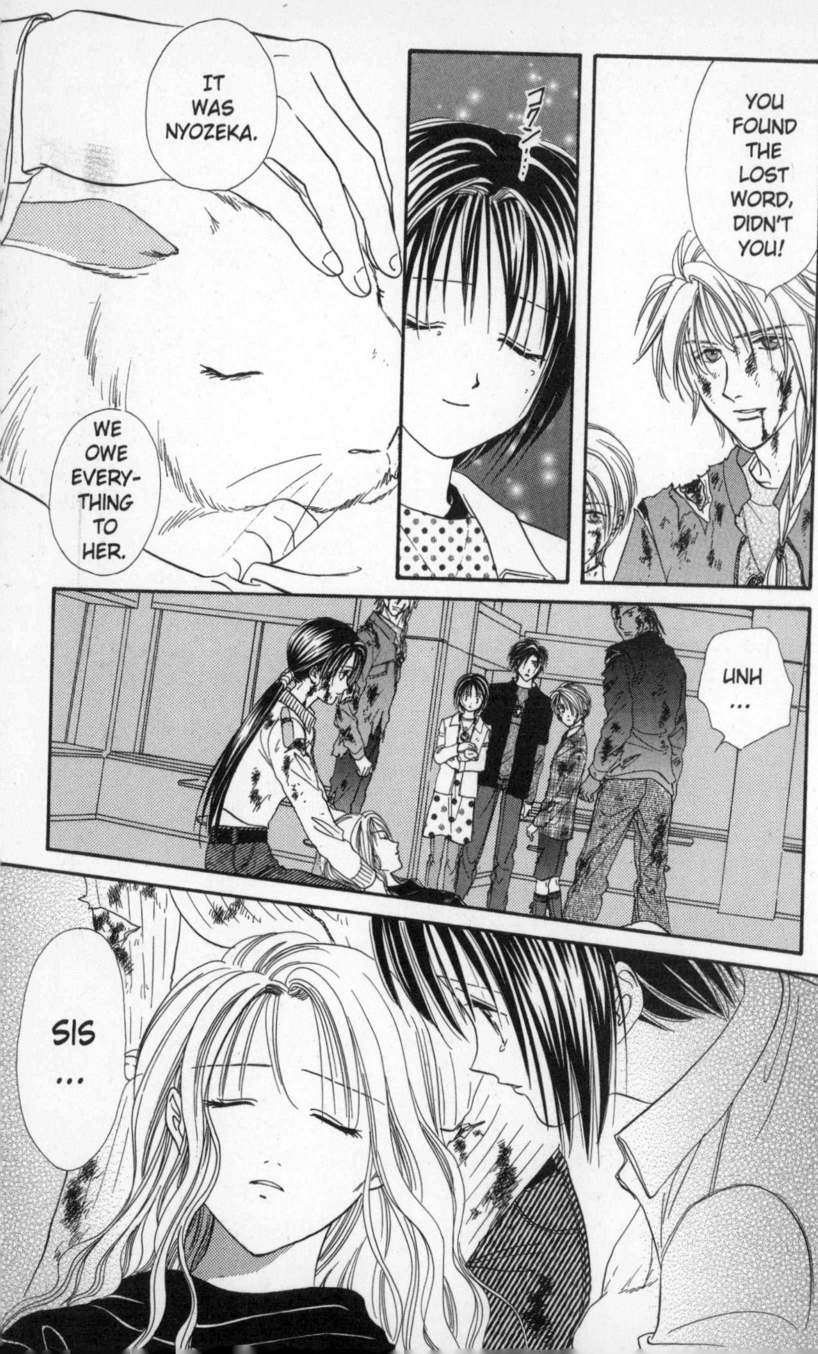
YOU FOUND THE LOST WORD, DIDN'T YOU!
IT WAS NYOZEKA.
WE OWE EVERYTHING TO HER.
UNH ...
SIS ...

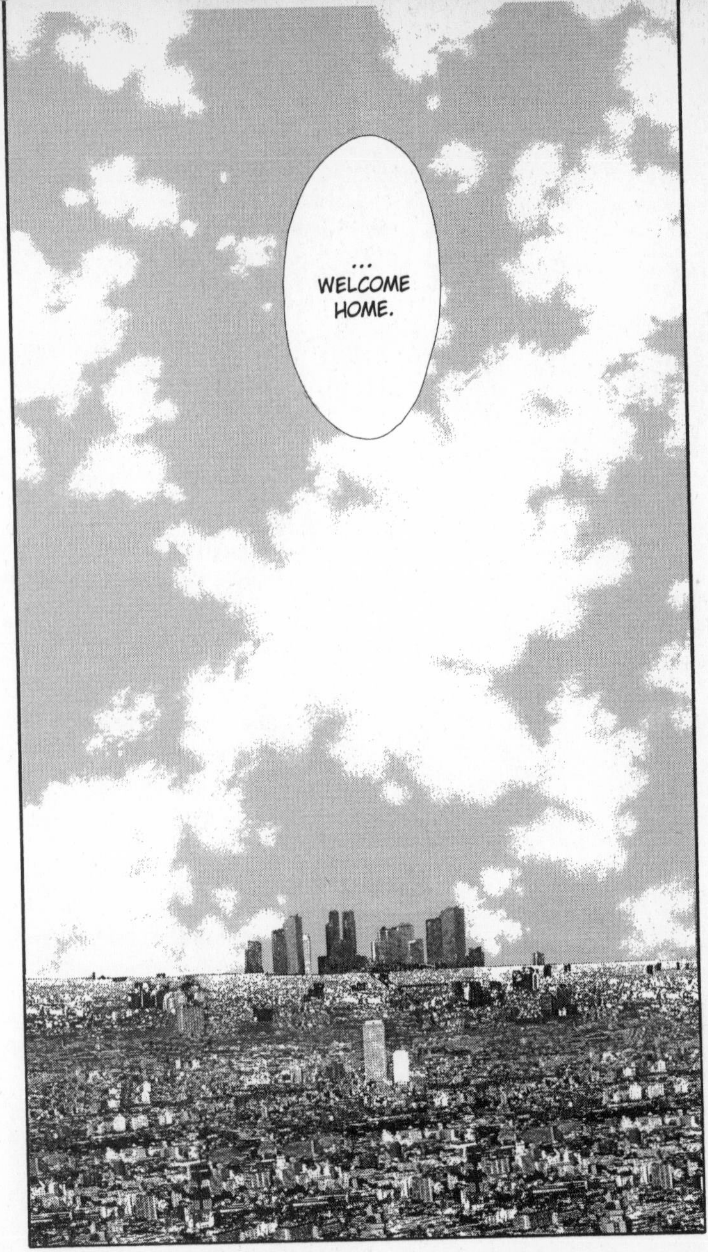
...
WELCOME
HOME.

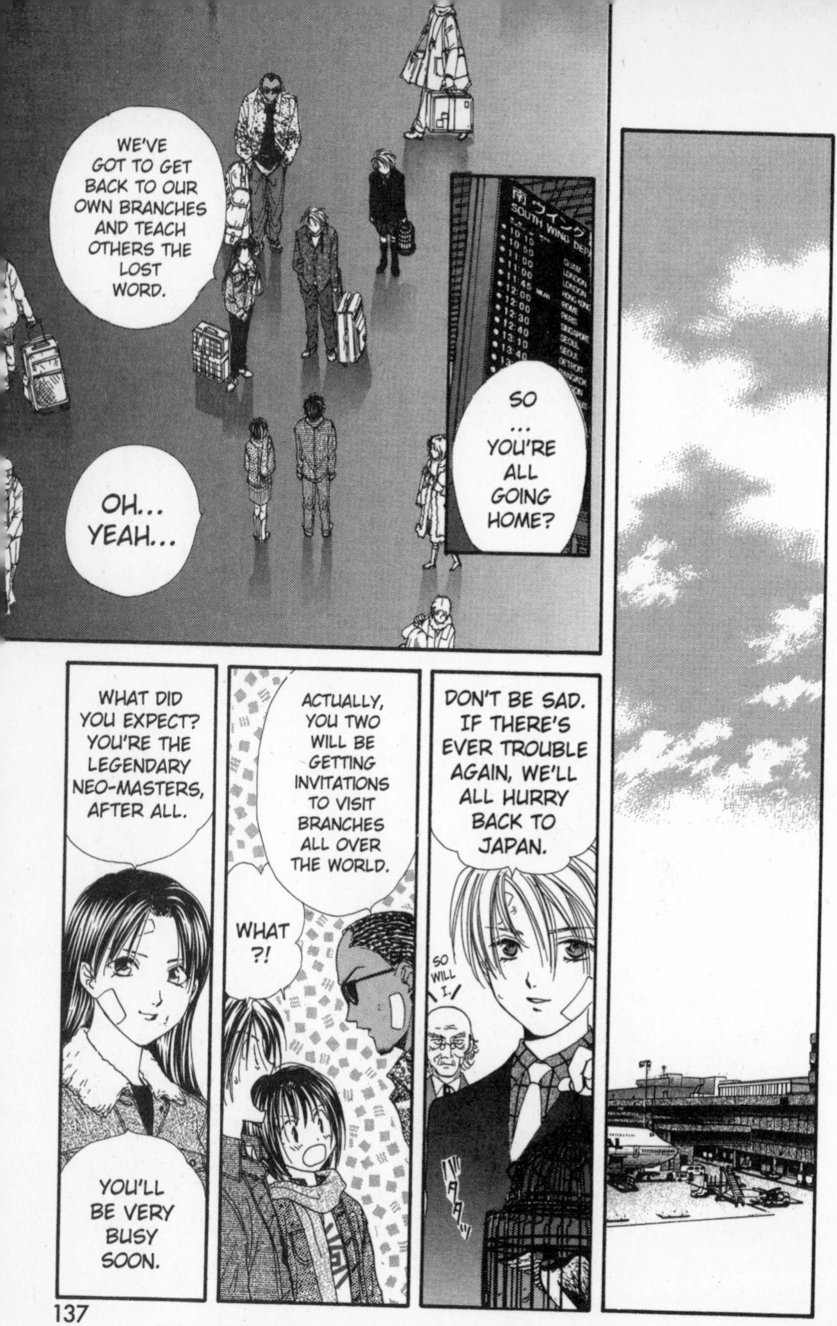
SO ... YOU'RE ALL GOING HOME?
WE'VE GOT TO GET BACK TO OUR OWN BRANCHES AND TEACH OTHERS THE LOST WORD.
OH... YEAH...
DON'T BE SAD. IF THERE'S EVER TROUBLE AGAIN, WE'LL ALL HURRY BACK TO JAPAN.
SO WILL I.
ACTUALLY, YOU TWO WILL BE GETTING INVITATIONS TO VISIT BRANCHES ALL OVER THE WORLD.
WHAT ?!
WHAT DID YOU EXPECT? YOU'RE THE LEGENDARY NEO-MASTERS, AFTER ALL.
YOU'LL BE VERY BUSY SOON.

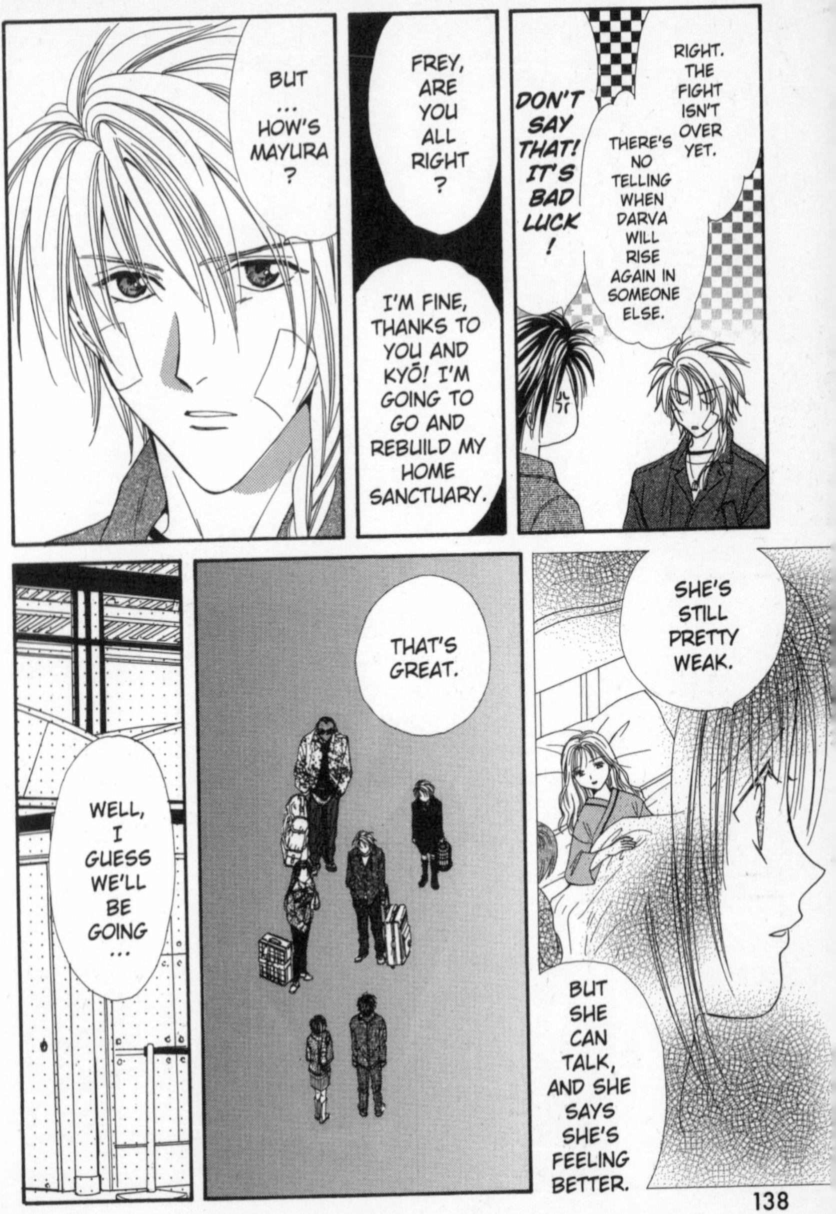
RIGHT. THE FIGHT ISN'T OVER YET.
THERE'S NO TELLING WHEN DARVA WILL RISE AGAIN IN SOMEONE ELSE.
DON'T SAY THAT! IT'S BAD LUCK!
FREY, ARE YOU ALL RIGHT?
I'M FINE, THANKS TO YOU AND KYŌ! I'M GOING TO GO AND REBUILD MY HOME SANCTUARY.
BUT ... HOW'S MAYURA?
SHE'S STILL PRETTY WEAK.
BUT SHE CAN TALK, AND SHE SAYS SHE'S FEELING BETTER.
THAT'S GREAT.
WELL, I GUESS WE'LL BE GOING ...

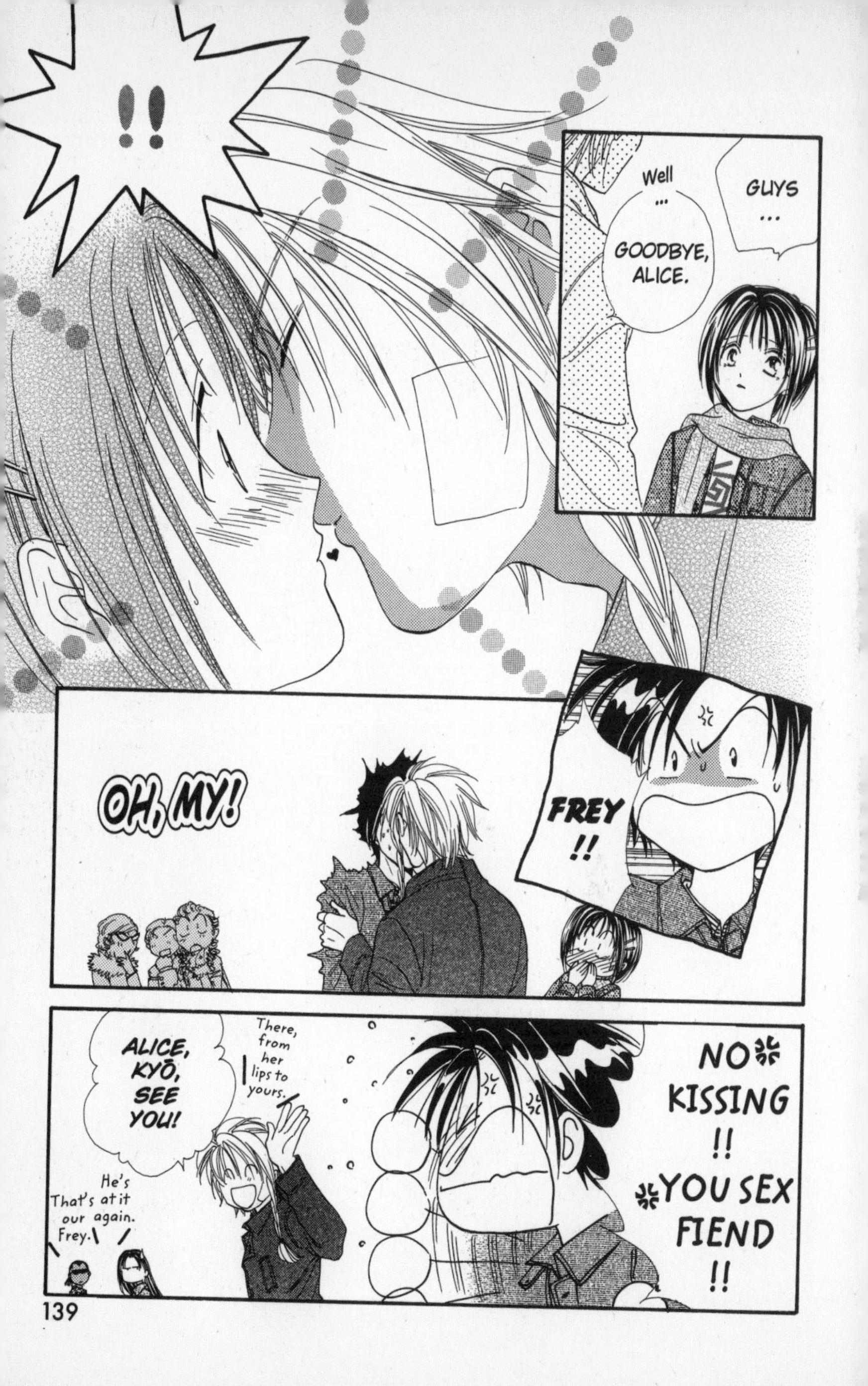
GUYS ...
Well ... GOODBYE, ALICE.
!!
FREY !!
OH, MY!
NO KISSING !! YOU SEX FIEND !!
There, from her lips to yours.
ALICE, KYŌ, SEE YOU!
He's at it again.
That's our Frey.

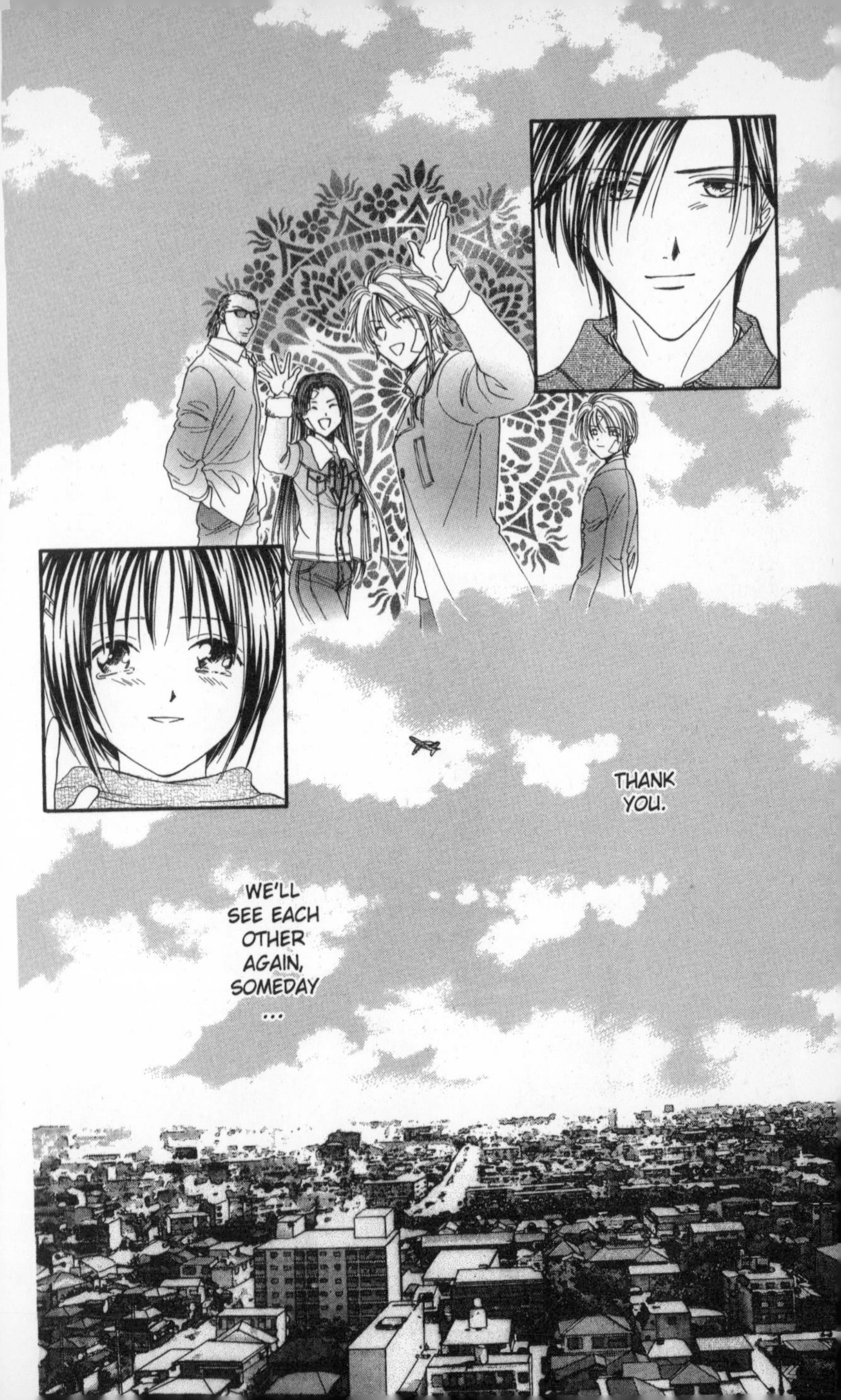
THANK YOU.
WE'LL SEE EACH OTHER AGAIN, SOMEDAY ...

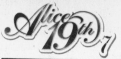

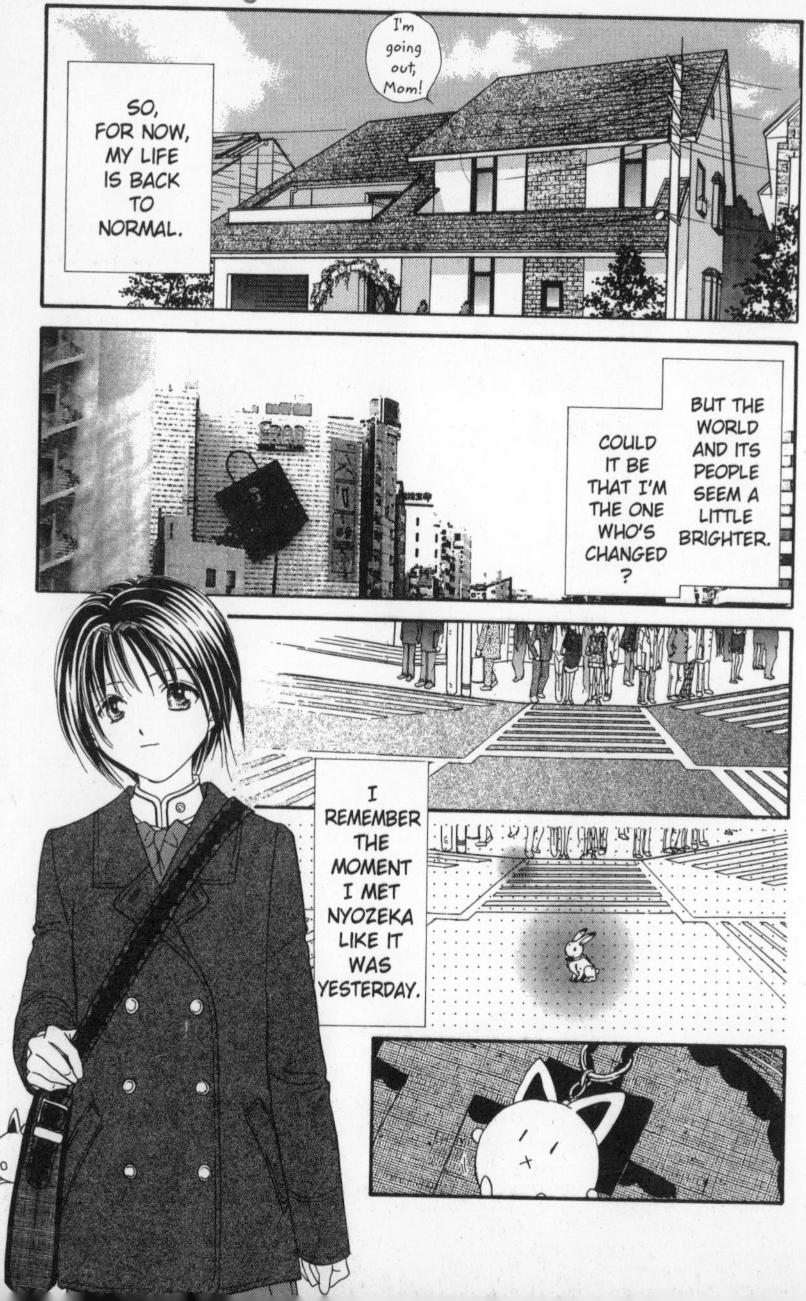
I'm going out, Mom!
SO, FOR NOW, MY LIFE IS BACK TO NORMAL.
BUT THE WORLD AND ITS PEOPLE SEEM A LITTLE BRIGHTER.
COULD IT BE THAT I'M THE ONE WHO'S CHANGED?
I REMEMBER THE MOMENT I MET NYOZEKA LIKE IT WAS YESTERDAY.

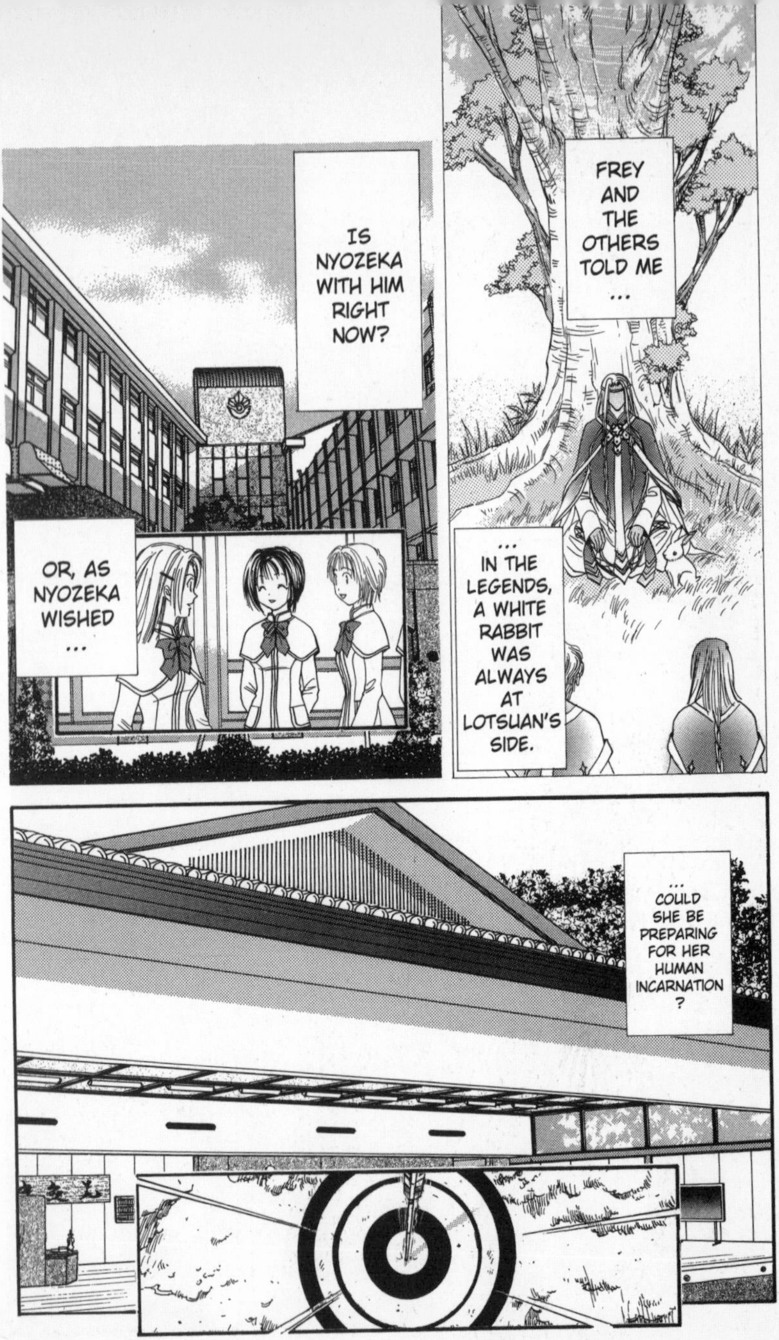
FREY AND THE OTHERS TOLD ME ...
... IN THE LEGENDS, A WHITE RABBIT WAS ALWAYS AT LOTSUAN'S SIDE.
IS NYOZEKA WITH HIM RIGHT NOW?
OR, AS NYOZEKA WISHED ...
... COULD SHE BE PREPARING FOR HER HUMAN INCARNATION ?

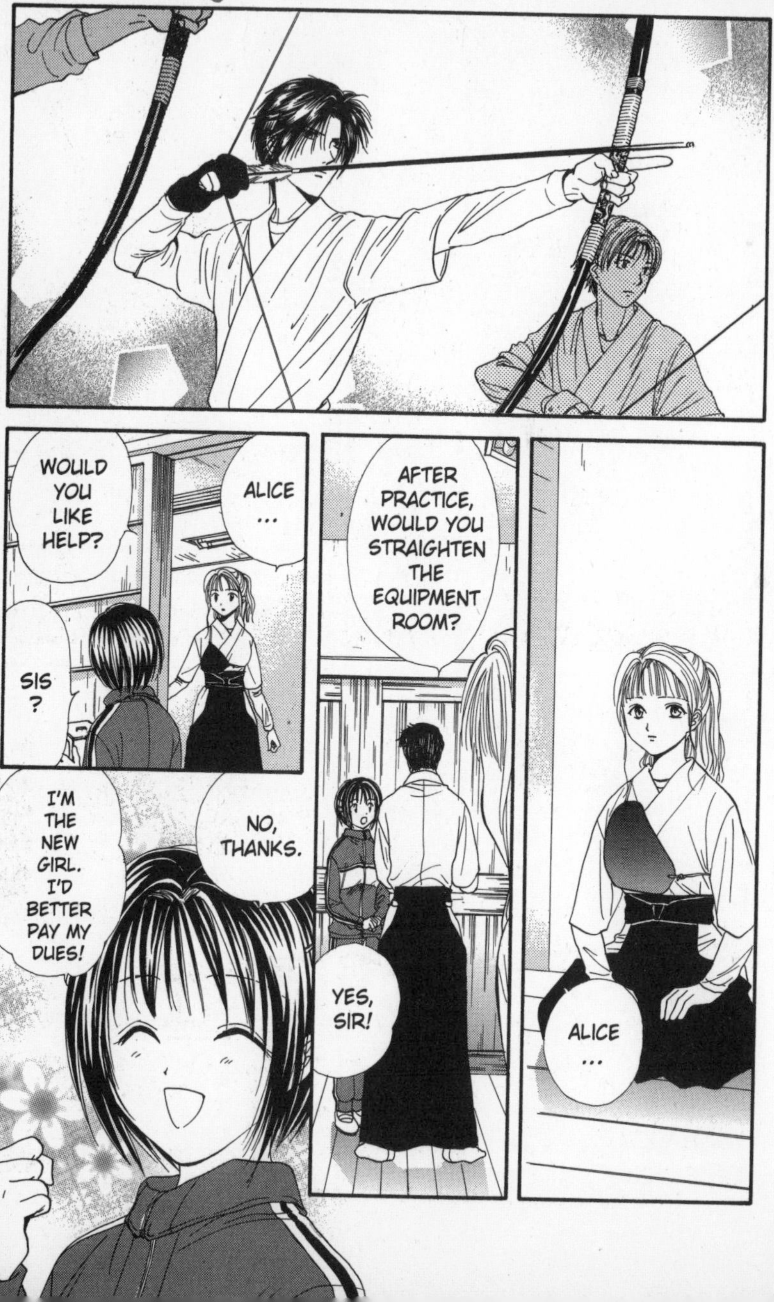
ALICE ...
AFTER PRACTICE, WOULD YOU STRAIGHTEN THE EQUIPMENT ROOM?
YES, SIR!
ALICE ...
WOULD YOU LIKE HELP?
SIS ?
NO, THANKS.
I'M THE NEW GIRL. I'D BETTER PAY MY DUES!

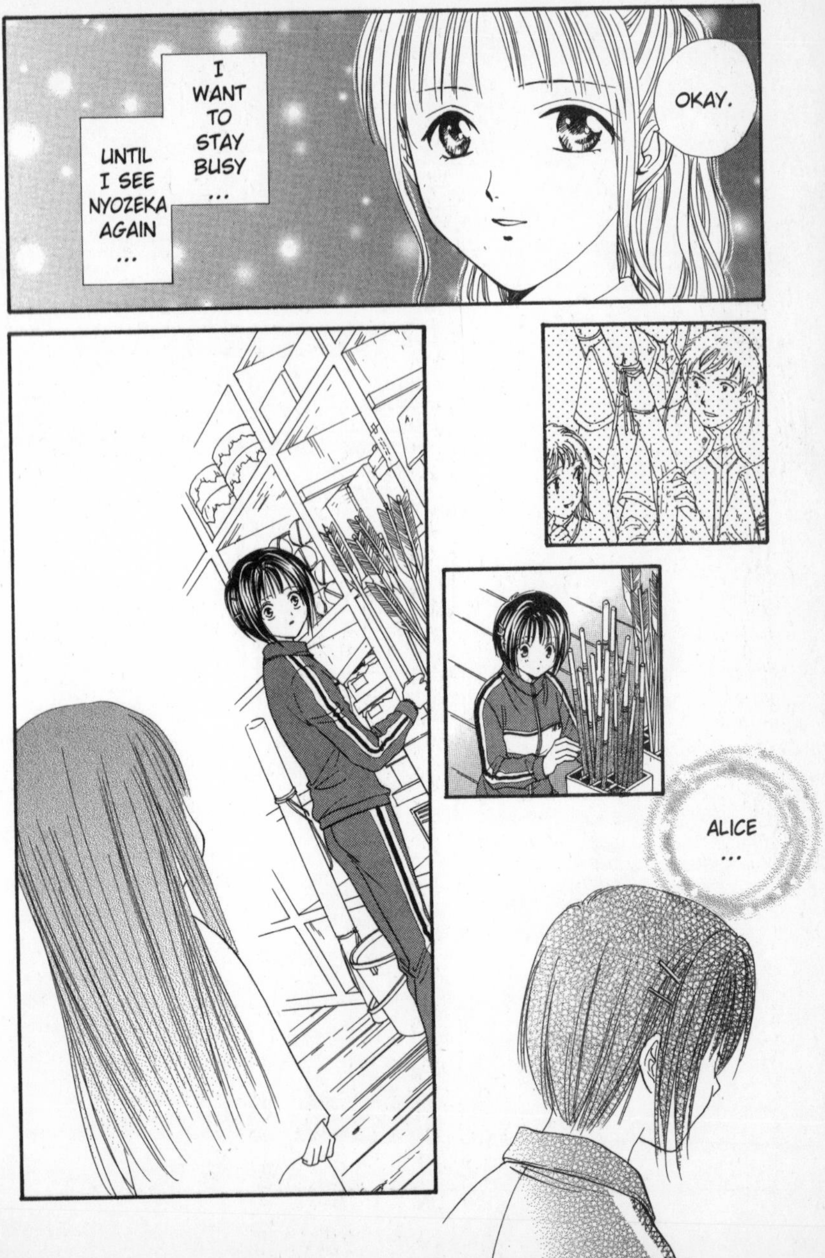
OKAY.
I WANT TO STAY BUSY...
UNTIL I SEE NYOZEKA AGAIN...
ALICE...

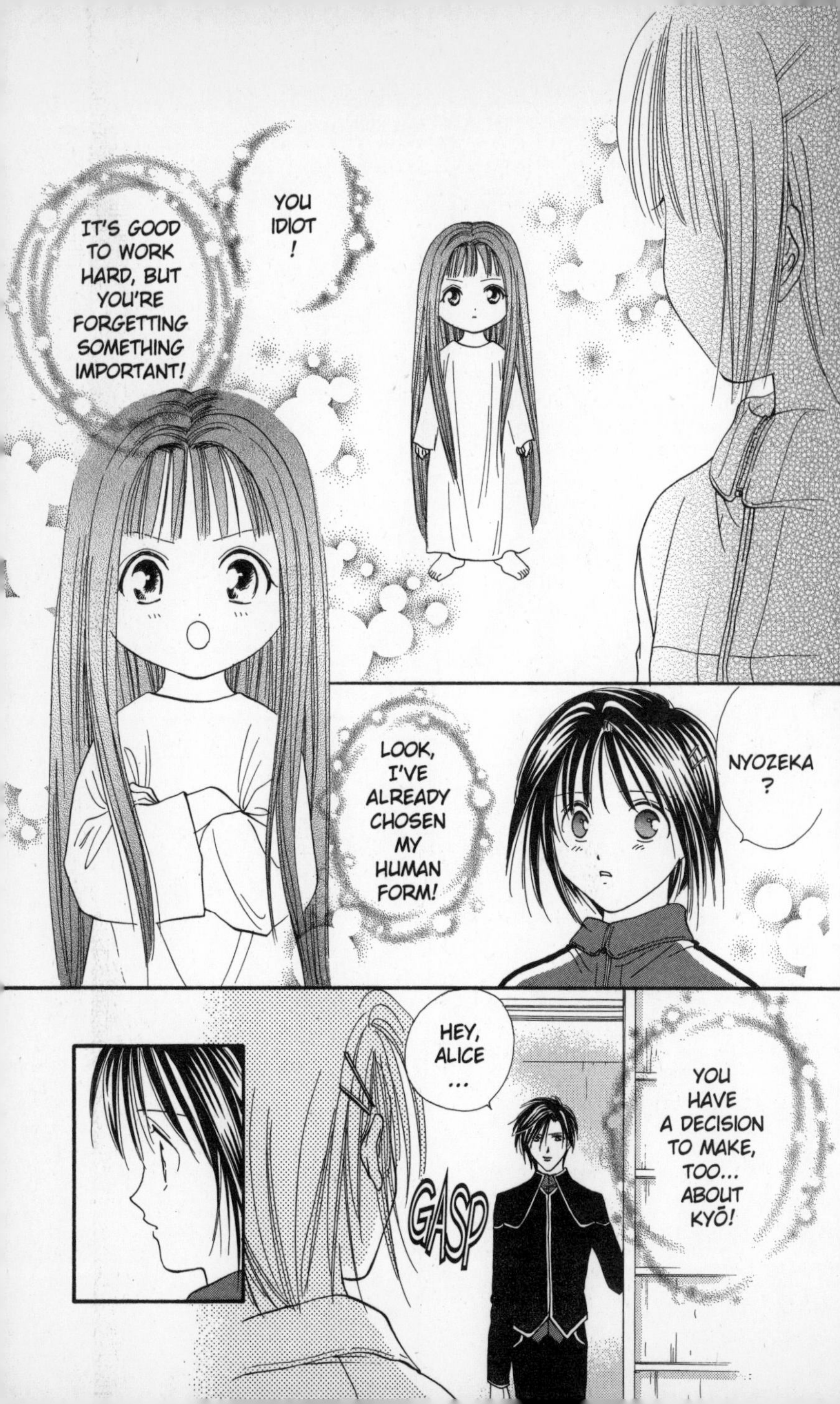
YOU IDIOT!
IT'S GOOD TO WORK HARD, BUT YOU'RE FORGETTING SOMETHING IMPORTANT!
NYOZEKA?
LOOK, I'VE ALREADY CHOSEN MY HUMAN FORM!
YOU HAVE A DECISION TO MAKE, TOO... ABOUT KYŌ!
HEY, ALICE...
GASP

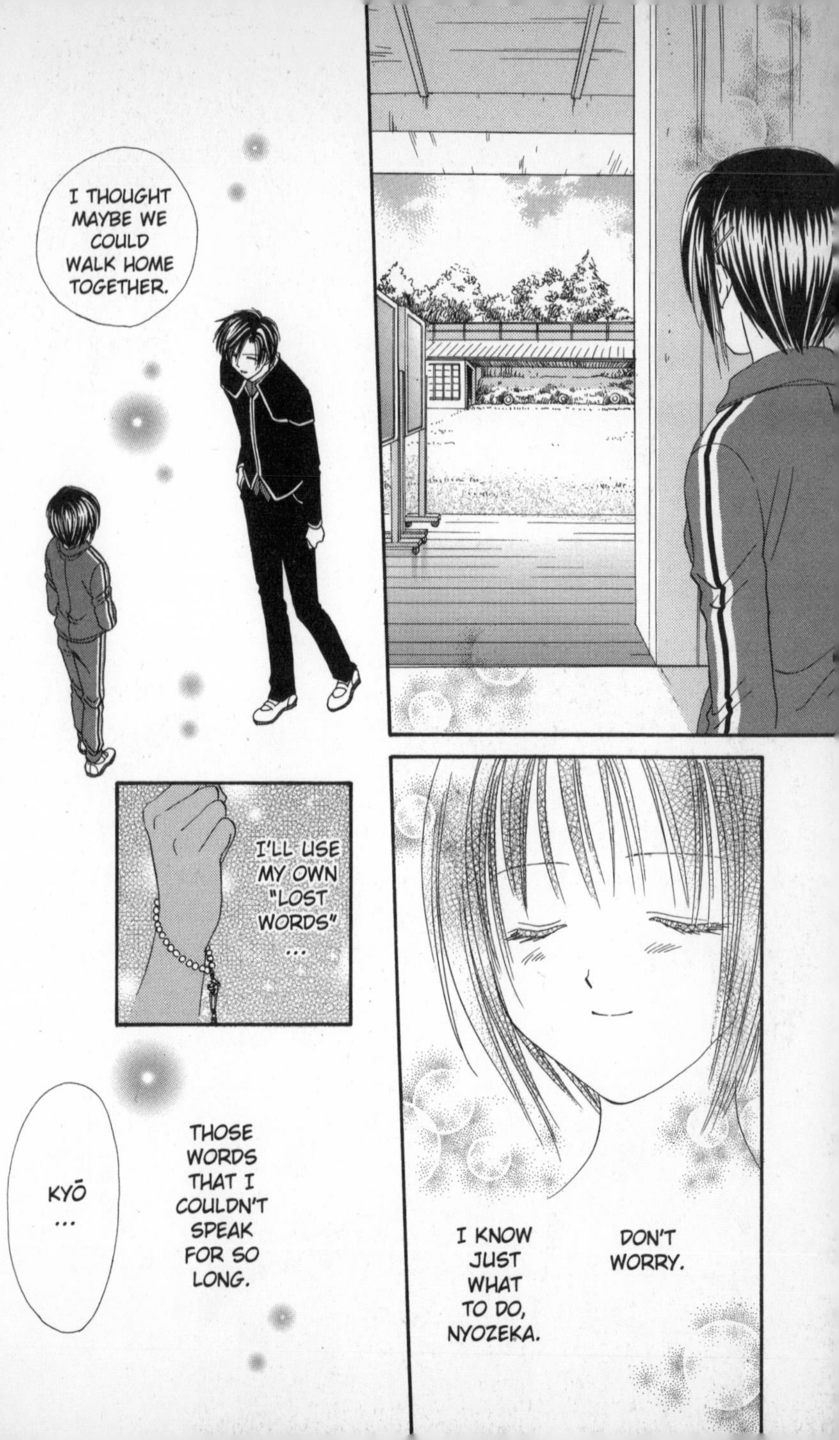
I THOUGHT MAYBE WE COULD WALK HOME TOGETHER.
DON'T WORRY.
I KNOW JUST WHAT TO DO, NYOZEKA.
I'LL USE MY OWN "LOST WORDS"...
THOSE WORDS THAT I COULDN'T SPEAK FOR SO LONG.
KYŌ...

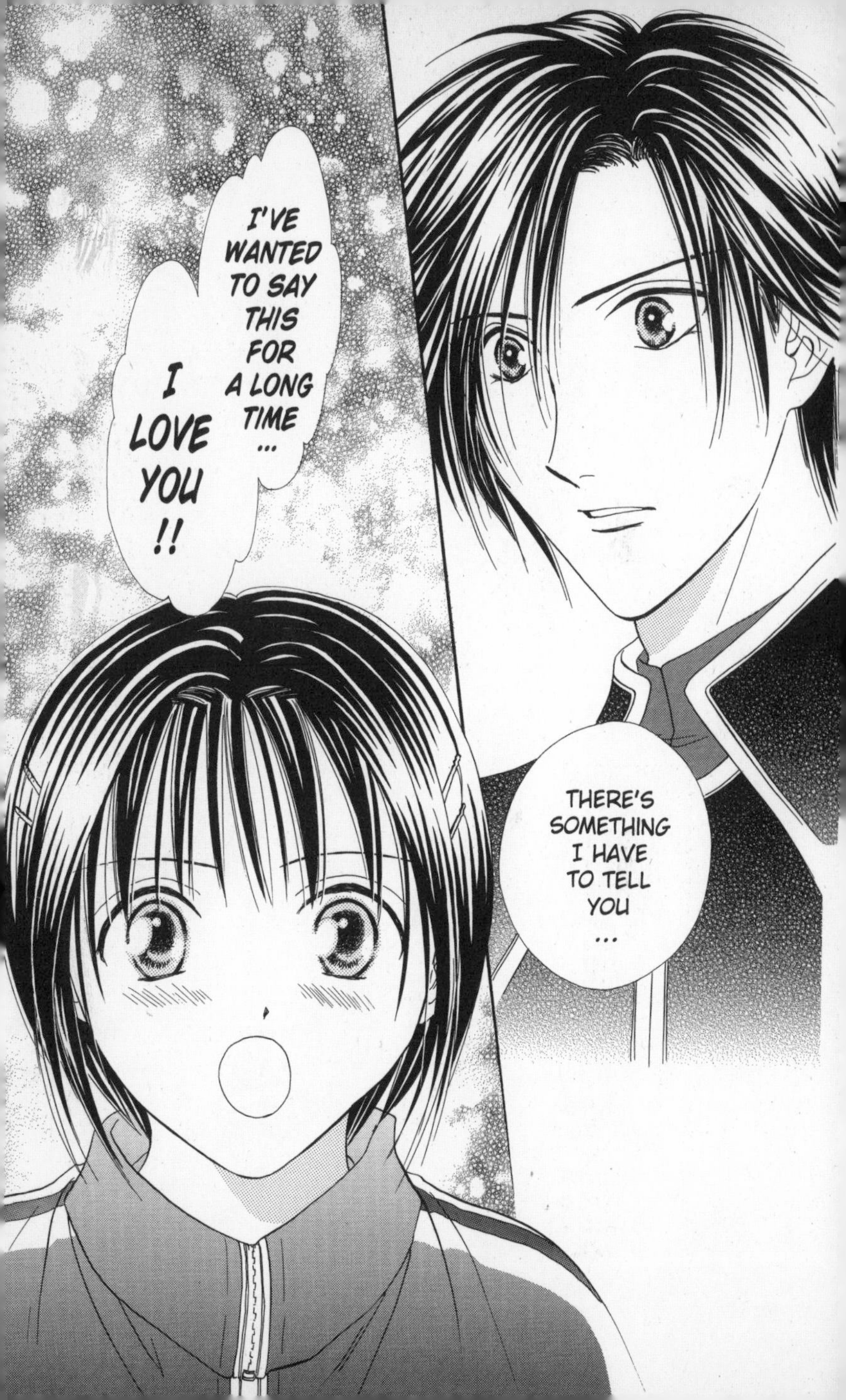
THERE'S SOMETHING I HAVE TO TELL YOU ...
I'VE WANTED TO SAY THIS FOR A LONG TIME ...
I LOVE YOU !!

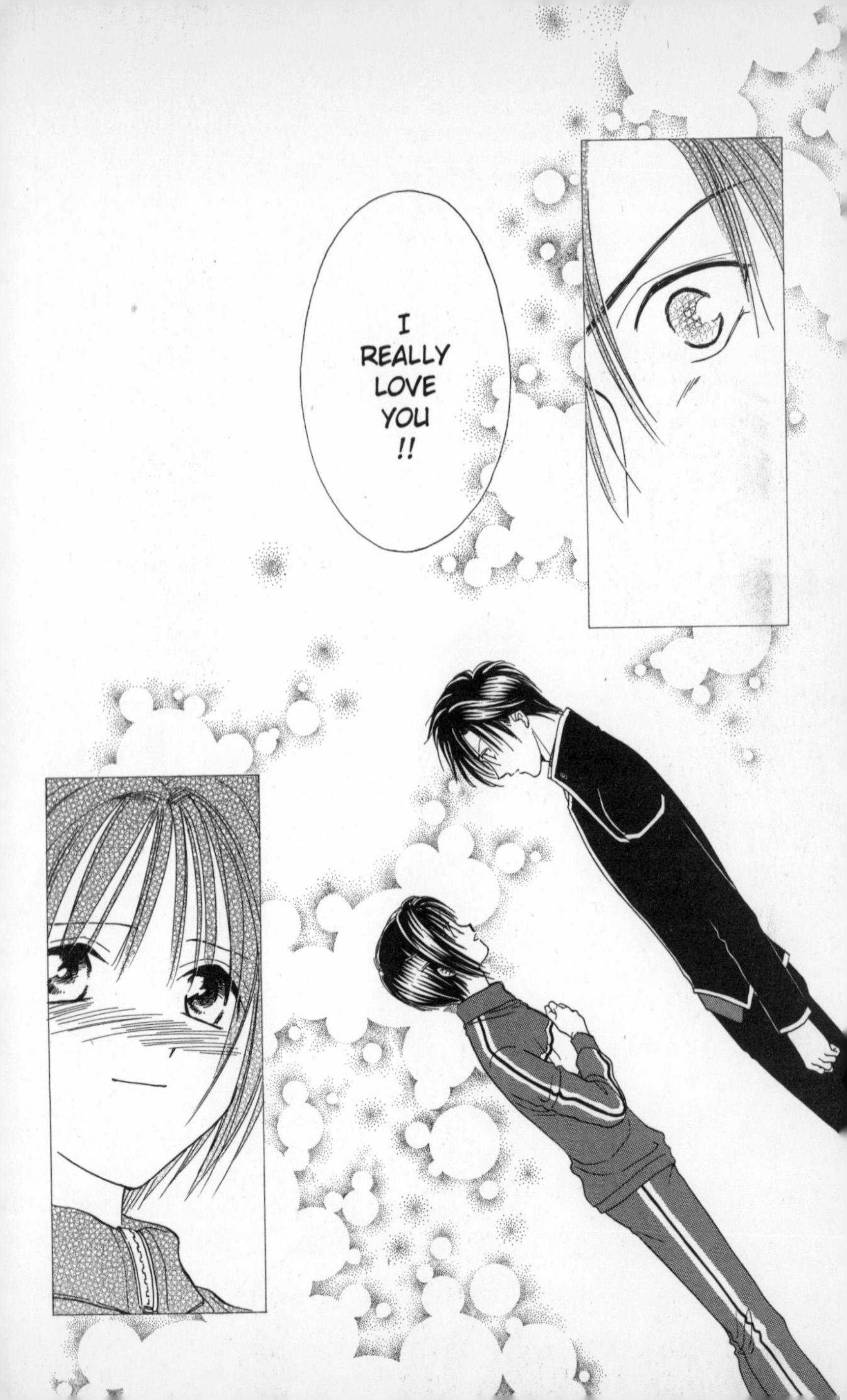
I REALLY LOVE YOU !!

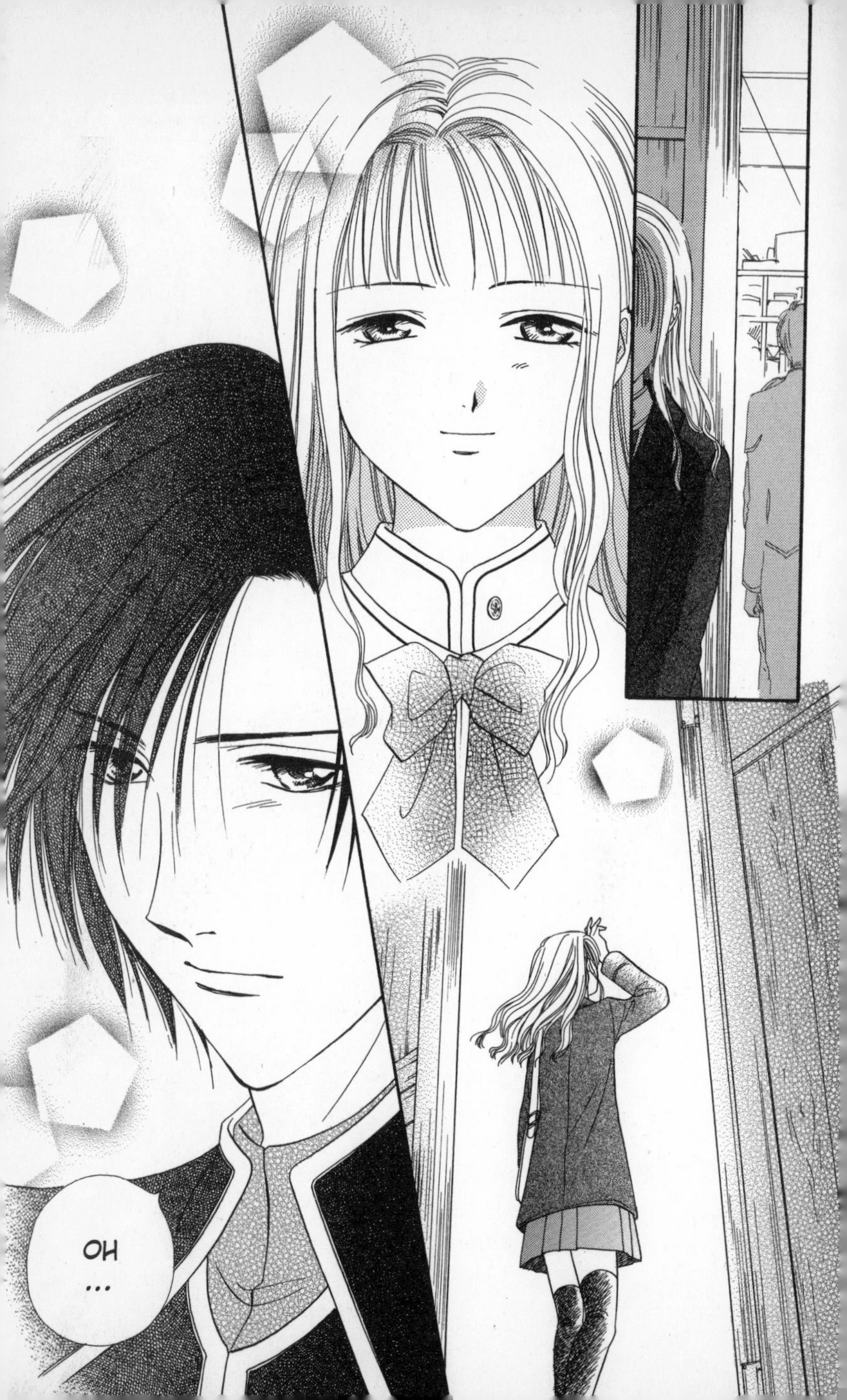
OH ...

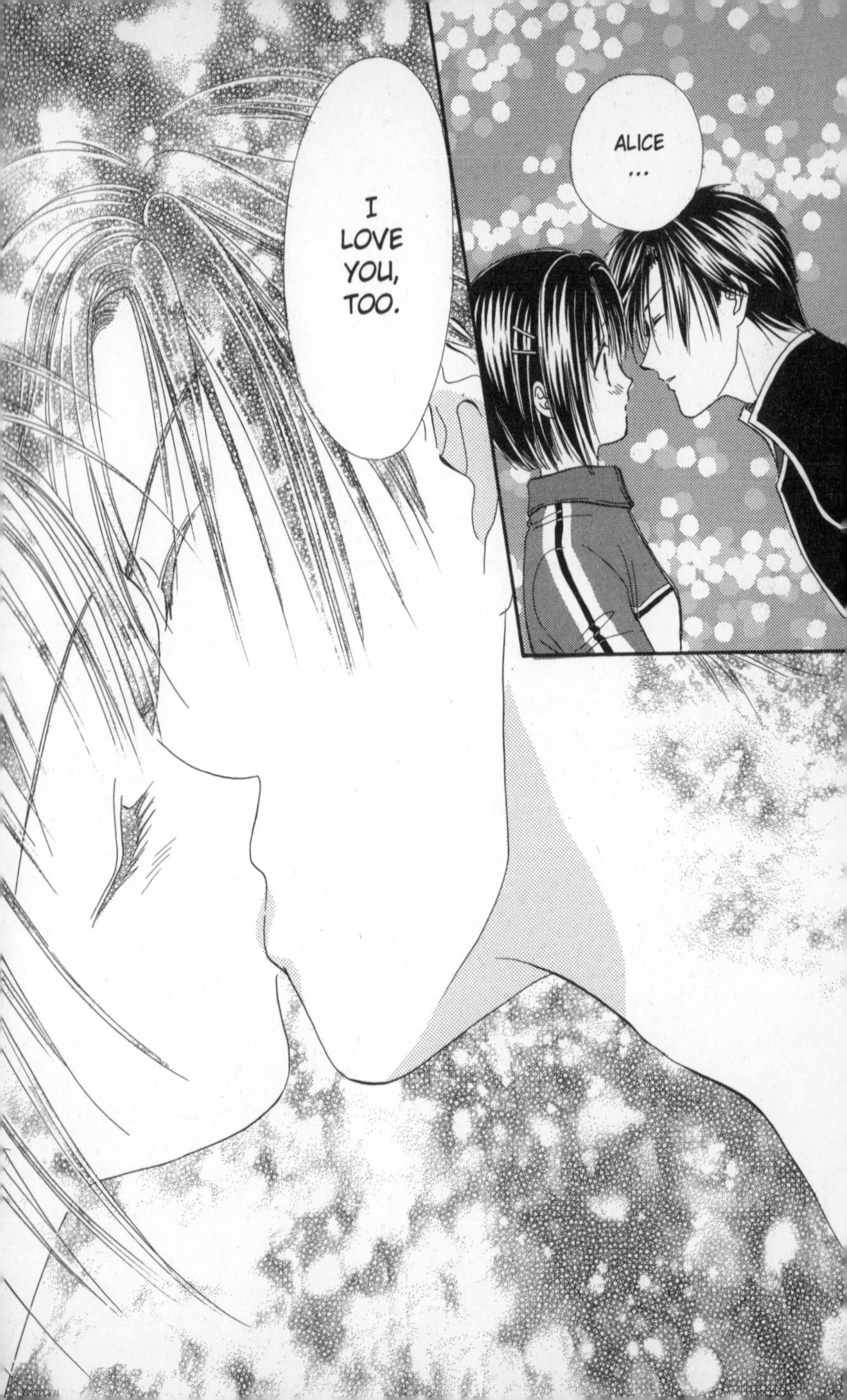
ALICE ...
I LOVE YOU, TOO.

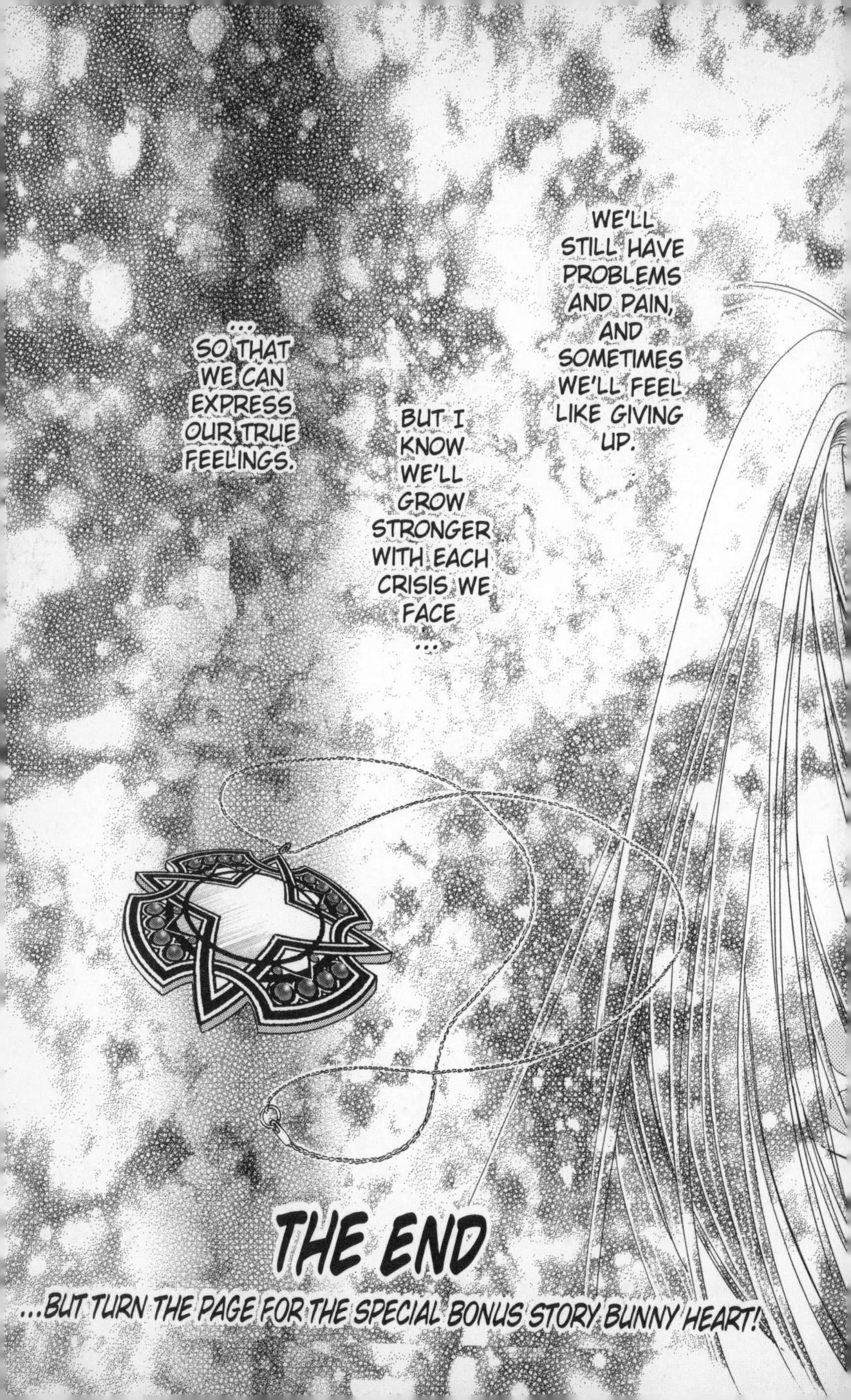
WE'LL STILL HAVE PROBLEMS AND PAIN, AND SOMETIMES WE'LL FEEL LIKE GIVING UP.
BUT I KNOW WE'LL GROW STRONGER WITH EACH CRISIS WE FACE...
...SO THAT WE CAN EXPRESS OUR TRUE FEELINGS.
THE END
...BUT TURN THE PAGE FOR THE SPECIAL BONUS STORY BUNNY HEART!

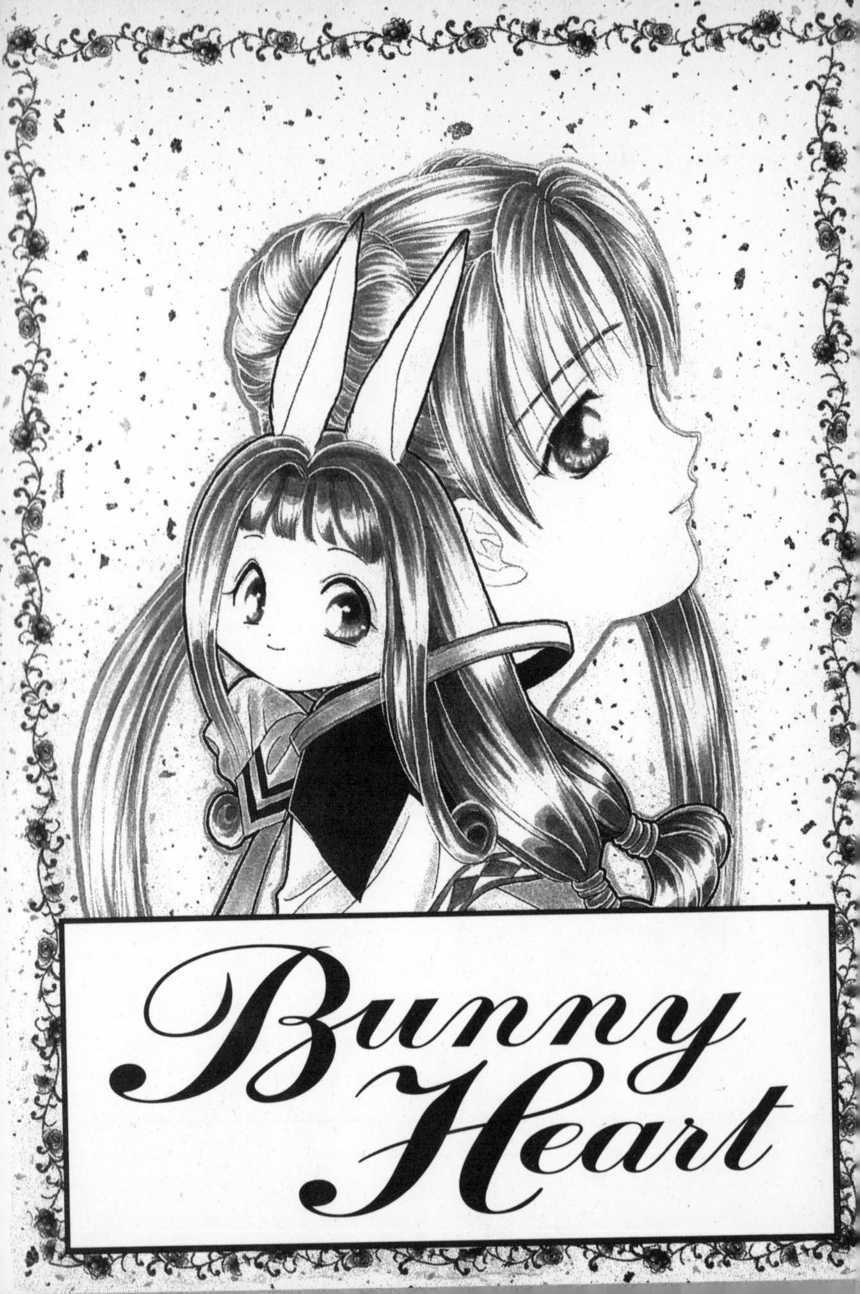
Bunny
Heart

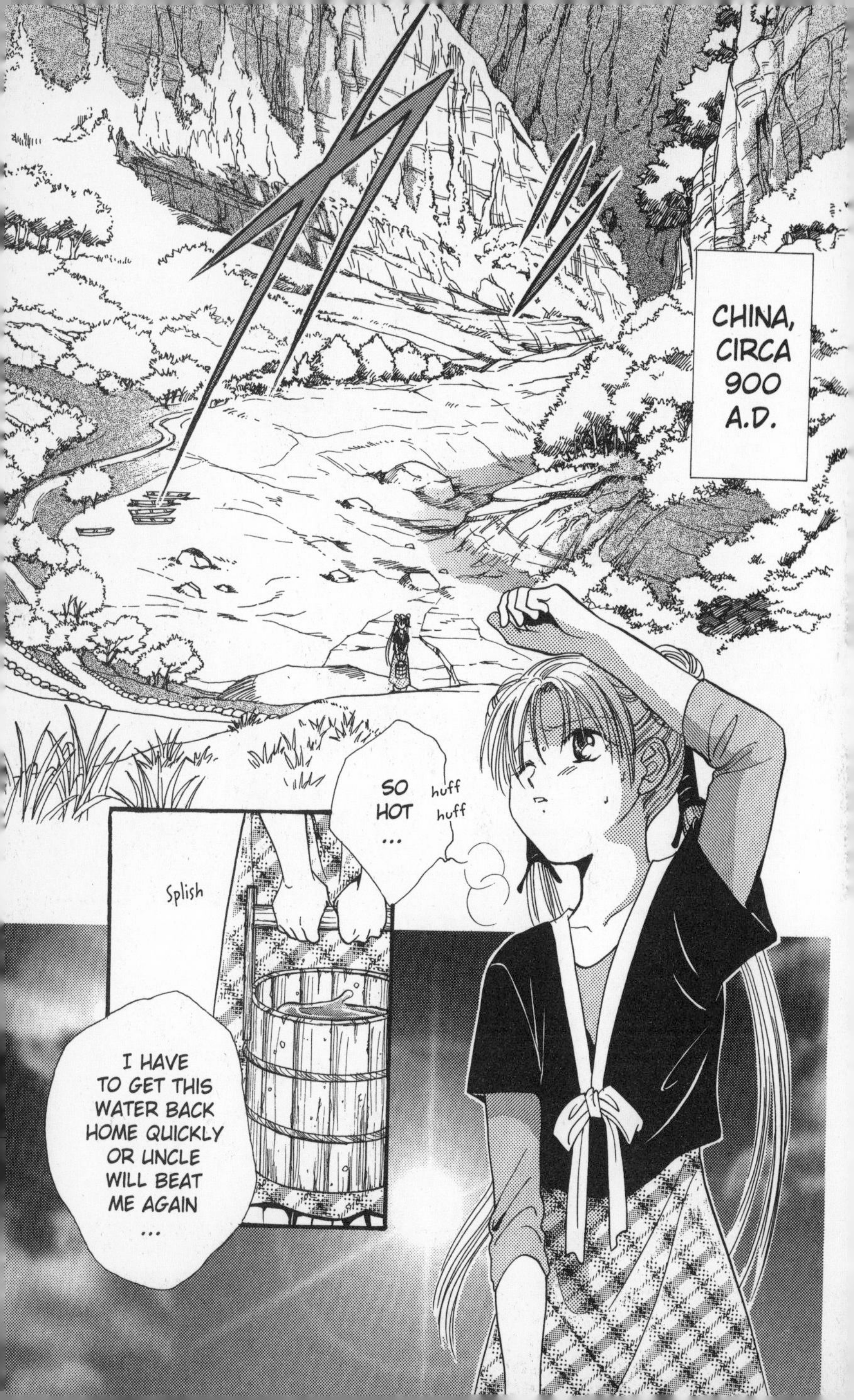
CHINA, CIRCA 900 A.D.
SO HOT ...
huff huff
Splish
I HAVE TO GET THIS WATER BACK HOME QUICKLY OR UNCLE WILL BEAT ME AGAIN ...

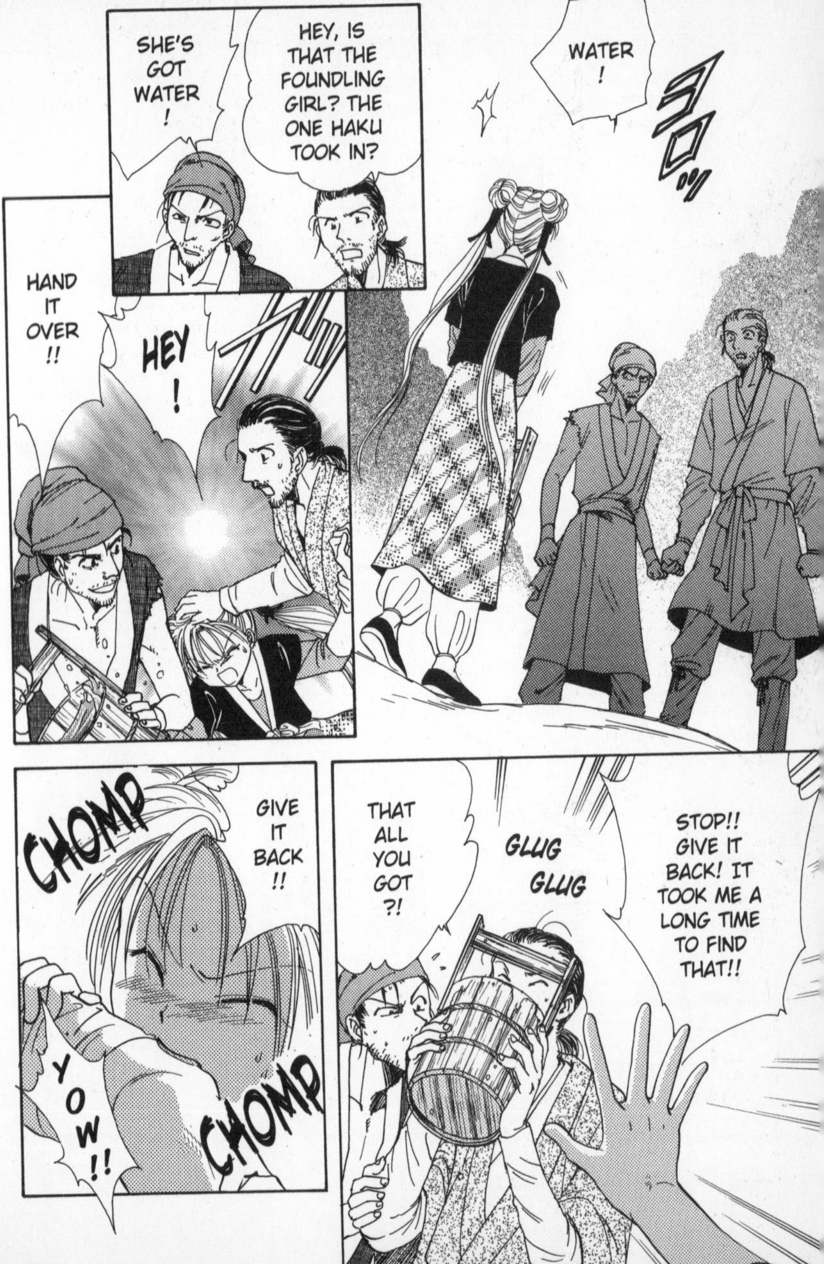
WATER!
ヨロッ
HEY, IS THAT THE FOUNDLING GIRL? THE ONE HAKU TOOK IN?
SHE'S GOT WATER!
HEY!
HAND IT OVER!!
STOP!! GIVE IT BACK! IT TOOK ME A LONG TIME TO FIND THAT!!
GLUG GLUG
THAT ALL YOU GOT?!
GIVE IT BACK!!
CHOMP
YOW!!
CHOMP

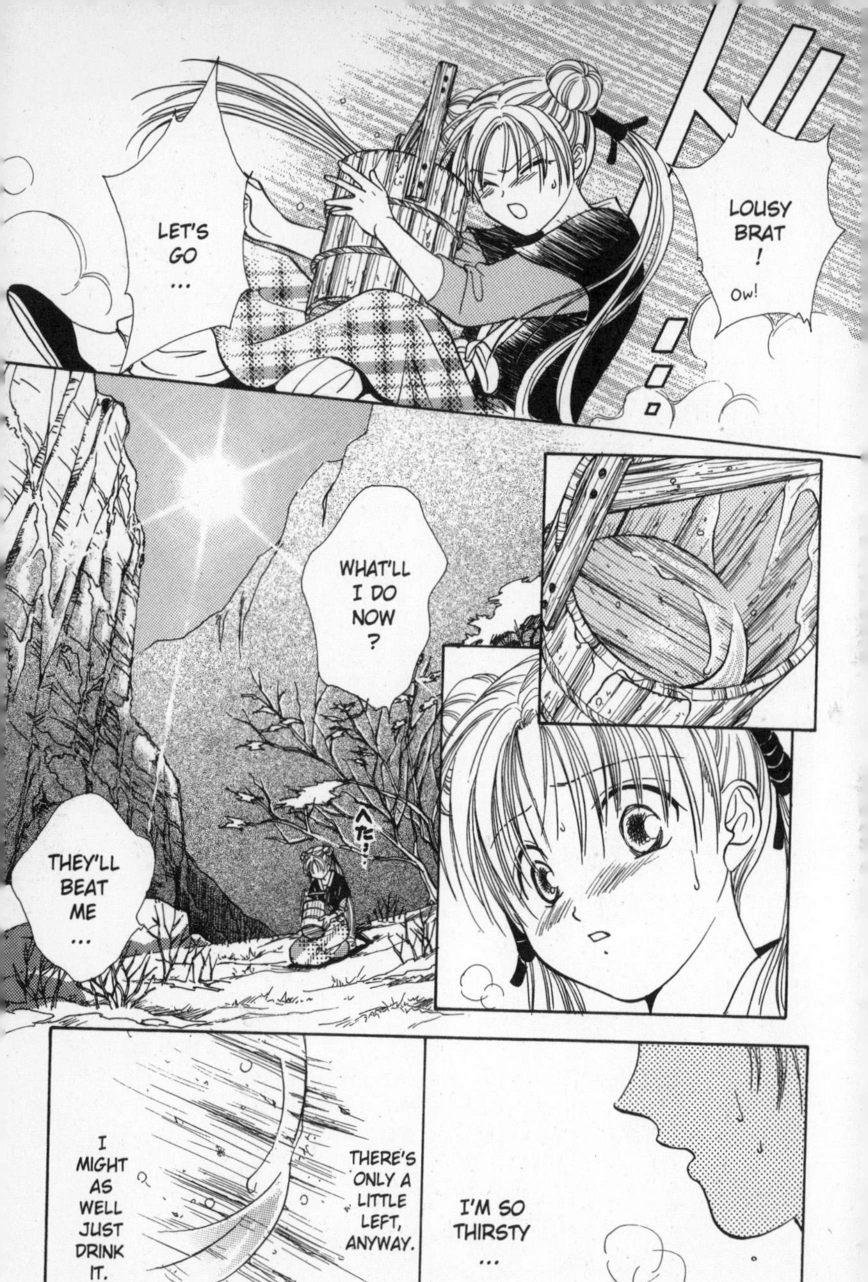

LOUSY BRAT!
Ow!
LET'S GO ...
WHAT'LL I DO NOW?
THEY'LL BEAT ME ...
I'M SO THIRSTY ...
THERE'S ONLY A LITTLE LEFT, ANYWAY.
I MIGHT AS WELL JUST DRINK IT.

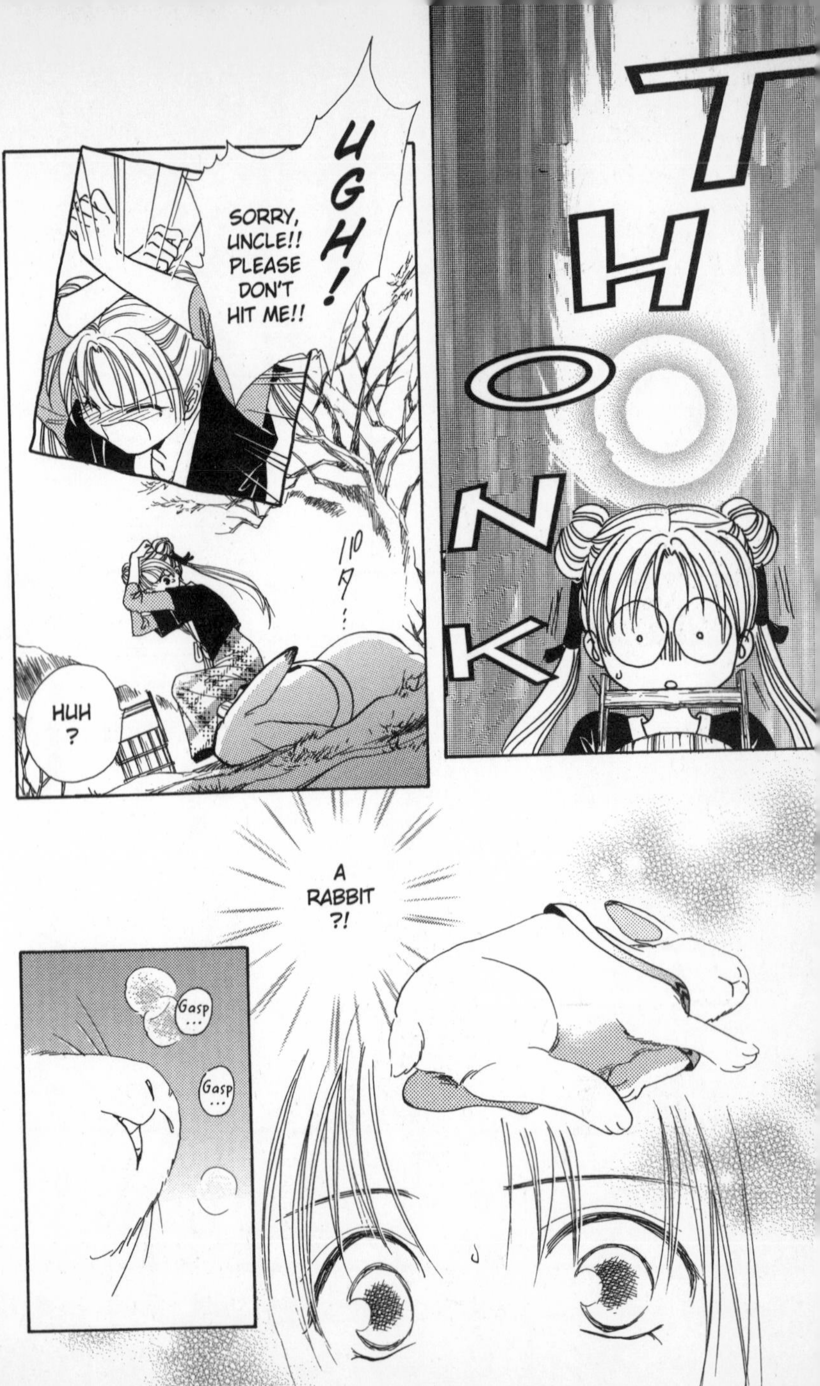
THONK
UGH!
SORRY, UNCLE!! PLEASE DON'T HIT ME!!
HUH?
A RABBIT?!
Gasp...
Gasp...

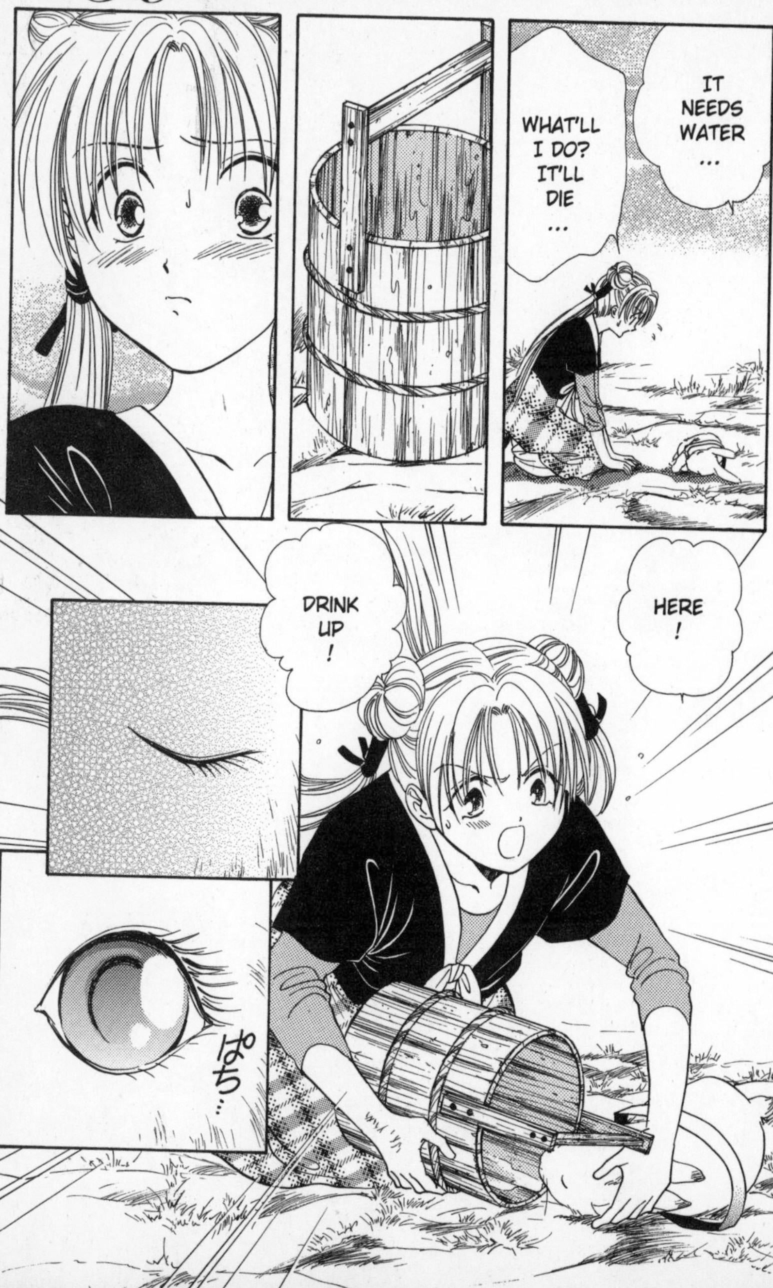
IT NEEDS WATER ...
WHAT'LL I DO? IT'LL DIE ...
HERE!
DRINK UP!
ぱち…

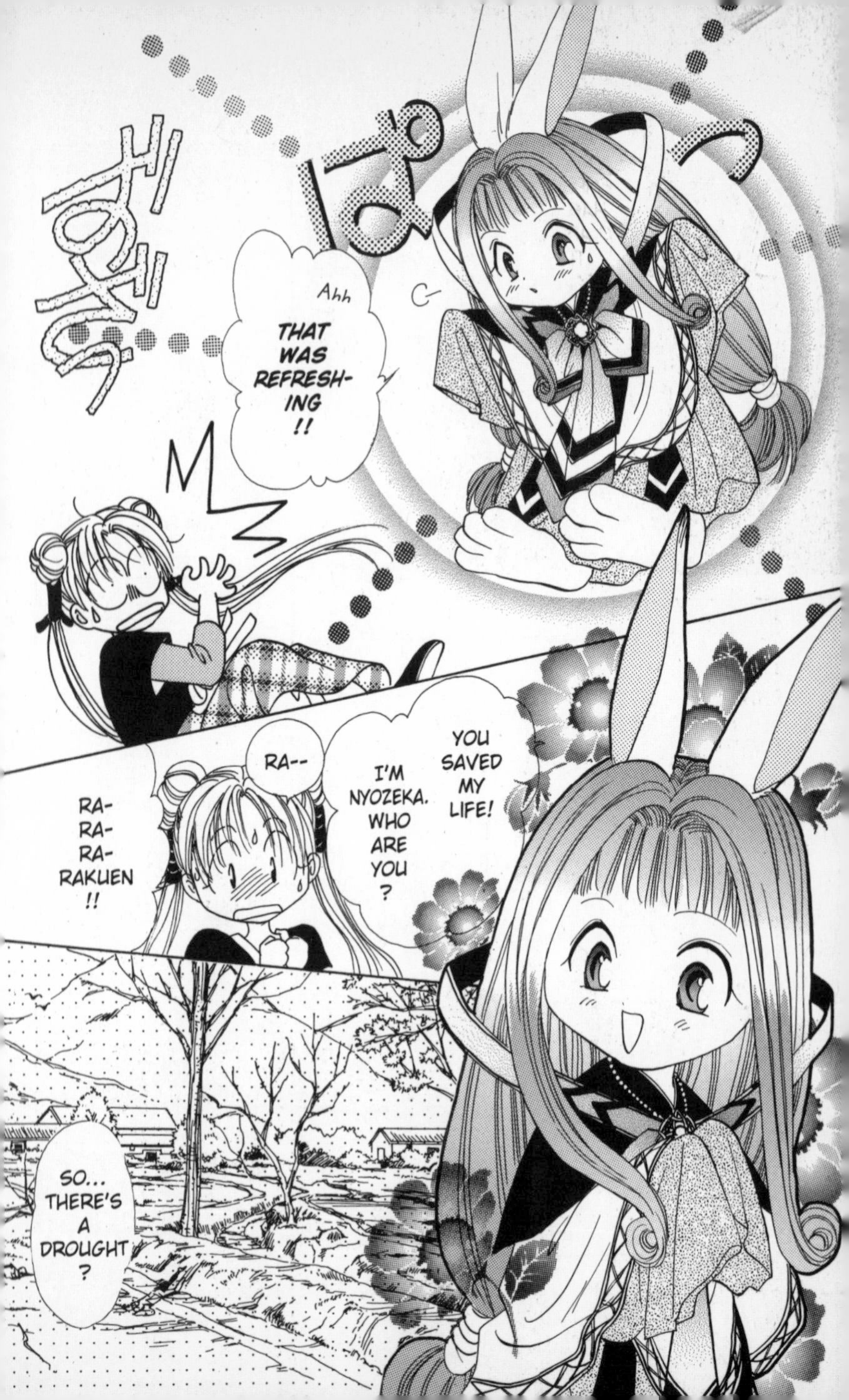
ぱっ
すぽっ
Ahh
THAT WAS REFRESHING!!
YOU SAVED MY LIFE!
I'M NYOZEKA. WHO ARE YOU?
RA--
RA-RA-RA-RAKUEN!!
SO... THERE'S A DROUGHT?

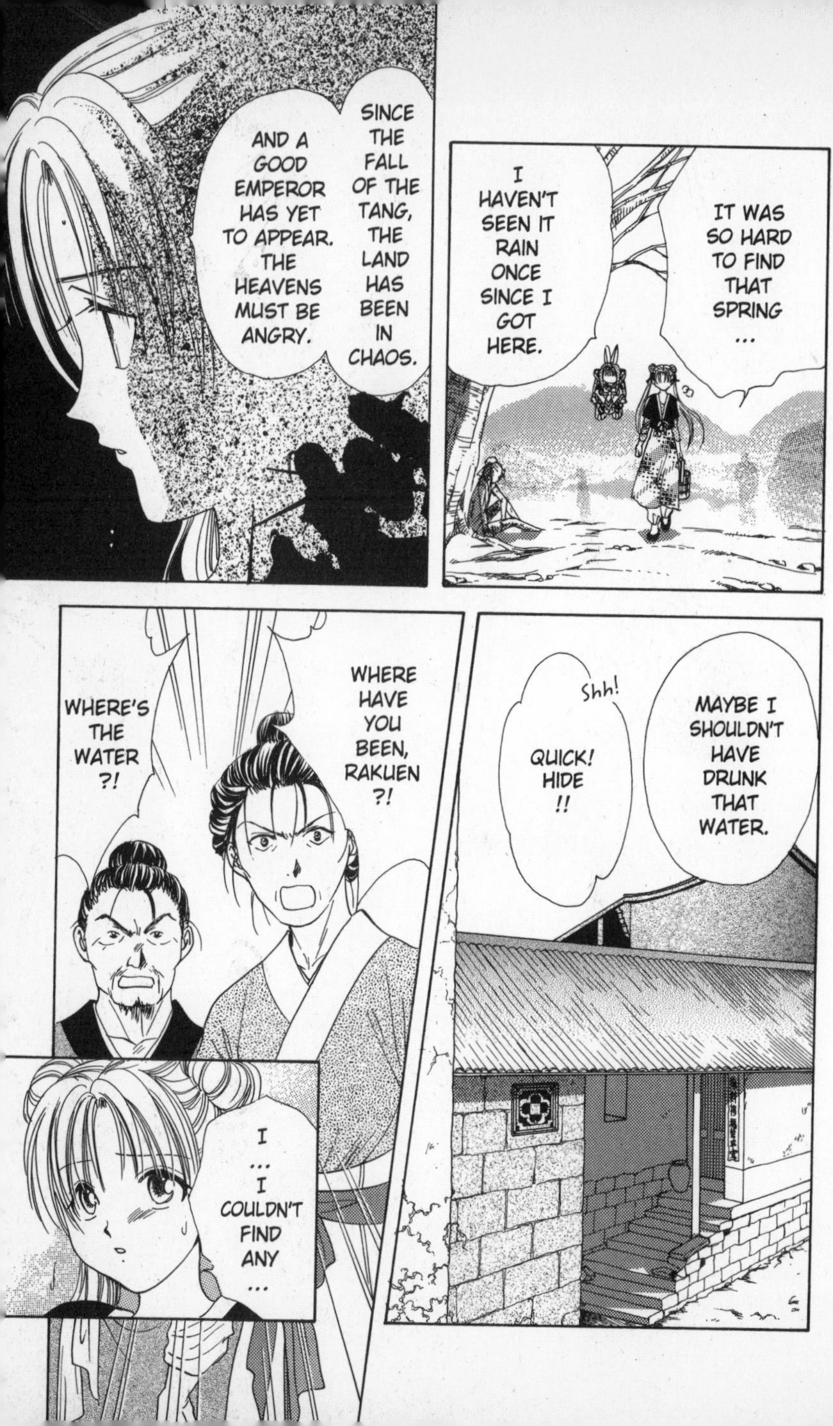
IT WAS SO HARD TO FIND THAT SPRING ...
I HAVEN'T SEEN IT RAIN ONCE SINCE I GOT HERE.
SINCE THE FALL OF THE TANG, THE LAND HAS BEEN IN CHAOS.
AND A GOOD EMPEROR HAS YET TO APPEAR. THE HEAVENS MUST BE ANGRY.
MAYBE I SHOULDN'T HAVE DRUNK THAT WATER.
Shh!
QUICK! HIDE !!
WHERE HAVE YOU BEEN, RAKUEN ?!
WHERE'S THE WATER ?!
I ... I COULDN'T FIND ANY ...

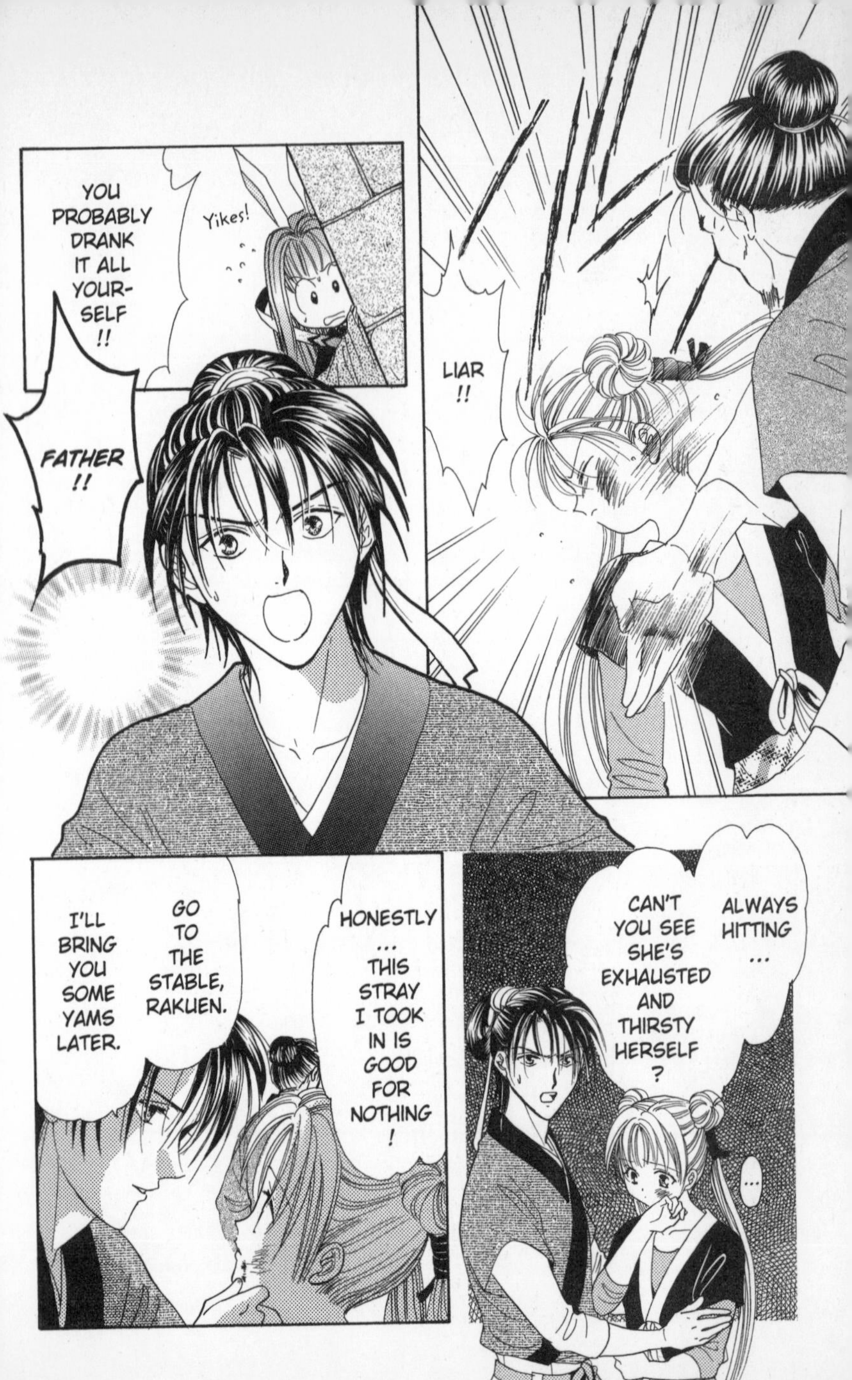
LIAR !!
Yikes!
YOU PROBABLY DRANK IT ALL YOUR-SELF !!
FATHER !!
ALWAYS HITTING ...
CAN'T YOU SEE SHE'S EXHAUSTED AND THIRSTY HERSELF ?
...
HONESTLY ... THIS STRAY I TOOK IN IS GOOD FOR NOTHING !
GO TO THE STABLE, RAKUEN.
I'LL BRING YOU SOME YAMS LATER.

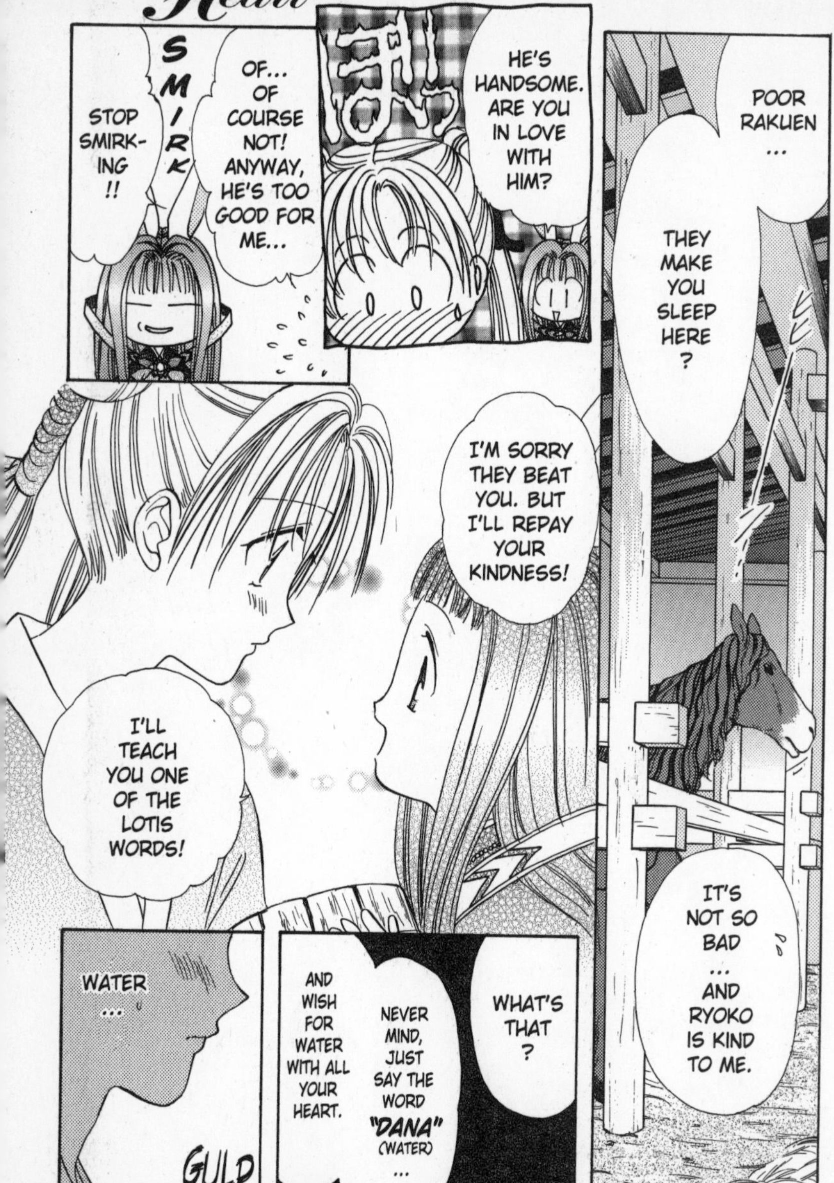
POOR RAKUEN ...
THEY MAKE YOU SLEEP HERE ?
IT'S NOT SO BAD ... AND RYOKO IS KIND TO ME.
HE'S HANDSOME. ARE YOU IN LOVE WITH HIM?
OF... OF COURSE NOT! ANYWAY, HE'S TOO GOOD FOR ME...
SMIRK
STOP SMIRK-ING !!
I'M SORRY THEY BEAT YOU. BUT I'LL REPAY YOUR KINDNESS!
I'LL TEACH YOU ONE OF THE LOTIS WORDS!
WHAT'S THAT ?
NEVER MIND, JUST SAY THE WORD "DANA" (WATER) ...
AND WISH FOR WATER WITH ALL YOUR HEART.
WATER ...
GULP

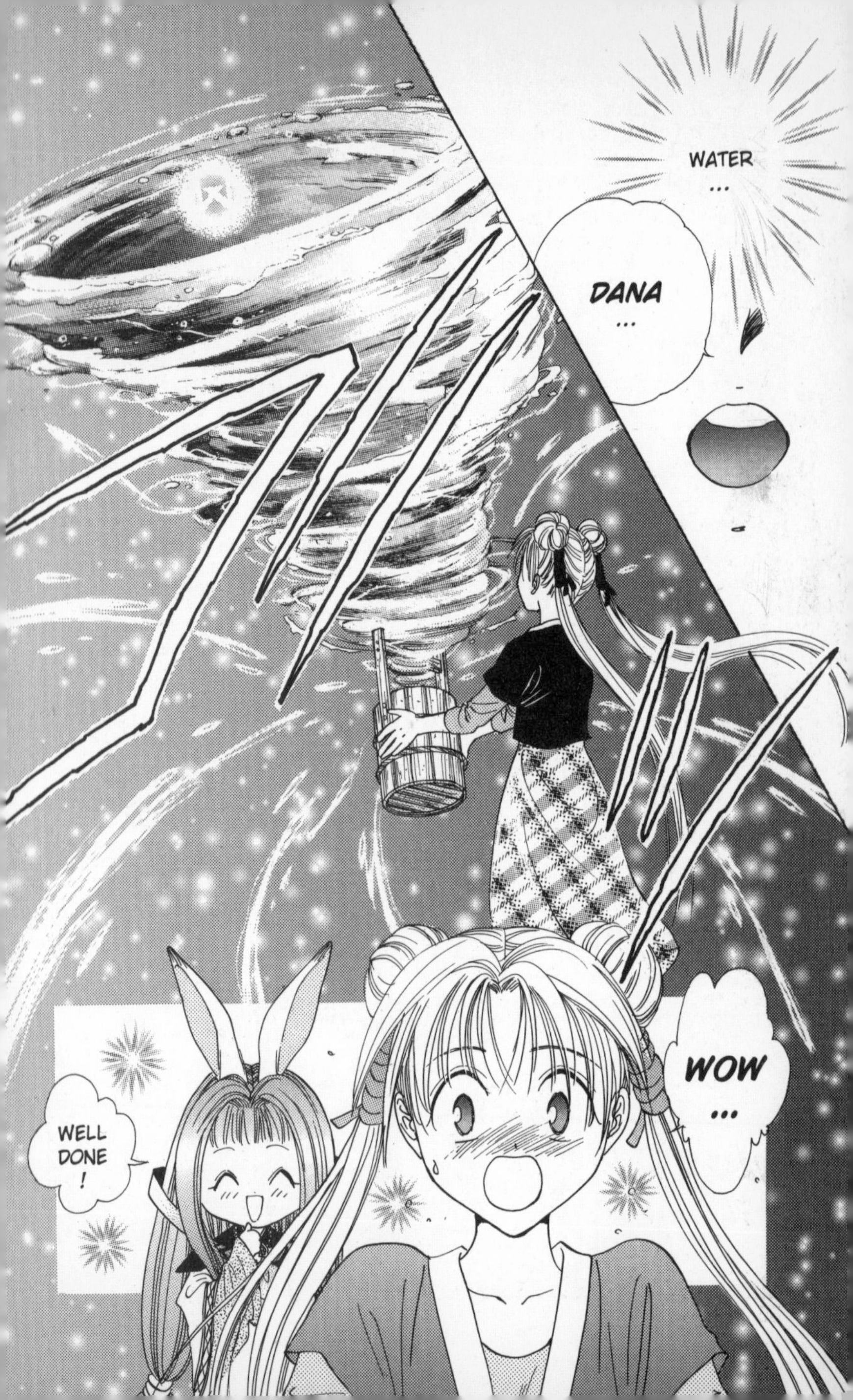
WATER ...
DANA ...
WOW ...
WELL DONE !

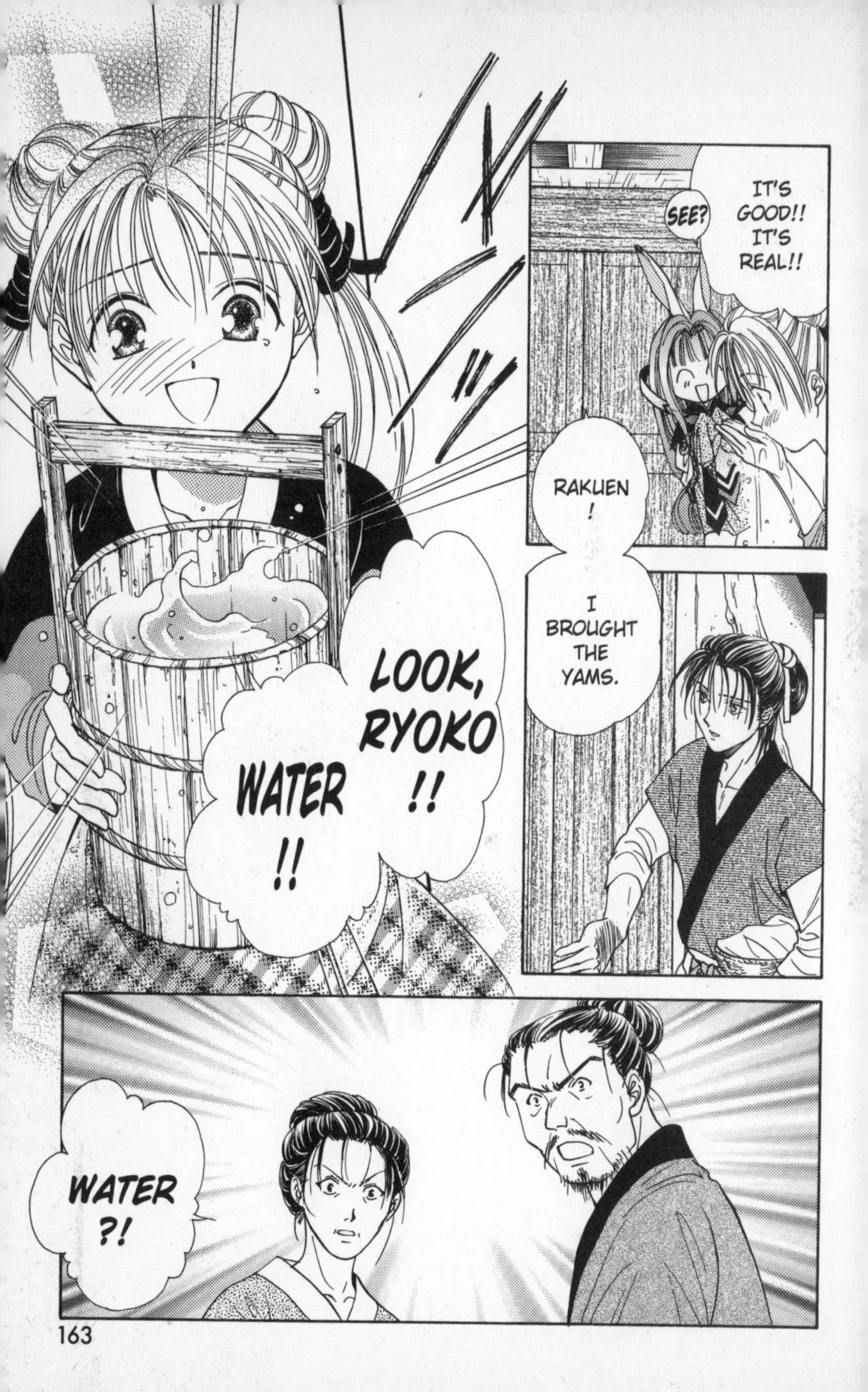

IT'S GOOD!! IT'S REAL!!
SEE?
RAKUEN!
I BROUGHT THE YAMS.
LOOK, RYOKO!!
WATER!!
WATER?!

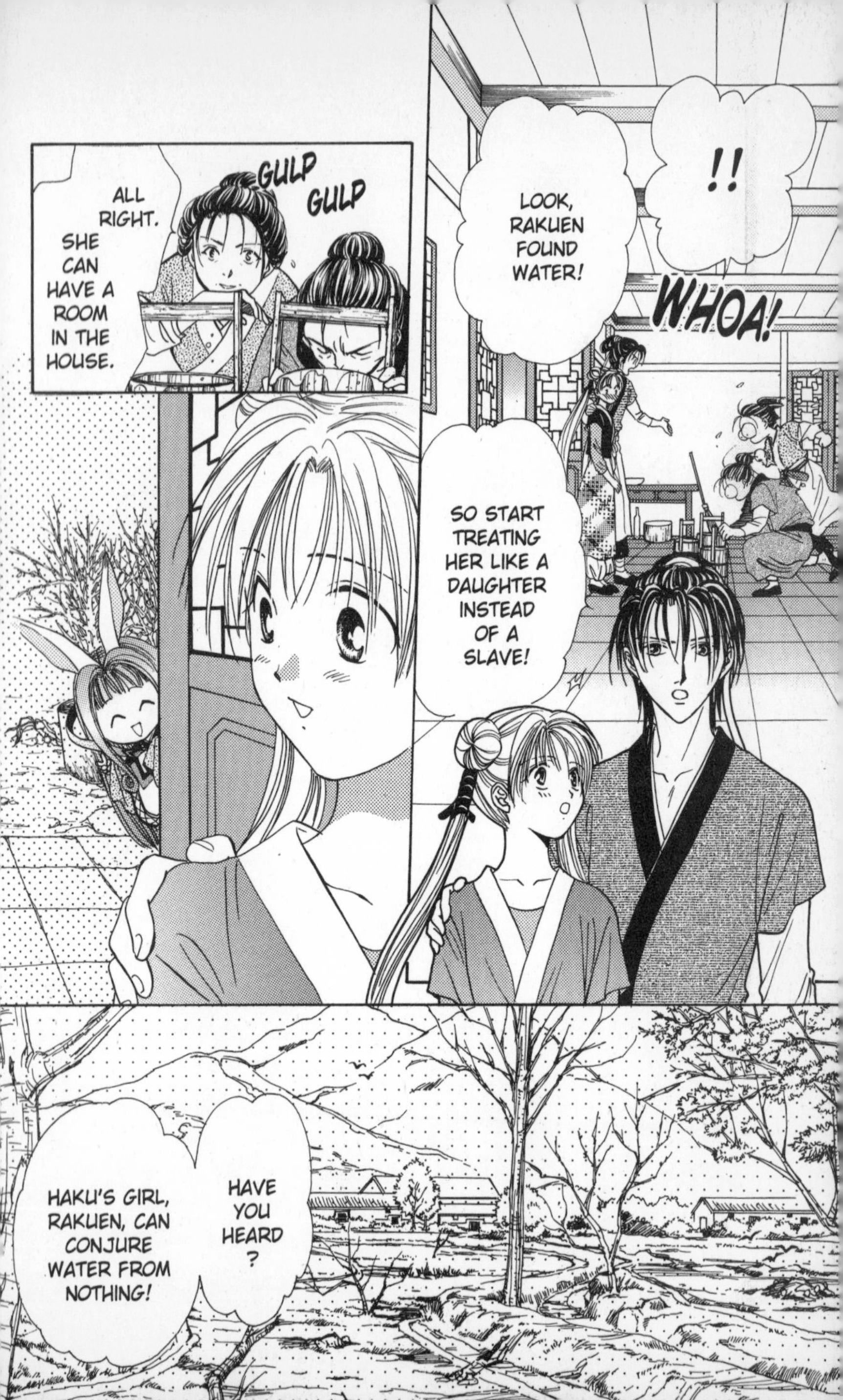
!!
LOOK, RAKUEN FOUND WATER!
WHOA!
SO START TREATING HER LIKE A DAUGHTER INSTEAD OF A SLAVE!
GULP GULP
ALL RIGHT. SHE CAN HAVE A ROOM IN THE HOUSE.
HAVE YOU HEARD?
HAKU'S GIRL, RAKUEN, CAN CONJURE WATER FROM NOTHING!

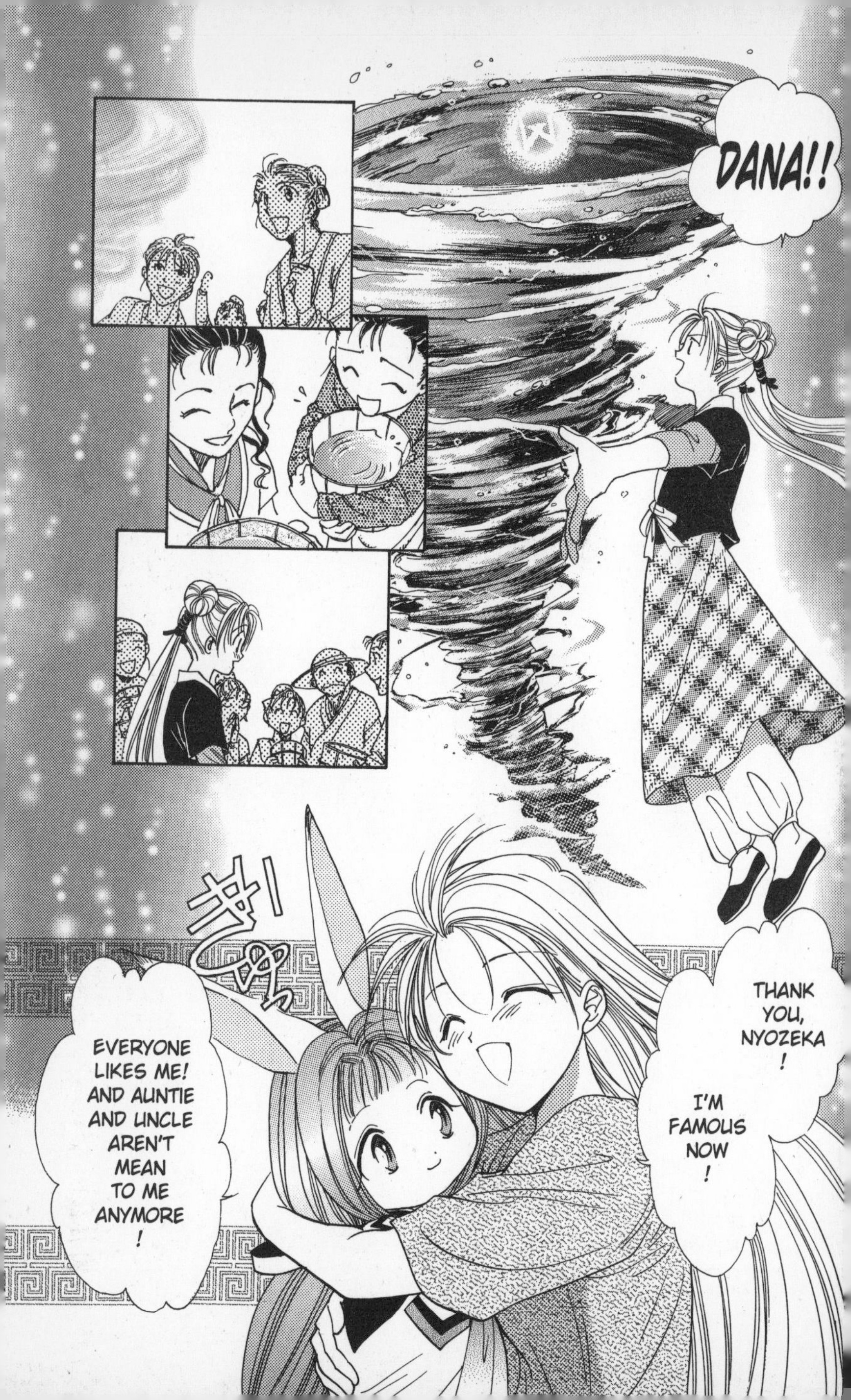
DANA!!
ぎゅー
THANK YOU, NYOZEKA!
I'M FAMOUS NOW!
EVERYONE LIKES ME! AND AUNTIE AND UNCLE AREN'T MEAN TO ME ANYMORE!

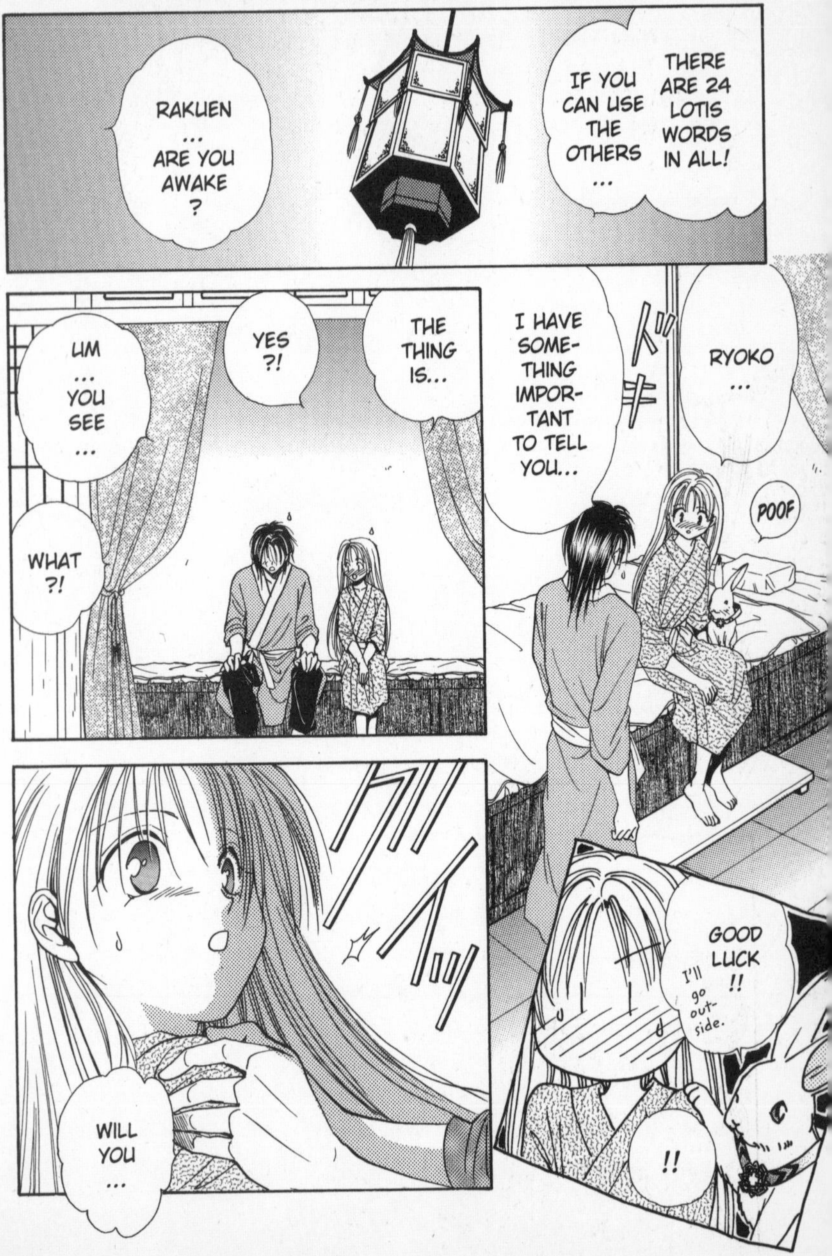
THERE ARE 24 LOTIS WORDS IN ALL!
IF YOU CAN USE THE OTHERS ...
RAKUEN ... ARE YOU AWAKE ?
RYOKO ...
I HAVE SOME-THING IMPOR-TANT TO TELL YOU...
POOF
THE THING IS...
YES ?!
UM ... YOU SEE ...
WHAT ?!
GOOD LUCK !!
I'll go out-side.
!!
WILL YOU ...

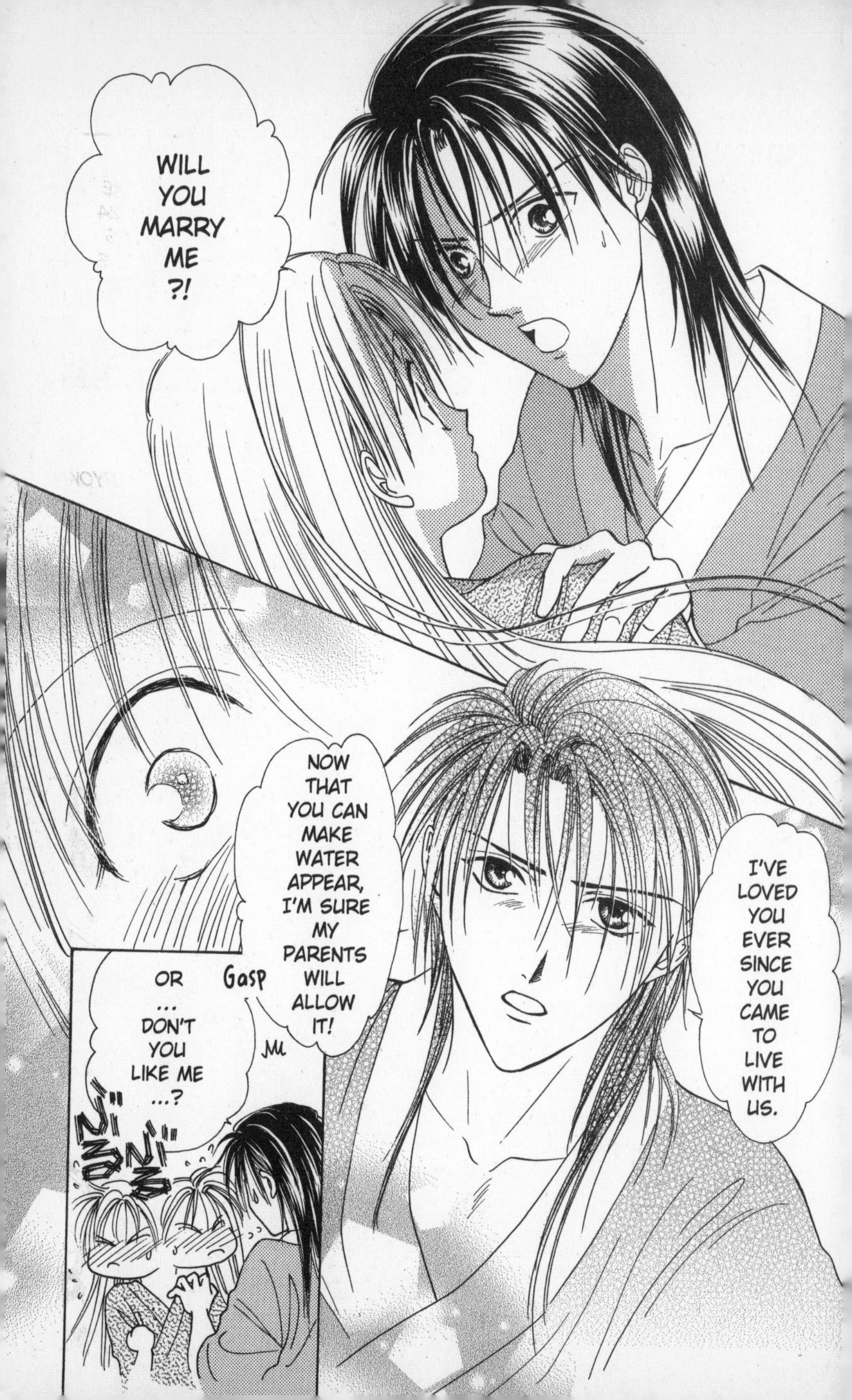
WILL YOU MARRY ME ?!
I'VE LOVED YOU EVER SINCE YOU CAME TO LIVE WITH US.
NOW THAT YOU CAN MAKE WATER APPEAR, I'M SURE MY PARENTS WILL ALLOW IT!
Gasp
OR ... DON'T YOU LIKE ME ...?

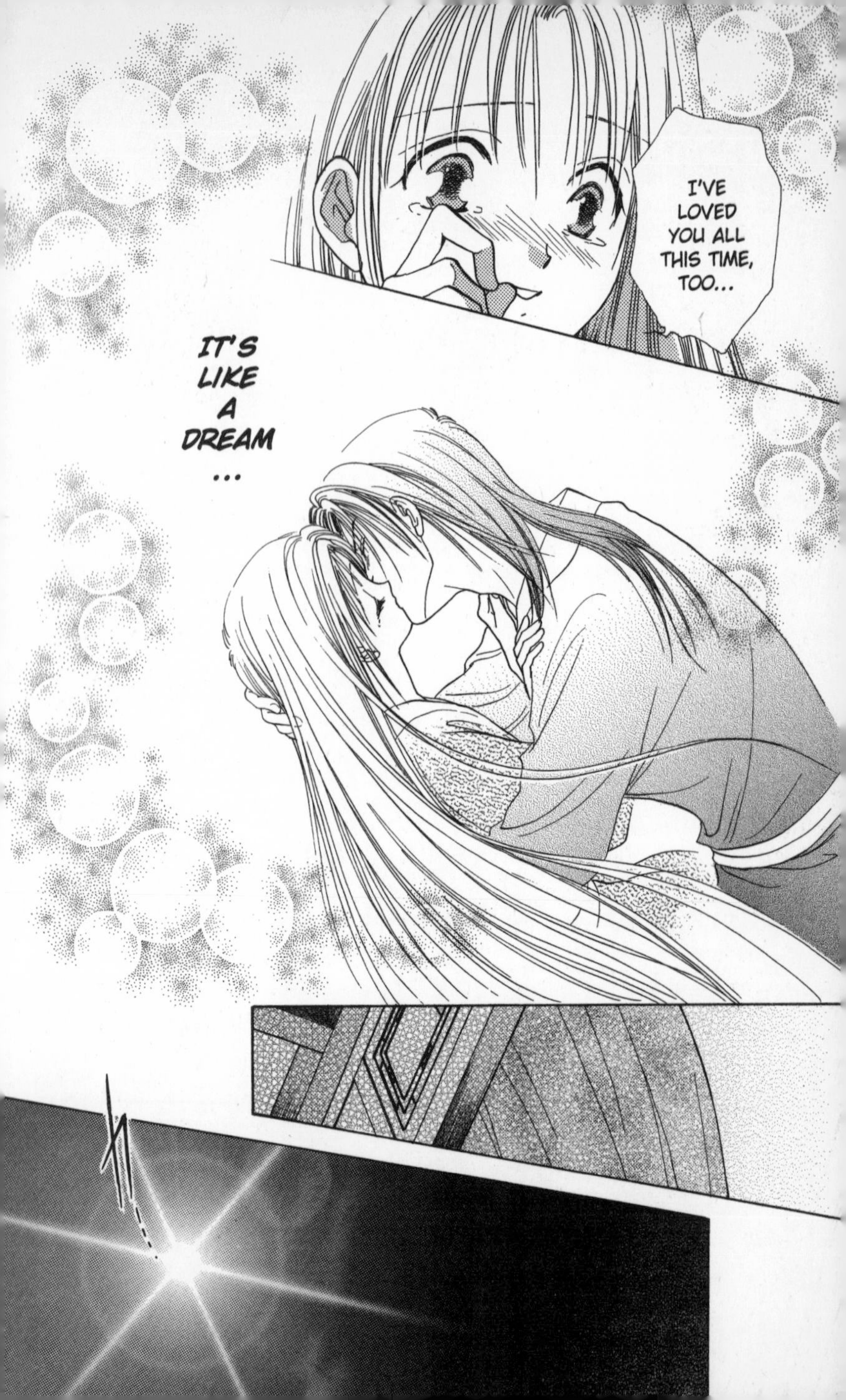
I'VE LOVED YOU ALL THIS TIME, TOO...
IT'S LIKE A DREAM...

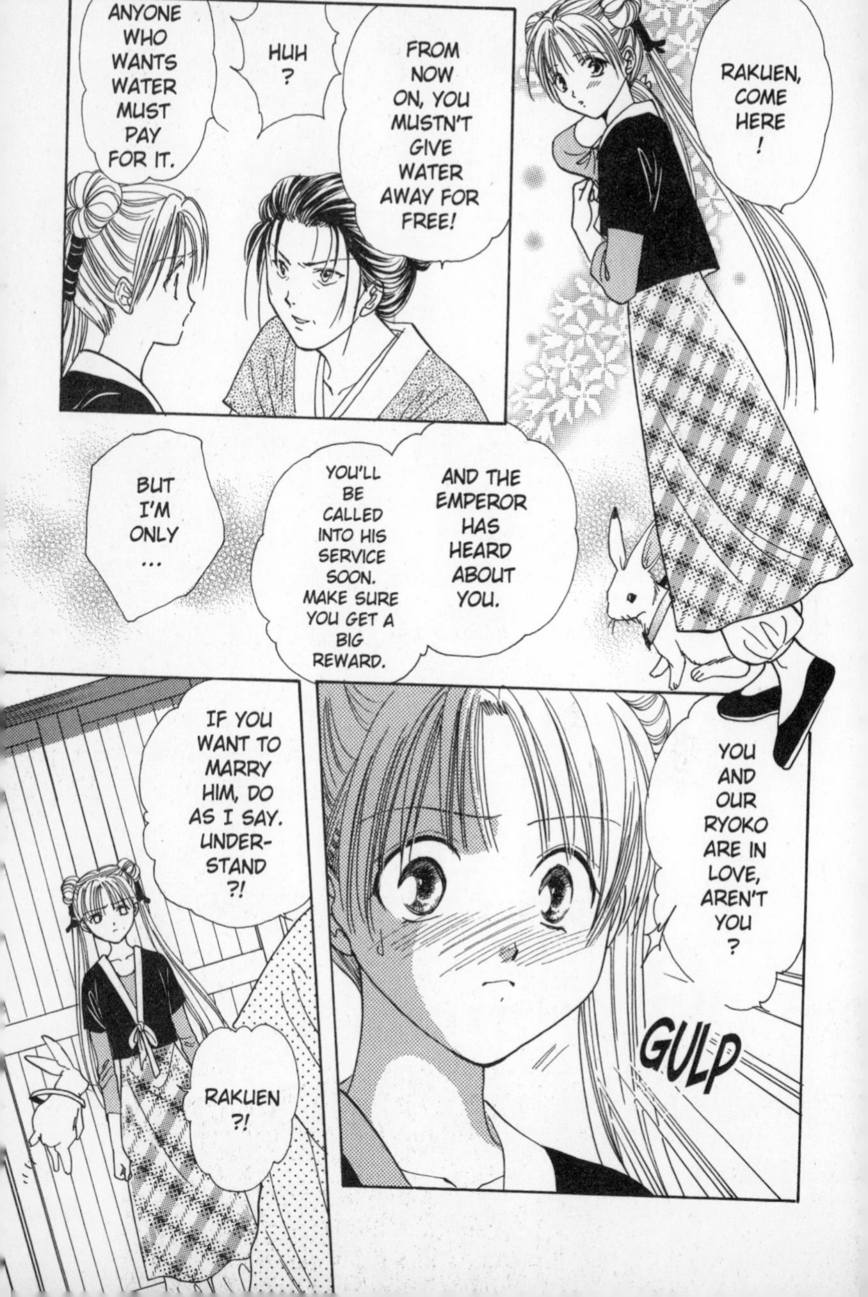
RAKUEN, COME HERE!
FROM NOW ON, YOU MUSTN'T GIVE WATER AWAY FOR FREE!
HUH?
ANYONE WHO WANTS WATER MUST PAY FOR IT.
AND THE EMPEROR HAS HEARD ABOUT YOU.
YOU'LL BE CALLED INTO HIS SERVICE SOON. MAKE SURE YOU GET A BIG REWARD.
BUT I'M ONLY ...
YOU AND OUR RYOKO ARE IN LOVE, AREN'T YOU?
GULP
IF YOU WANT TO MARRY HIM, DO AS I SAY. UNDER-STAND?!
RAKUEN?!

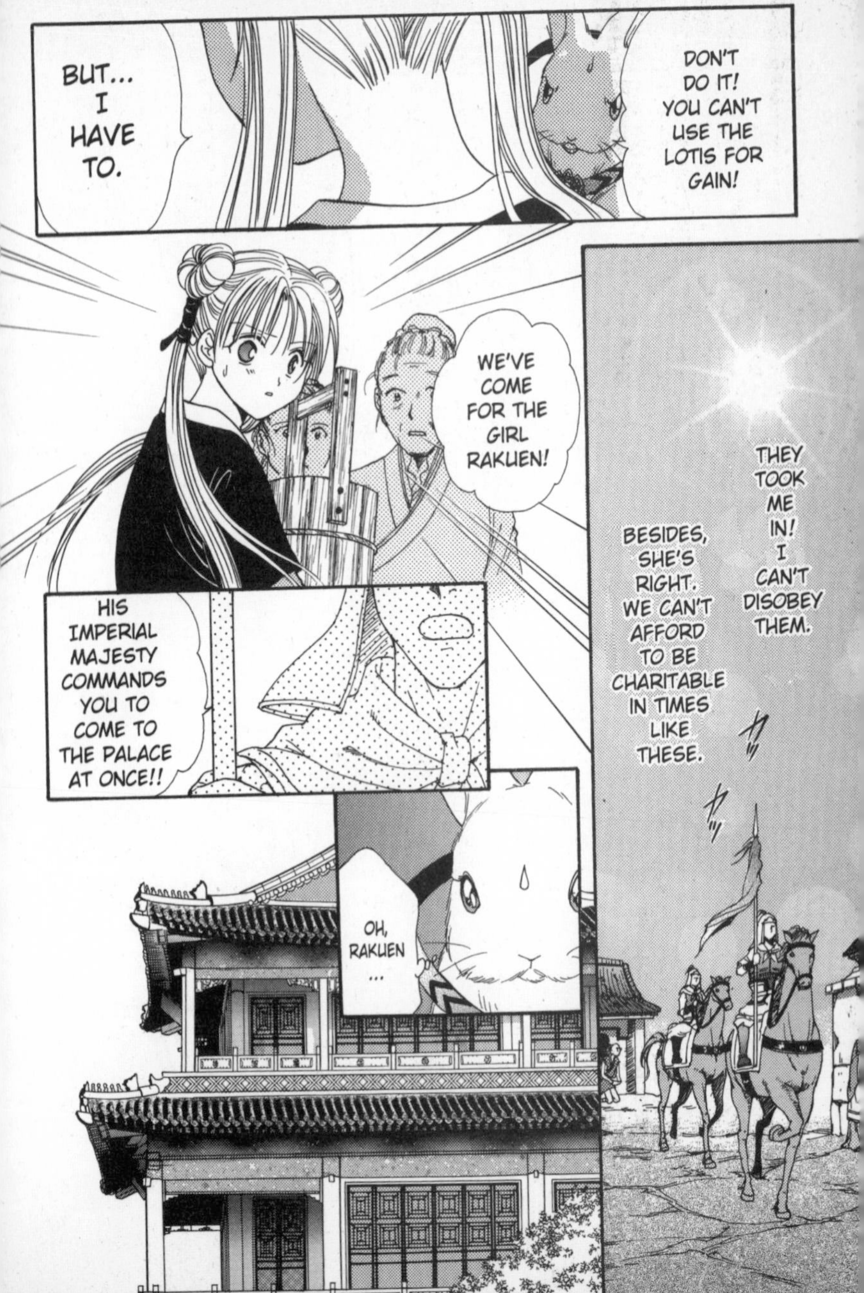
DON'T DO IT! YOU CAN'T USE THE LOTIS FOR GAIN!
BUT... I HAVE TO.
THEY TOOK ME IN! I CAN'T DISOBEY THEM.
BESIDES, SHE'S RIGHT. WE CAN'T AFFORD TO BE CHARITABLE IN TIMES LIKE THESE.
WE'VE COME FOR THE GIRL RAKUEN!
HIS IMPERIAL MAJESTY COMMANDS YOU TO COME TO THE PALACE AT ONCE!!
OH, RAKUEN ...

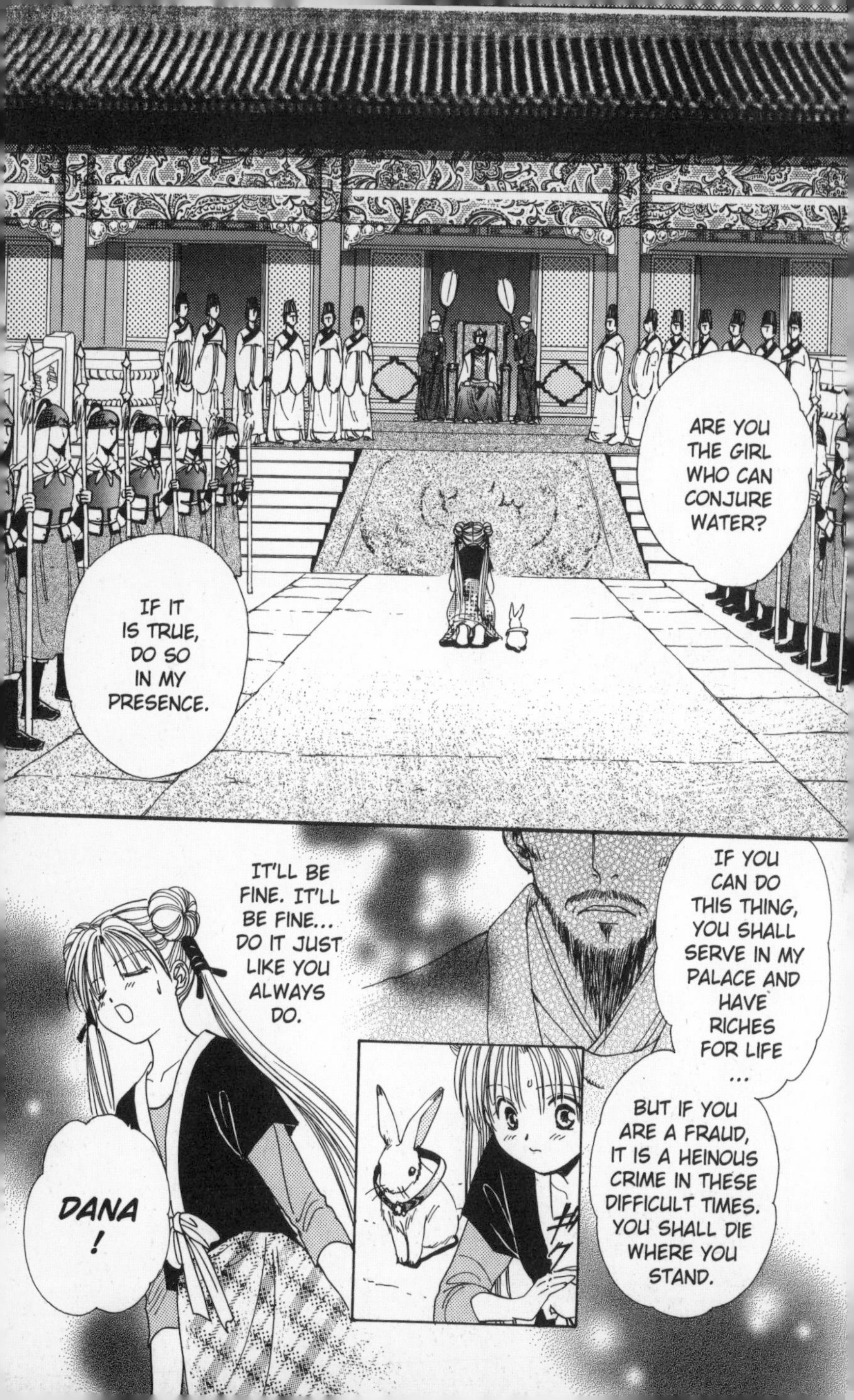
ARE YOU THE GIRL WHO CAN CONJURE WATER?
IF IT IS TRUE, DO SO IN MY PRESENCE.
IF YOU CAN DO THIS THING, YOU SHALL SERVE IN MY PALACE AND HAVE RICHES FOR LIFE ...
BUT IF YOU ARE A FRAUD, IT IS A HEINOUS CRIME IN THESE DIFFICULT TIMES. YOU SHALL DIE WHERE YOU STAND.
IT'LL BE FINE. IT'LL BE FINE... DO IT JUST LIKE YOU ALWAYS DO.
DANA!

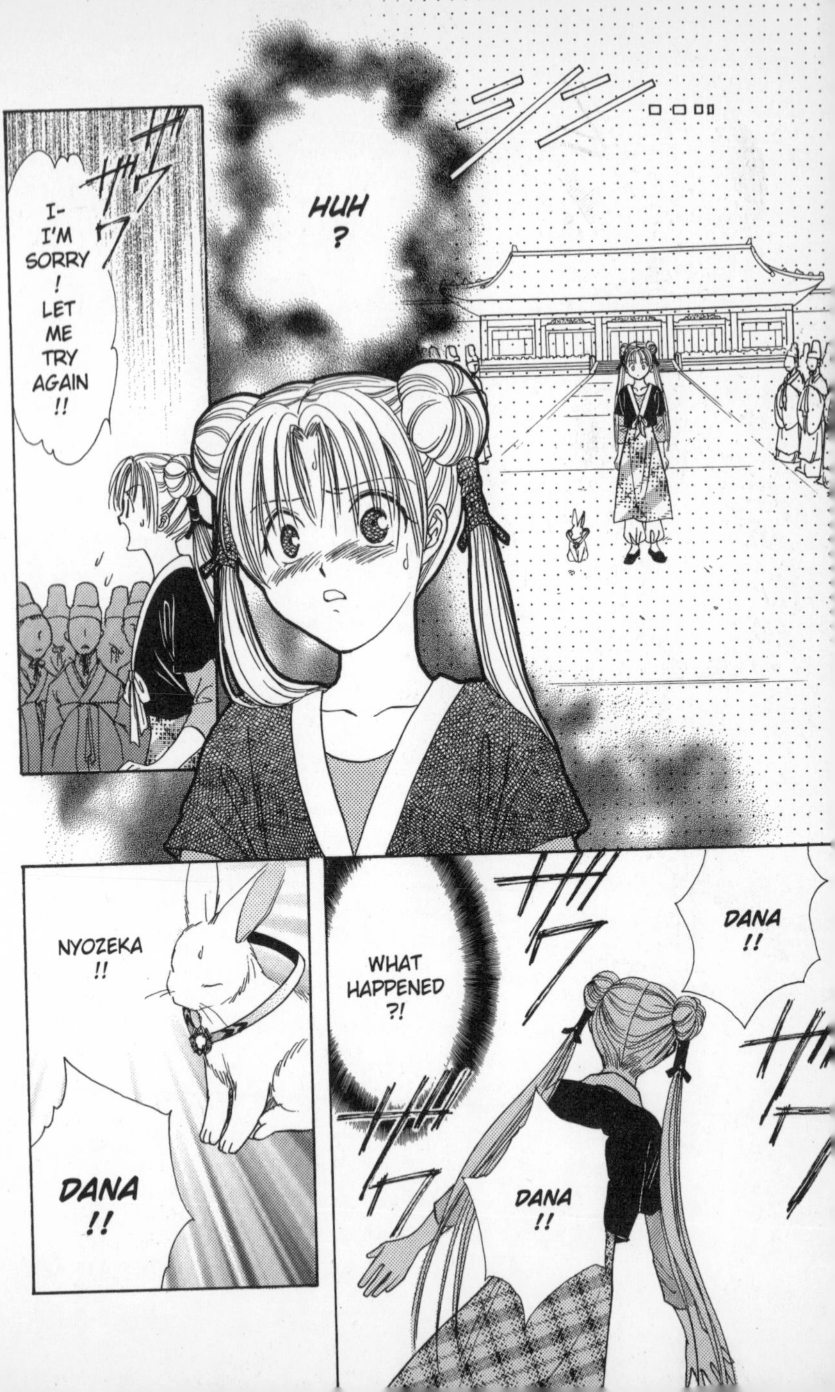
HUH?
I- I'M SORRY! LET ME TRY AGAIN!!
DANA!!
WHAT HAPPENED?!
DANA!!
NYOZEKA!!
DANA!!

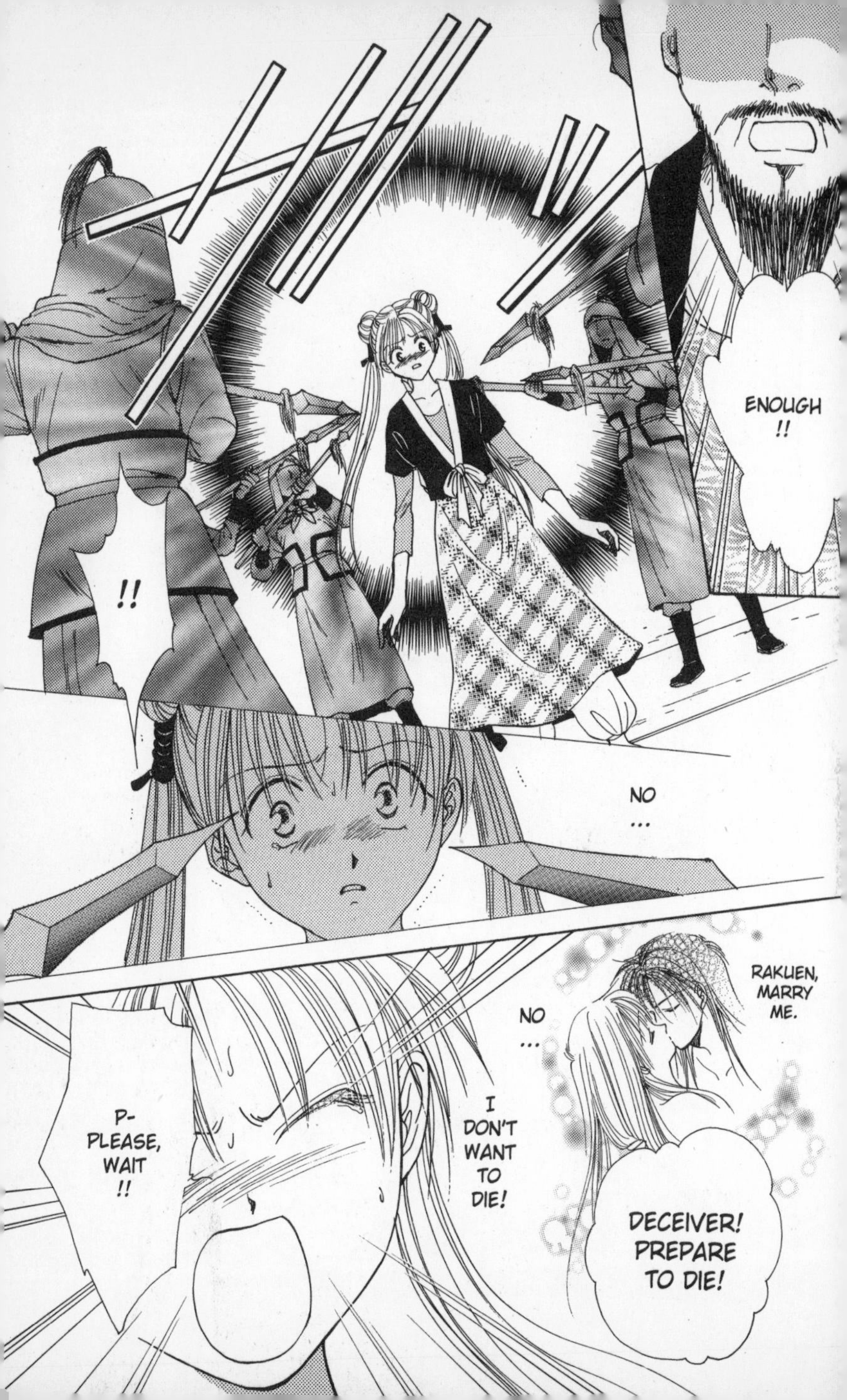

ENOUGH !!
!!
NO ...
RAKUEN, MARRY ME.
NO ...
DECEIVER! PREPARE TO DIE!
I DON'T WANT TO DIE!
P-PLEASE, WAIT !!

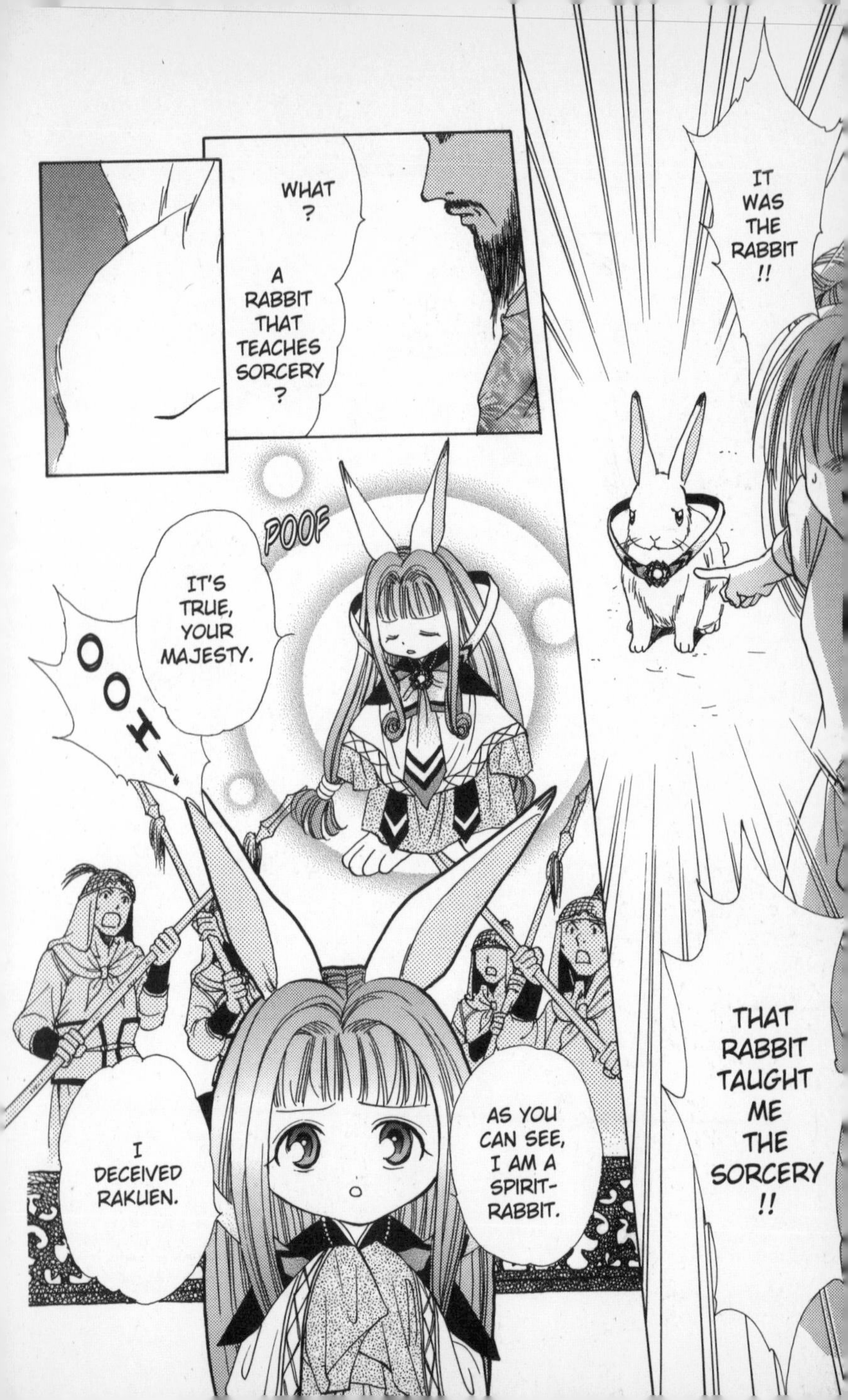
IT WAS THE RABBIT!!
THAT RABBIT TAUGHT ME THE SORCERY!!
WHAT? A RABBIT THAT TEACHES SORCERY?
POOF
IT'S TRUE, YOUR MAJESTY.
OOH!
AS YOU CAN SEE, I AM A SPIRIT-RABBIT.
I DECEIVED RAKUEN.

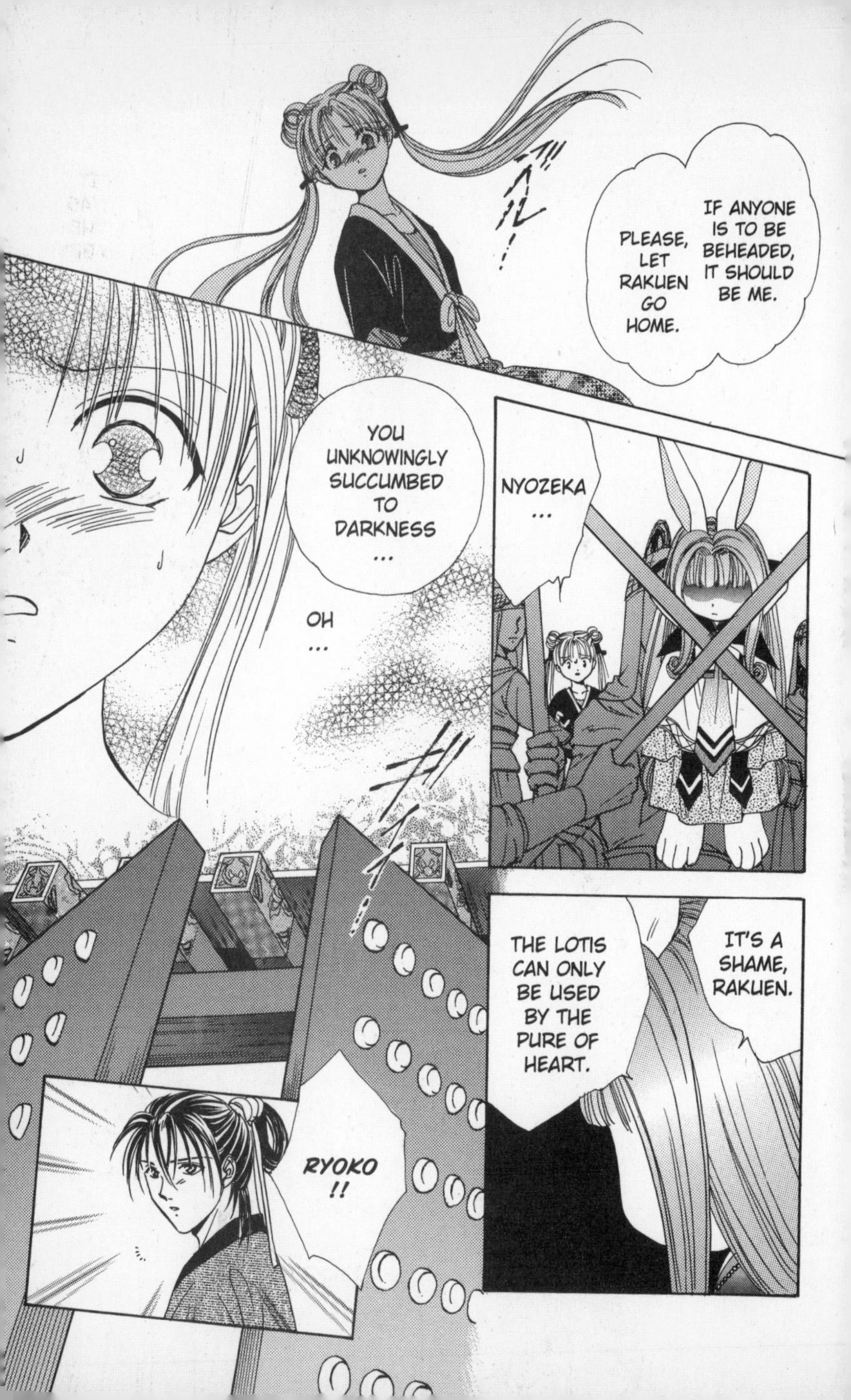
IF ANYONE IS TO BE BEHEADED, IT SHOULD BE ME.
PLEASE, LET RAKUEN GO HOME.
NYOZEKA ...
YOU UNKNOWINGLY SUCCUMBED TO DARKNESS ...
OH ...
IT'S A SHAME, RAKUEN.
THE LOTIS CAN ONLY BE USED BY THE PURE OF HEART.
RYOKO !!

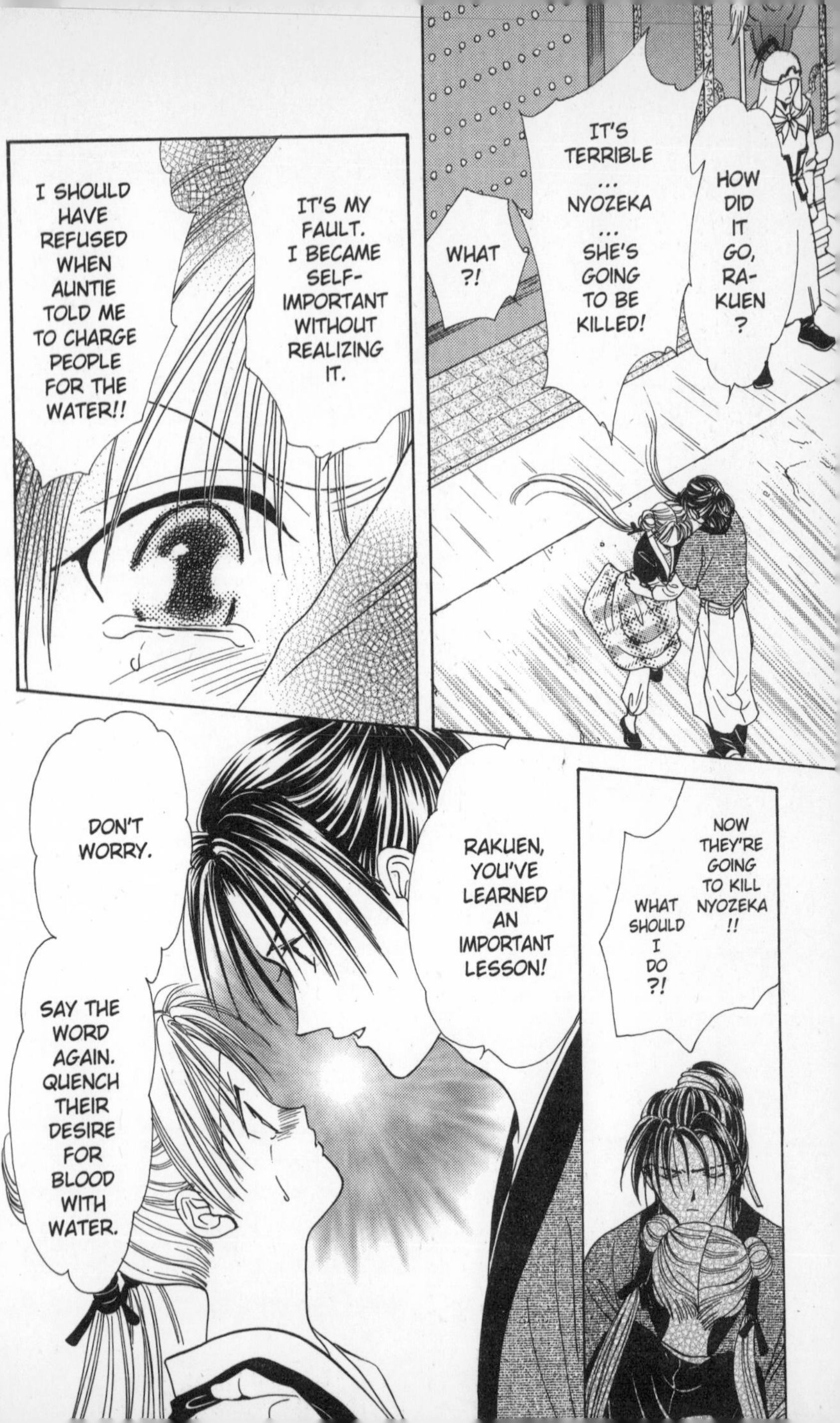
HOW DID IT GO, RAKUEN?
IT'S TERRIBLE... NYOZEKA... SHE'S GOING TO BE KILLED!
WHAT?!
IT'S MY FAULT. I BECAME SELF-IMPORTANT WITHOUT REALIZING IT.
I SHOULD HAVE REFUSED WHEN AUNTIE TOLD ME TO CHARGE PEOPLE FOR THE WATER!!
NOW THEY'RE GOING TO KILL NYOZEKA!!
WHAT SHOULD I DO?!
RAKUEN, YOU'VE LEARNED AN IMPORTANT LESSON!
DON'T WORRY.
SAY THE WORD AGAIN. QUENCH THEIR DESIRE FOR BLOOD WITH WATER.

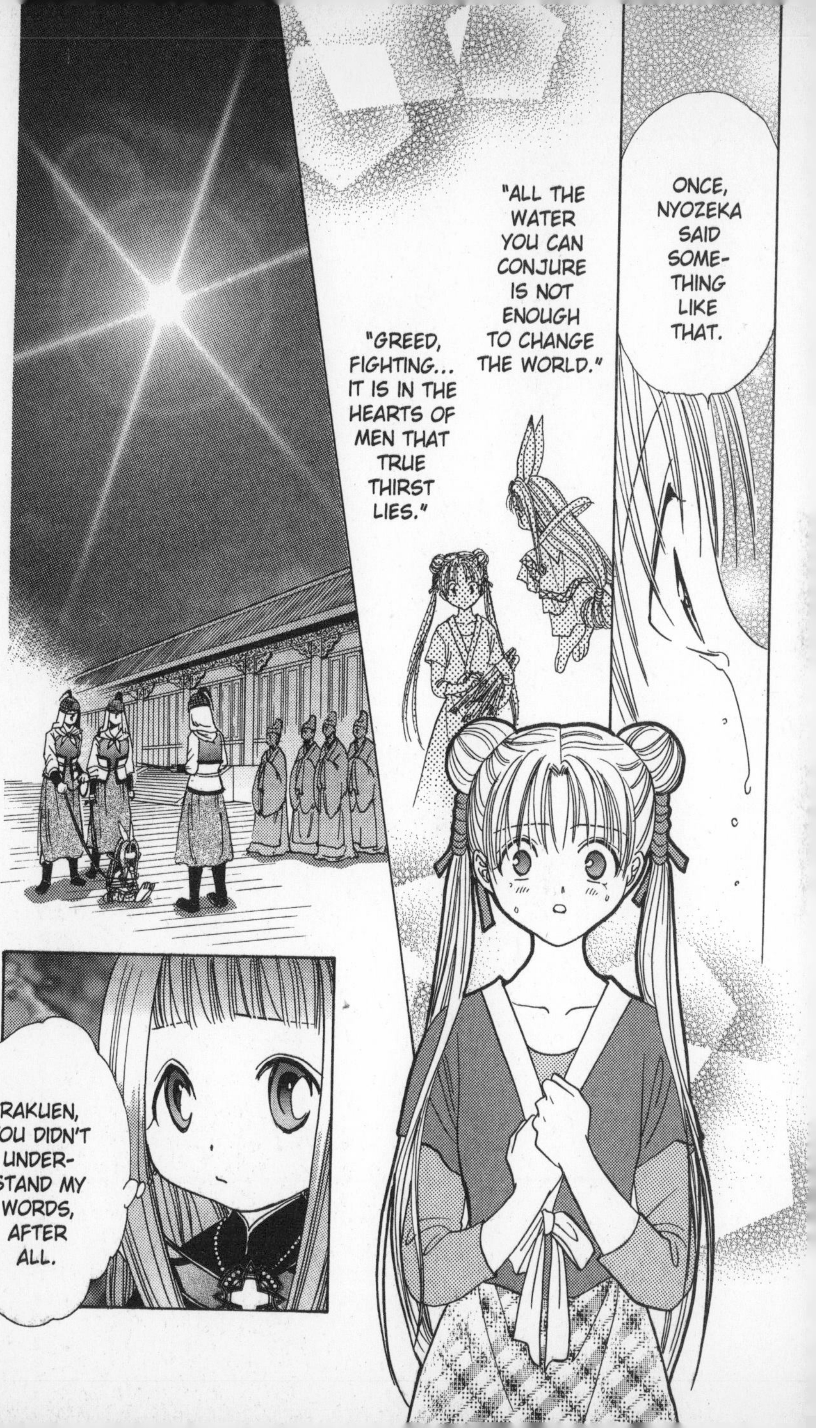
ONCE, NYOZEKA SAID SOME-THING LIKE THAT.
"ALL THE WATER YOU CAN CONJURE IS NOT ENOUGH TO CHANGE THE WORLD."
"GREED, FIGHTING... IT IS IN THE HEARTS OF MEN THAT TRUE THIRST LIES."
RAKUEN, YOU DIDN'T UNDER-STAND MY WORDS, AFTER ALL.

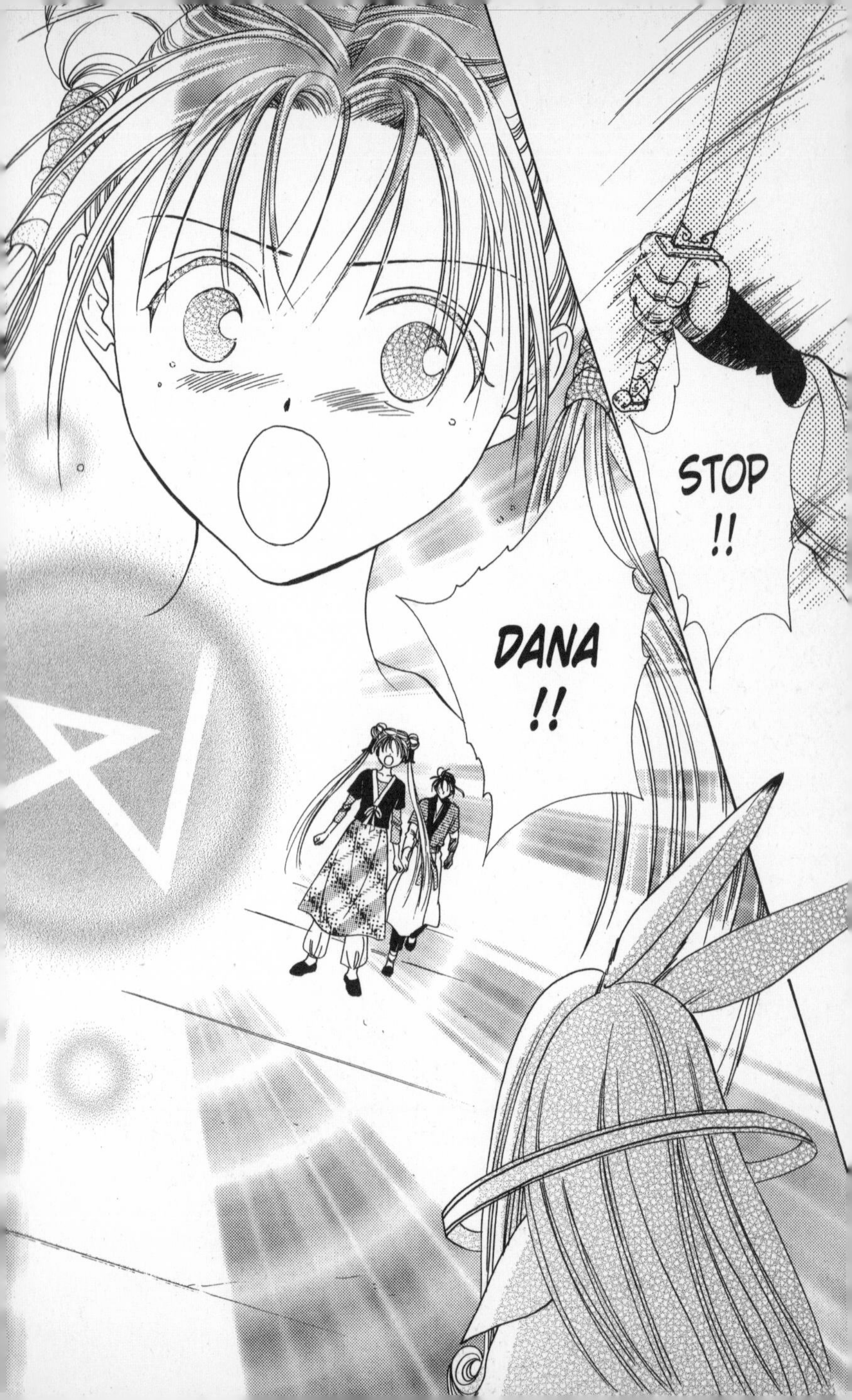
STOP !!
DANA !!

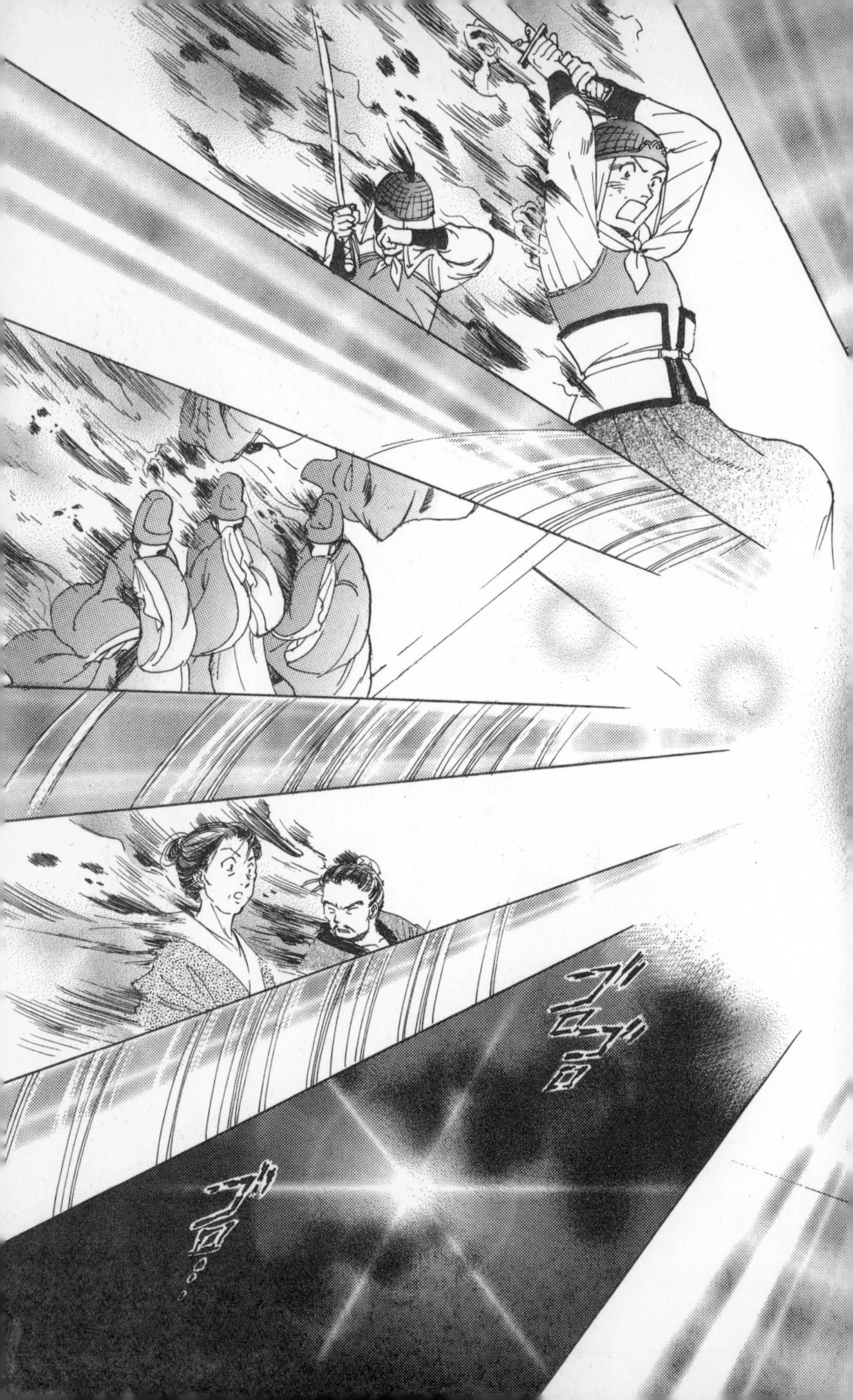
ゴロゴロ
ゴロ。。。

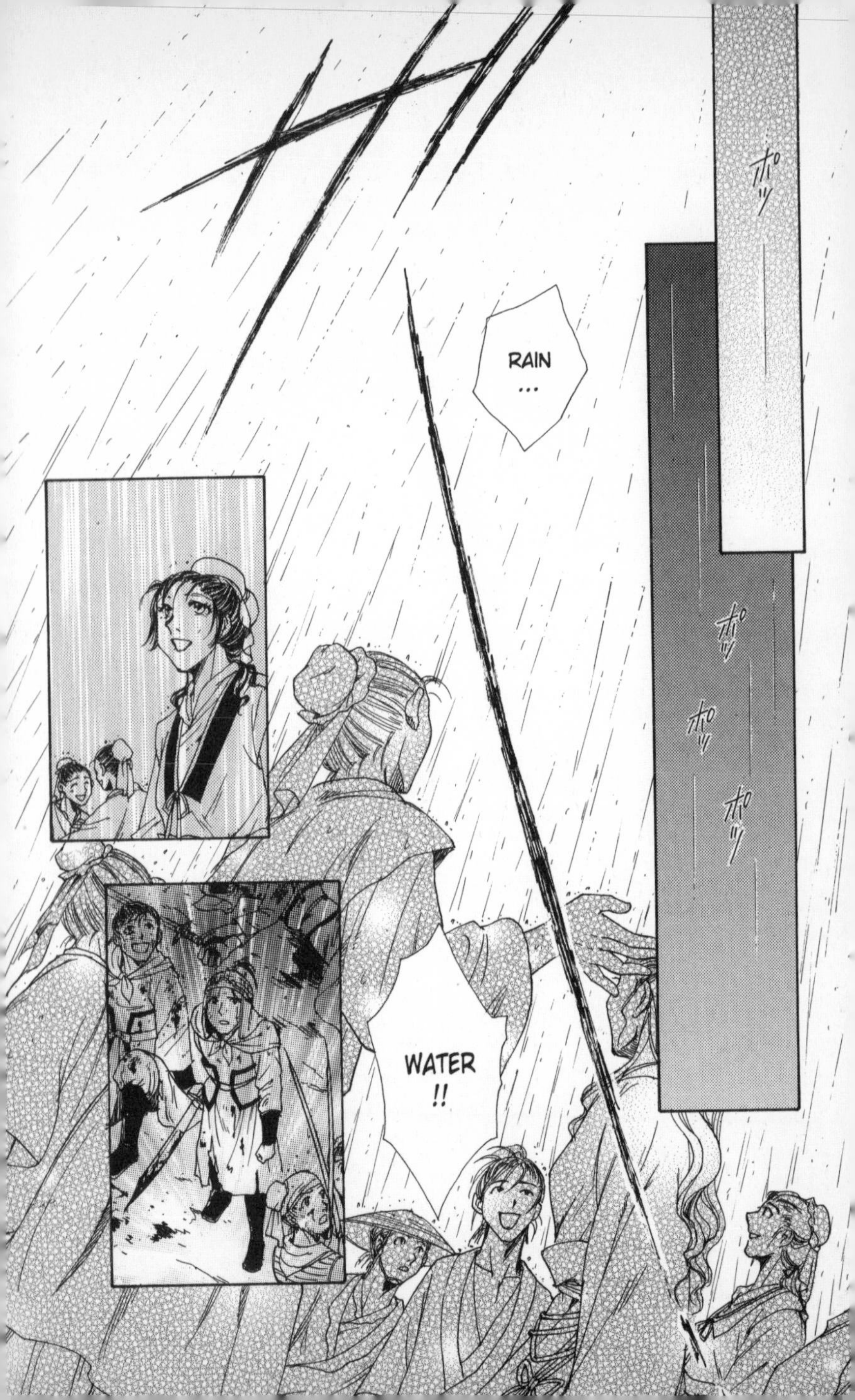
ポッ
RAIN ...
ポッ
ポッ
ポッ
WATER !!

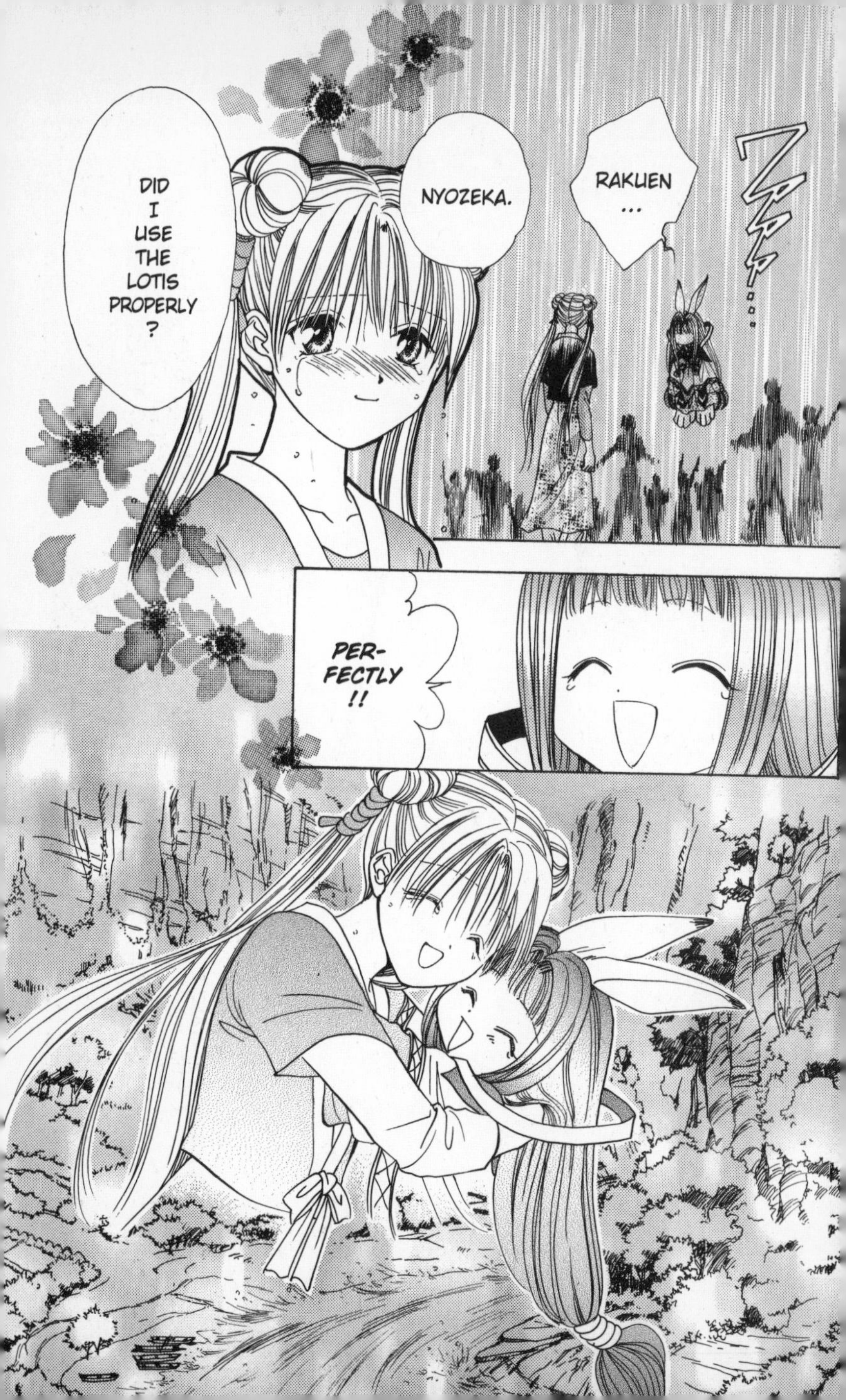
RAKUEN ...
NYOZEKA.
DID I USE THE LOTIS PROPERLY ?
PER-FECTLY !!

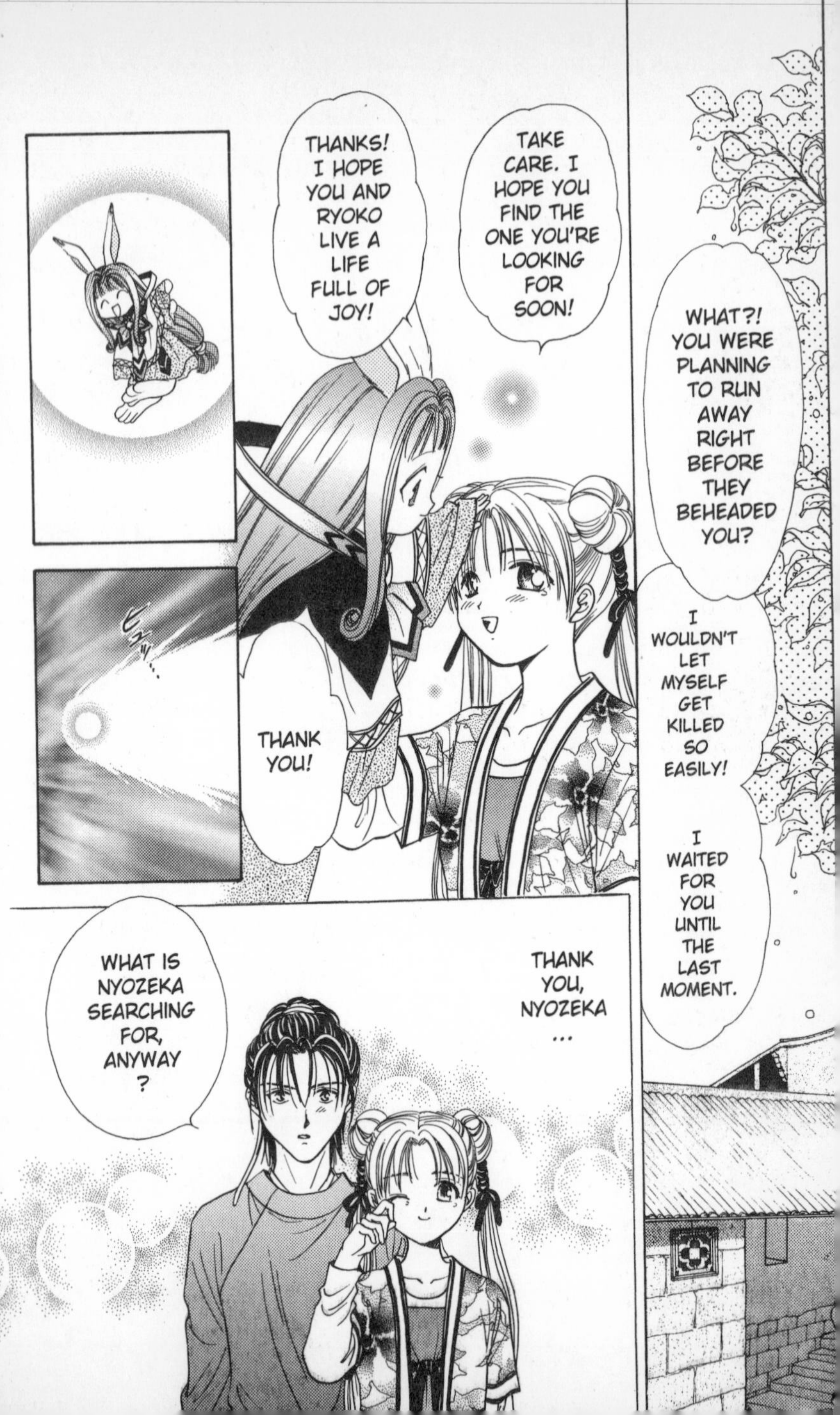
WHAT?! YOU WERE PLANNING TO RUN AWAY RIGHT BEFORE THEY BEHEADED YOU?
I WOULDN'T LET MYSELF GET KILLED SO EASILY!
I WAITED FOR YOU UNTIL THE LAST MOMENT.
TAKE CARE. I HOPE YOU FIND THE ONE YOU'RE LOOKING FOR SOON!
THANKS! I HOPE YOU AND RYOKO LIVE A LIFE FULL OF JOY!
THANK YOU!
THANK YOU, NYOZEKA ...
WHAT IS NYOZEKA SEARCHING FOR, ANYWAY?

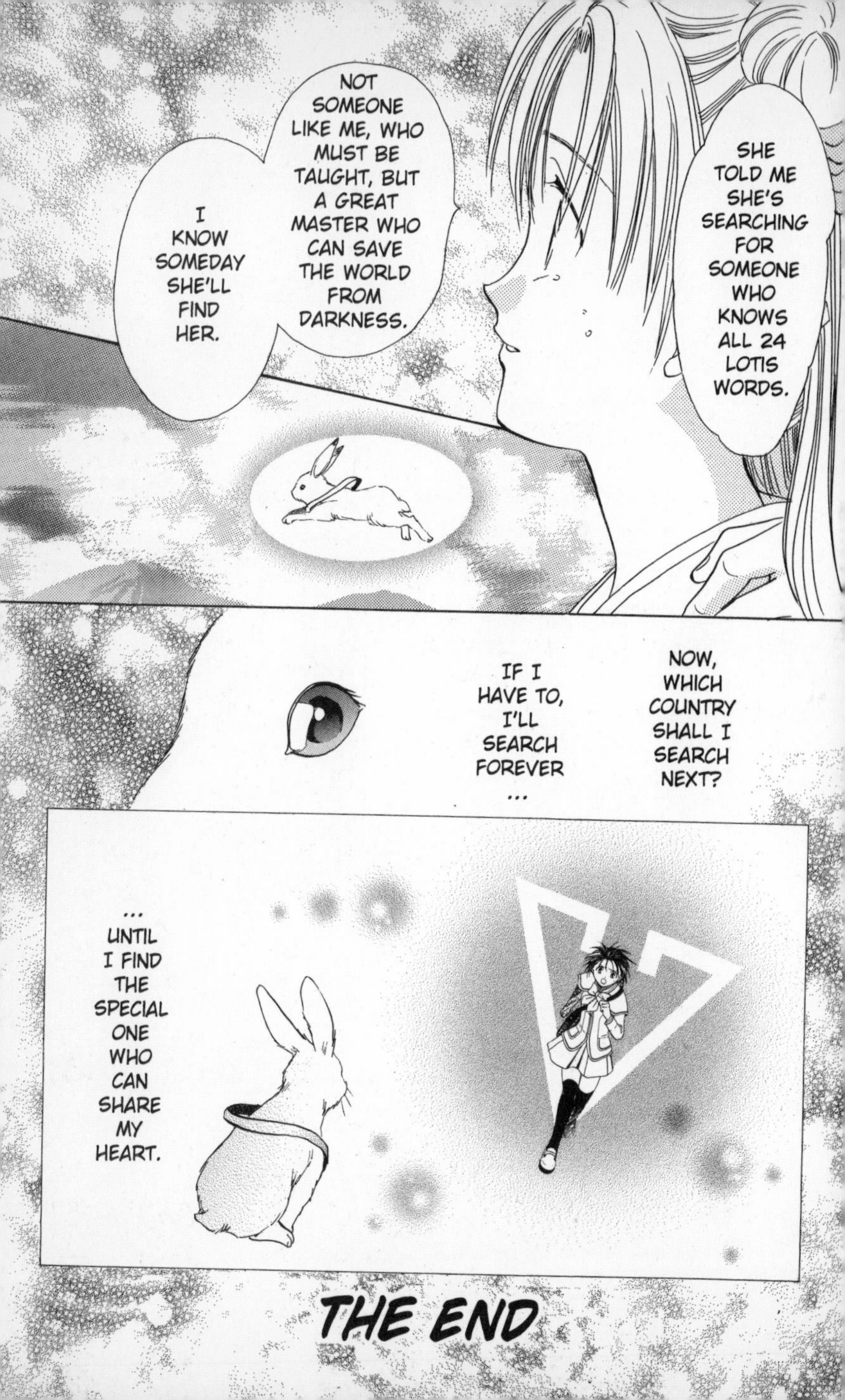
SHE TOLD ME SHE'S SEARCHING FOR SOMEONE WHO KNOWS ALL 24 LOTIS WORDS.
NOT SOMEONE LIKE ME, WHO MUST BE TAUGHT, BUT A GREAT MASTER WHO CAN SAVE THE WORLD FROM DARKNESS.
I KNOW SOMEDAY SHE'LL FIND HER.
NOW, WHICH COUNTRY SHALL I SEARCH NEXT?
IF I HAVE TO, I'LL SEARCH FOREVER ...
... UNTIL I FIND THE SPECIAL ONE WHO CAN SHARE MY HEART.
THE END

🌀 17 YEARS OLD

🌀 BLOOD TYPE: O

🌀 ASTROLOGICAL SIGN: LEO

🌀 HEIGHT: 5'6"

🌀 BIRTHPLACE: CHINA

🌀 LIVES ALONE IN A CONDO IN SHANGHAI. ASPIRING STARLET WITH A TALENT AGENCY.

🌀 SHE'S THE BIG-SISTER TYPE--OPEN-HEARTED, BOLD, WITH A STRONG SENSE OF JUSTICE--SO SHE HAS MANY FEMALE FRIENDS. HER LAMENT IS THAT SHE CAN'T FIND A BOYFRIEND, MAYBE BECAUSE OF HER STRONG PERSONALITY.

🌀 SPECIAL TALENT: TAI CHI

🌀 LOVES THE OUTDOORS. ON DAYS OFF, DEVOTES HERSELF TO SPORTS.

PAI MEI LIN

NYOZEKA'S MINI-MINI LOTIS CLASS

YUGU

NUMBER 10

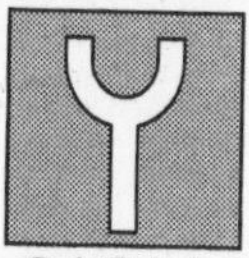

THE 24TH LOTIS WORD MEANS "FULFILLMENT" AND "TREE." FREY USED IT IN OISHI'S INNER HEART TO MAKE A PLACE OF REST FOR KYŌ.

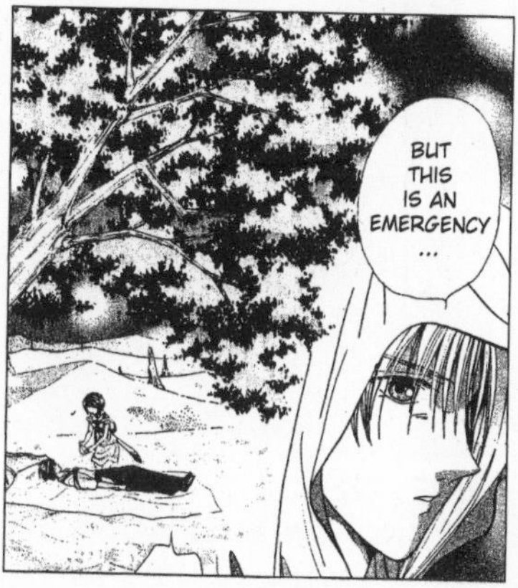
BUT THIS IS AN EMERGENCY ...

NUMBER 11

IRU

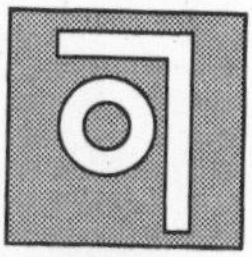

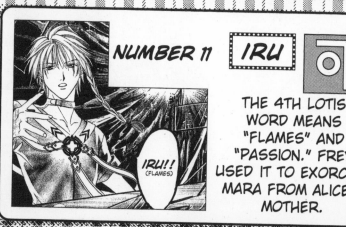

THE 4TH LOTIS WORD MEANS "FLAMES" AND "PASSION." FREY USED IT TO EXORCISE MARA FROM ALICE'S MOTHER.

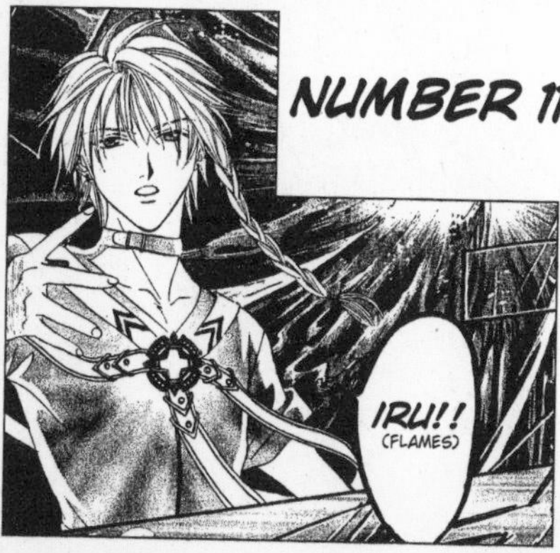
IRU!! (FLAMES)

NUMBER 12 SAN

THE 15TH LOTIS WORD MEANS "FRIENDSHIP," "COMRADE," AND "CIRCLE." KYŌ USED IT TO BREAK THE MARA'S SPELL ON KAZUKI.

SAN! (FRIEND-SHIP)

UTI  NUMBER 13

THE 20TH LOTIS WORD MEANS "SEE," "TO SEE THROUGH," AND "AWAKEN." MEI LIN USED IT TO REPEL THE MARAM MASTERS.

UTEI!! (AWAKEN)

PASA

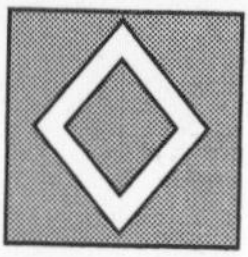

NUMBER 14

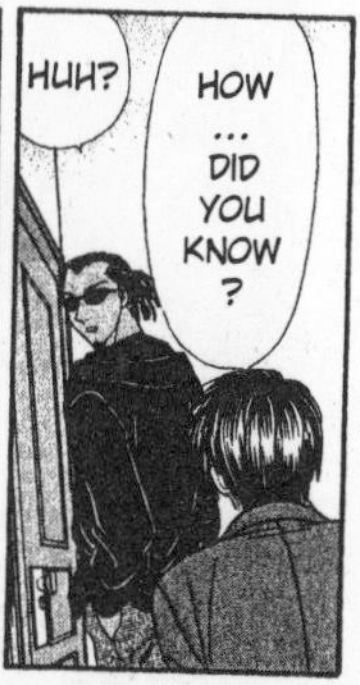
HUH?
HOW ... DID YOU KNOW ?

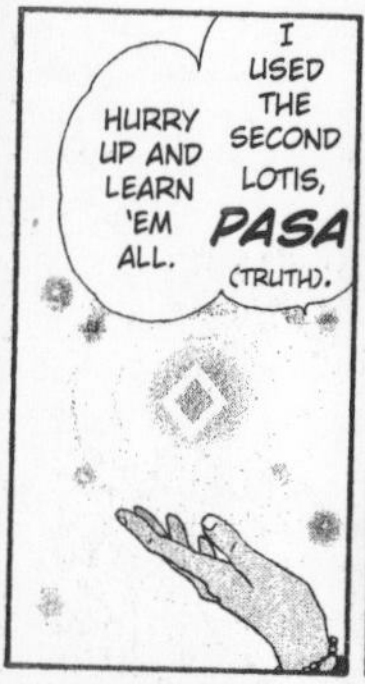
I USED THE SECOND LOTIS, PASA (TRUTH).
HURRY UP AND LEARN 'EM ALL.

THE 2ND LOTIS WORD MEANS "TRUTH," "SINCERITY," AND "DETERMINATION." BILLY USED THIS WORD TO FIND OUT ABOUT THE MARAM WORD BURNED INTO KYŌ'S HEART.

NUMBER 15

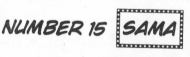

SAMA

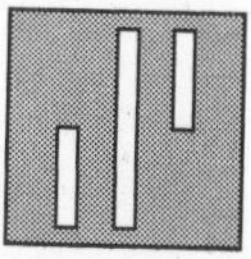

THE 22ND LOTIS WORD MEANS "PATH," "GUIDE," AND "POSSIBILITY." ALICE USED IT TO OPEN THE WAY TO MAYURA.

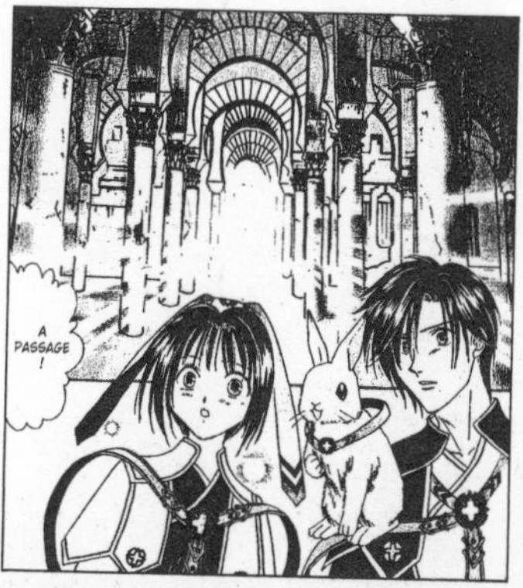
A PASSAGE !

NUMBER 16

JETA

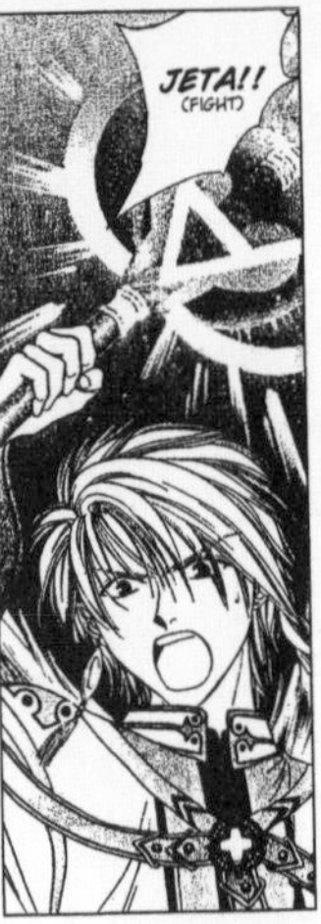
JETA!!
(FIGHT)

THE 6TH LOTIS WORD MEANS "VICTORY," "FIGHT," "WAR," AND "JUSTICE." FREY USED IT TO REPEL THE ENEMY.

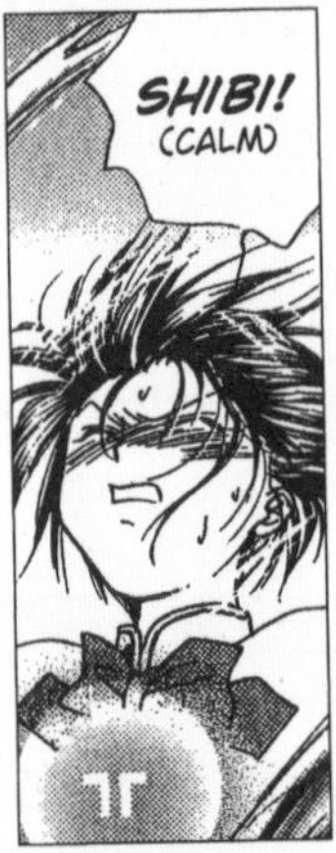
SHIBI!
(CALM)

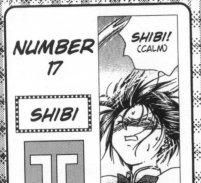

NUMBER 17

SHIBI

THE 13TH LOTIS WORD MEANS "PEACE," "CALM," AND "TRANQUILITY." ALICE USED THIS TO PROTECT HERSELF FROM MAYURA'S ATTACK.

NUMBER 18

UIDO

THE 10TH LOTIS WORD MEANS "TRUST," "APPRECIATION," AND "SELF-SACRIFICE." KYŌ USED IT TO EXORCISE THE MARA FROM HIS UNCLE.

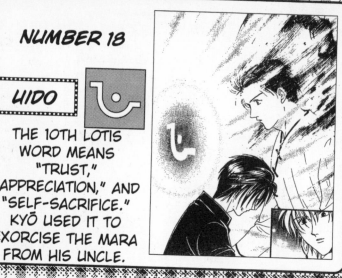

NUMBER 19

ALETO

THE 9TH LOTIS WORD MEANS "TO CLEANSE," "PURITY," AND "REASON." THIS WAS USED TO PURIFY THE MARAM MASTERS SAMUEL AND KAYNA.

RANA NUMBER 20

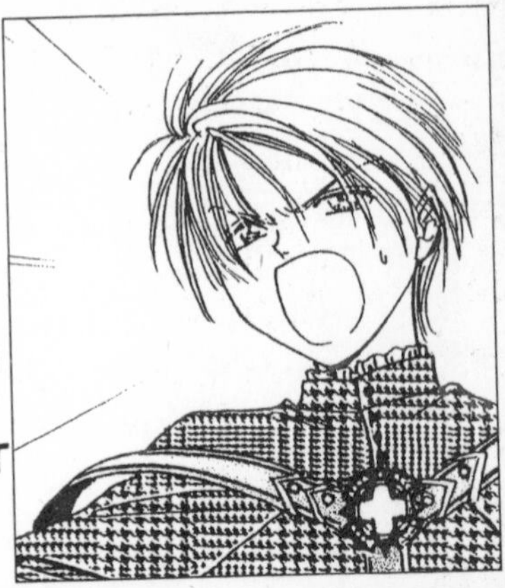

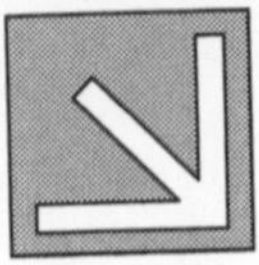

THE 8TH LOTIS WORD MEANS "HOPE," "JOY," "GLORY," AND "HAPPINESS." CHRIS USED IT TO SAVE MAYURA.

NUMBER 21 **SHETO**

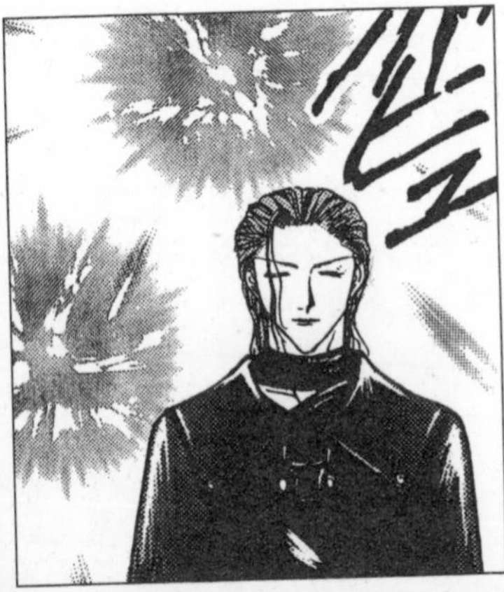

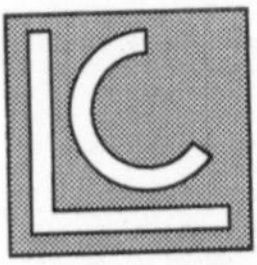

THE 21ST LOTIS WORD MEANS "LIFE," "LONGEVITY," AND "FATE." CHRIS USED THIS TO SAVE MAYURA.

NUMBER 22

SAKUA

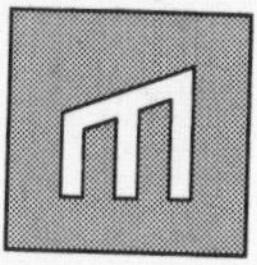

THE 5TH LOTIS WORD MEANS "WISDOM," "LISTEN," "KNOWLEDGE," AND "UNDERSTANDING."

NUMBER 23

SARTO

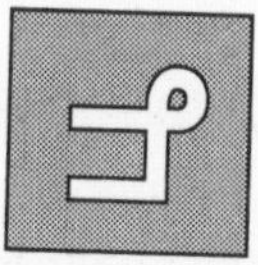

THE 12TH LOTIS WORD MEANS "BEAUTY," "UPRIGHT-NESS," "COMPLETE-NESS," "ONENESS."

NUMBER 24

FORA

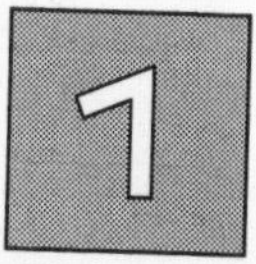

THE 18TH LOTIS WORD MEANS "TIME," "FLOW," "CONTINUITY," AND "ETERNITY."

Alice 19th
volume 7 The Lost Word
shôjo edition

STORY & ART BY
Yû Watase

English Adaptation/Lance Caselman
Translation/JN Productions
Touch-Up Art & Lettering/Walden Wong
Cover Design & Layout/Judi Roubideaux
Editor/Frances E. Wall

Managing Editor/Annette Roman
Editorial Director/Alvin Lu
Director of Production/Noboru Watanabe
Sr. Director of Licensing & Acquisitions/Rika Inouye
Vice President of Sales & Marketing/Liza Coppola
Executive Vice President/Hyoe Narita
Publisher/Seiji Horibuchi

Printed in Canada

Published by VIZ, LLC
P.O. Box 77010 · San Francisco, CA 94107

10 9 8 7 6 5 4 3 2
First printing, October 2004
Second printing, December 2004

www.viz.com   storeviz.com   ANIMERICA
ANIME & MANGA MONTHLY

EDITOR'S NOTE

My high school Japanese teacher once told our class that when Japanese people look up at the full moon, instead of seeing the Man in the Moon, they see a rabbit. Tsukimi ("moon viewing") is a traditional Chinese and Japanese holiday of thanksgiving for the bountiful autumn harvest. It falls on the 15th day of the eighth month of the lunar calendar, or around mid-September, when it is believed that the largest, brightest full moon of the year shines in the sky. To celebrate, people make rice dumplings called *tsukimi-dango* as offerings to the rabbit on the moon and gather together with loved ones to sit outside to enjoy the moon's beauty. The next time you go outside at night and see a full moon, maybe you'll think of Nyozeka!

—Frances E. Wall
Editor, *Alice 19th*

If you're enjoying this story and are in the mood for more, here are three manga titles that you should check out:

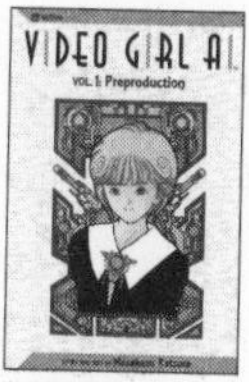
VIDEO GIRL AI
VOL. 1: Preproduction

VIDEO GIRL AI ©1989 by MASAKAZU KATSURA/ SHUEISHA Inc.

VIDEO GIRL AI When Moemi, the object of Yota's incurable crush, turns out to be in love with the dashing and popular Takashi, poor Yota is devastated. He rents a video to distract himself, but Ai, the hottie featured on the tape, magically bursts out of the TV and into Yota's world. Ai's mission is to fix Yota's hopeless love life, but when Ai develops romantic feelings towards Yota, things get complicated. A true manga classic, sweet and hilarious!

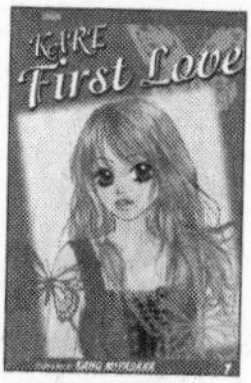
KARE
First Love

© 2002 Kaho Miyasaka / Shogakukan, Inc.

KARE FIRST LOVE Sixteen-year-old plain-Jane Karin finds herself torn between keeping the friendship of her classmate Yuka and entertaining the advances of a boy named Kiriya, who also happens to be the object of Yuka's affections. Living happily ever after in high school isn't on the curriculum, as Karin soon finds herself the center of Kiriya's attention, as well as the bull's-eye in embittered pal Yuka's dartboard of hate. Experience the spine-tingling roller coaster ride of Karin's first experiences in love!

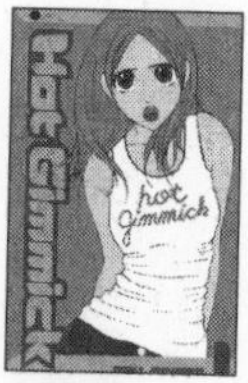
Hot Gimmick
hot gimmick

© 2001 Miki Aihara / Shogakukan, Inc.

HOT GIMMICK High-school girl Hatsumi lives in an apartment complex owned by her father's company and ruled with a tight fist by the rumor-mongering, self-righteous Mrs. Tachibana. When Hatsumi goes to surreptitiously buy a pregnancy test for her precocious younger sister Akane, a cruel bully named Ryoki (who also happens to be Mrs. Tachibana's son) catches her and blackmails her into becoming his slave in exchange for protecting her sister's devastating secret. Hatsumi is experiencing the joy of a budding romance with her crush Azusa, but Ryoki won't let poor Hatsumi forget that he is her master and the keeper of the secret that could ruin the lives of everyone in Hatsumi's family!

Glossary of Sound Effects, Signs, and other Miscellaneous Notes

Each entry includes: the location, indicated by page number and panel number (so 3.1 means page 3, panel number 1); the phonetic romanization of the original Japanese; and our English "translation"—we offer as close an English equivalent as we can.

40.1	FX:	Ba (blam)
42.1	FX:	Don (bang)
44.2	FX:	Pikun (startle)
45.4	FX:	Ha (gasp)
47.3	FX:	Yoro (wobble)
49.5	FX:	Fu… (a weight is lifted)
54.1	FX:	Zaaa (flying apart)
54.3	FX:	Fu (disappearing)
57.1	FX:	Fu (disappearing)
57.2	FX:	Pan (blam)
58.2	FX:	Dokun dokun (heartbeats)
58.4	FX:	Dokun (heartbeat)
59.1	FX:	Gaba (jumping out)
59.2	FX:	Go go go (rumble)
63.2	FX:	Gyu (squeeze)
64.1-3	FX:	Dokun dokun dokun dokun (heartbeats)
65.2-3	FX:	Ka (glow)
66.2	FX:	Ba (slash)
66.4	FX:	Don (blam)
67.2	FX:	Go (blam)
67.5-6	FX:	Goooh (monster appearing)

4.1	FX:	Basha (splash of footstep)
4.2	FX:	Basha basha (footsteps)
6.2	FX:	Pasha (splash)
10.2	FX:	Za (hand motion to stop)
12.2	FX:	Dokun dokun (heartbeats)
13.1	FX:	Dokun dokun (heartbeats)
15.3	FX:	Doki (shock or jolt)
16.2	FX:	Bua (evil force attacking)
18.2	FX:	Gu (squeeze tightly)
21.1	FX:	Suru (slip off)
21.3	FX:	To (shaking off)
22.1	FX:	Dokun (shocked heartbeat)
24.2	FX:	Hiso hiso (whispering)
25.3-4	FX:	Gashan (crash)
28.3	FX:	Zuru (sink down or slump)
31.1	FX:	Zuzu (something ominously appears)
34.3	FX:	Gaku (sink to knees)
35.3	FX:	Gura (feeling faint)
37.2	FX:	Zuzu (web unfurls)
38.3	FX:	Ba (blam)
39.2	FX:	To (running)

68.1—FX: Gabaaa (opening mouth)

69.1-4—FX: Zu zu zu zu zu (growing or expanding)

70.1 —FX: Dosha (slamming against something)

72.2 —FX: Gooh (evil force)

73.1-2—FX: Dokun dokun dokun dokun (heartbeats)

75.1—FX: Gyu (squeeze)

78.2—FX: Tosa (falls)

82.3—FX: Yoro (wobble)

84.1—FX: Ka (glow)

84.4—FX: Pan (crash)

85.1—FX: Zuza (skid or slide)

87.1 —FX: Zu zu zu (growing)

91.1 —FX: Gabaa (swallows up)

92.1-3—FX: Zuzu zuzu (sliding closer)

93.1-2—FX: Dokun dokun dokun (heartbeats)

94.4—FX: Ba (blam)

95.4 —FX: Zuru (sinks down)

96.2—FX: Zuba (blast)

97.1 —FX: Tosa (falls)

98.3-4—FX: Zu zu zu zu (slithering closer)

99.1-4—FX: Dokun dokun dokun dokun (heartbeats)

99.3-4—FX: Doro doro (slime)

100.1 —FX: Zubu (latching on)

100.4—FX: Fu (goes dark)

101.1 —FX: Kakun (head falls)

103.1 —FX: Zuru (sinks down)

104.1 —FX: Ha (gasp)

105.1-3 –FX: Go (forceful blast)

108.1 —FX: Pi...chichichi... (birds chirping)

108.2 —FX: Sawa (breeze blowing)

108.3 —FX: Fura (shakily stands)

108.6—FX: Pyokon, pyokon (hop, hop)

109.3 —FX: Sawa (rustle of leaves)

112.4 —FX: Su (injuries vanish, appearance returns to normal)

116.2—FX: Dokun dokun dokun (heartbeats)

123.1 —FX: Piku (Frey twitches)

123.5—FX: Ta (dash)

126.2—FX: Ba (Alice comes blasting through)

127.2—FX: Ba (gunk gets blasted away)

129.2 —FX: Guaaaa (monster's death cry)

130.2—FX: Gyu (squeezes hand)

131.1 —FX: Go (flash of light)

134.5 —FX: Yoro (wobble)

172.1 —FX: Shin (silence)

172.3 —FX: Zawa zawa
(crowd murmuring in surprise)

172.4 —FX: Zawa zawa zawa (crowd
murmuring)

173.2 —FX: Za
(spears pointed at Rakuen)

175.1 —FX: Zuru (reacts with a start)

175.4 —FX: Gii (gate opens)

179.4—FX: Goro goro goro
(rumbling in the sky)

180.1 —FX: Potsu (rain drop)

180.2—FX: Potsu potsu potsu
(pitter patter of rain drops)

180.3—FX: Za (downpour)

181.1 —FX: Waa (happy yelling)

182.4—FX: Hyu (takes off or vanishes)

135.2—FX: Kokun (nod)

137.4 —FX: Batata (flapping wings)

153.1 —FX: Ka (glare of hot sun)

154.1 —FX: Yoro
(wobble, weak from thirst)

154.3 —FX: Ga (grab)

155.1 —FX: Do (thud)

155.4 —FX: Heta (sinks to ground)

156.3 —FX: Pata (plop or soft thud)

157.6 —FX: Pachi (eyes open)

158.1 —FX: Pa! (poof)

158.1 —FX: Zuza (jumps back)

160.1 —FX: Bashi (slap)

161.1 —FX: Hihiin (horse whinny)

161.2 —FX: Bo (shock)

162.2—FX: Go (water appearing)

163.3 —FX: Ban (door bangs open)

165.5 —FX: Gyu (squeeze)

166.2 —FX: Doki (heart skips a beat)

166.5 —FX: Gui (grab)

167.3 —FX: Buru buru
(shaking her head "no")

168.4—FX: Ka (glare of sun)

170.2 —FX: Katsu katsu (clop of the
horses' hooves on stone)

171.3—FX: Giku (cracking knuckles)

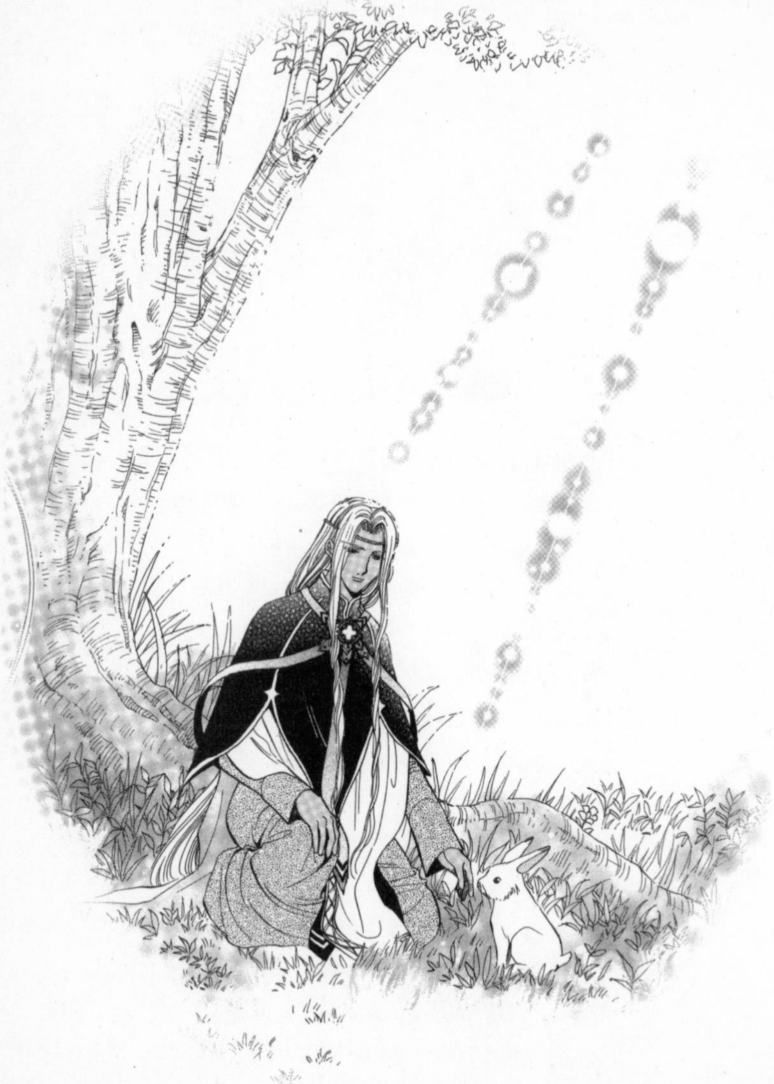

About the Author:

Yû Watase was born on March 5 in a town near Osaka, Japan, and she was raised there before moving to Tokyo to follow her dream of creating manga. In the decade since her debut short story, *PAJAMA DE OJAMA* ("An Intrusion in Pajamas"), she has produced more than 50 compiled volumes of short stories and continuing series. Her latest series, *ZETTAI KARESHI* ("He'll Be My Boyfriend"), is currently running in the anthology magazine *SHÔJO COMIC*. Watase's long-running horror/romance story *CERES: CELESTIAL LEGEND*, her historical fantasy *FUSHIGI YÛGI*, and her more recent series *IMADOKI! (NOWADAYS)* are all available in North America, published by VIZ. She loves science fiction, fantasy and comedy.

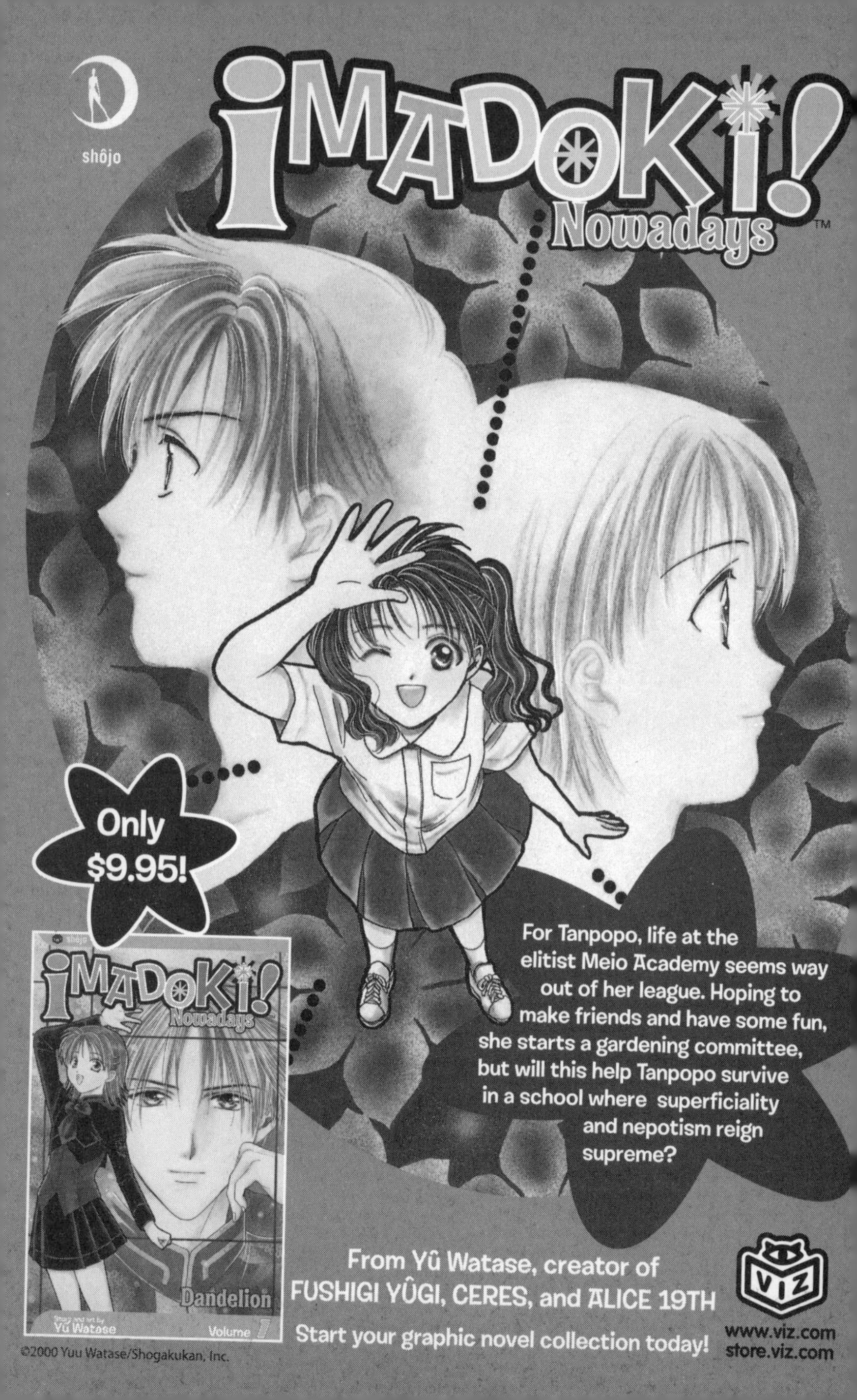
shôjo
Imadoki! Nowadays™
Only $9.95!
Imadoki! Nowadays
Dandelion
Story and art by Yû Watase
Volume 1
For Tanpopo, life at the elitist Meio Academy seems way out of her league. Hoping to make friends and have some fun, she starts a gardening committee, but will this help Tanpopo survive in a school where superficiality and nepotism reign supreme?
From Yû Watase, creator of FUSHIGI YÛGI, CERES, and ALICE 19TH
Start your graphic novel collection today!
VIZ
www.viz.com
store.viz.com
©2000 Yuu Watase/Shogakukan, Inc.

a Heavenly Maiden
From Yû Watase, creator of ALICE 19TH, FUSHIGI YÛGI, and IMADOKI!–complete your collection today!
CERES
Celestial Legend
Ceres
Celestial Legend
Manga only $9.95
VIZ
www.viz.com
store.viz.com
©1997 Yuu Watase/Shogakukan, Inc.

Hell Hath No Fury Like
When an angel named Ceres is reincarnated in 16-year-old Aya Mikage, Aya becomes a liability to her family's survival. Not only does Ceres want revenge against the Mikage family for past wrongs, but her power is also about to manifest itself. Can Aya control Ceres' hold on her, or will her family mark her for death?
Complete anime series on two DVD box sets– 12 episodes per volume
only $49.98 each!
©Yuu Watase / Shogakukan • Bandai Visual • Studio Pierrot

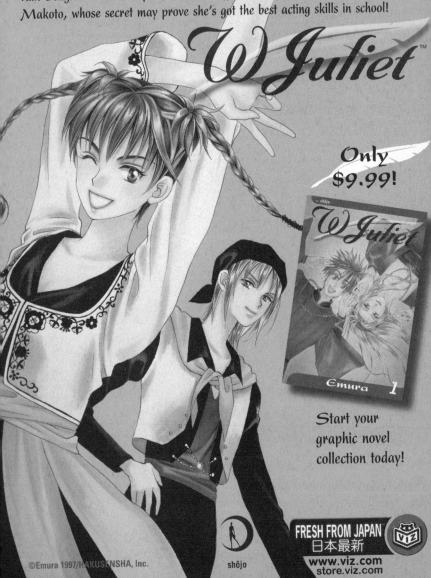

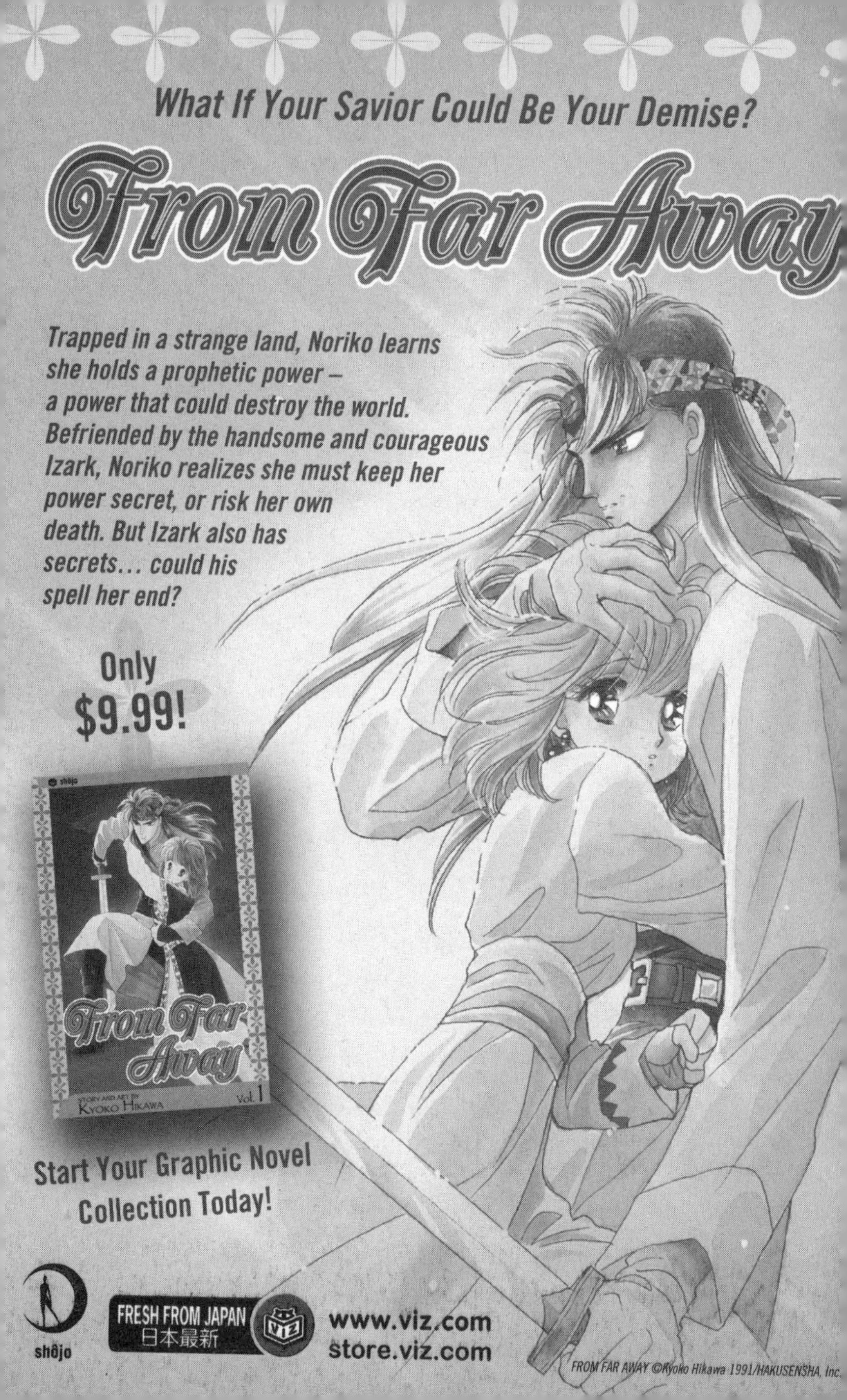
What If Your Savior Could Be Your Demise?
From Far Away
Trapped in a strange land, Noriko learns she holds a prophetic power – a power that could destroy the world. Befriended by the handsome and courageous Izark, Noriko realizes she must keep her power secret, or risk her own death. But Izark also has secrets… could his spell her end?
Only $9.99!
shôjo
From Far Away
Story and Art by Kyoko Hikawa
Vol. 1
Start Your Graphic Novel Collection Today!
shôjo
FRESH FROM JAPAN
日本最新
VIZ
www.viz.com
store.viz.com
FROM FAR AWAY ©Kyoko Hikawa 1991/HAKUSENSHA, Inc.

COMPLETE OUR SURVEY AND LET
US KNOW WHAT YOU THINK!

☐ Please do NOT send me information about VIZ products, news and events, special offers, or other information.

☐ Please do NOT send me information from VIZ's trusted business partners.

Name: _____

Address: _____

City: _____ **State:** _____ **Zip:** _____

E-mail: _____

☐ Male ☐ Female **Date of Birth** (mm/dd/yyyy): ___ / ___ / ___ (Under 13? Parental consent required)

What race/ethnicity do you consider yourself? (please check one)

☐ Asian/Pacific Islander ☐ Black/African American ☐ Hispanic/Latino

☐ Native American/Alaskan Native ☐ White/Caucasian ☐ Other: _____

What VIZ product did you purchase? (check all that apply and indicate title purchased)

☐ DVD/VHS _____

☐ Graphic Novel _____

☐ Magazines _____

☐ Merchandise _____

Reason for purchase: (check all that apply)

☐ Special offer ☐ Favorite title ☐ Gift

☐ Recommendation ☐ Other _____

Where did you make your purchase? (please check one)

☐ Comic store ☐ Bookstore ☐ Mass/Grocery Store

☐ Newsstand ☐ Video/Video Game Store ☐ Other: _____

☐ Online (site: _____)

What other VIZ properties have you purchased/own? _____

_____

How many anime and/or manga titles have you purchased in the last year? How many were VIZ titles? **(please check one from each column)**

ANIME	MANGA	VIZ
☐ None	☐ None	☐ None
☐ 1-4	☐ 1-4	☐ 1-4
☐ 5-10	☐ 5-10	☐ 5-10
☐ 11+	☐ 11+	☐ 11+

I find the pricing of VIZ products to be: **(please check one)**

☐ Cheap ☐ Reasonable ☐ Expensive

What genre of manga and anime would you like to see from VIZ? **(please check two)**

☐ Adventure ☐ Comic Strip ☐ Science Fiction ☐ Fighting
☐ Horror ☐ Romance ☐ Fantasy ☐ Sports

What do you think of VIZ's new look?

☐ Love It ☐ It's OK ☐ Hate It ☐ Didn't Notice ☐ No Opinion

Which do you prefer? **(please check one)**

☐ Reading right-to-left
☐ Reading left-to-right

Which do you prefer? **(please check one)**

☐ Sound effects in English
☐ Sound effects in Japanese with English captions
☐ Sound effects in Japanese only with a glossary at the back

THANK YOU! Please send the completed form to:

NJW Research
42 Catharine St.
Poughkeepsie, NY 12601

All information provided will be used for internal purposes only. We promise not to sell or otherwise divulge your information.